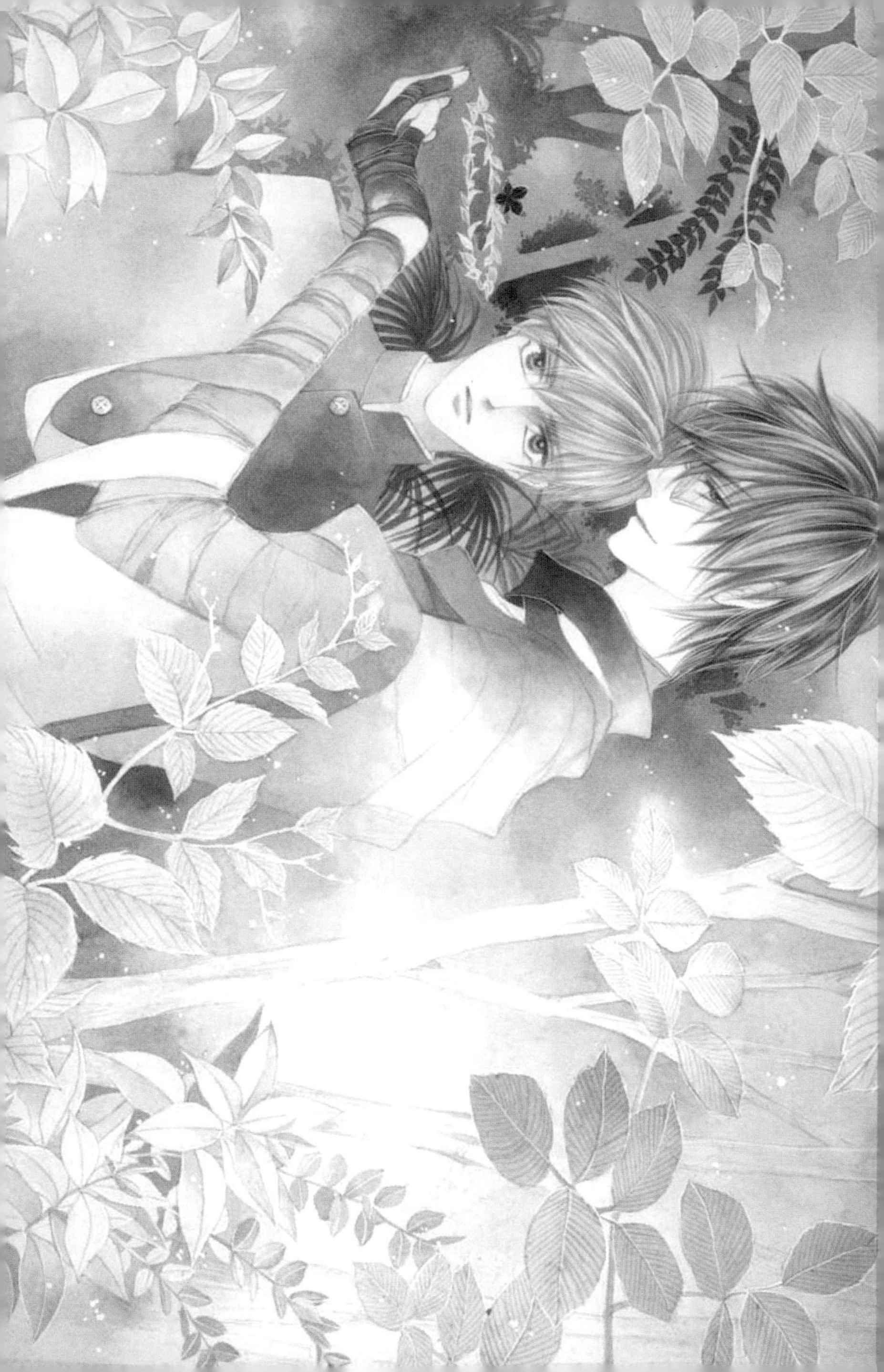

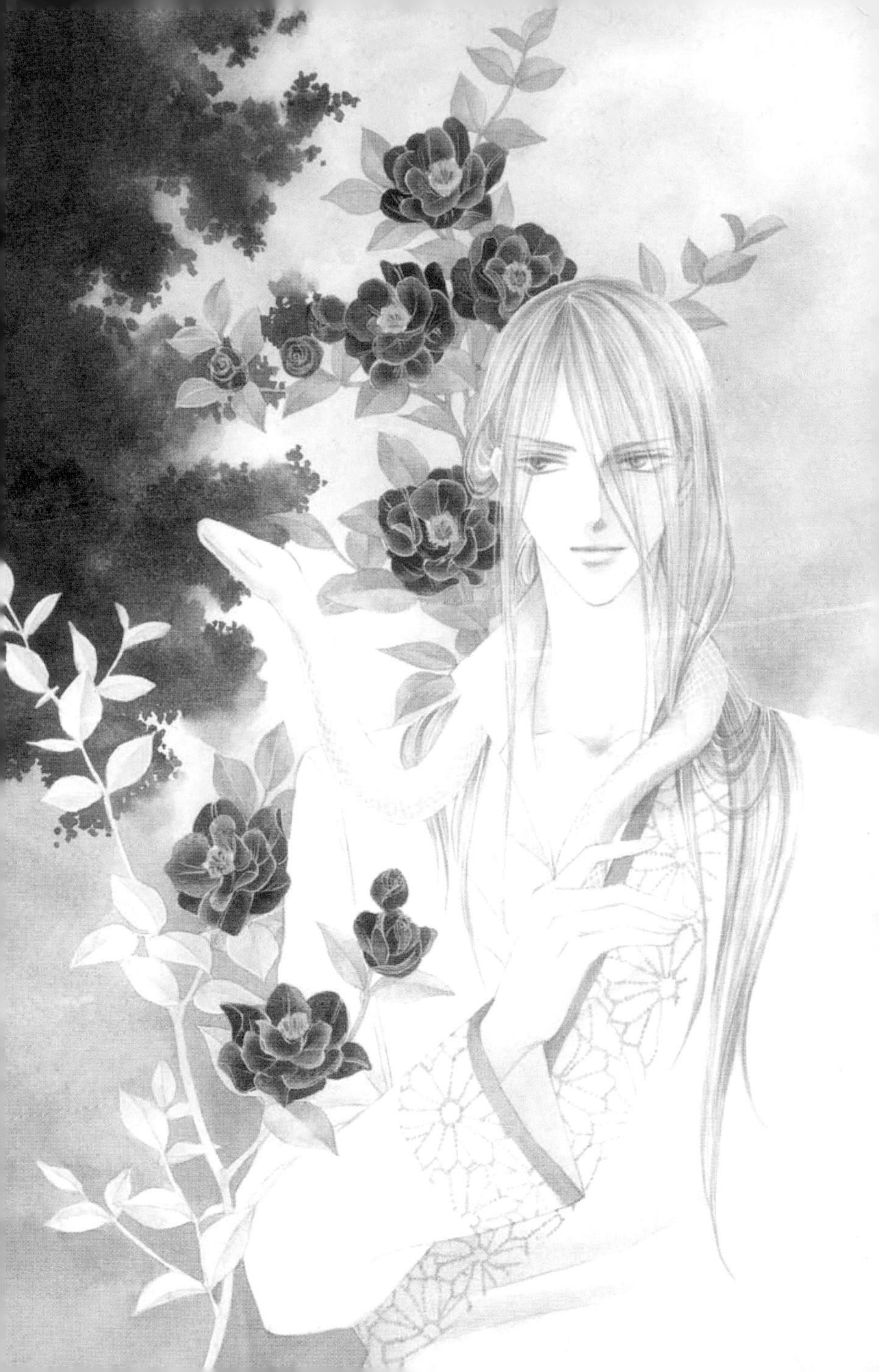

silver diamond

1: silver seed

By Shiho Sugiura

HAMBURG // LONDON // LOS ANGELES // TOKYO

SILVER DIAMOND Vol. 1
Created by Shiho Sugiura

Translation - Shirley Kubo
English Adaptation - Karen S. Ahlstrom
Fan Consultant - The SD Fan Advisory Group
Retouch and Lettering - Erica Terriquez, Star Print Brokers
Production Artist - Mike Estacio
Graphic Designer - Chelsea Windlinger

Editor - Alexis Kirsch
Digital Imaging Manager - Chris Buford
Pre-Production Supervisor - Lucas Riveras
Production Manager - Elisabeth Brizzi
Managing Editor - Vy Nguyen
Creative Director - Anne Marie Horne
Editor-in-Chief - Rob Tokar
Publisher - Mike Kiley
President and C.O.O. - John Parker
C.E.O. and Chief Creative Officer - Stu Levy

A **TOKYOPOP** Manga

TOKYOPOP and are trademarks or registered trademarks of TOKYOPOP Inc.

TOKYOPOP Inc.
5900 Wilshire Blvd. Suite 2000
Los Angeles, CA 90036

E-mail: info@TOKYOPOP.com
Come visit us online at www.TOKYOPOP.com

ISBN: 978-1-4278-0965-0

First TOKYOPOP printing: July 2008
10 9 8 7 6 5 4 3 2 1
Printed in the USA

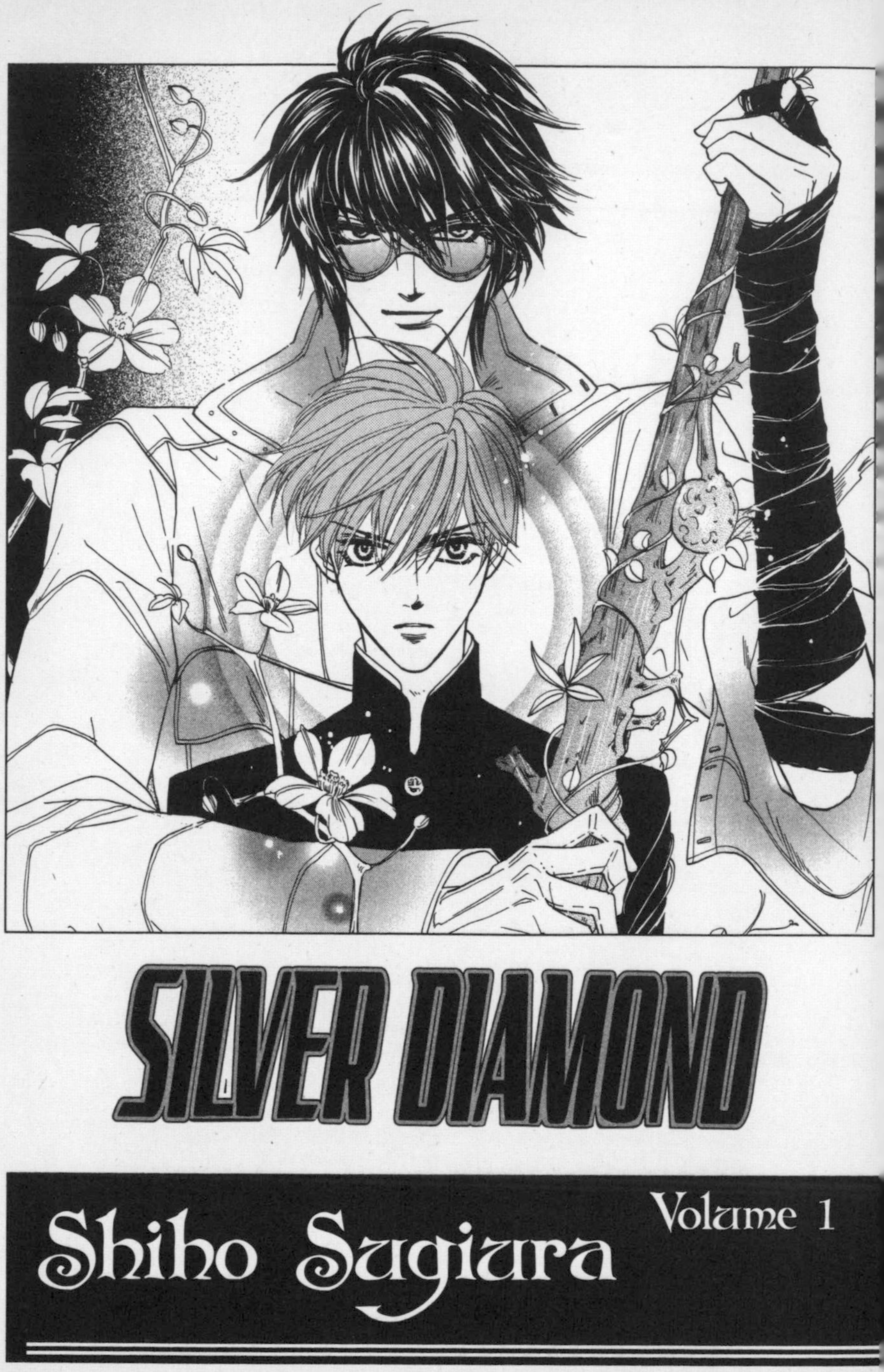

SILVER DIAMOND

Volume 1

Shiho Sugiura

Contents

Silver Diamond

**TO KEEP *SILVER DIAMOND* AS AUTHENTIC AS POSSIBLE, JAPANESE NAME ORDER (FAMILY NAME FIRST) AND HONORIFICS WILL BE MAINTAINED THROUGHOUT THE TEXT. FOR FURTHER EXPLANATIONS OF SPECIALLY-MARKED DIALOGUE(*), PLEASE CHECK THE GLOSSARY AT THE END OF THE VOLUME.

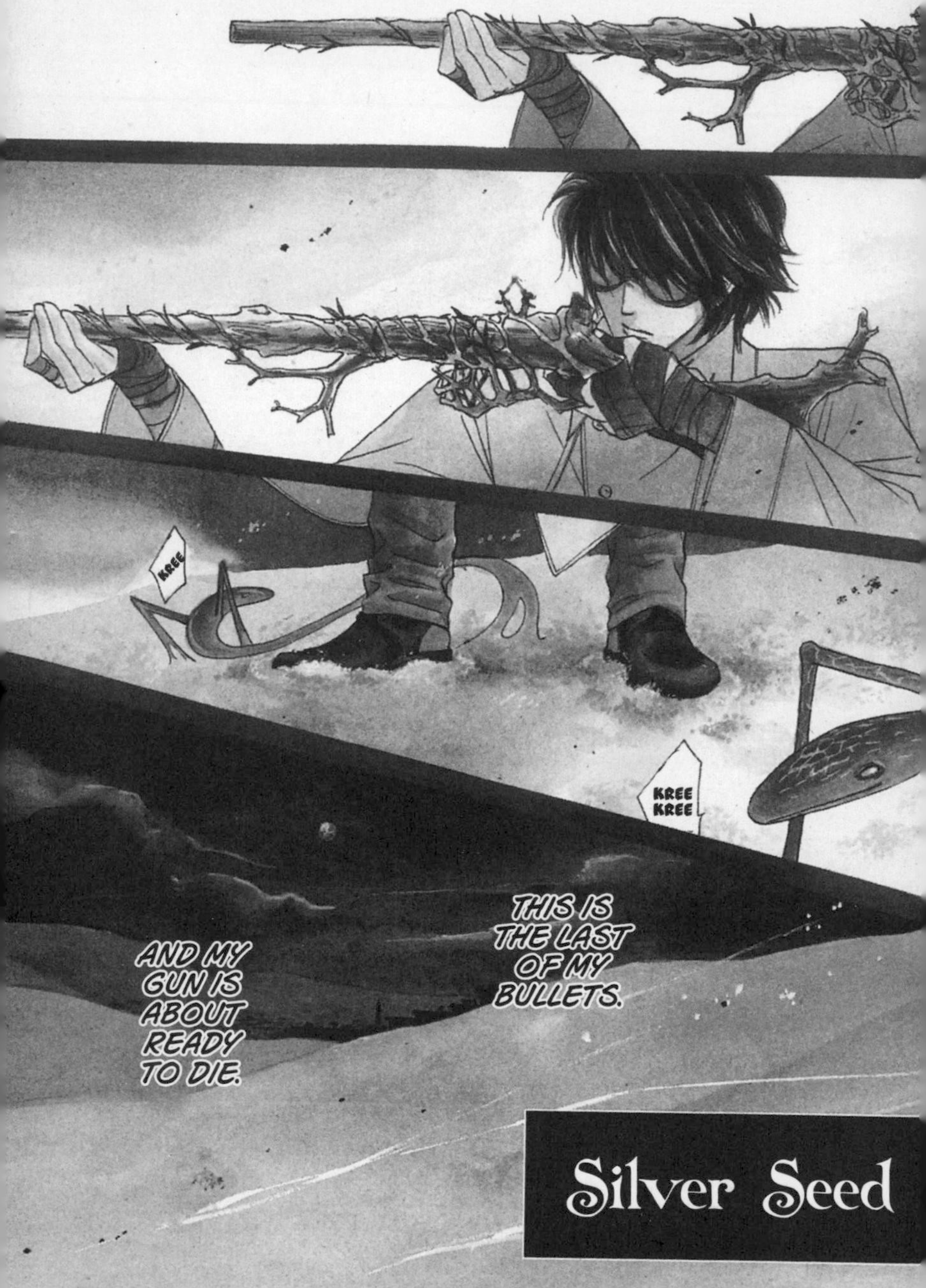

KREE
KREE KREE
THIS IS THE LAST OF MY BULLETS.
AND MY GUN IS ABOUT READY TO DIE.
Silver Seed

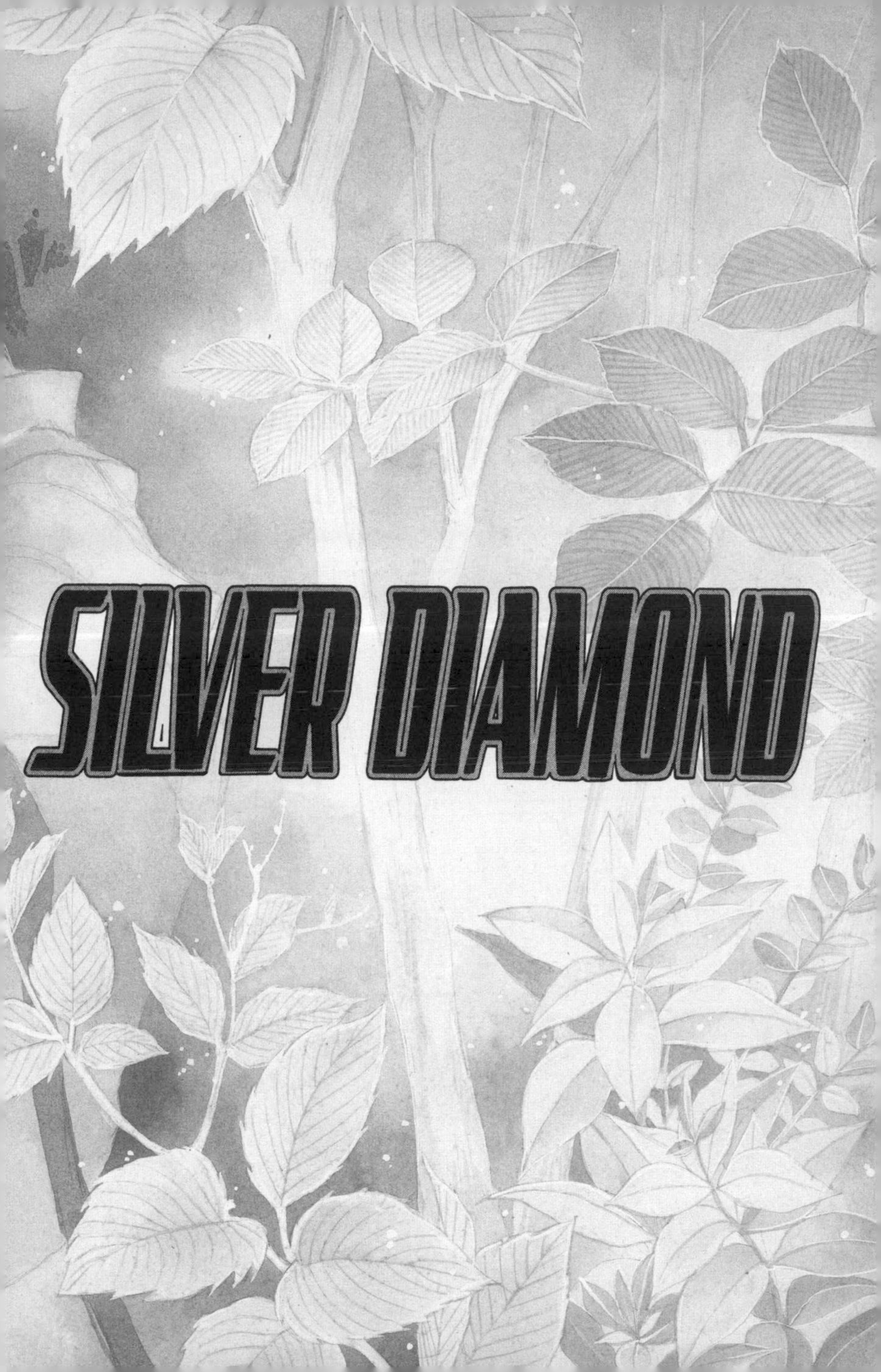
SILVER DIAMOND

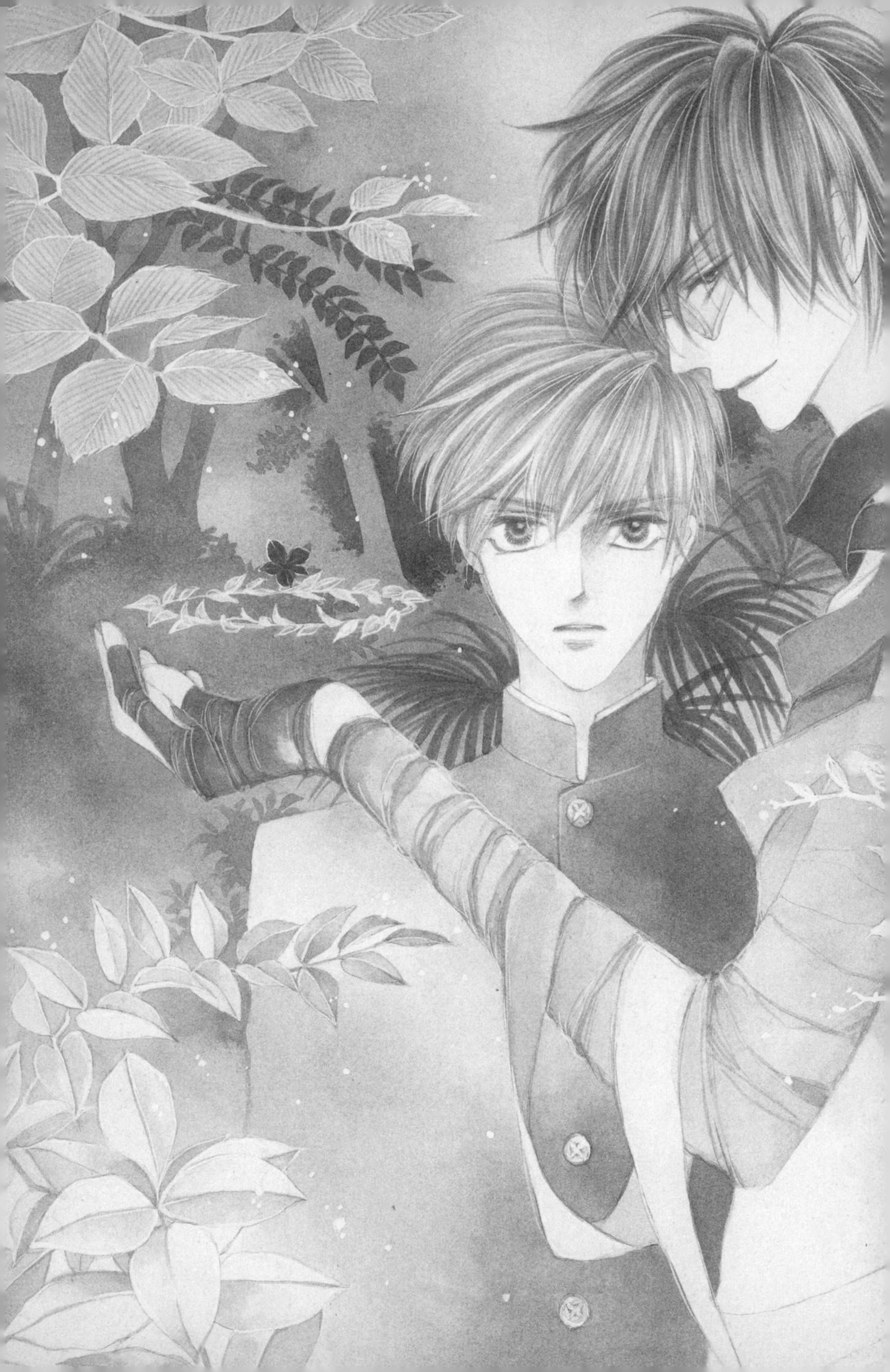

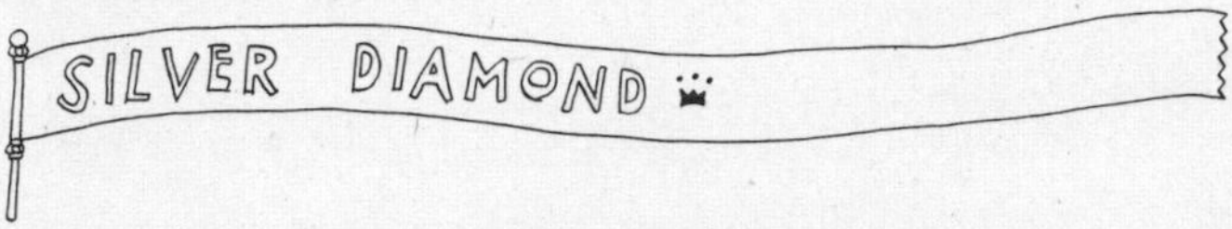
SILVER DIAMOND

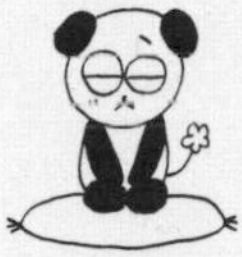

For those I'm meeting for the first time, and those that I've seen not so long ago... Hello, all! My name is Sugiura. Thank you so much for acquiring the first volume of *Silver Diamond.* To tell you the truth, I'm not very confident (it's been x years since I've started a new series, and I feel like a complete newbie). Now, to be serious, I plan on getting through this with hard work and enthusiasm, just like I did when I first started my previous series *Koori No Mamono No Monogatari* (The Ice-Cold Demon's Tale), so please join me if you'd like!

Incidentally, I ended up creating a title that's just as difficult to shorten as the old "Mamono." What to do? If I shorten it to "SD" I automatically think of the other manga series, *Slam Dunk.* I guess "Silver" would work.

I'm sure those of you who are familiar with my work will read this story and think, "How typical," but it would make me happy if you can enjoy it by thinking, "Oh, this is totally Sugiura's work!" I only know how to write exaggerated manga. Ha ha.

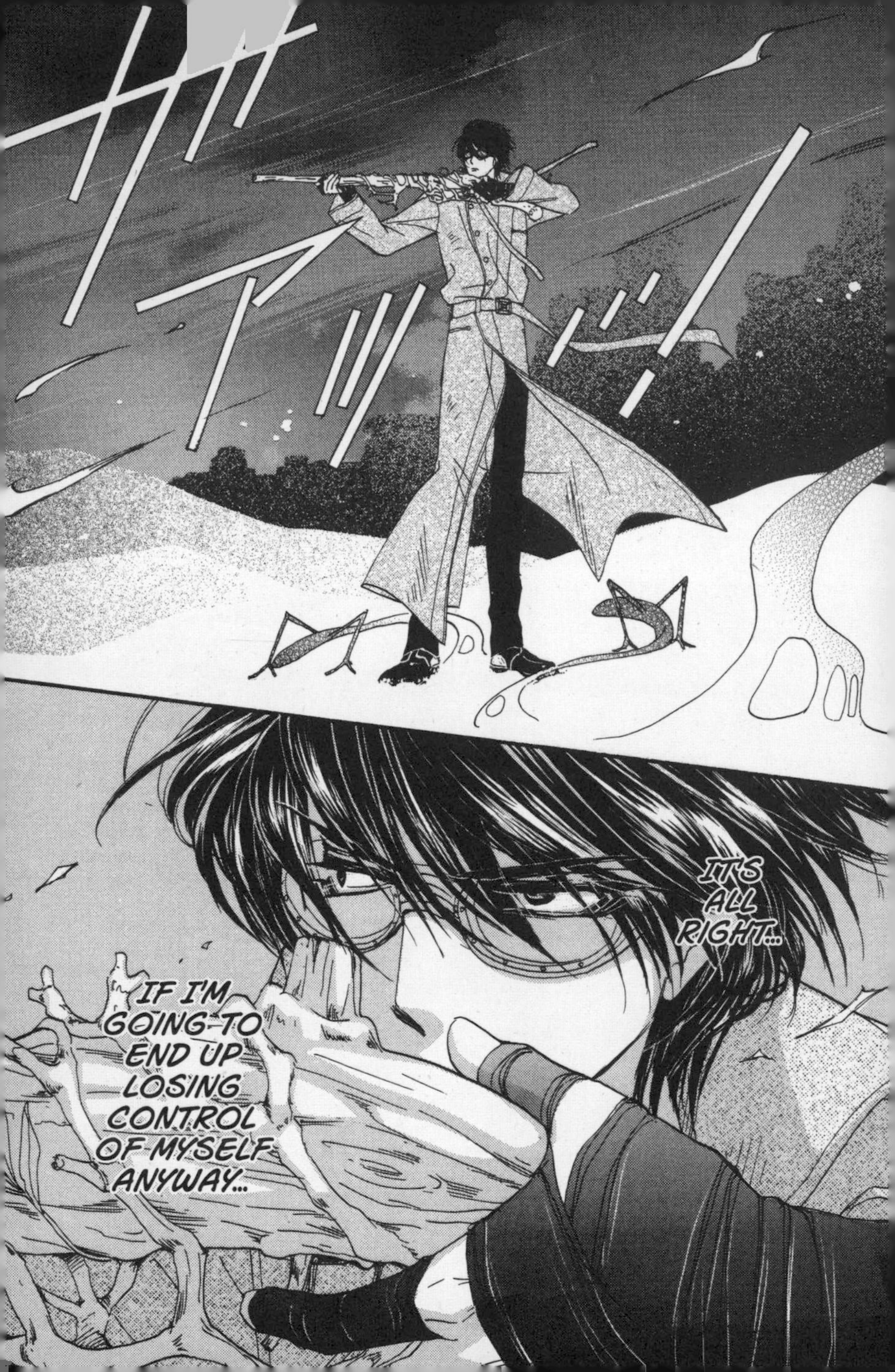
IT'S ALL RIGHT...
IF I'M GOING TO END UP LOSING CONTROL OF MYSELF ANYWAY...

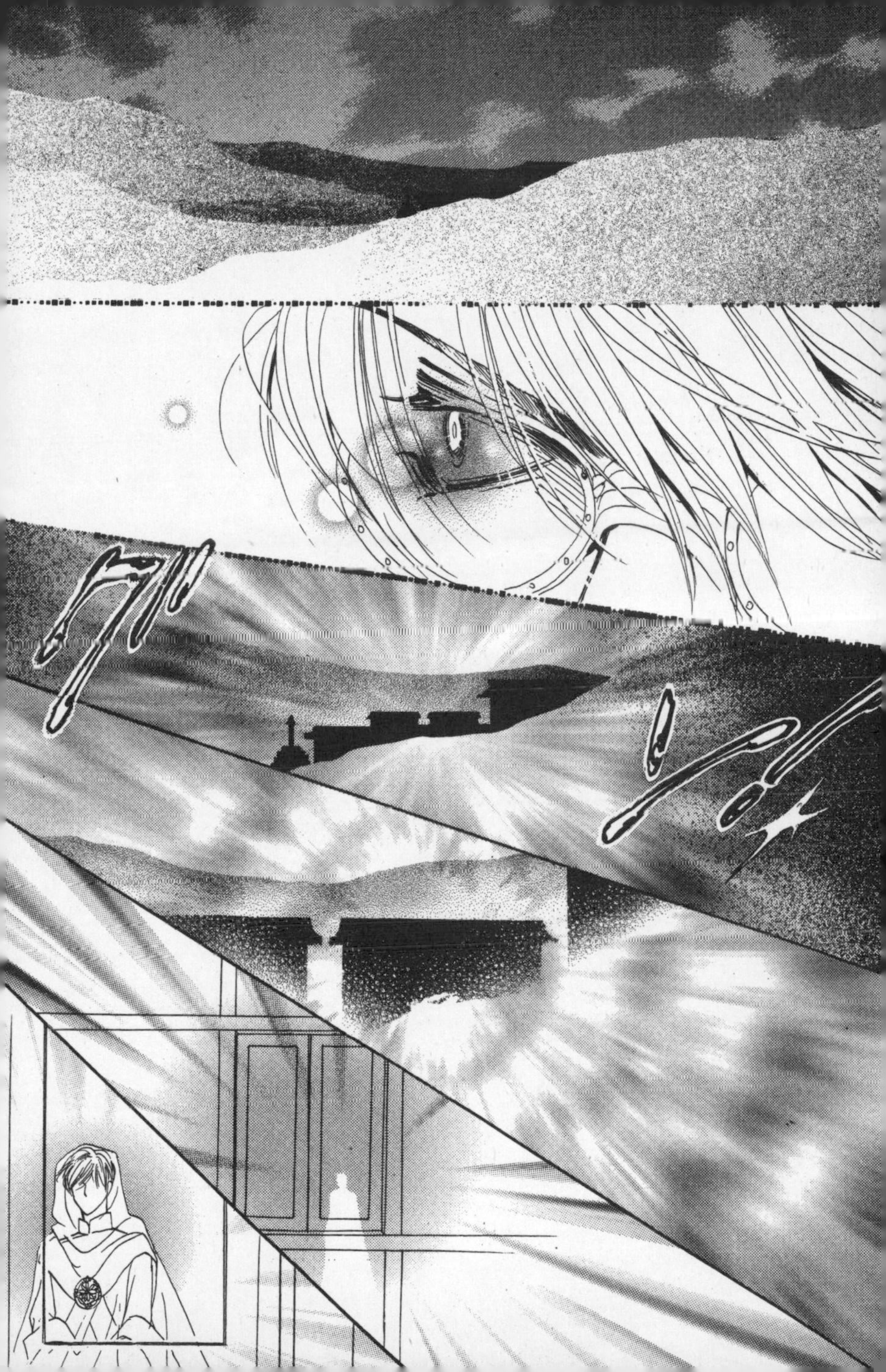

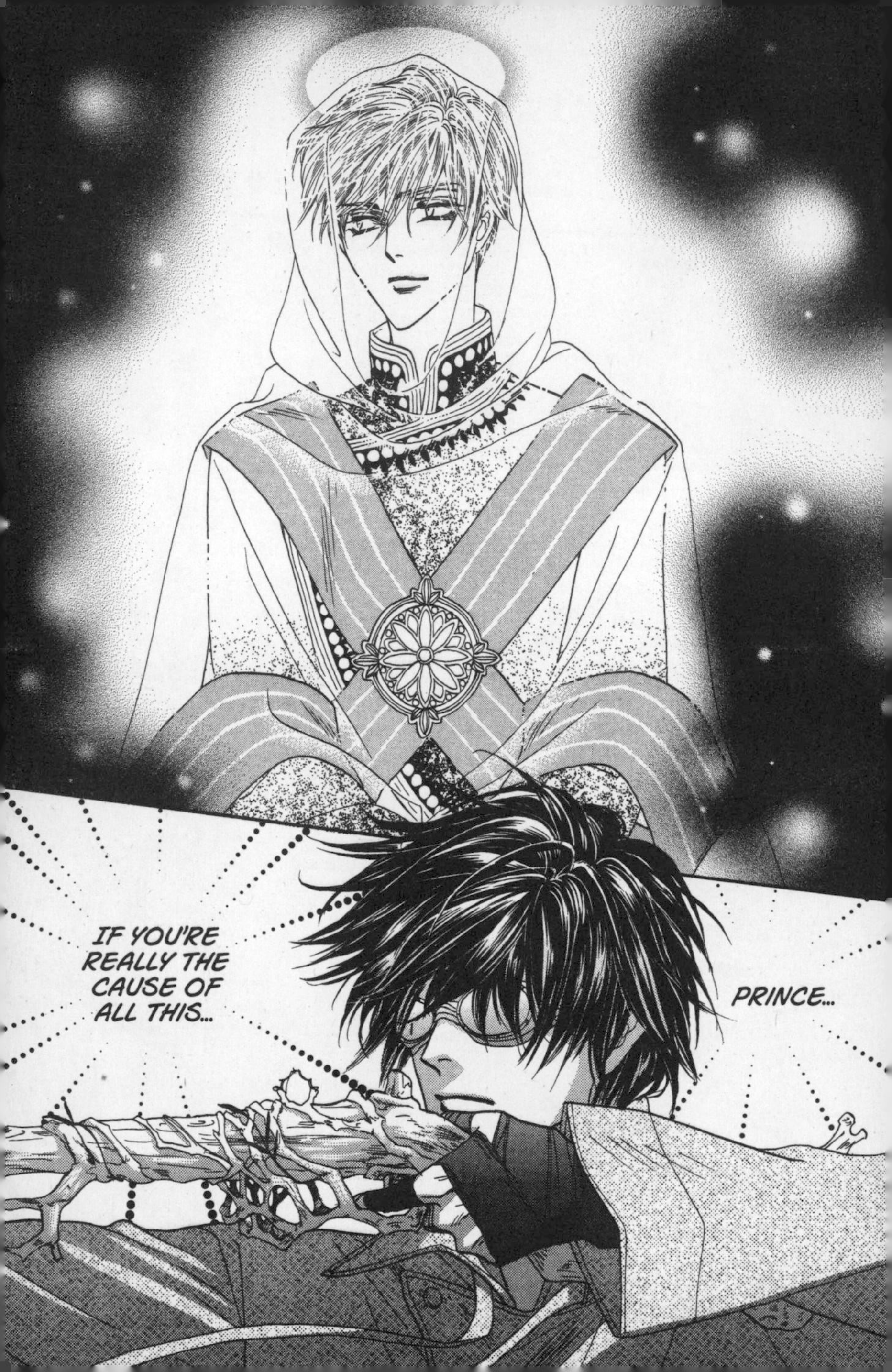
PRINCE...
IF YOU'RE REALLY THE CAUSE OF ALL THIS...

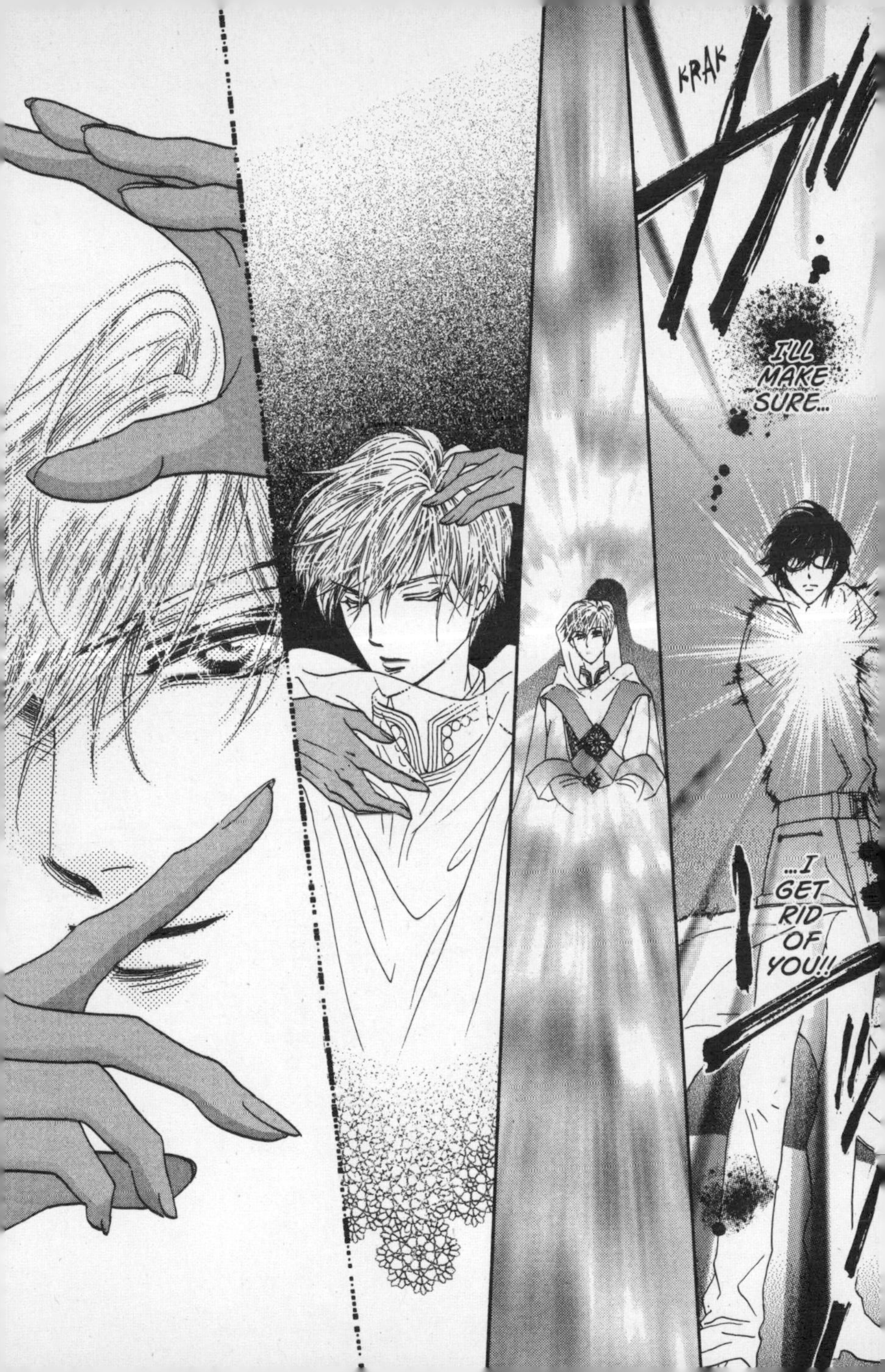
KRAK
I'LL MAKE SURE...
...I GET RID OF YOU!!

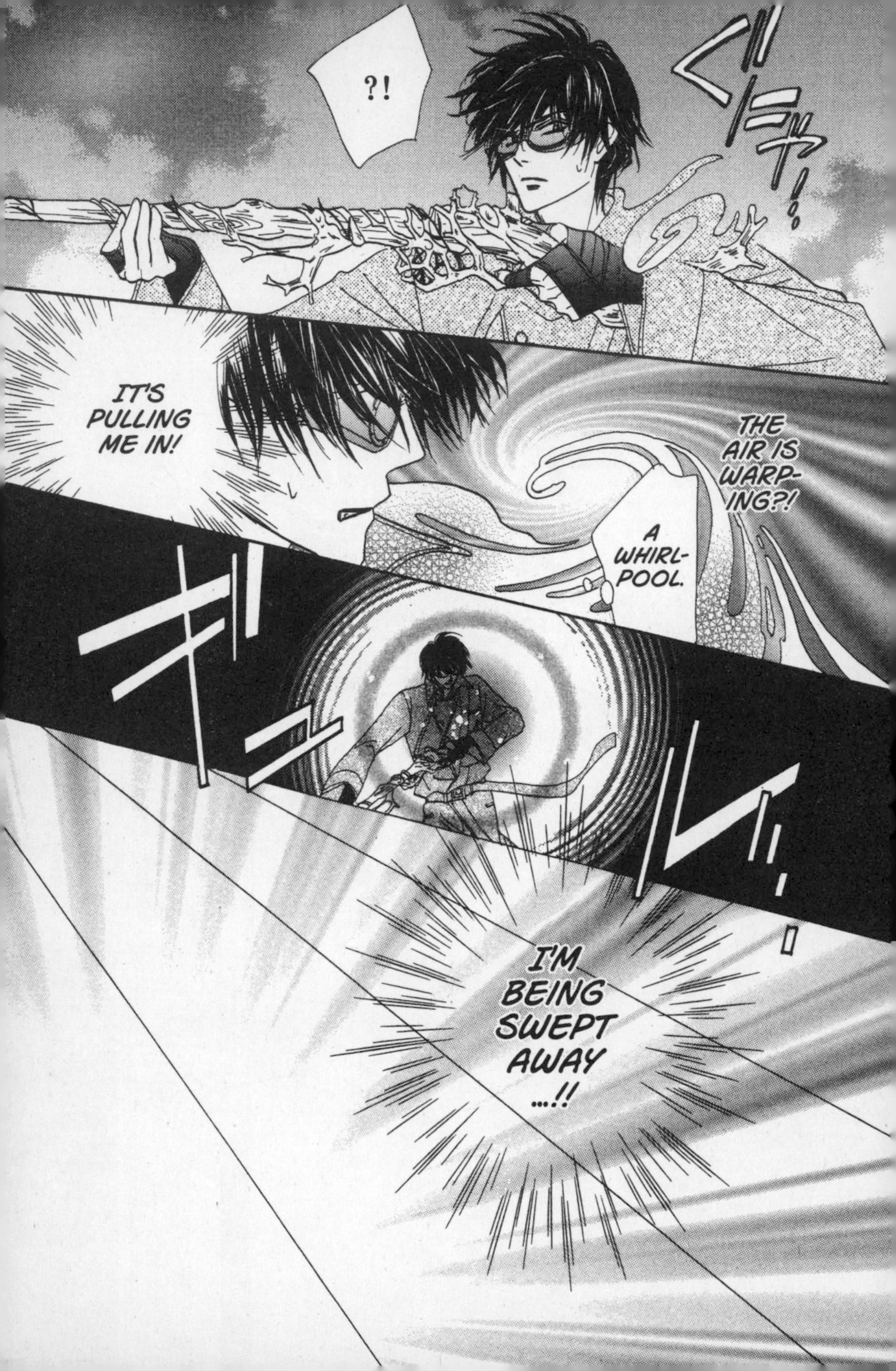

?!
ぐにゃ!!
THE AIR IS WARPING?!
A WHIRLPOOL.
IT'S PULLING ME IN!
I'M BEING SWEPT AWAY ...!!

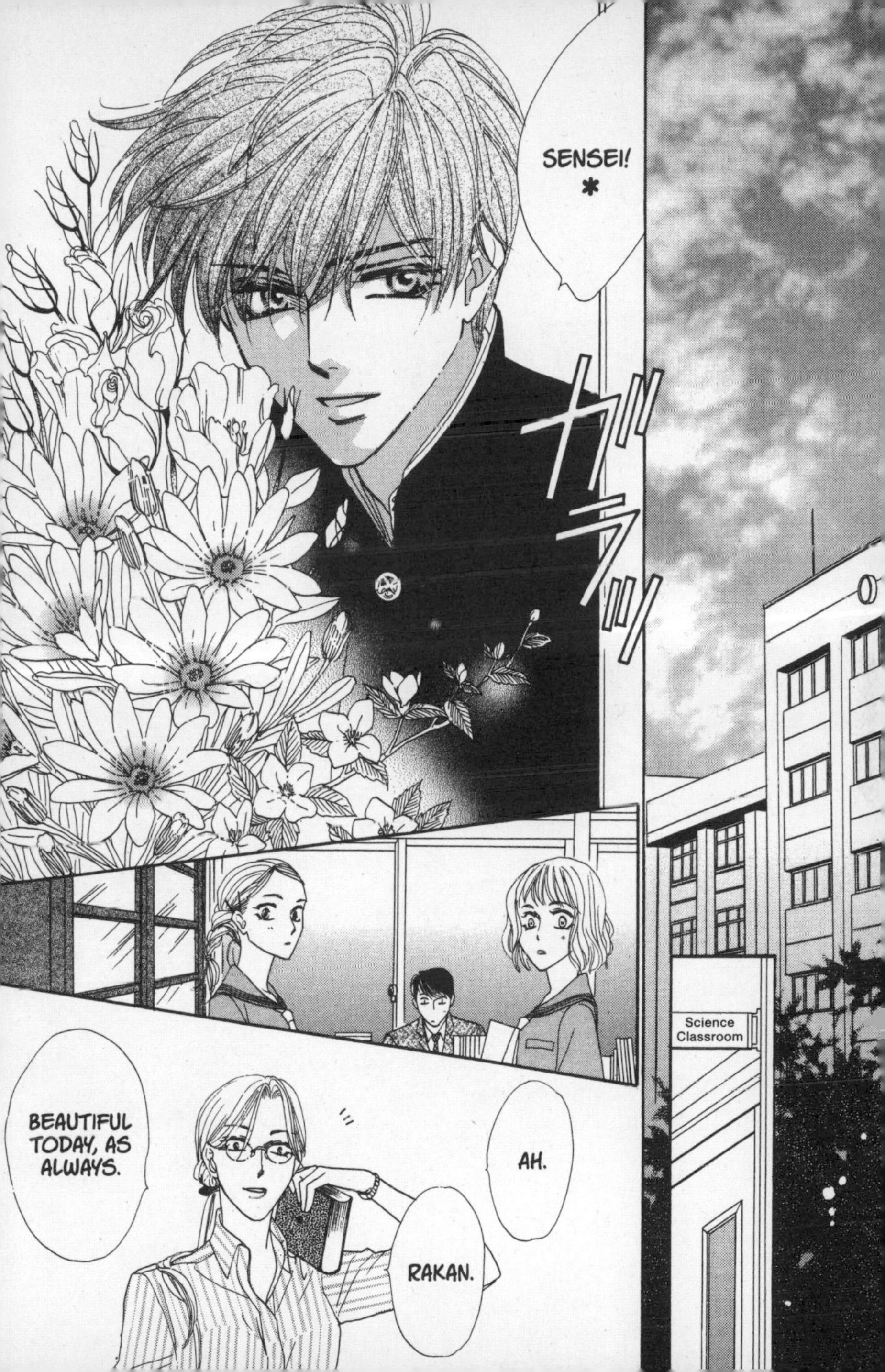
Science Classroom
SENSEI!
*
ガラッ
AH.
RAKAN.
BEAUTIFUL TODAY, AS ALWAYS.

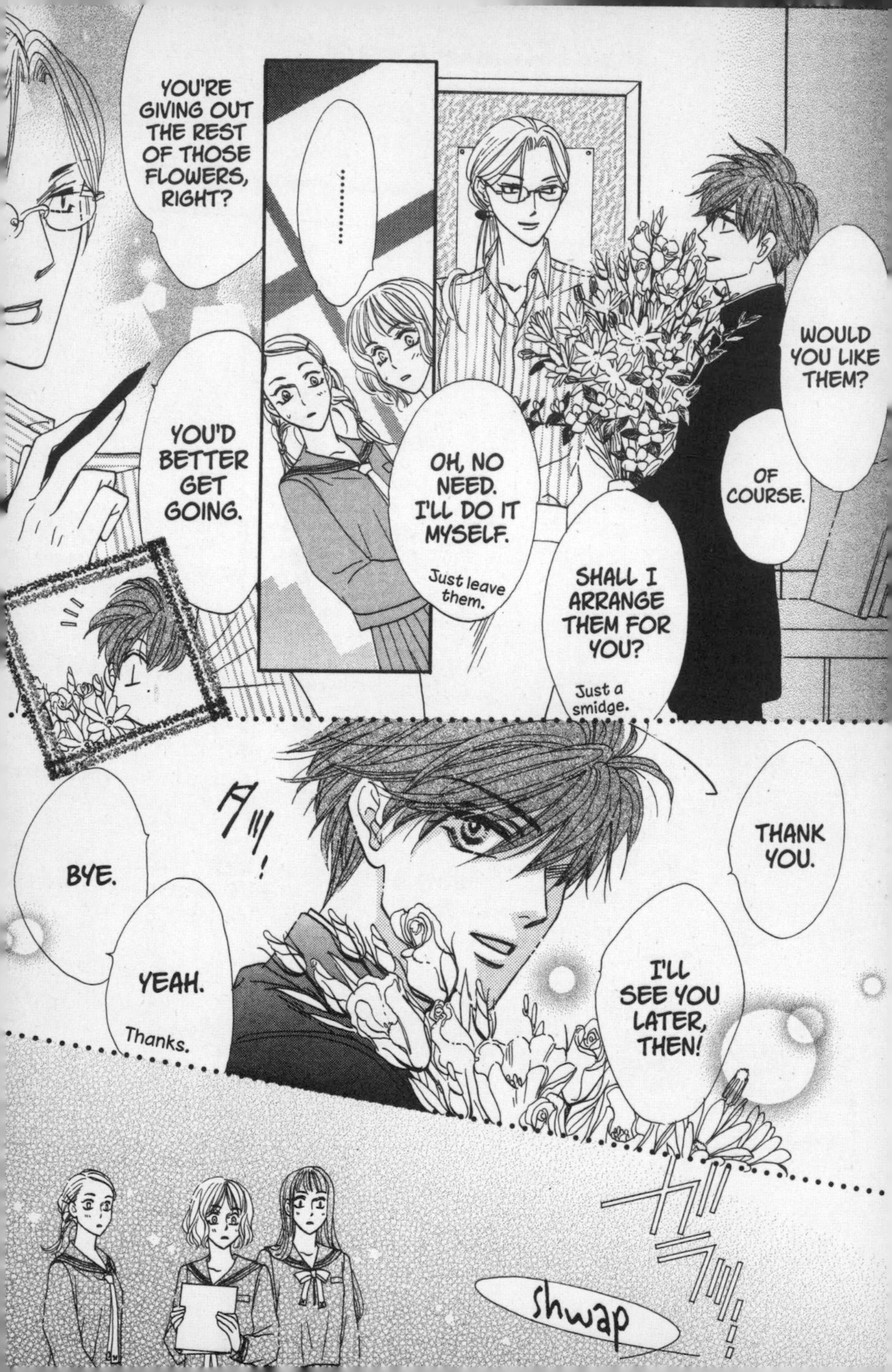

WOULD YOU LIKE THEM?
OF COURSE.
SHALL I ARRANGE THEM FOR YOU?
Just a smidge.
OH, NO NEED. I'LL DO IT MYSELF.
Just leave them.
......
YOU'RE GIVING OUT THE REST OF THOSE FLOWERS, RIGHT?
YOU'D BETTER GET GOING.
THANK YOU.
I'LL SEE YOU LATER, THEN!
BYE.
YEAH.
Thanks.
shwap

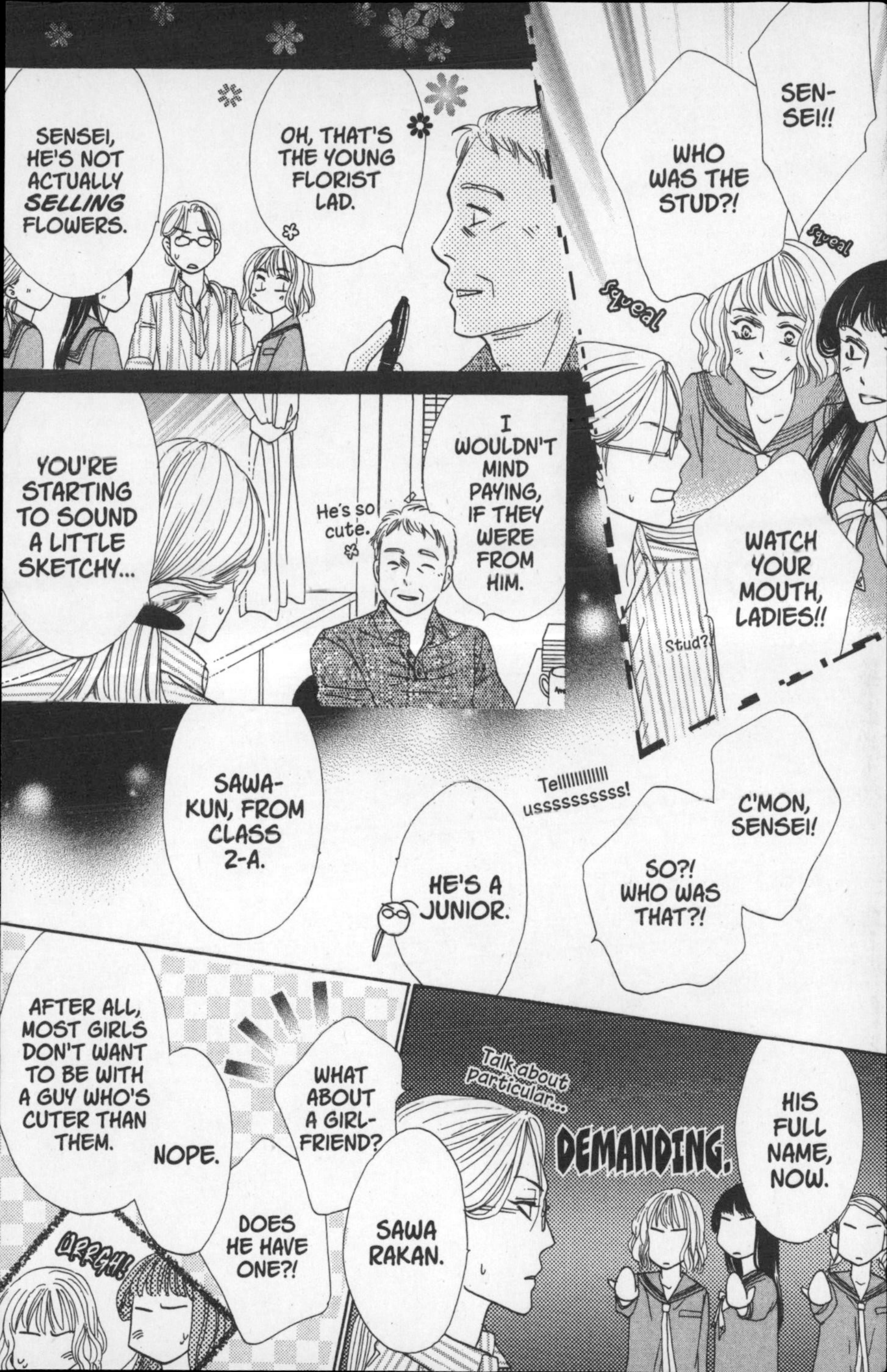
SEN-SEI!!
WHO WAS THE STUD?!
squeal
squeal
WATCH YOUR MOUTH, LADIES!!
Stud?
OH, THAT'S THE YOUNG FLORIST LAD.
SENSEI, HE'S NOT ACTUALLY *SELLING* FLOWERS.
I WOULDN'T MIND PAYING, IF THEY WERE FROM HIM.
He's so cute.
YOU'RE STARTING TO SOUND A LITTLE SKETCHY...
C'MON, SENSEI!
Tellllllllllll usssssssss!
SO?! WHO WAS THAT?!
HE'S A JUNIOR.
SAWA-KUN, FROM CLASS 2-A.
HIS FULL NAME, NOW.
DEMANDING.
Talk about particular...
SAWA RAKAN.
WHAT ABOUT A GIRL-FRIEND?
DOES HE HAVE ONE?!
NOPE.
AFTER ALL, MOST GIRLS DON'T WANT TO BE WITH A GUY WHO'S CUTER THAN THEM.
URRGH!

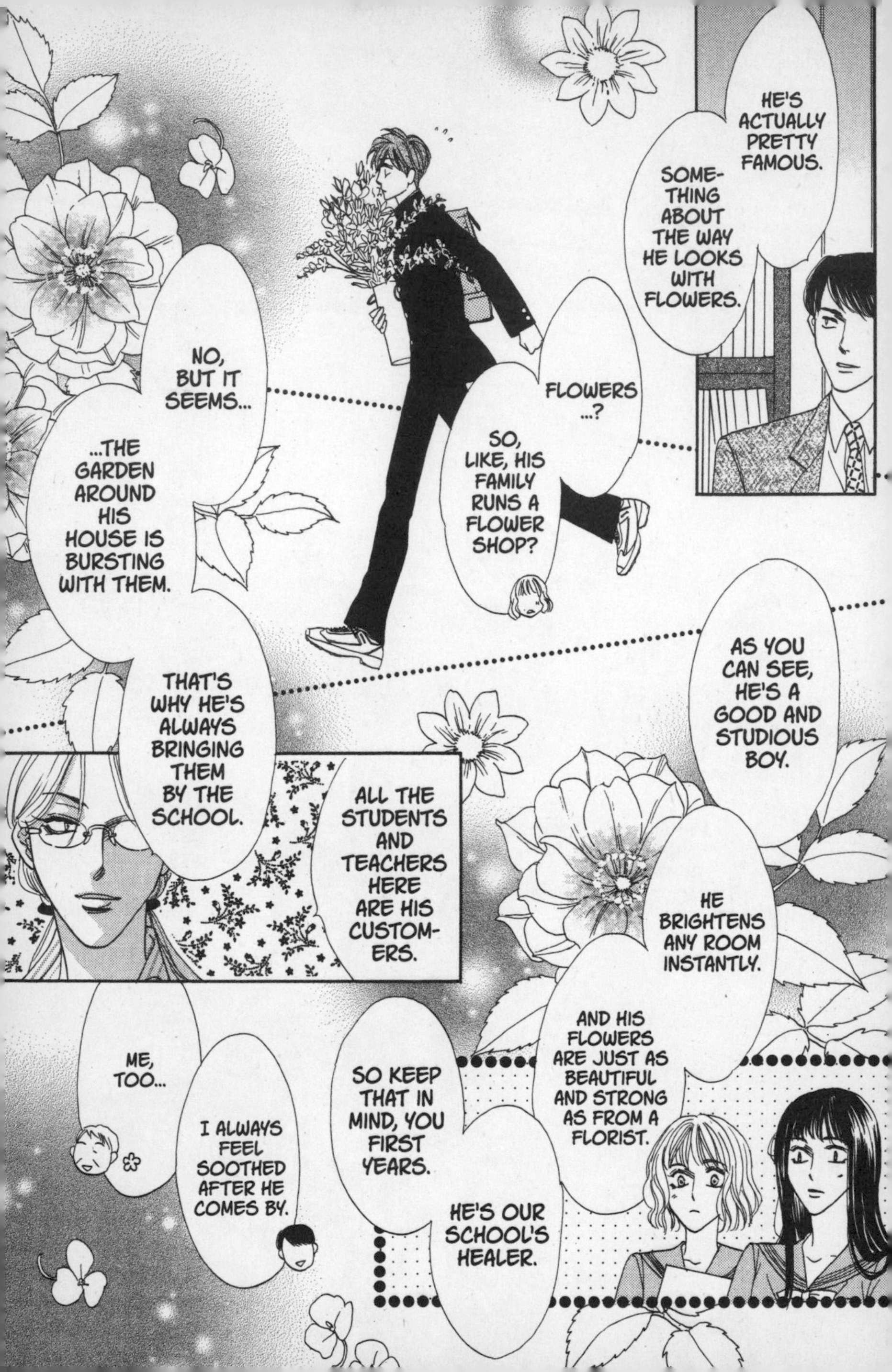
HE'S ACTUALLY PRETTY FAMOUS.
SOME-THING ABOUT THE WAY HE LOOKS WITH FLOWERS.
FLOWERS ...?
SO, LIKE, HIS FAMILY RUNS A FLOWER SHOP?
NO, BUT IT SEEMS...
...THE GARDEN AROUND HIS HOUSE IS BURSTING WITH THEM.
AS YOU CAN SEE, HE'S A GOOD AND STUDIOUS BOY.
THAT'S WHY HE'S ALWAYS BRINGING THEM BY THE SCHOOL.
ALL THE STUDENTS AND TEACHERS HERE ARE HIS CUSTOM-ERS.
HE BRIGHTENS ANY ROOM INSTANTLY.
AND HIS FLOWERS ARE JUST AS BEAUTIFUL AND STRONG AS FROM A FLORIST.
SO KEEP THAT IN MIND, YOU FIRST YEARS.
HE'S OUR SCHOOL'S HEALER.
I ALWAYS FEEL SOOTHED AFTER HE COMES BY.
ME, TOO...

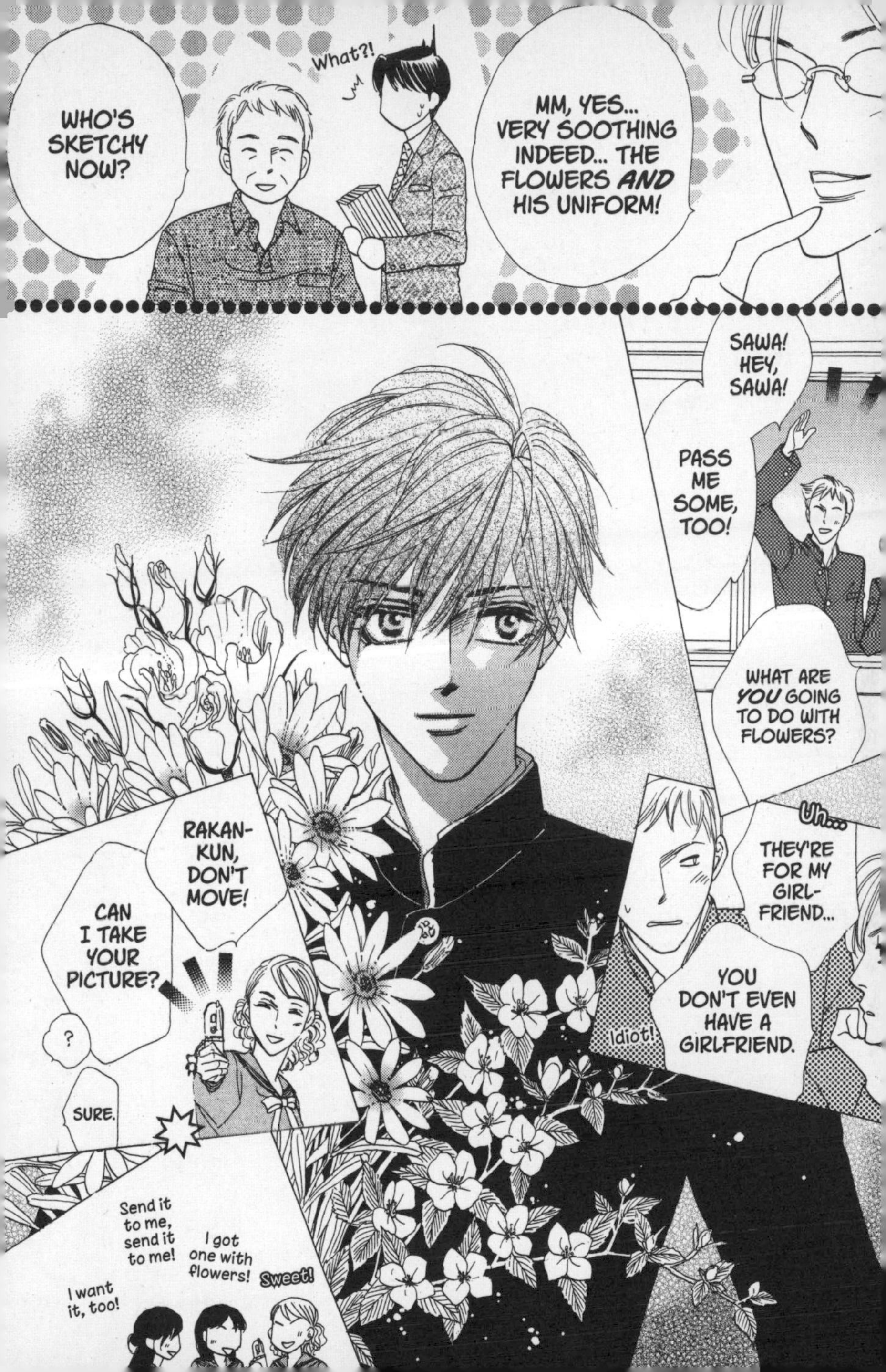
MM, YES... VERY SOOTHING INDEED... THE FLOWERS AND HIS UNIFORM!
What?!
WHO'S SKETCHY NOW?
SAWA! HEY, SAWA!
PASS ME SOME, TOO!
WHAT ARE YOU GOING TO DO WITH FLOWERS?
Uh...
THEY'RE FOR MY GIRL-FRIEND...
YOU DON'T EVEN HAVE A GIRLFRIEND.
Idiot!
RAKAN-KUN, DON'T MOVE!
CAN I TAKE YOUR PICTURE?
?
SURE.
Sweet!
I got one with flowers!
Send it to me, send it to me!
I want it, too!

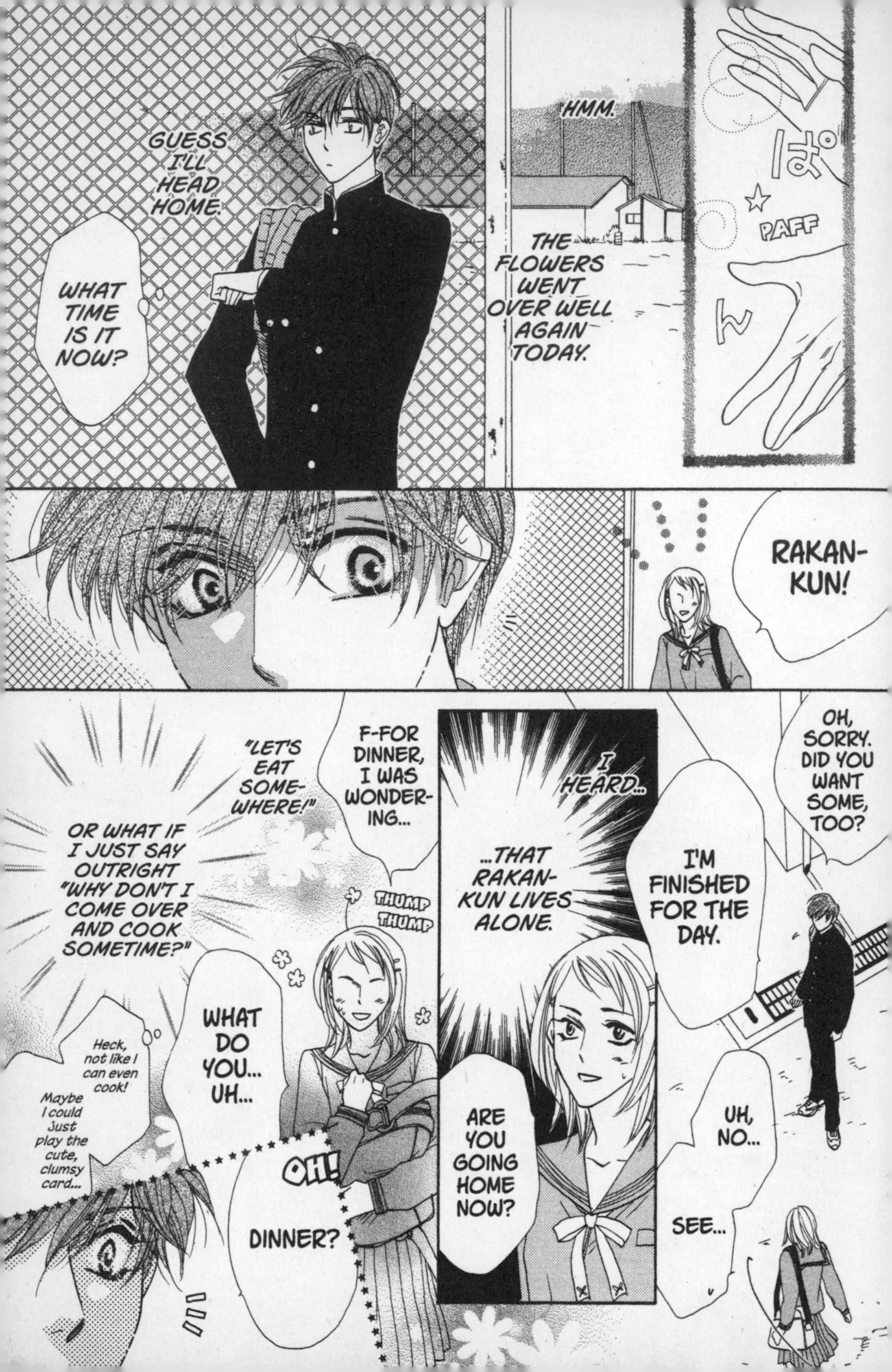
ぱ
PAFF
ん
HMM.
THE FLOWERS WENT OVER WELL AGAIN TODAY.
GUESS I'LL HEAD HOME.
WHAT TIME IS IT NOW?
RAKAN-KUN!
OH, SORRY. DID YOU WANT SOME, TOO?
I'M FINISHED FOR THE DAY.
UH, NO...
SEE...
I HEARD...
...THAT RAKAN-KUN LIVES ALONE.
ARE YOU GOING HOME NOW?
F-FOR DINNER, I WAS WONDERING...
"LET'S EAT SOMEWHERE!"
OR WHAT IF I JUST SAY OUTRIGHT "WHY DON'T I COME OVER AND COOK SOMETIME?"
THUMP THUMP
WHAT DO YOU... UH...
Heck, not like I can even cook!
Maybe I could just play the cute, clumsy card...
OH!
DINNER?

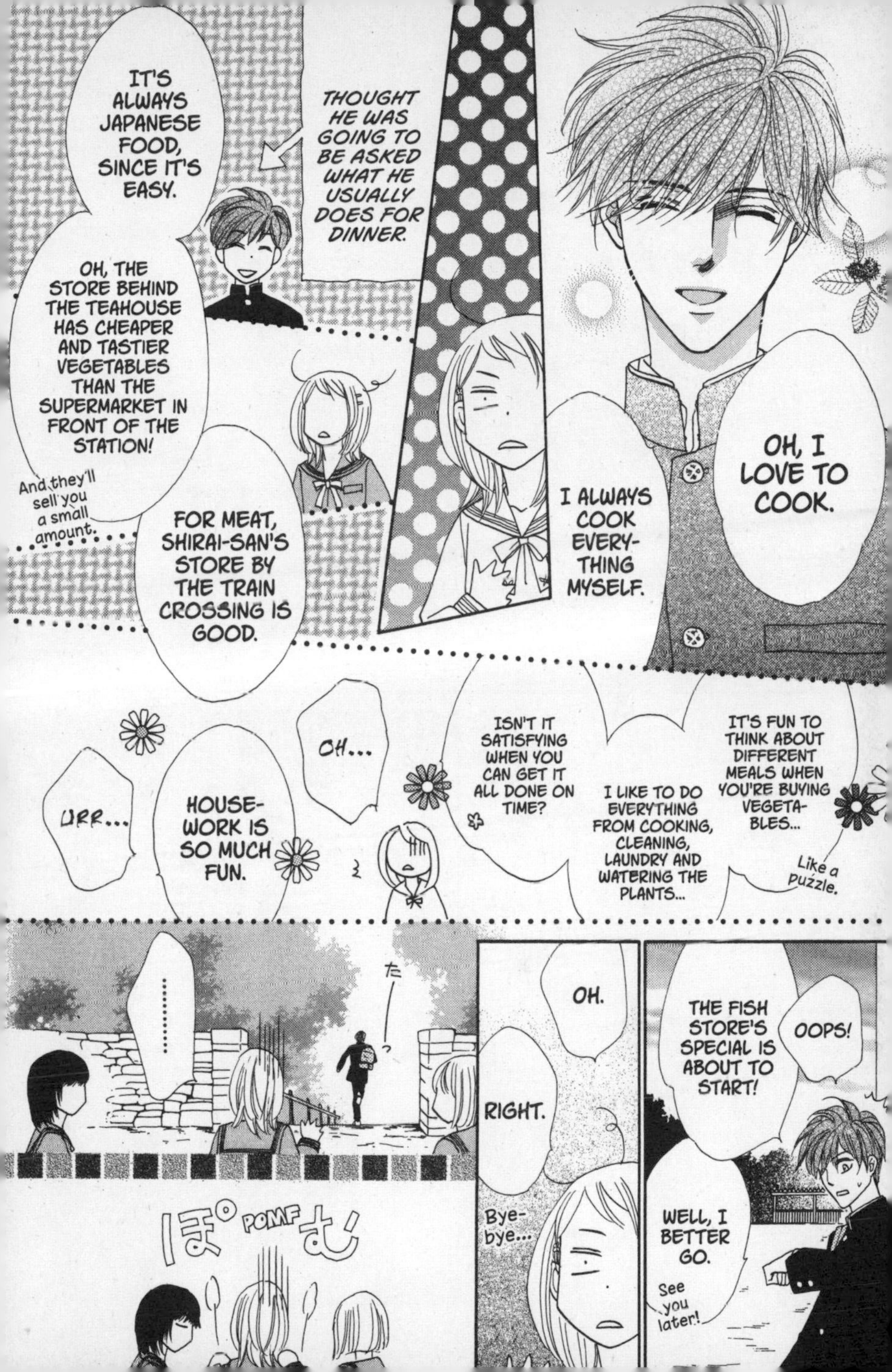
OH, I LOVE TO COOK.
I ALWAYS COOK EVERYTHING MYSELF.
THOUGHT HE WAS GOING TO BE ASKED WHAT HE USUALLY DOES FOR DINNER.
IT'S ALWAYS JAPANESE FOOD, SINCE IT'S EASY.
OH, THE STORE BEHIND THE TEAHOUSE HAS CHEAPER AND TASTIER VEGETABLES THAN THE SUPERMARKET IN FRONT OF THE STATION!
And they'll sell you a small amount.
FOR MEAT, SHIRAI-SAN'S STORE BY THE TRAIN CROSSING IS GOOD.
IT'S FUN TO THINK ABOUT DIFFERENT MEALS WHEN YOU'RE BUYING VEGETABLES...
Like a puzzle.
I LIKE TO DO EVERYTHING FROM COOKING, CLEANING, LAUNDRY AND WATERING THE PLANTS...
ISN'T IT SATISFYING WHEN YOU CAN GET IT ALL DONE ON TIME?
OH...
HOUSEWORK IS SO MUCH FUN.
URR...
OOPS!
THE FISH STORE'S SPECIAL IS ABOUT TO START!
WELL, I BETTER GO.
See you later!
OH.
RIGHT.
Bye-bye...
たー
....
?
ぽ POMF む!

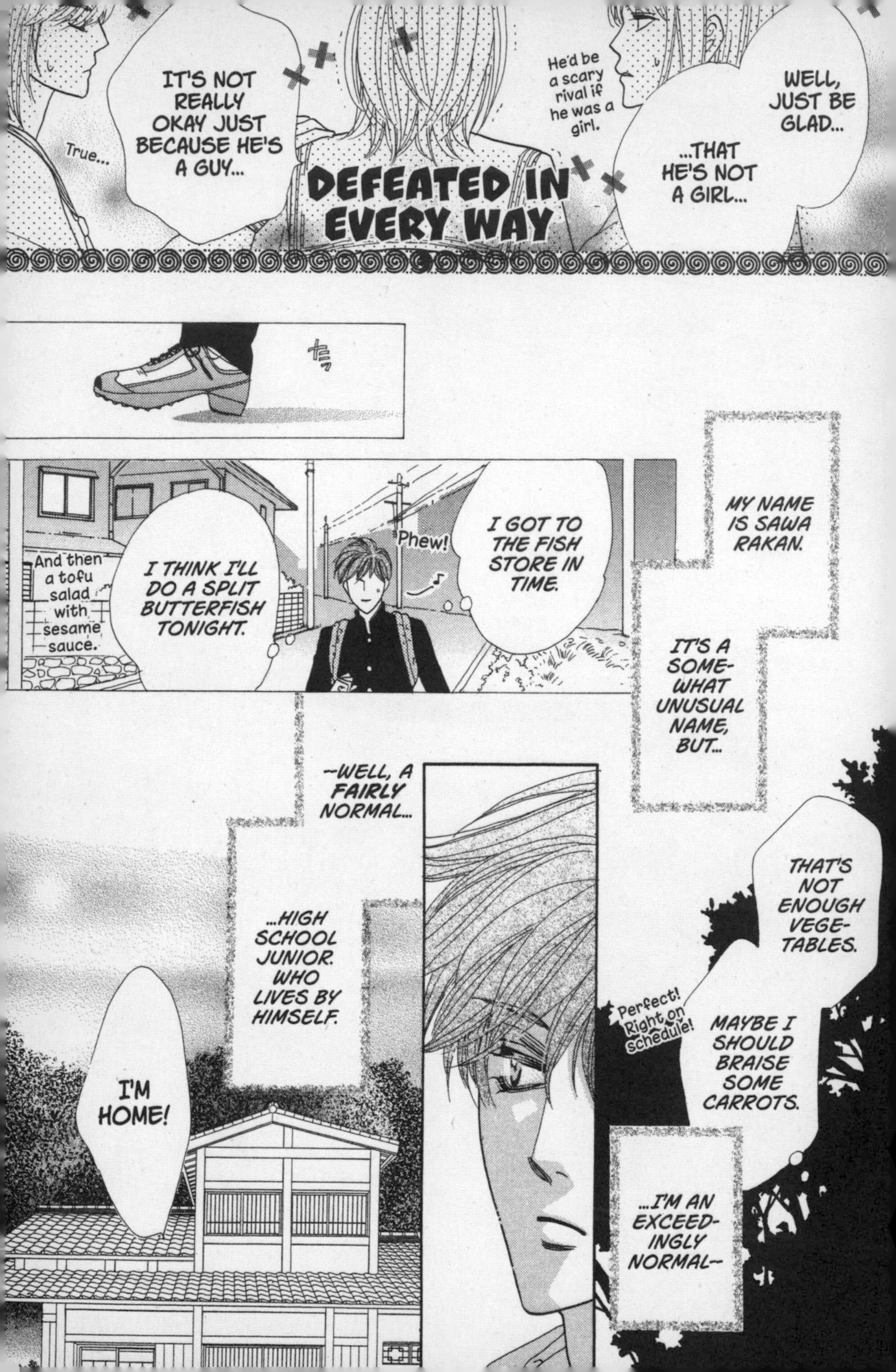
WELL, JUST BE GLAD...
...THAT HE'S NOT A GIRL...
He'd be a scary rival if he was a girl.
DEFEATED IN EVERY WAY
IT'S NOT REALLY OKAY JUST BECAUSE HE'S A GUY...
True...
MY NAME IS SAWA RAKAN.
IT'S A SOME-WHAT UNUSUAL NAME, BUT...
I GOT TO THE FISH STORE IN TIME.
Phew!
I THINK I'LL DO A SPLIT BUTTERFISH TONIGHT.
And then a tofu salad with sesame sauce.
THAT'S NOT ENOUGH VEGE-TABLES.
MAYBE I SHOULD BRAISE SOME CARROTS.
Perfect! Right on schedule!
...I'M AN EXCEED-INGLY NORMAL--
--WELL, A FAIRLY NORMAL...
...HIGH SCHOOL JUNIOR. WHO LIVES BY HIMSELF.
I'M HOME!

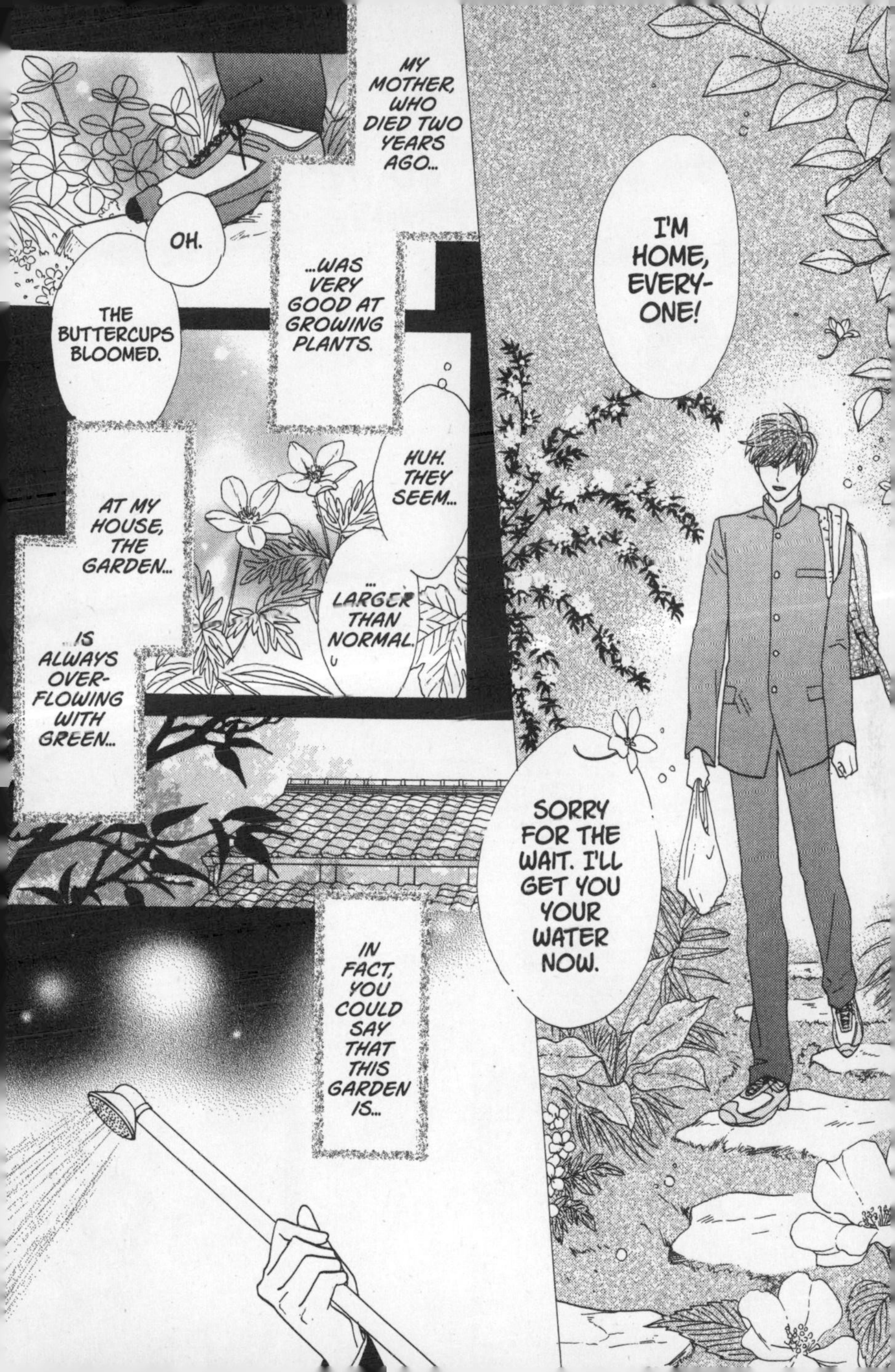
I'M HOME, EVERY-ONE!
SORRY FOR THE WAIT. I'LL GET YOU YOUR WATER NOW.
MY MOTHER, WHO DIED TWO YEARS AGO...
OH.
THE BUTTERCUPS BLOOMED.
...WAS VERY GOOD AT GROWING PLANTS.
HUH. THEY SEEM...
...LARGER THAN NORMAL.
AT MY HOUSE, THE GARDEN...
...IS ALWAYS OVER-FLOWING WITH GREEN...
IN FACT, YOU COULD SAY THAT THIS GARDEN IS...

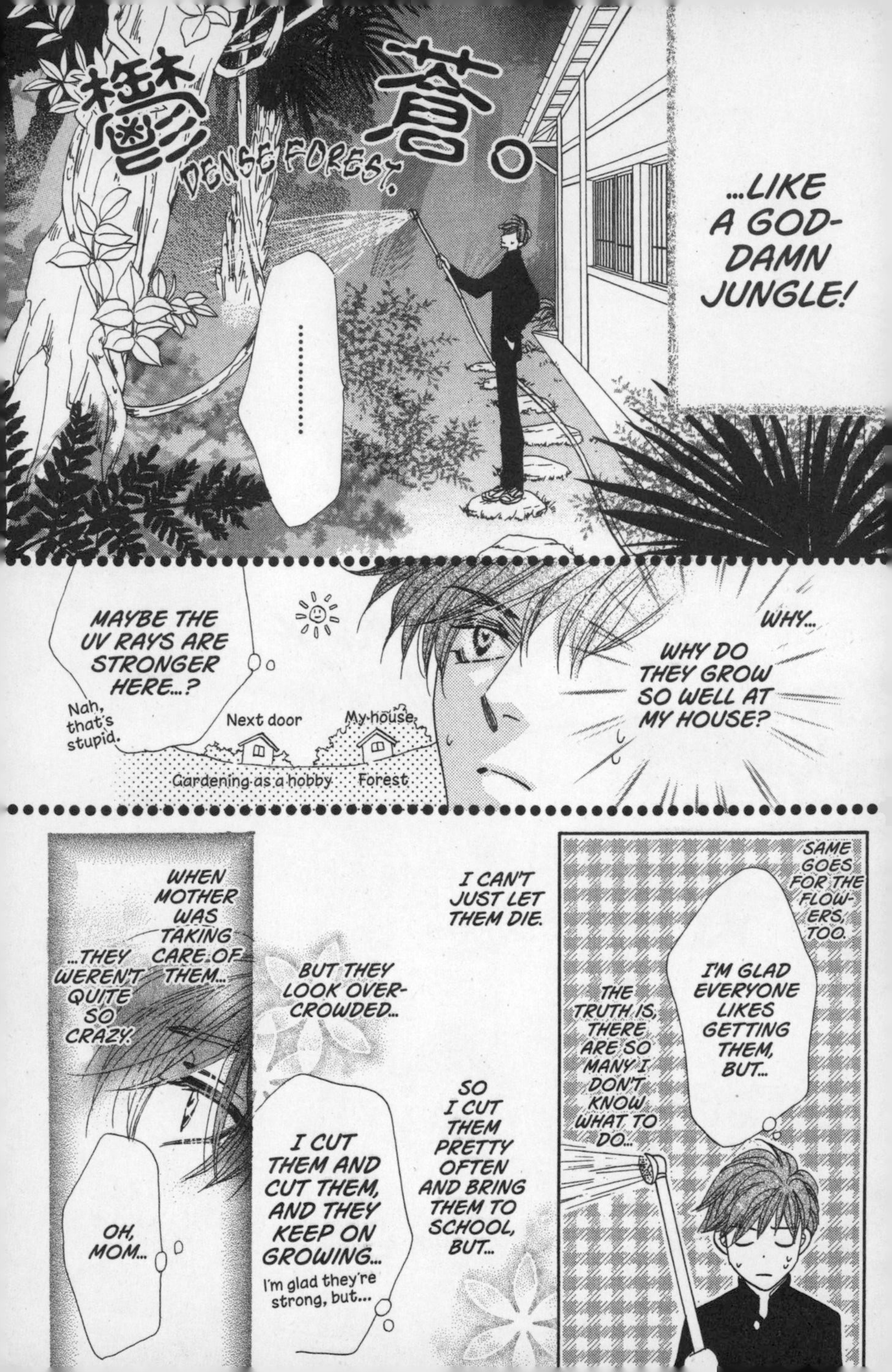
...LIKE A GOD-DAMN JUNGLE!
鬱蒼。
DENSE FOREST.
......
WHY...
WHY DO THEY GROW SO WELL AT MY HOUSE?
MAYBE THE UV RAYS ARE STRONGER HERE...?
Nah, that's stupid.
My house
Next door
Forest
Gardening as a hobby
SAME GOES FOR THE FLOWERS, TOO.
I'M GLAD EVERYONE LIKES GETTING THEM, BUT...
THE TRUTH IS, THERE ARE SO MANY I DON'T KNOW WHAT TO DO...
I CAN'T JUST LET THEM DIE.
BUT THEY LOOK OVER-CROWDED...
SO I CUT THEM PRETTY OFTEN AND BRING THEM TO SCHOOL, BUT...
I CUT THEM AND CUT THEM, AND THEY KEEP ON GROWING...
I'm glad they're strong, but...
WHEN MOTHER WAS TAKING CARE OF THEM...
...THEY WEREN'T QUITE SO CRAZY.
OH, MOM...

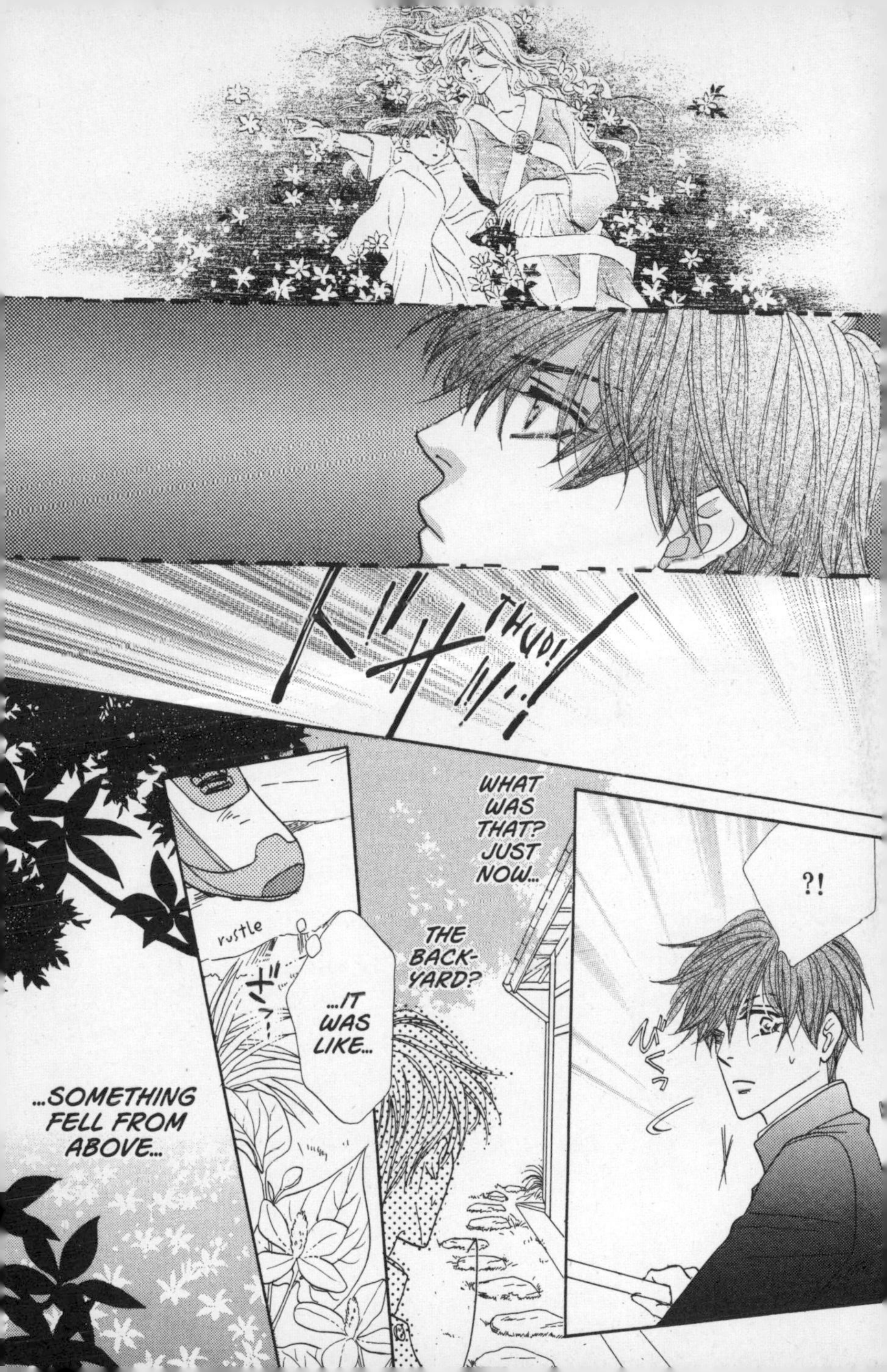
THUD!
?!
WHAT WAS THAT? JUST NOW...
THE BACK-YARD?
...IT WAS LIKE...
rustle
...SOMETHING FELL FROM ABOVE...

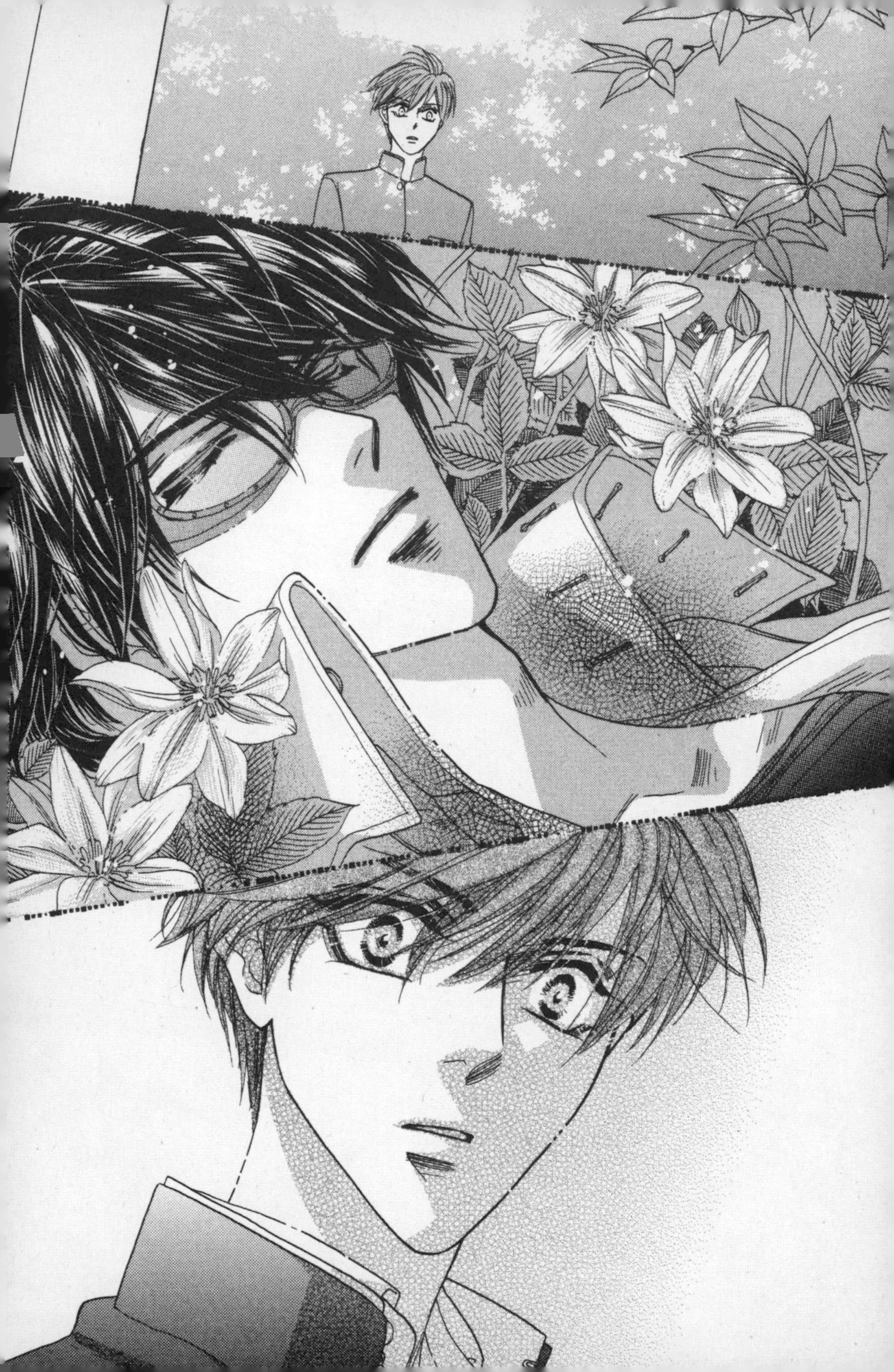

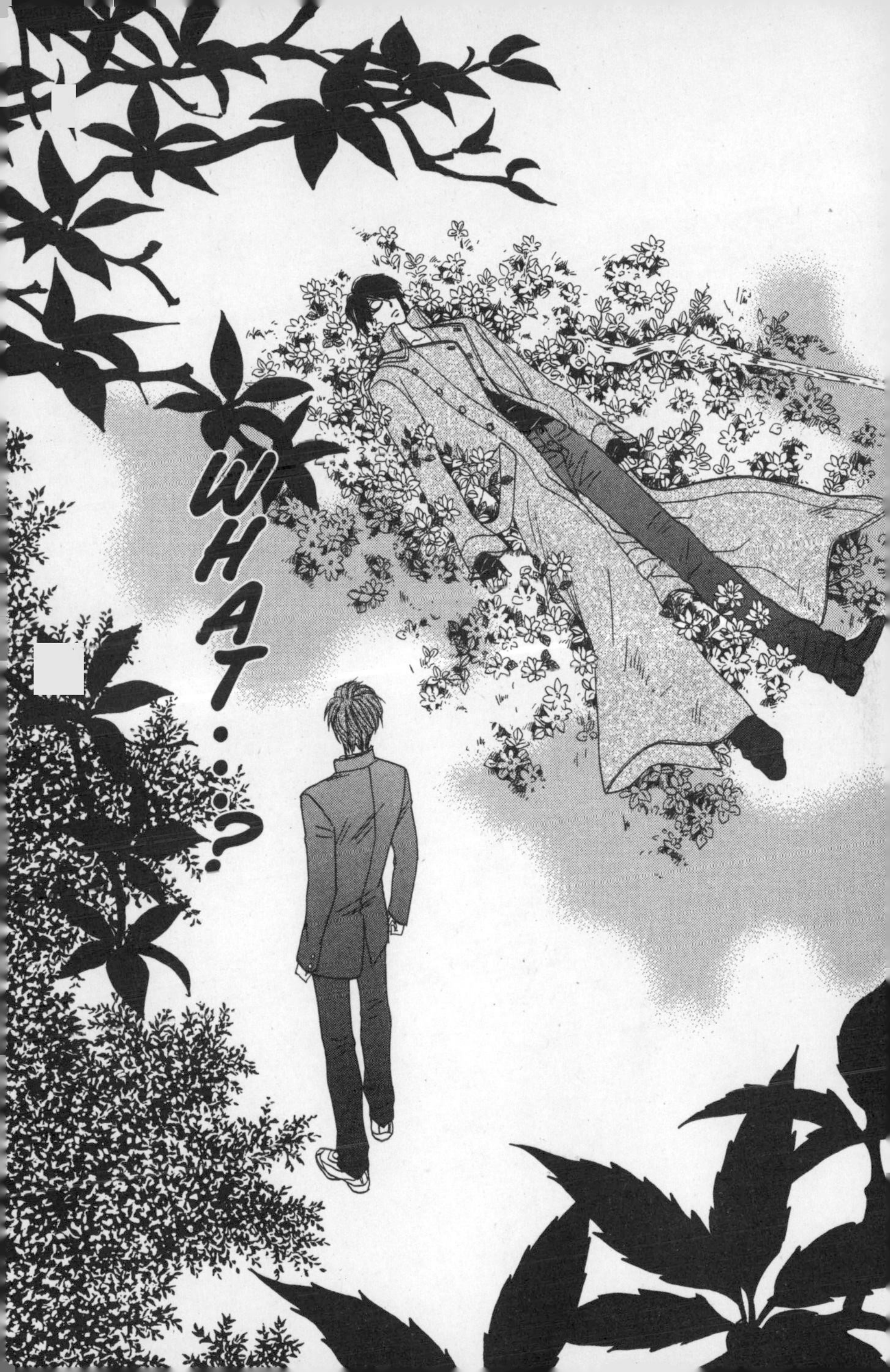
WHAT...?

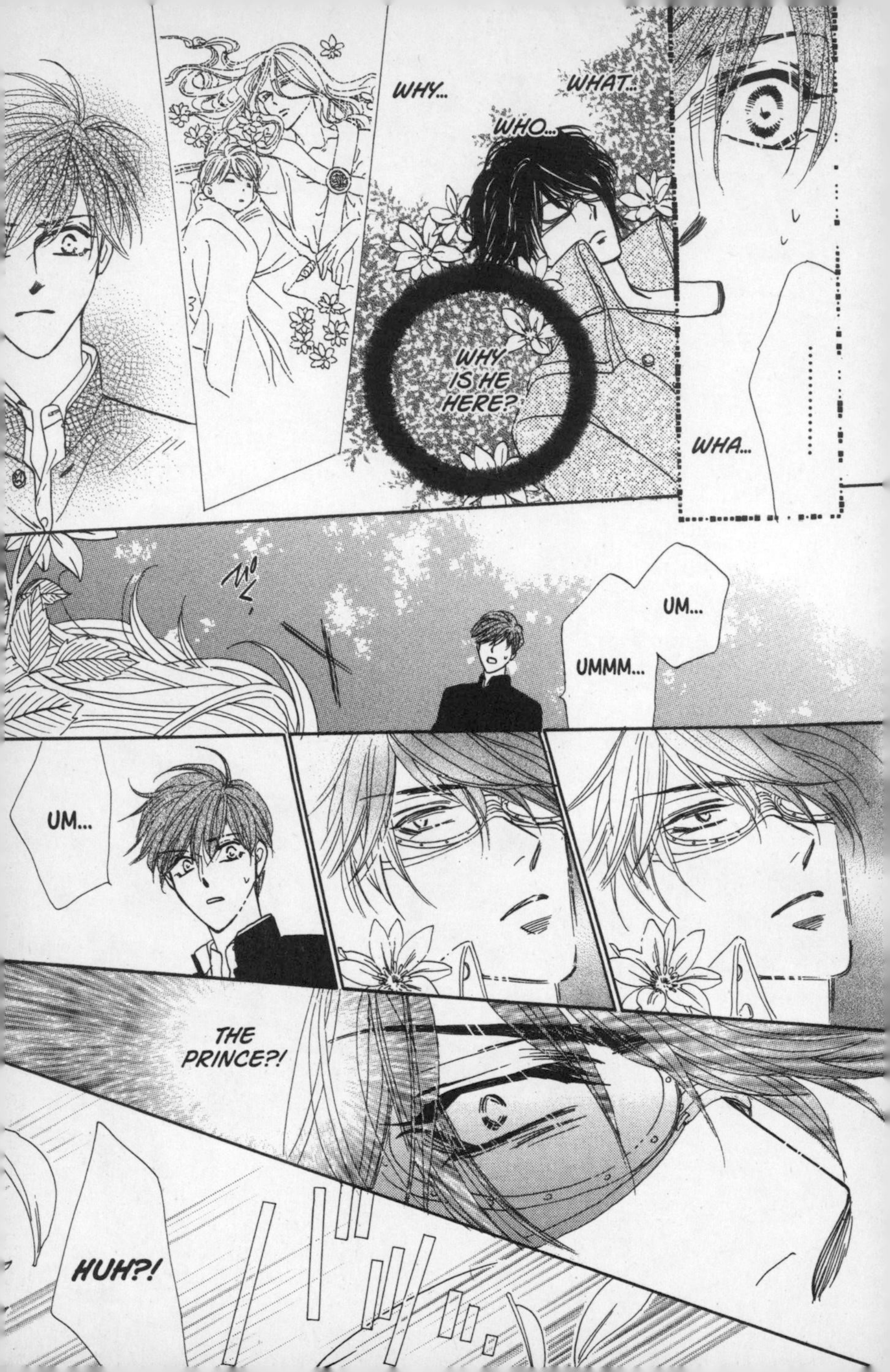
WHA...
WHAT...
WHO...
WHY...
WHY IS HE HERE?
UM...
UMMM...
UM...
THE PRINCE?!
HUH?!

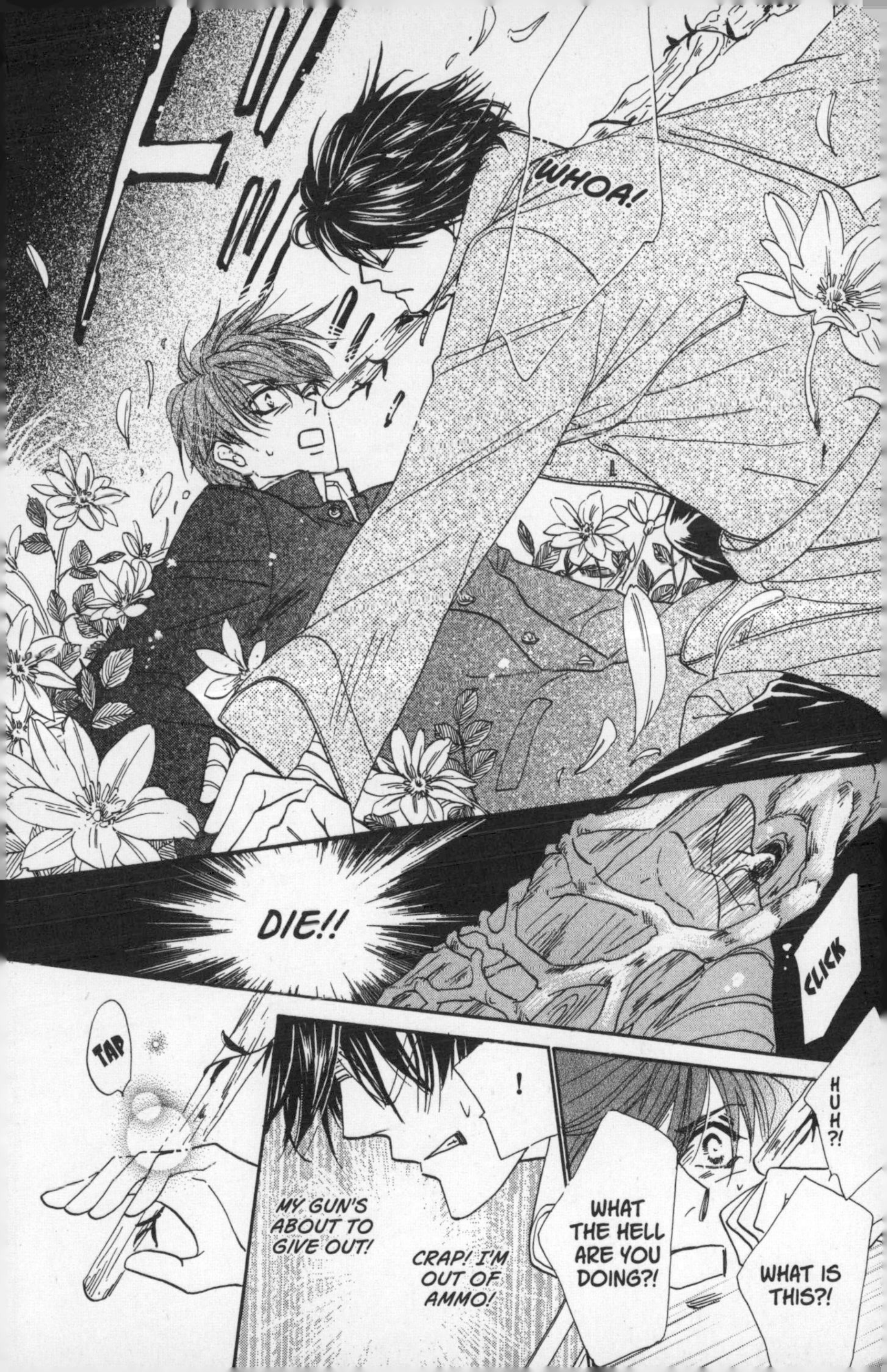
WHOA!
DIE!!
CLICK
HUH?!
WHAT IS THIS?!
WHAT THE HELL ARE YOU DOING?!
!
CRAP! I'M OUT OF AMMO!
MY GUN'S ABOUT TO GIVE OUT!
TAP

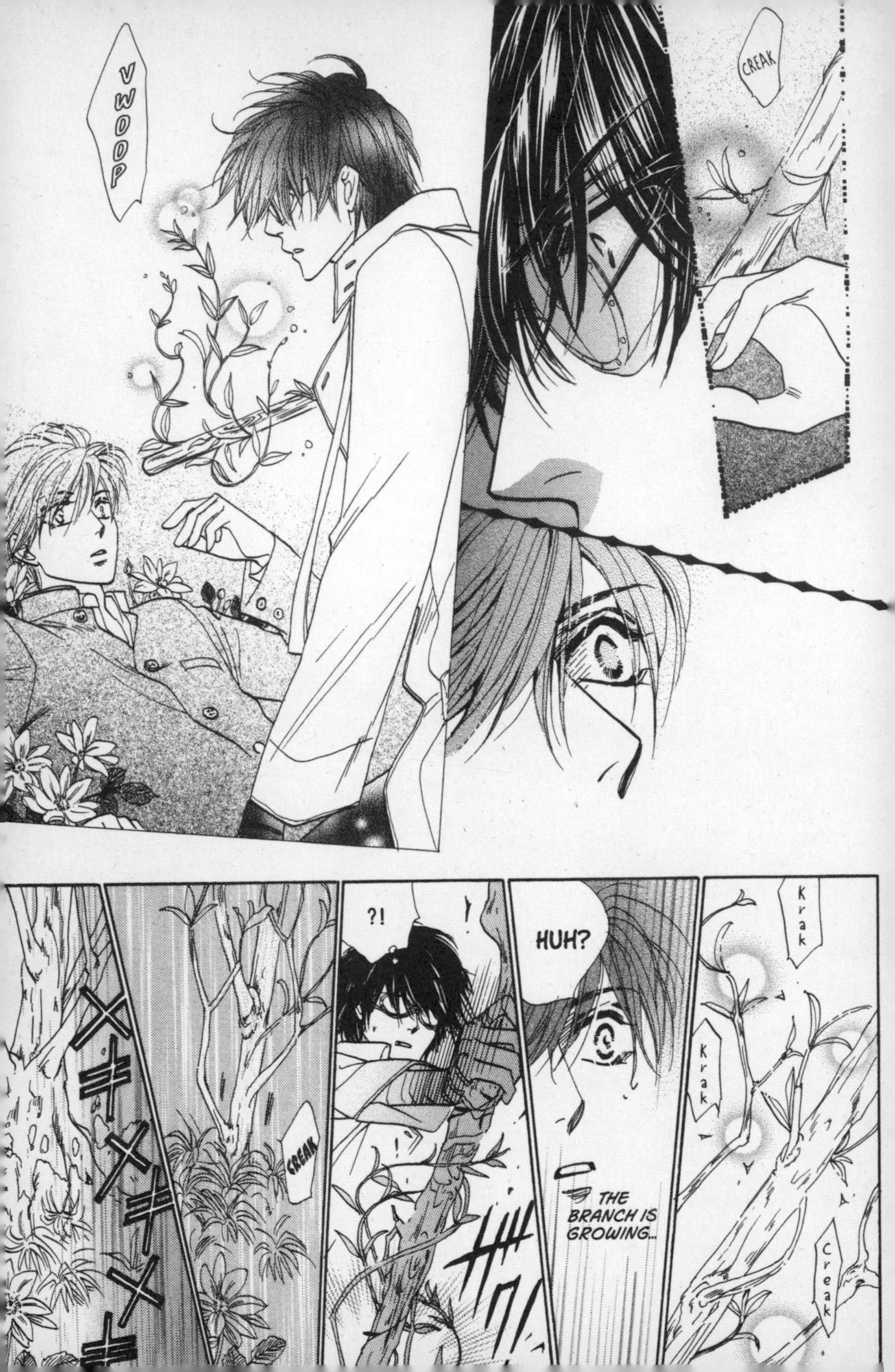
CREAK
VWOOP
Krak
Krak
Creak
HUH?
THE BRANCH IS GROWING...
!
?!
!
CREAK

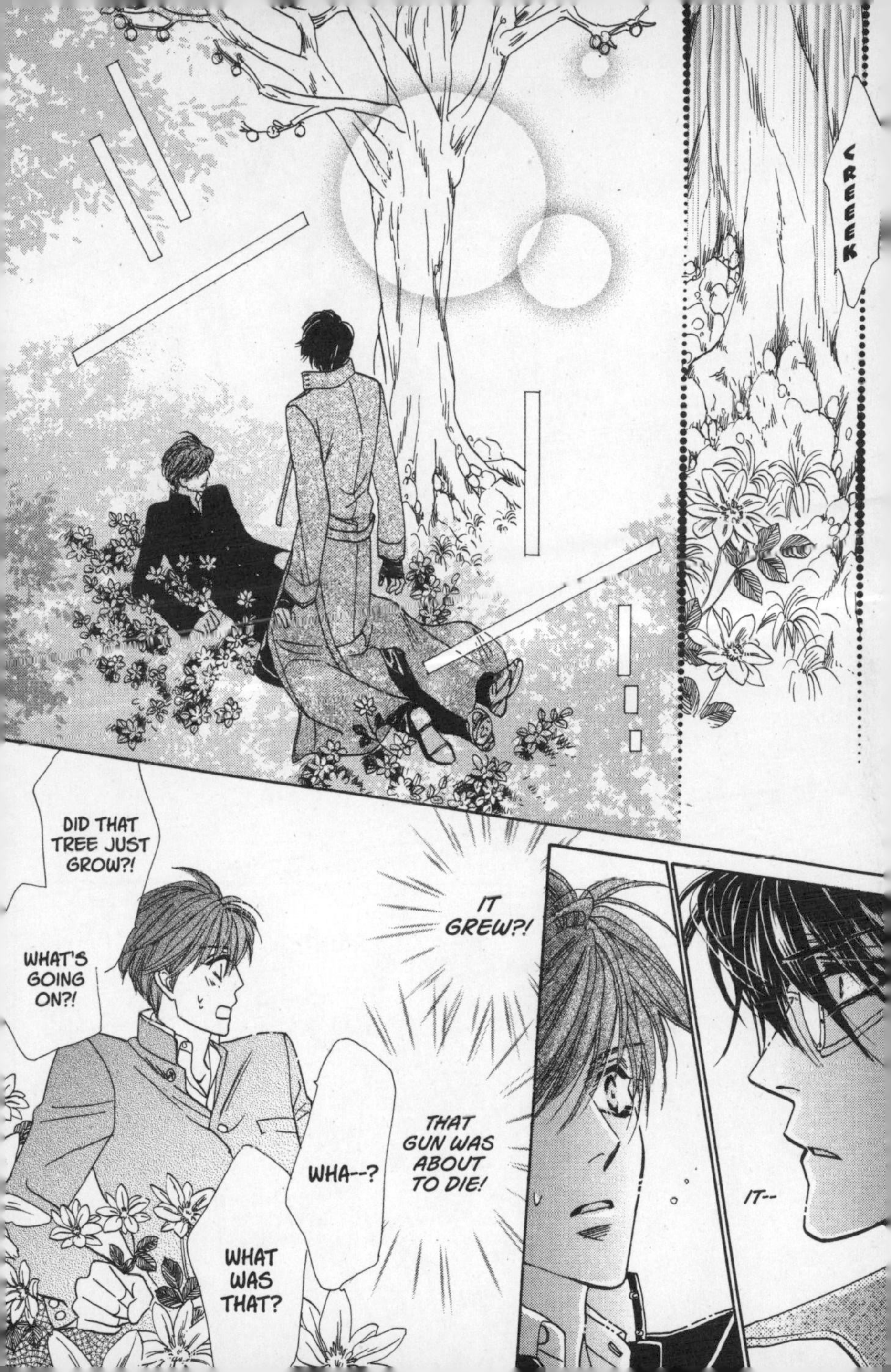
CREEEK
IT--
IT GREW?!
THAT GUN WAS ABOUT TO DIE!
DID THAT TREE JUST GROW?!
WHAT'S GOING ON?!
WHA--?
WHAT WAS THAT?

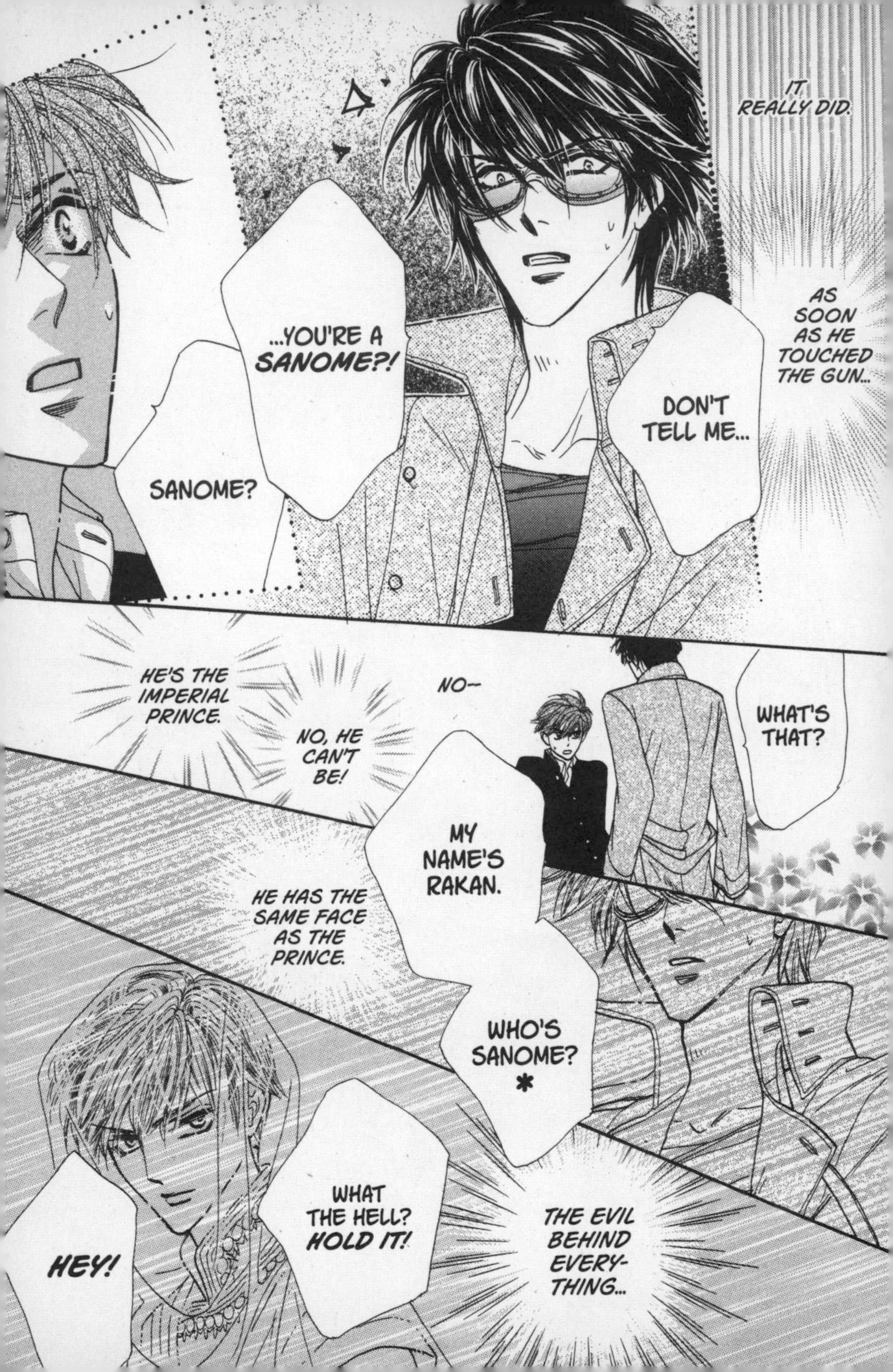

IT REALLY DID.
AS SOON AS HE TOUCHED THE GUN...
DON'T TELL ME...
...YOU'RE A *SANOME?!*
SANOME?
WHAT'S THAT?
HE'S THE IMPERIAL PRINCE.
NO--
NO, HE CAN'T BE!
MY NAME'S RAKAN.
WHO'S SANOME? *
HE HAS THE SAME FACE AS THE PRINCE.
THE EVIL BEHIND EVERY-THING...
WHAT THE HELL? *HOLD IT!*
HEY!

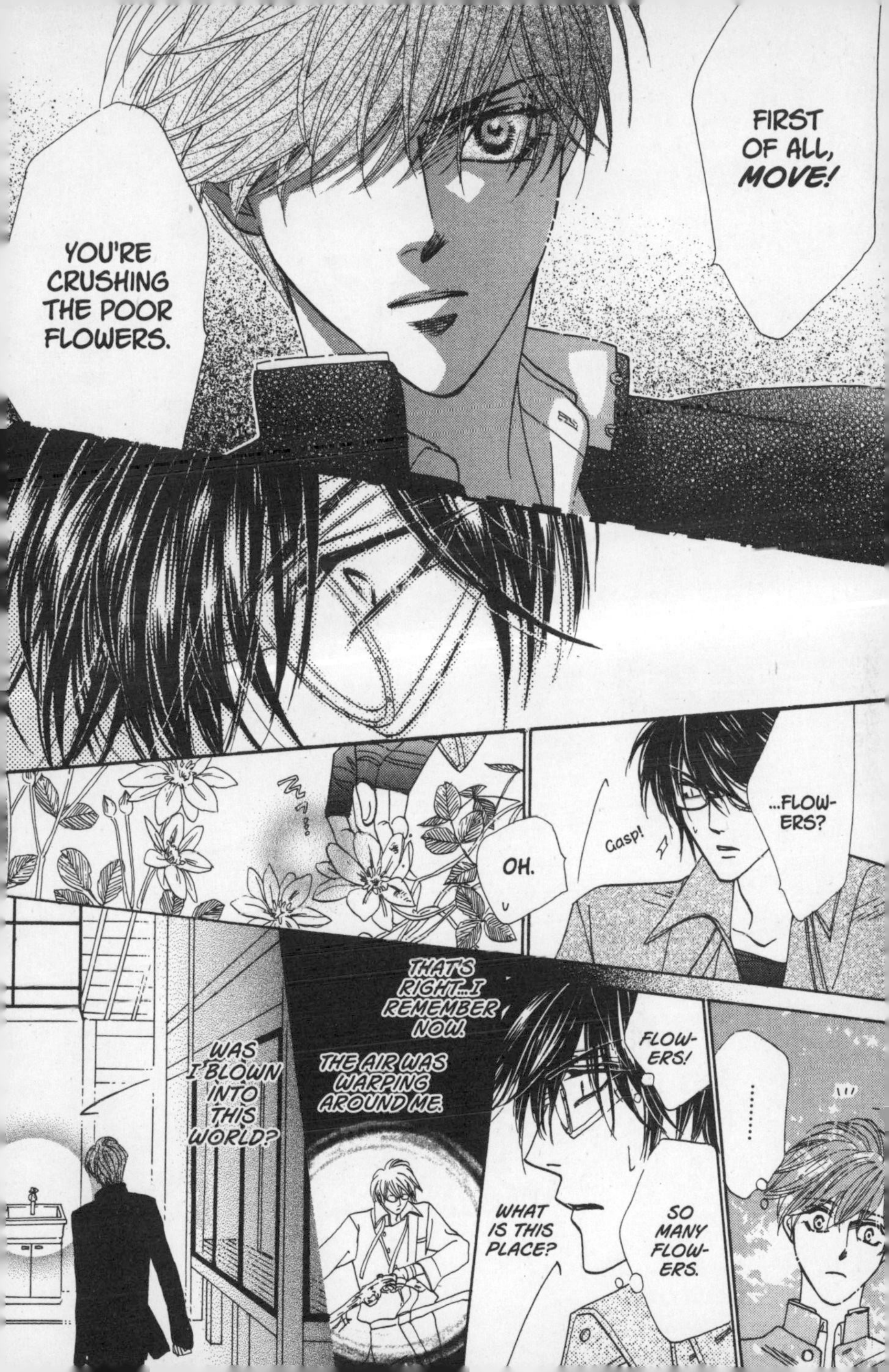

FIRST OF ALL, *MOVE!*
YOU'RE CRUSHING THE POOR FLOWERS.
...FLOWERS?
Gasp!
OH.
......
FLOWERS!
SO MANY FLOWERS.
WHAT IS THIS PLACE?
THAT'S RIGHT...I REMEMBER NOW.
THE AIR WAS WARPING AROUND ME.
WAS I BLOWN INTO THIS WORLD?

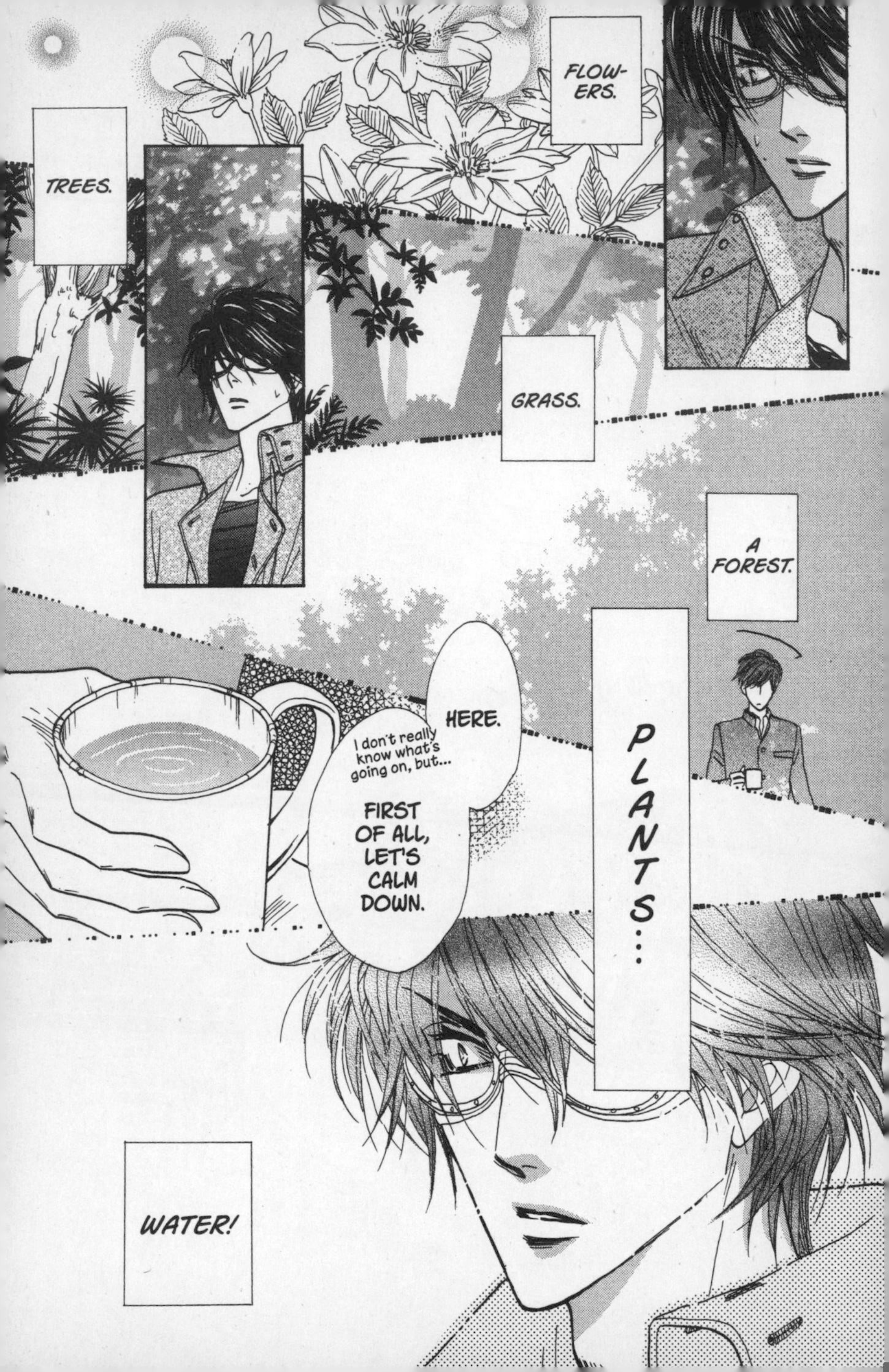
FLOW-
ERS.
TREES.
GRASS.
A FOREST.
PLANTS...
HERE.
I don't really know what's going on, but...
FIRST OF ALL, LET'S CALM DOWN.
WATER!

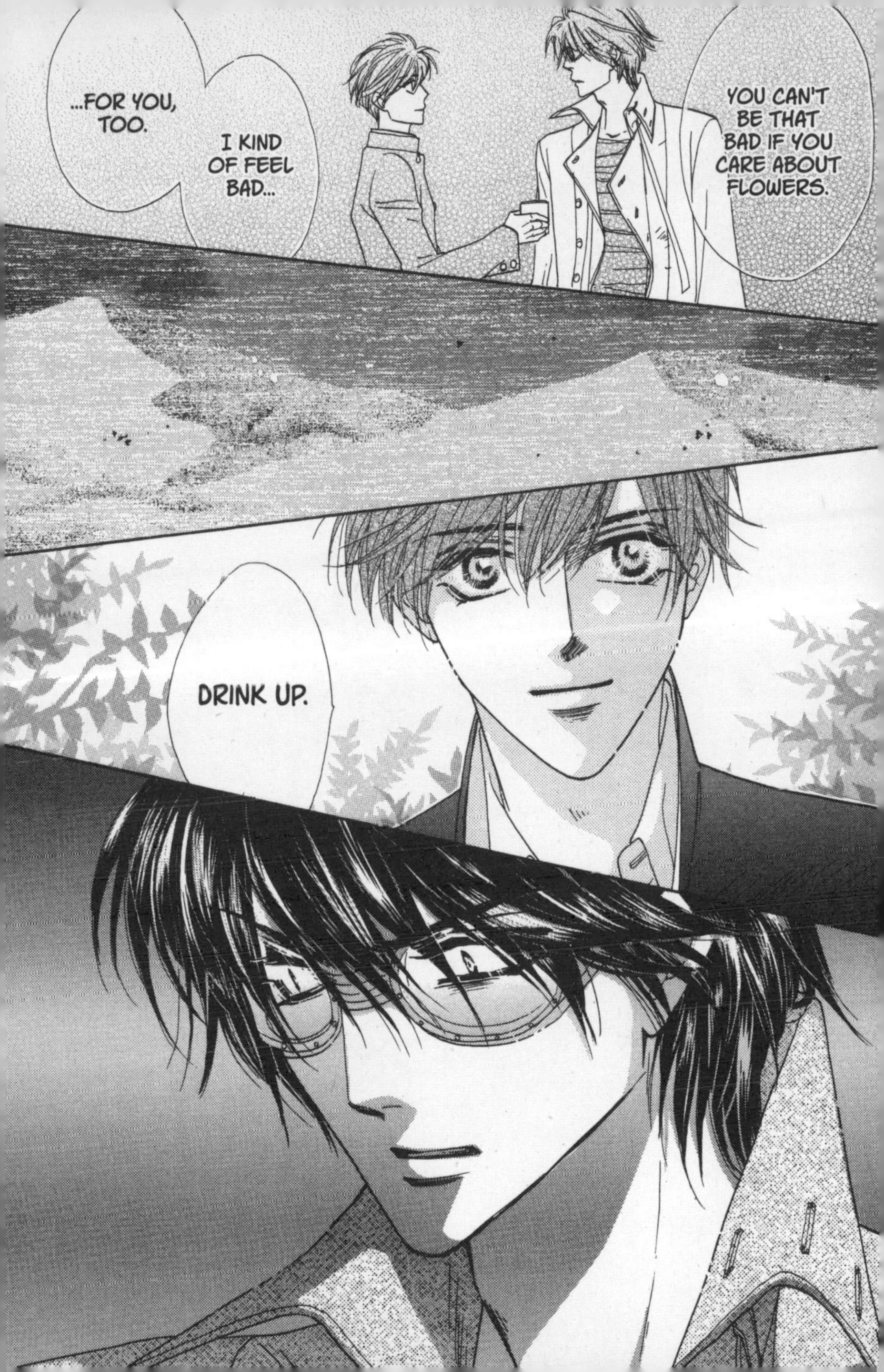
YOU CAN'T BE THAT BAD IF YOU CARE ABOUT FLOWERS.
I KIND OF FEEL BAD...
...FOR YOU, TOO.
DRINK UP.

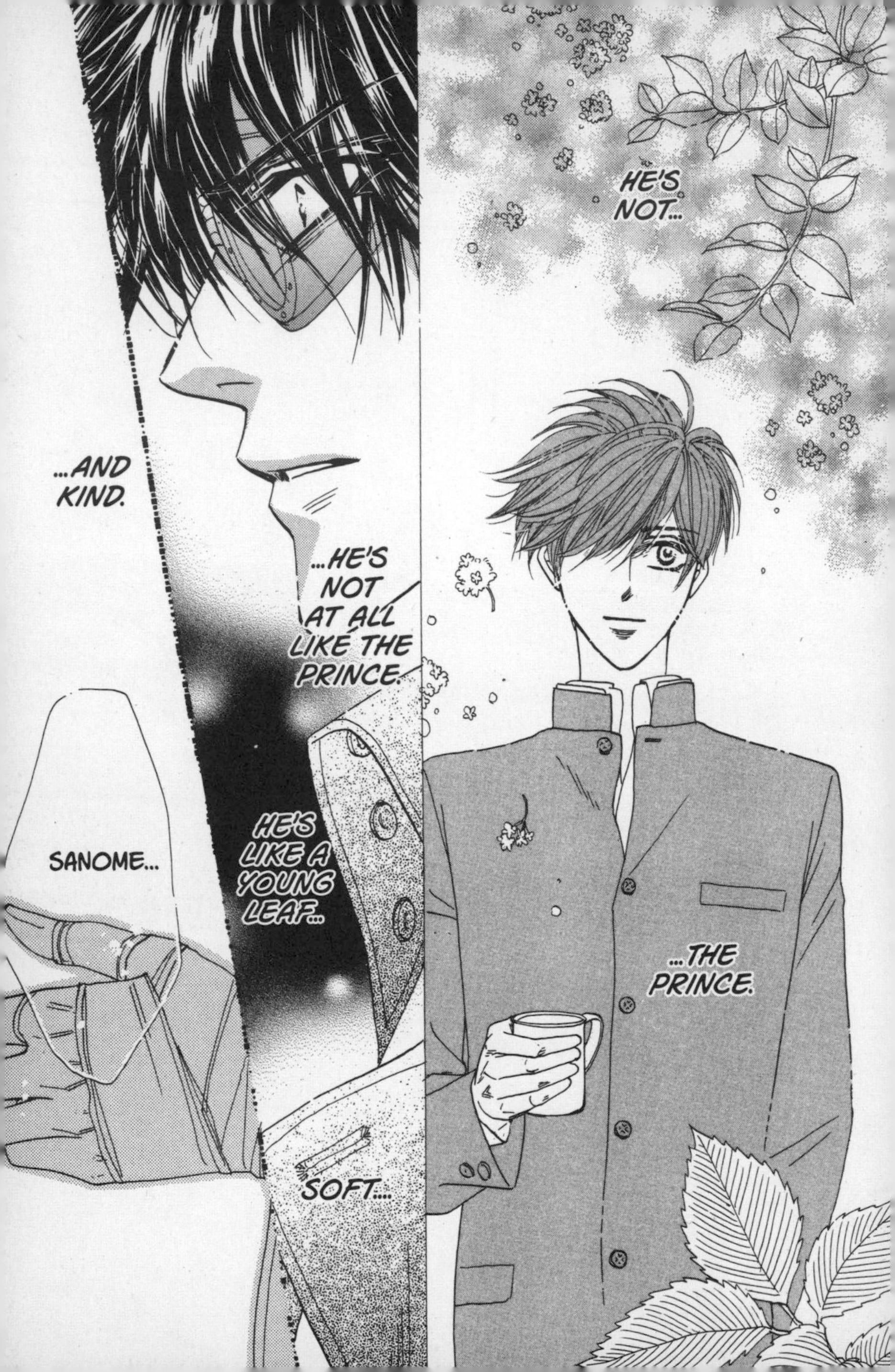
HE'S NOT...
...THE PRINCE.
...HE'S NOT AT ALL LIKE THE PRINCE.
HE'S LIKE A YOUNG LEAF...
SOFT....
...AND KIND.
SANOME...

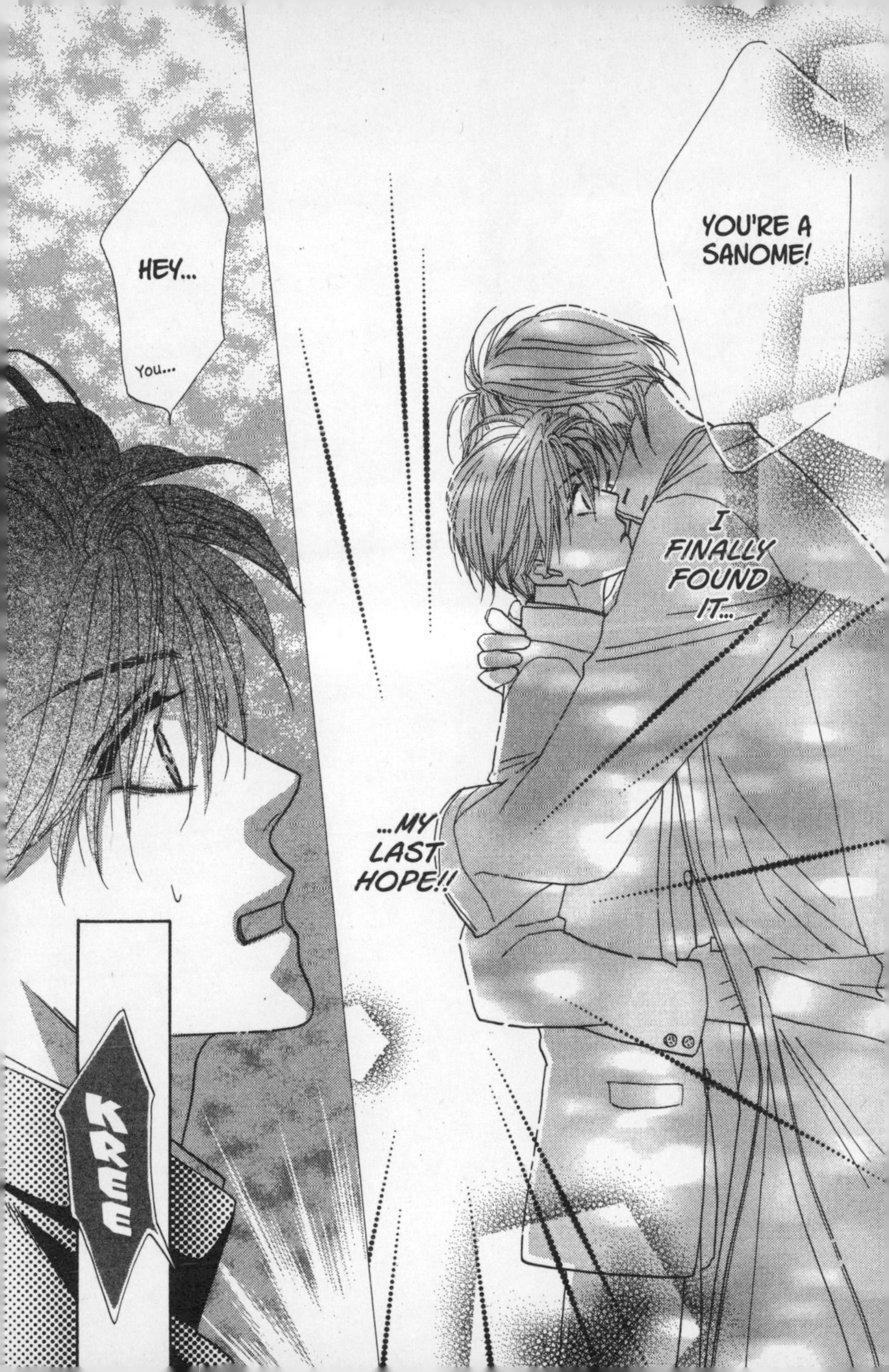
YOU'RE A SANOME!
I FINALLY FOUND IT...
...MY LAST HOPE!!
HEY...
You...
KREE

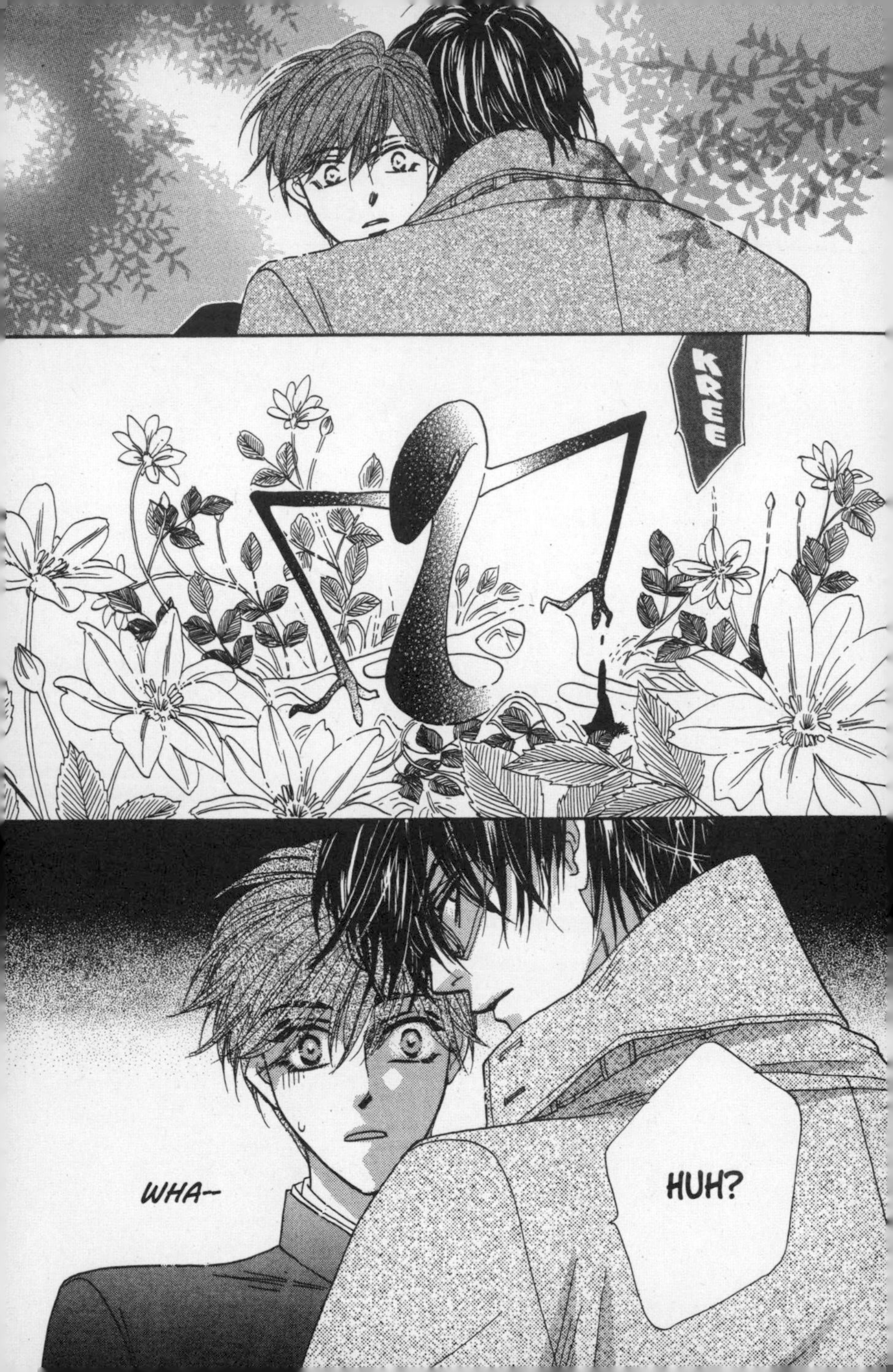
KREE
HUH?
WHA-

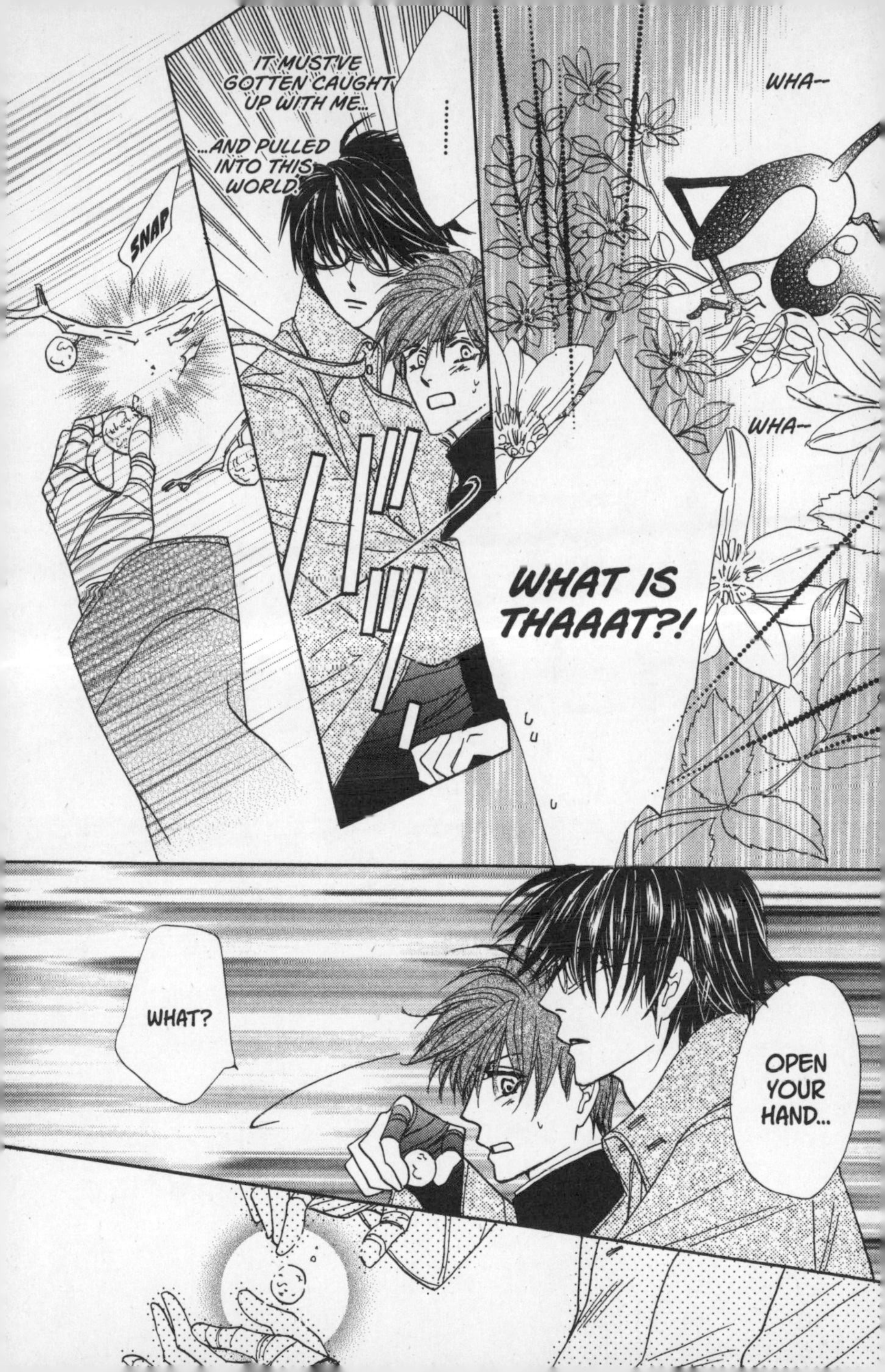

WHA--
WHA--
WHAT IS THAAAT?!
......
IT MUST'VE GOTTEN CAUGHT UP WITH ME...
...AND PULLED INTO THIS WORLD.
SNAP
OPEN YOUR HAND...
WHAT?

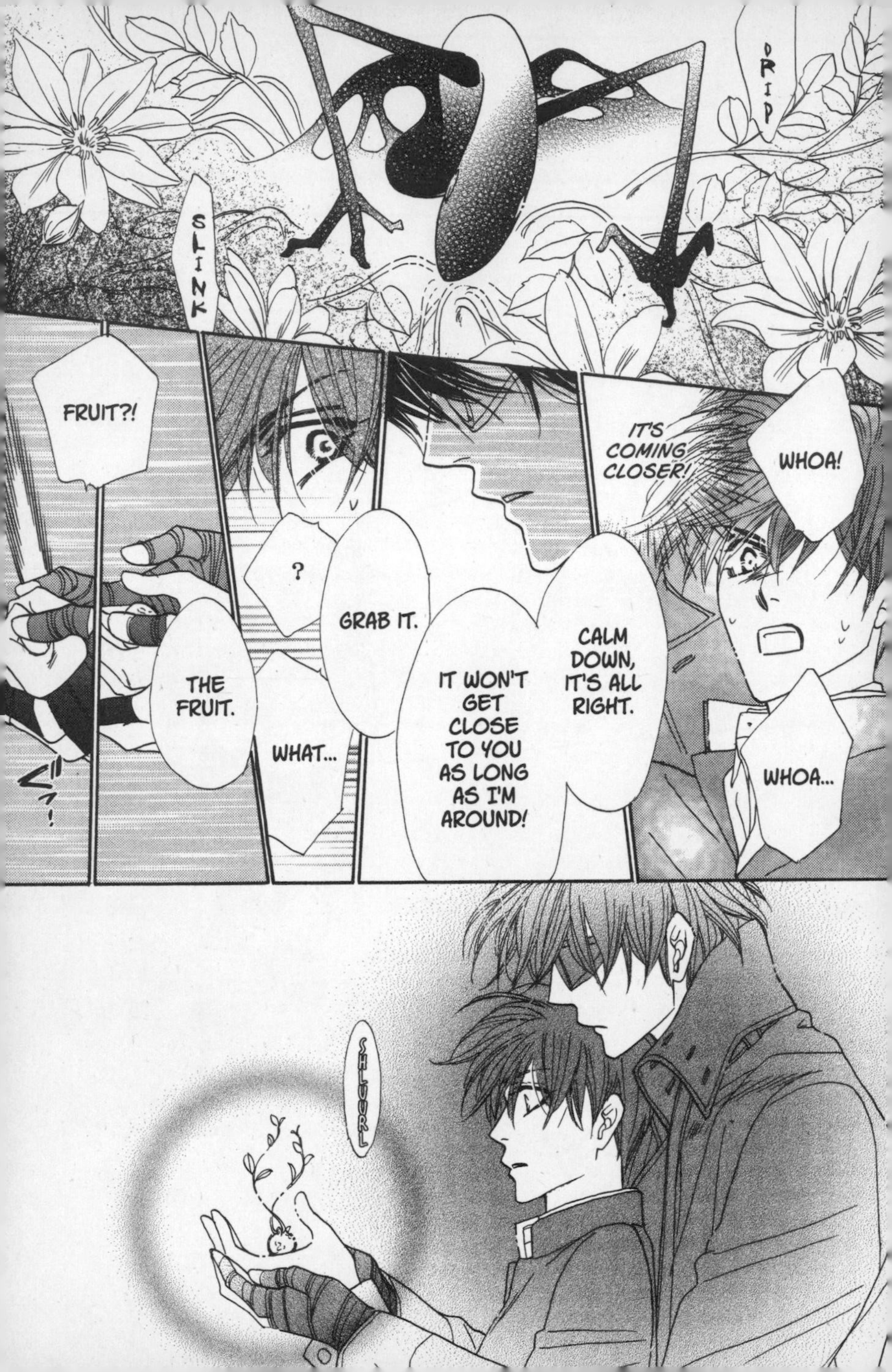
DRIP
SLINK
WHOA!
IT'S COMING CLOSER!
WHOA...
CALM DOWN, IT'S ALL RIGHT.
IT WON'T GET CLOSE TO YOU AS LONG AS I'M AROUND!
GRAB IT.
?
WHAT...
FRUIT?!
THE FRUIT.
SHLUURL

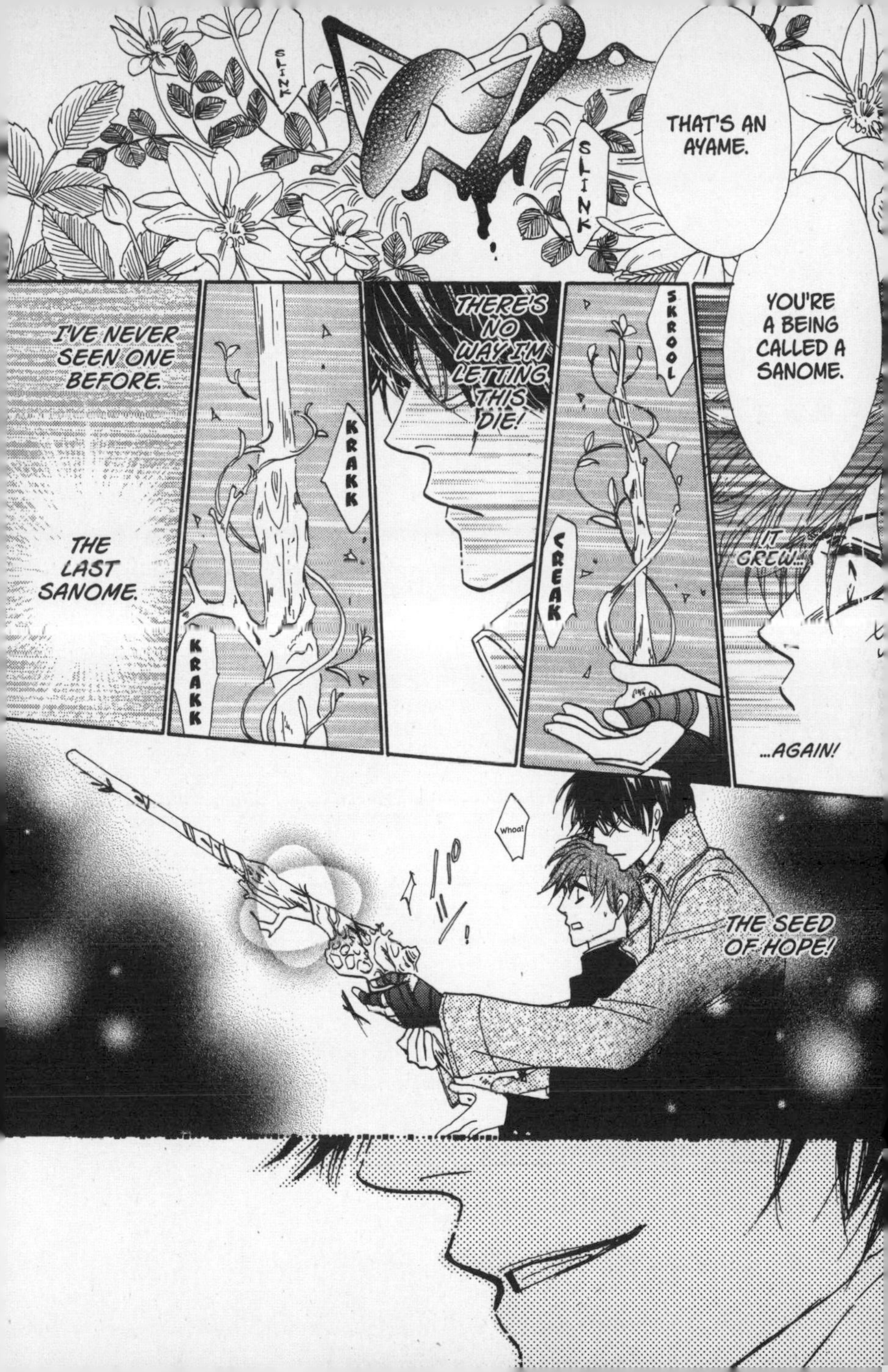
THAT'S AN AYAME.
SLINK
SLINK
YOU'RE A BEING CALLED A SANOME.
IT GREW...
...AGAIN!
SKROOL
CREAK
THERE'S NO WAY I'M LETTING THIS DIE!
KRAKK
KRAKK
I'VE NEVER SEEN ONE BEFORE.
THE LAST SANOME.
THE SEED OF HOPE!
Whoa!

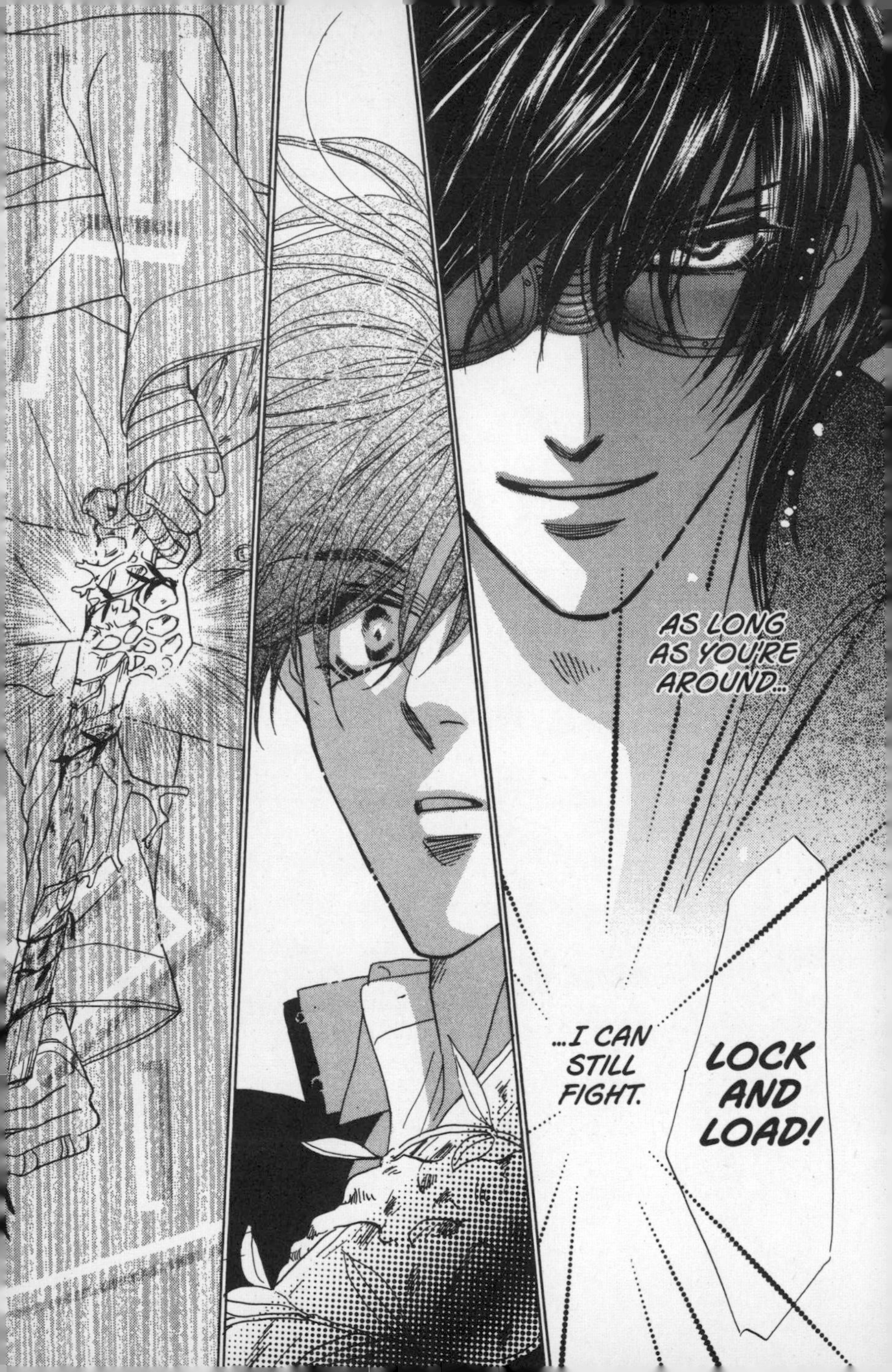
AS LONG AS YOU'RE AROUND...
...I CAN STILL FIGHT.
LOCK AND LOAD!

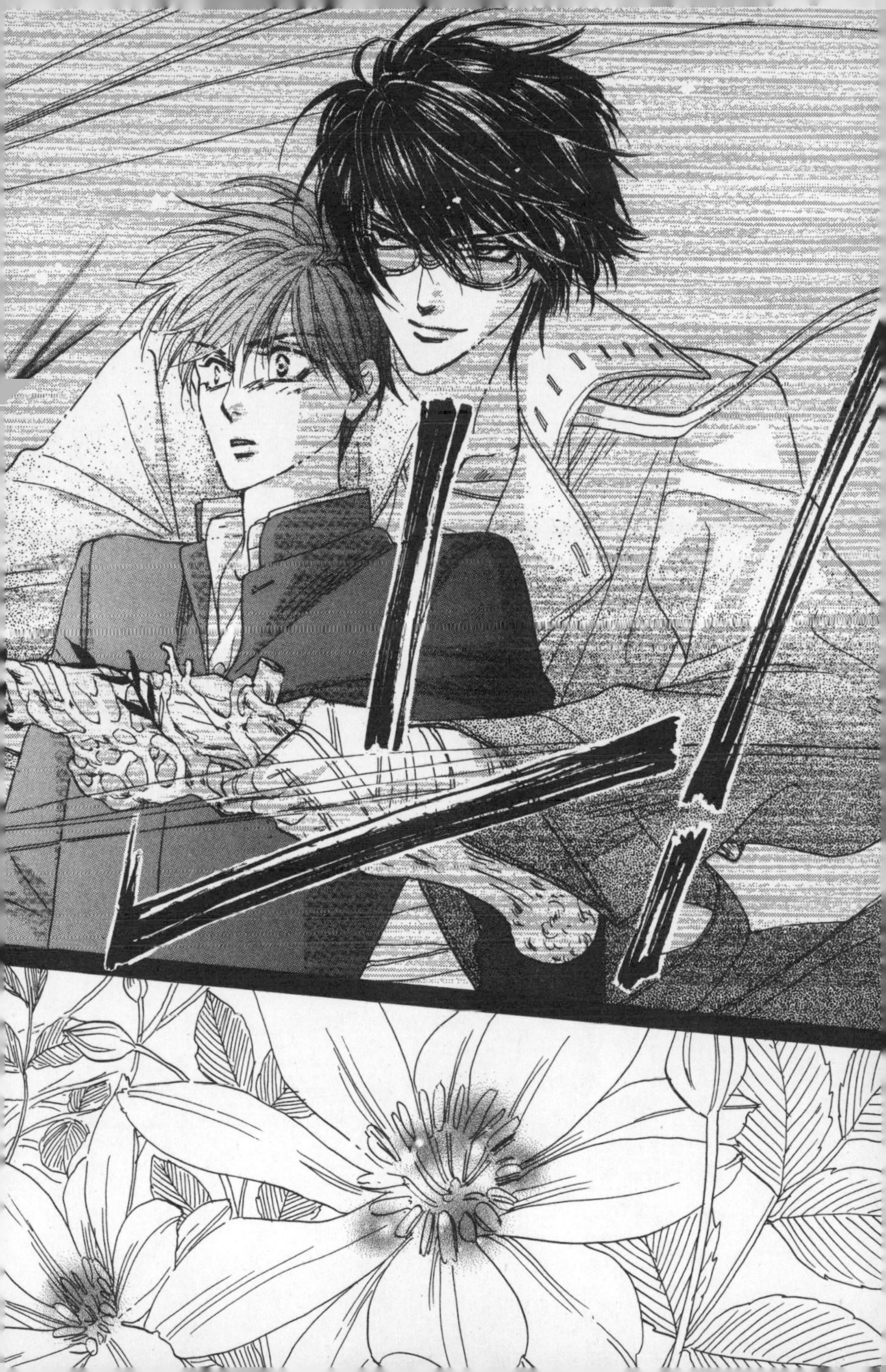

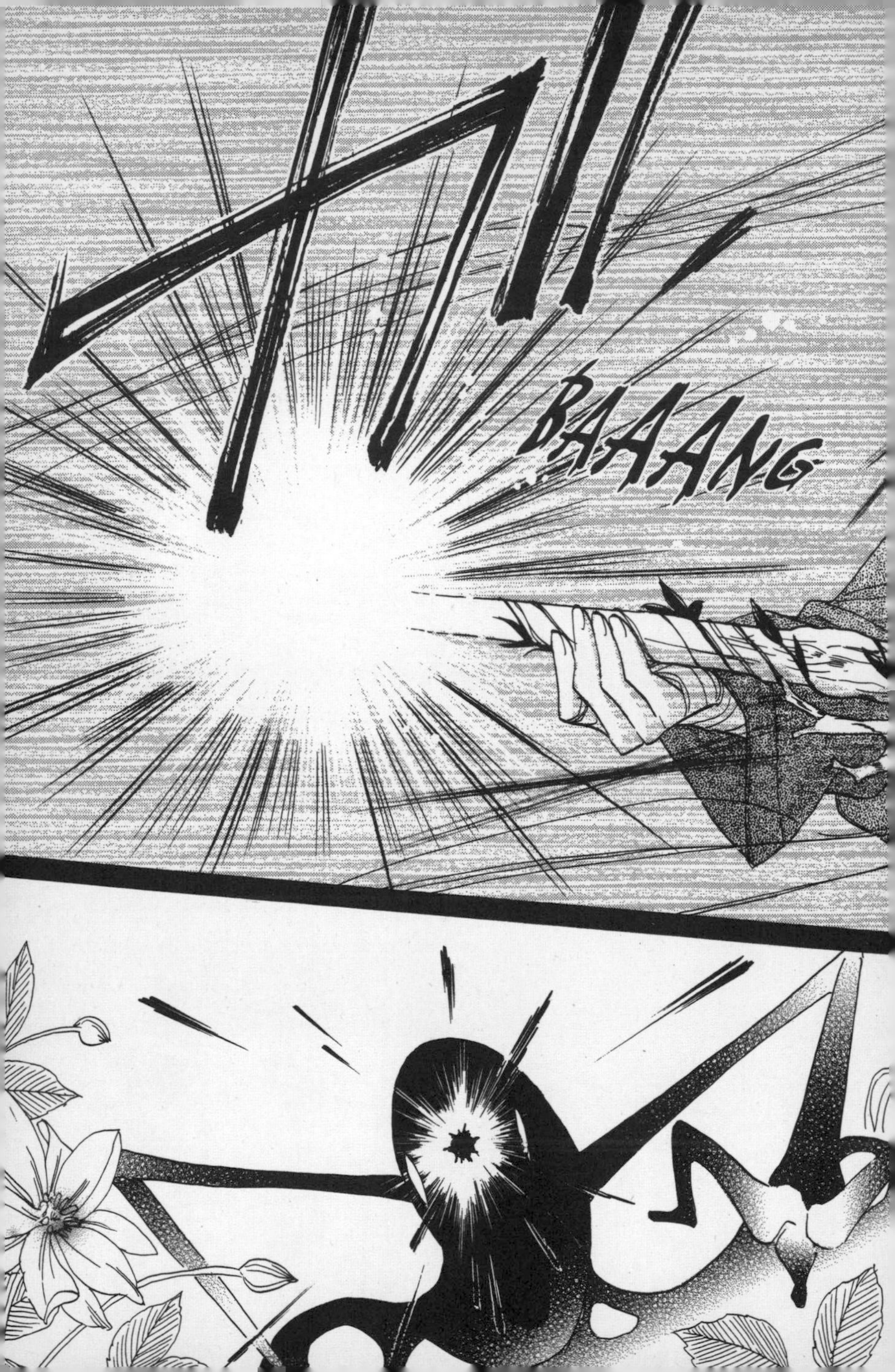
BAAAANG

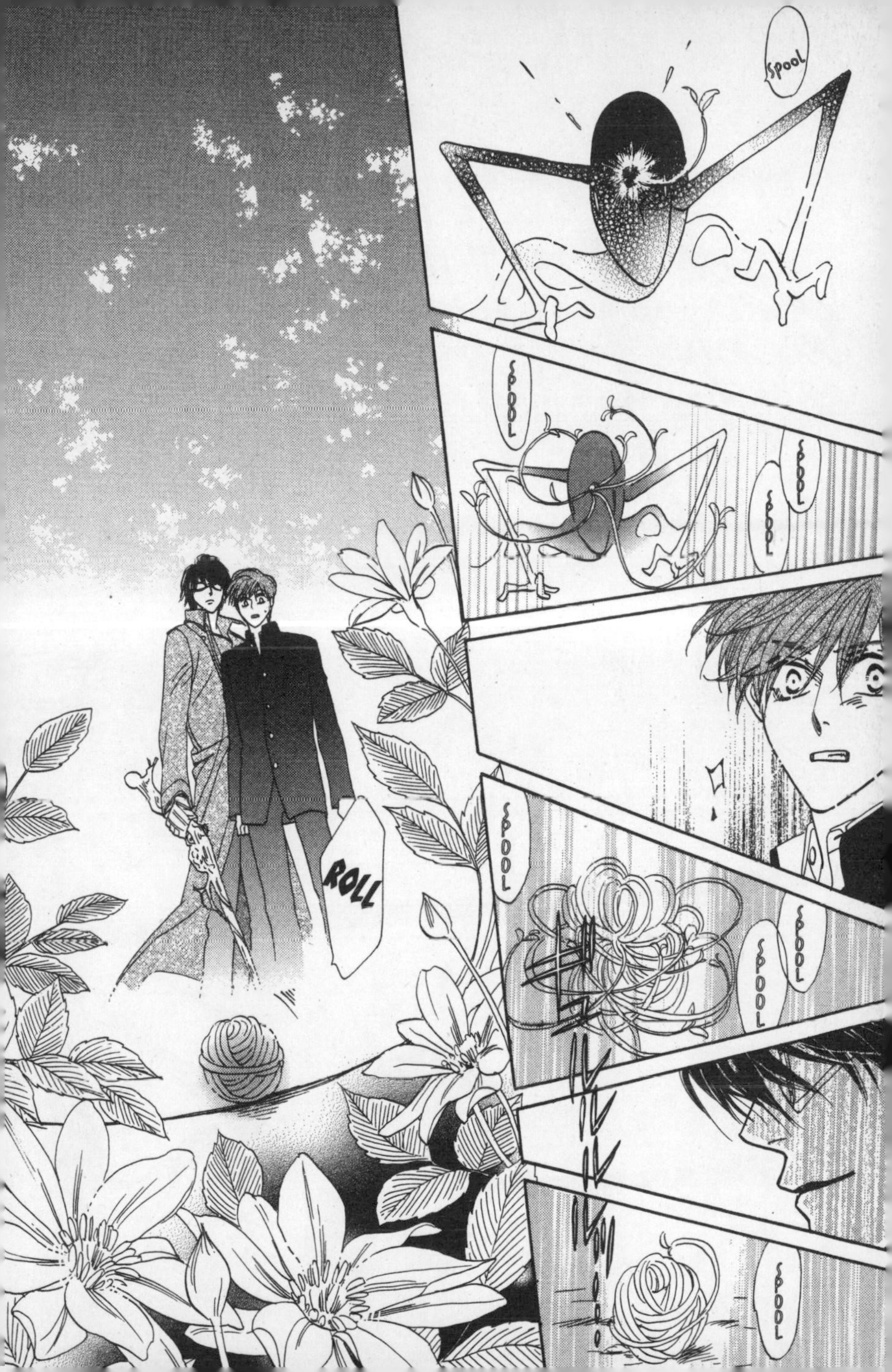
SPOOL
SPOOL
SPOOL
SPOOL
SPOOL
SPOOL
SPOOL
SPOOL
ROLL

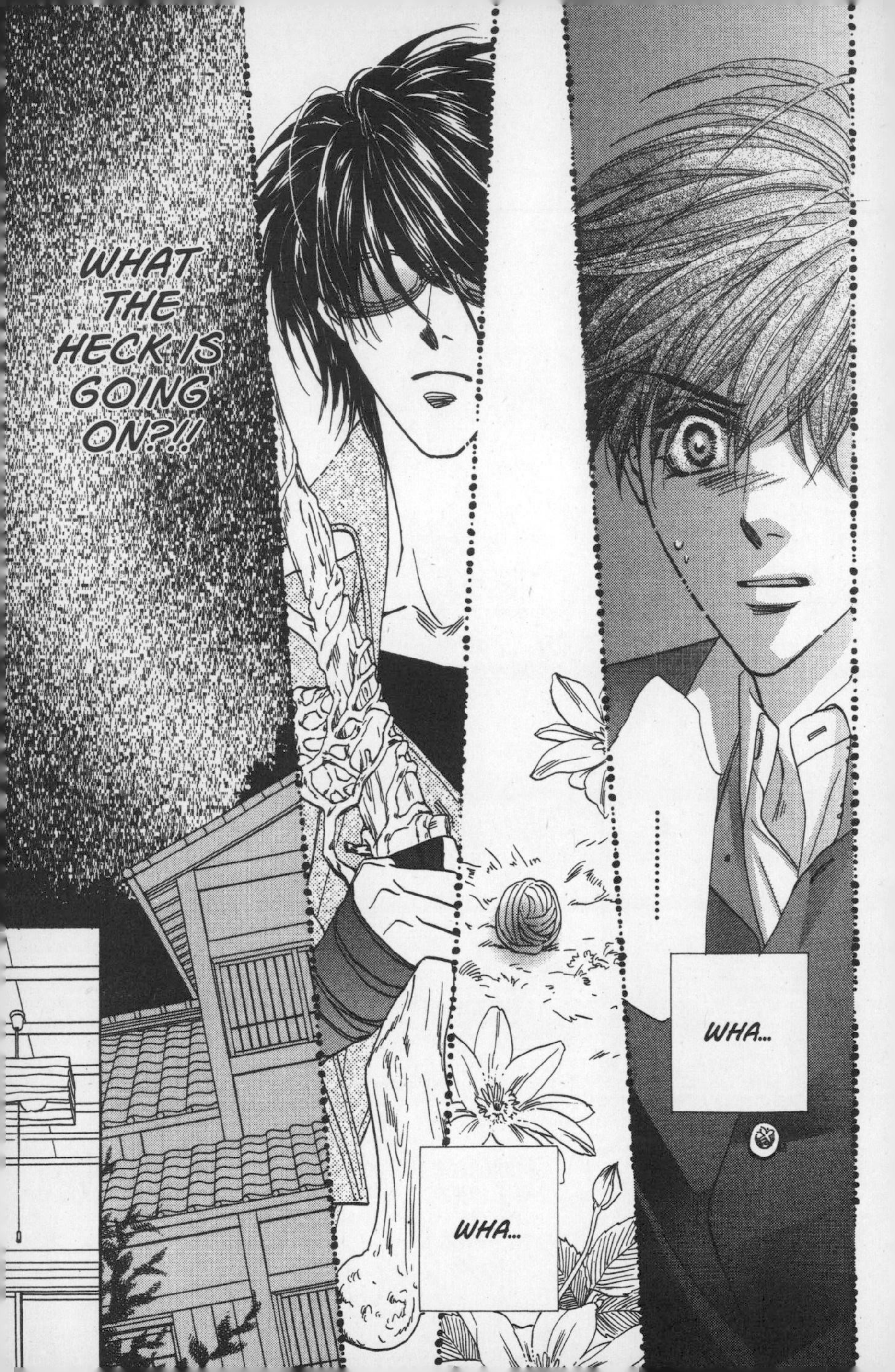
......
WHA...
WHA...
WHAT THE HECK IS GOING ON?!!

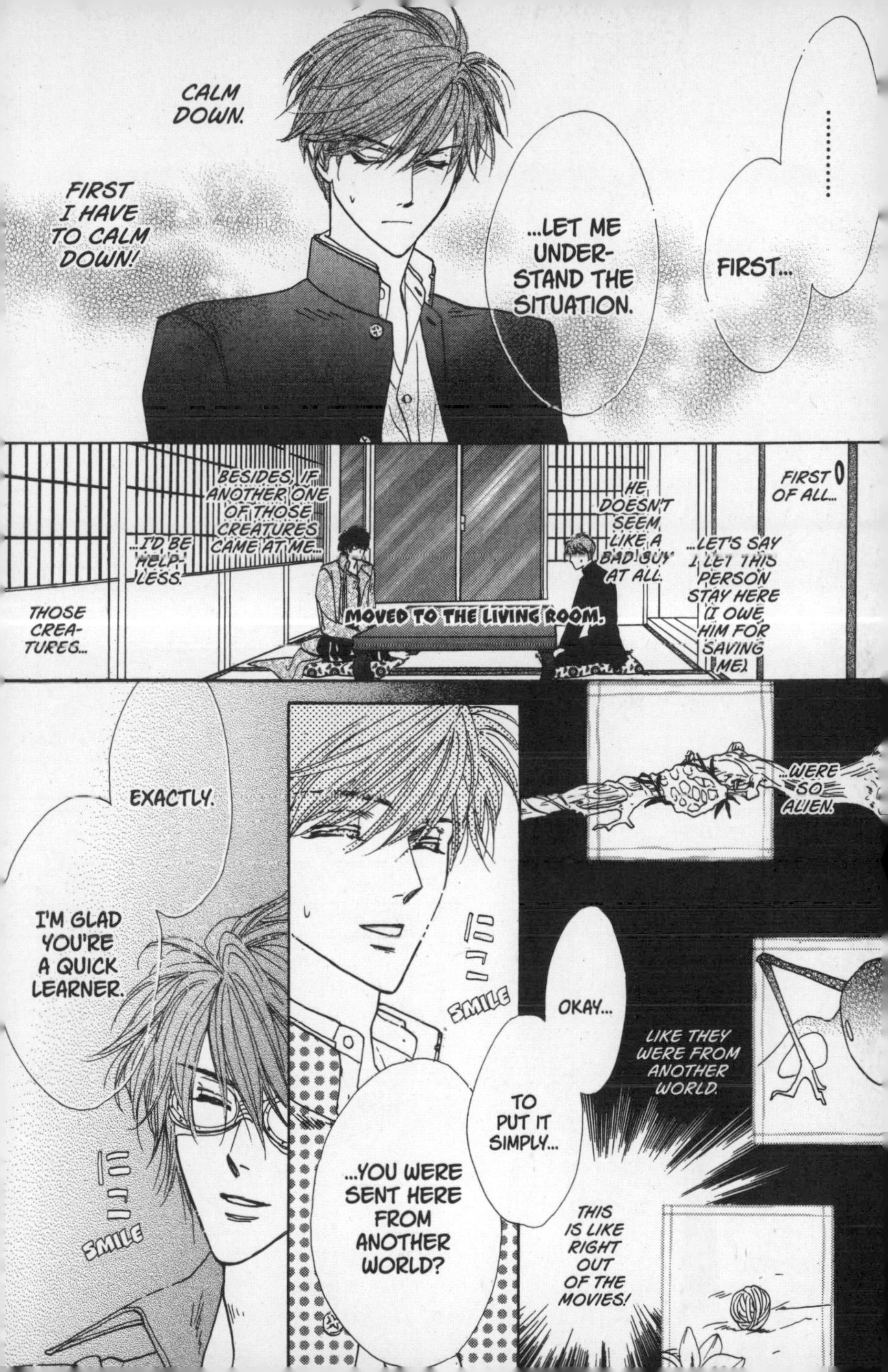
......
FIRST...
...LET ME UNDERSTAND THE SITUATION.
CALM DOWN.
FIRST I HAVE TO CALM DOWN!
FIRST OF ALL...
...LET'S SAY I LET THIS PERSON STAY HERE (I OWE HIM FOR SAVING ME).
HE DOESN'T SEEM LIKE A BAD GUY AT ALL.
BESIDES, IF ANOTHER ONE OF THOSE CREATURES CAME AT ME...
...I'D BE HELPLESS.
MOVED TO THE LIVING ROOM.
THOSE CREATURES...
...WERE SO ALIEN.
LIKE THEY WERE FROM ANOTHER WORLD.
THIS IS LIKE RIGHT OUT OF THE MOVIES!
OKAY...
TO PUT IT SIMPLY...
...YOU WERE SENT HERE FROM ANOTHER WORLD?
SMILE
EXACTLY.
I'M GLAD YOU'RE A QUICK LEARNER.
SMILE

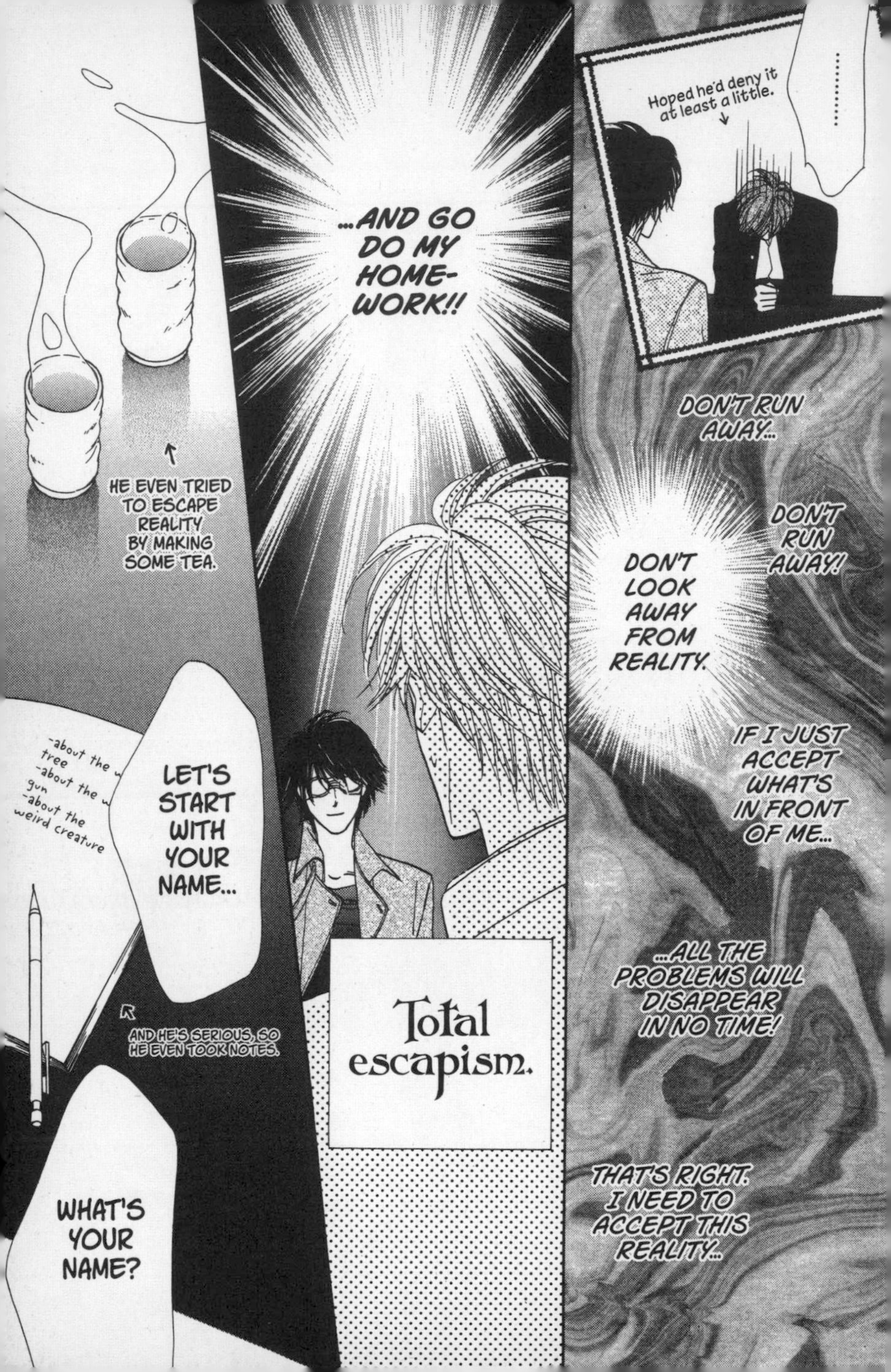
......
Hoped he'd deny it at least a little.
DON'T RUN AWAY...
DON'T RUN AWAY!
DON'T LOOK AWAY FROM REALITY.
IF I JUST ACCEPT WHAT'S IN FRONT OF ME...
...ALL THE PROBLEMS WILL DISAPPEAR IN NO TIME!
THAT'S RIGHT. I NEED TO ACCEPT THIS REALITY...
...AND GO DO MY HOMEWORK!!
Total escapism.
HE EVEN TRIED TO ESCAPE REALITY BY MAKING SOME TEA.
LET'S START WITH YOUR NAME...
-about the weird creature
AND HE'S SERIOUS, SO HE EVEN TOOK NOTES.
WHAT'S YOUR NAME?

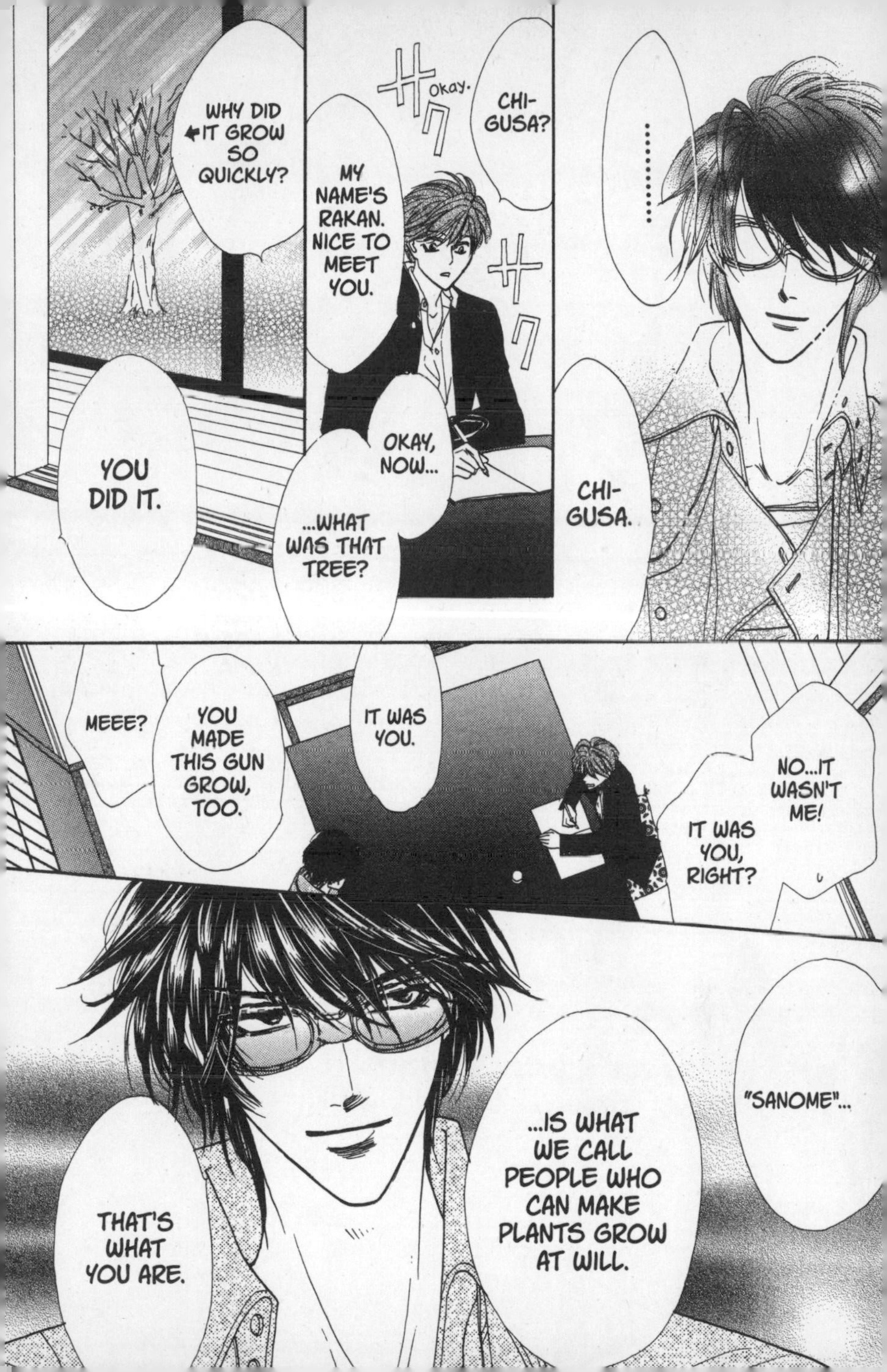
......
CHI-GUSA.
CHI-GUSA?
Okay.
MY NAME'S RAKAN. NICE TO MEET YOU.
OKAY, NOW...
...WHAT WAS THAT TREE?
WHY DID IT GROW SO QUICKLY?
YOU DID IT.
NO...IT WASN'T ME!
IT WAS YOU, RIGHT?
IT WAS YOU.
YOU MADE THIS GUN GROW, TOO.
MEEE?
"SANOME"...
...IS WHAT WE CALL PEOPLE WHO CAN MAKE PLANTS GROW AT WILL.
THAT'S WHAT YOU ARE.

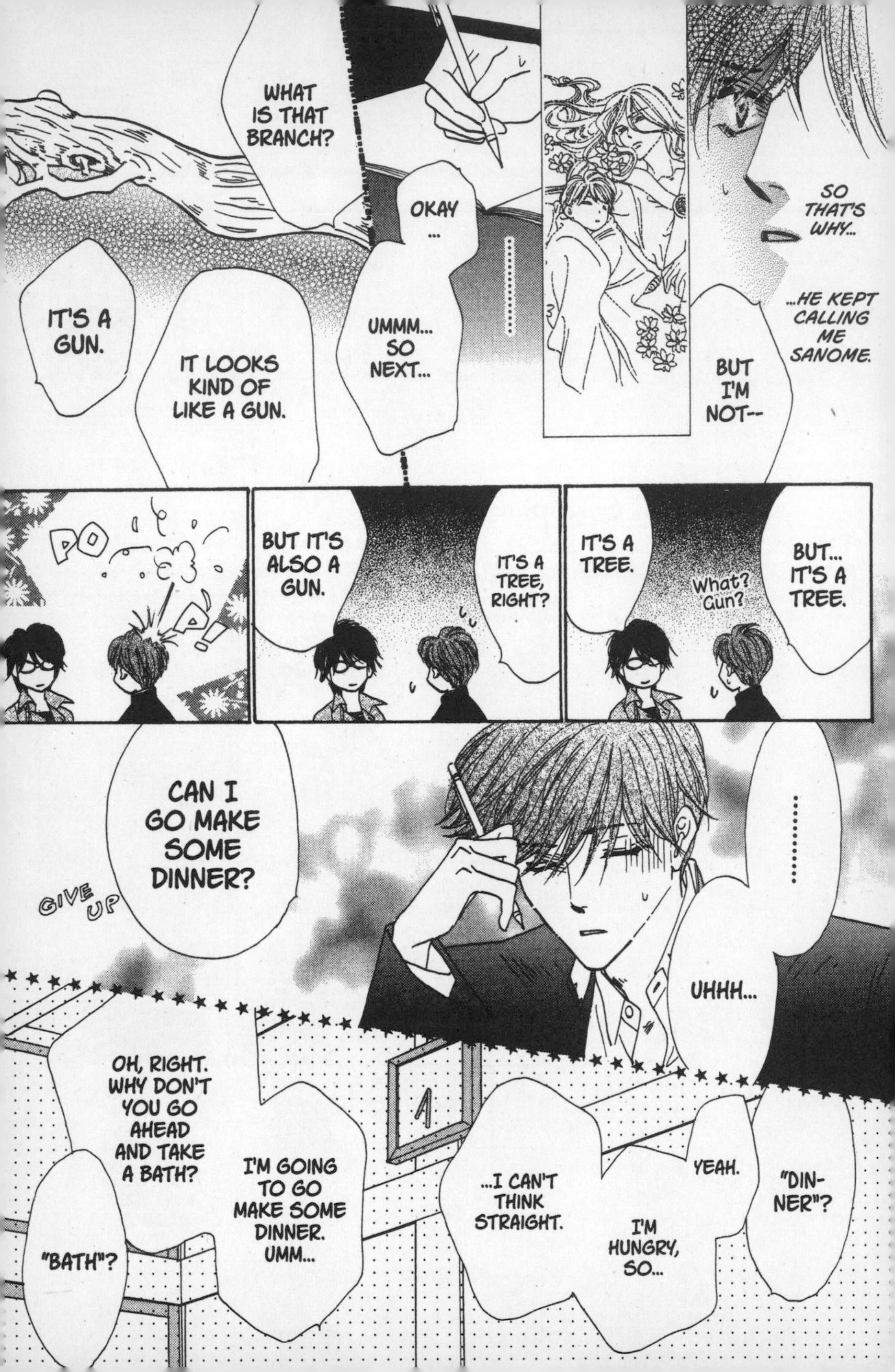
SO THAT'S WHY...
...HE KEPT CALLING ME SANOME.
BUT I'M NOT--
WHAT IS THAT BRANCH?
OKAY ...
......
UMMM... SO NEXT...
IT LOOKS KIND OF LIKE A GUN.
IT'S A GUN.
BUT... IT'S A TREE.
What? Gun?
IT'S A TREE.
IT'S A TREE, RIGHT?
BUT IT'S ALSO A GUN.
PO
P!
......
UHHH...
CAN I GO MAKE SOME DINNER?
GIVE UP
"DIN-NER"?
YEAH.
I'M HUNGRY, SO...
...I CAN'T THINK STRAIGHT.
I'M GOING TO GO MAKE SOME DINNER. UMM...
OH, RIGHT. WHY DON'T YOU GO AHEAD AND TAKE A BATH?
"BATH"?

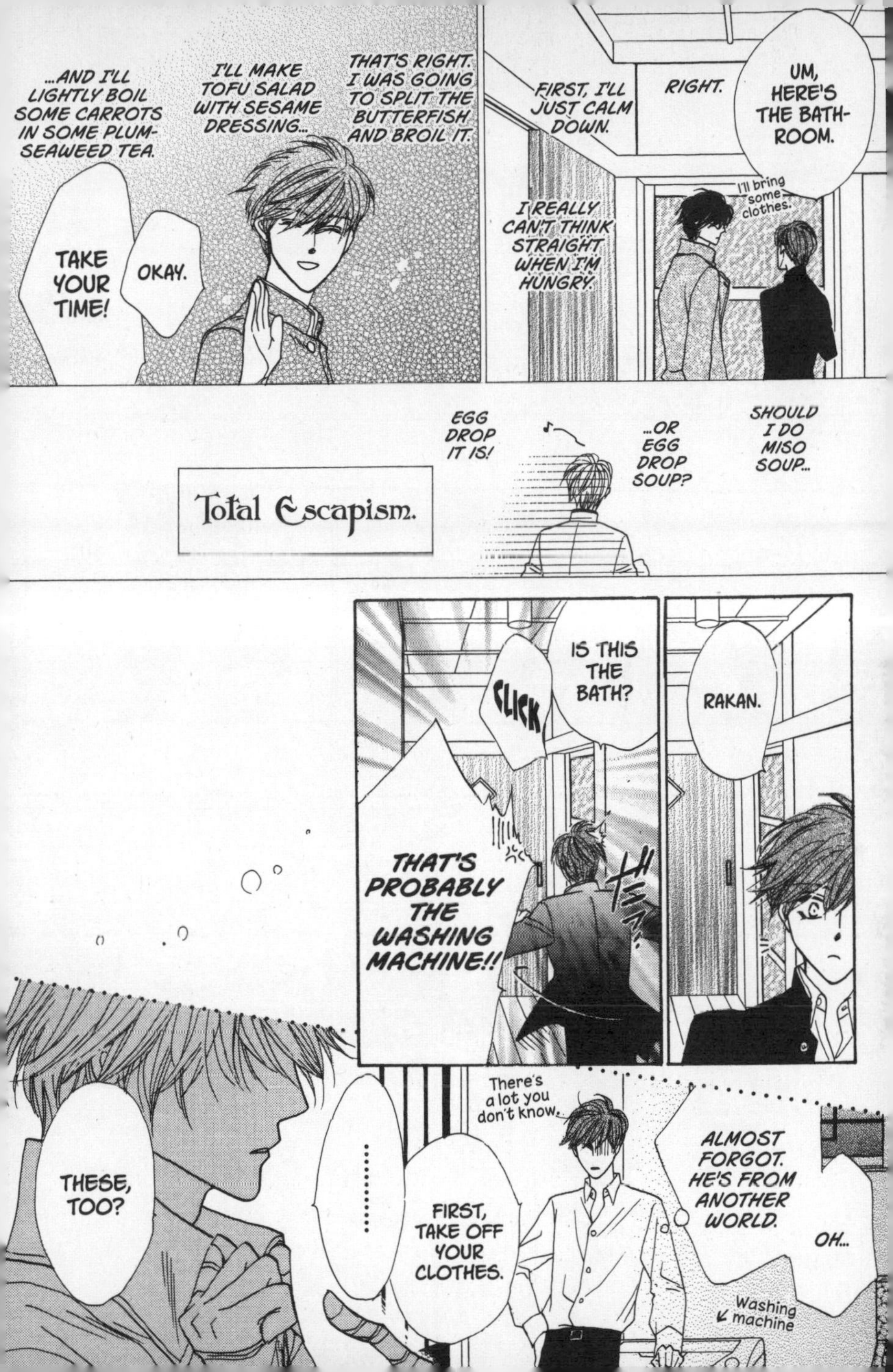
UM, HERE'S THE BATH-ROOM.
I'll bring some clothes.
RIGHT.
FIRST, I'LL JUST CALM DOWN.
I REALLY CAN'T THINK STRAIGHT WHEN I'M HUNGRY.
THAT'S RIGHT. I WAS GOING TO SPLIT THE BUTTERFISH AND BROIL IT.
I'LL MAKE TOFU SALAD WITH SESAME DRESSING...
...AND I'LL LIGHTLY BOIL SOME CARROTS IN SOME PLUM-SEAWEED TEA.
OKAY.
TAKE YOUR TIME!
SHOULD I DO MISO SOUP...
...OR EGG DROP SOUP?
EGG DROP IT IS!
Total Escapism.
RAKAN.
IS THIS THE BATH?
CLICK
THAT'S PROBABLY THE WASHING MACHINE!!
OH...
ALMOST FORGOT. HE'S FROM ANOTHER WORLD.
There's a lot you don't know.
Washing machine
FIRST, TAKE OFF YOUR CLOTHES.
......
THESE, TOO?

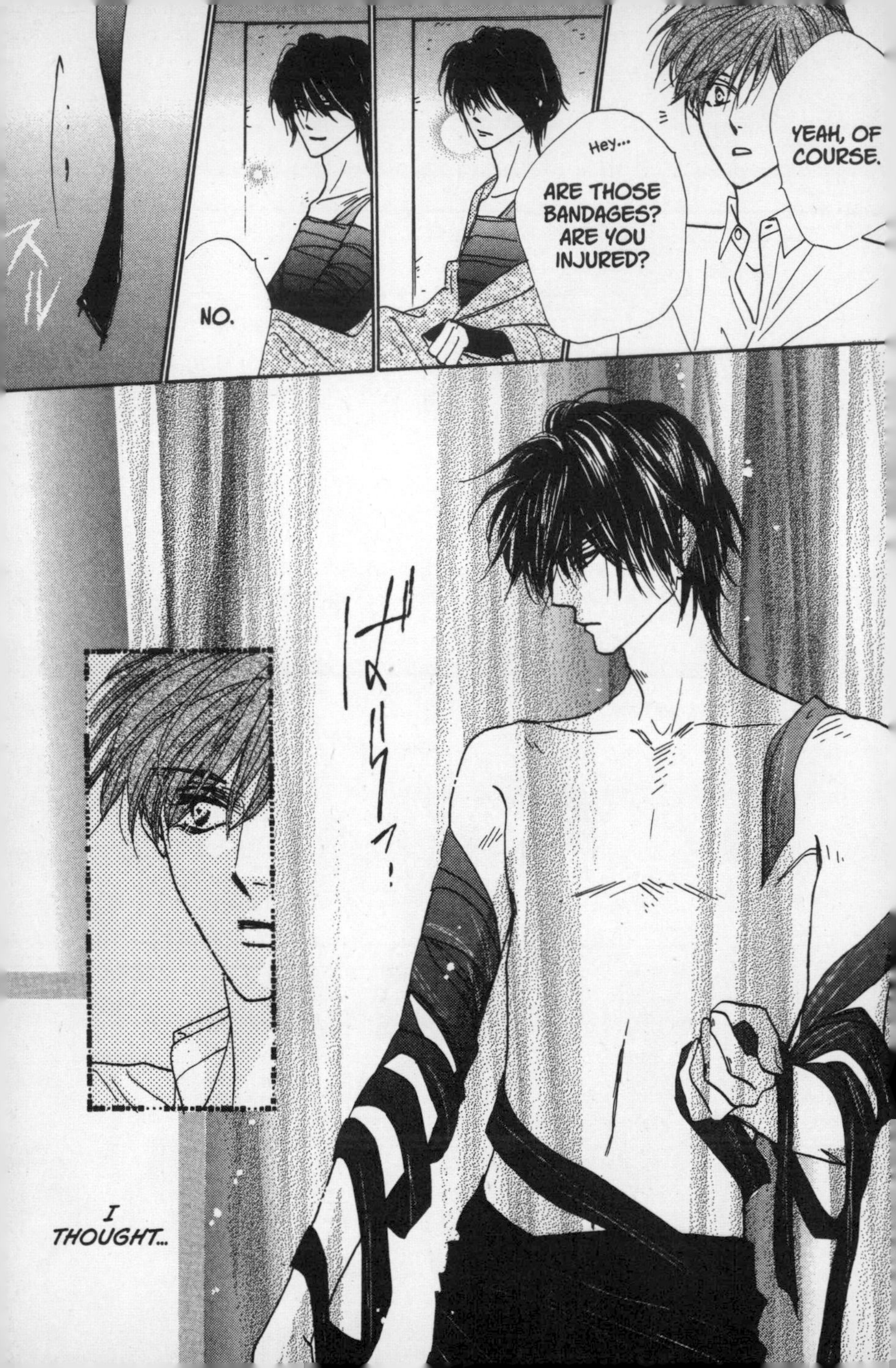
YEAH, OF COURSE.
Hey...
ARE THOSE BANDAGES? ARE YOU INJURED?
NO.
スル
ばらっ
I THOUGHT...

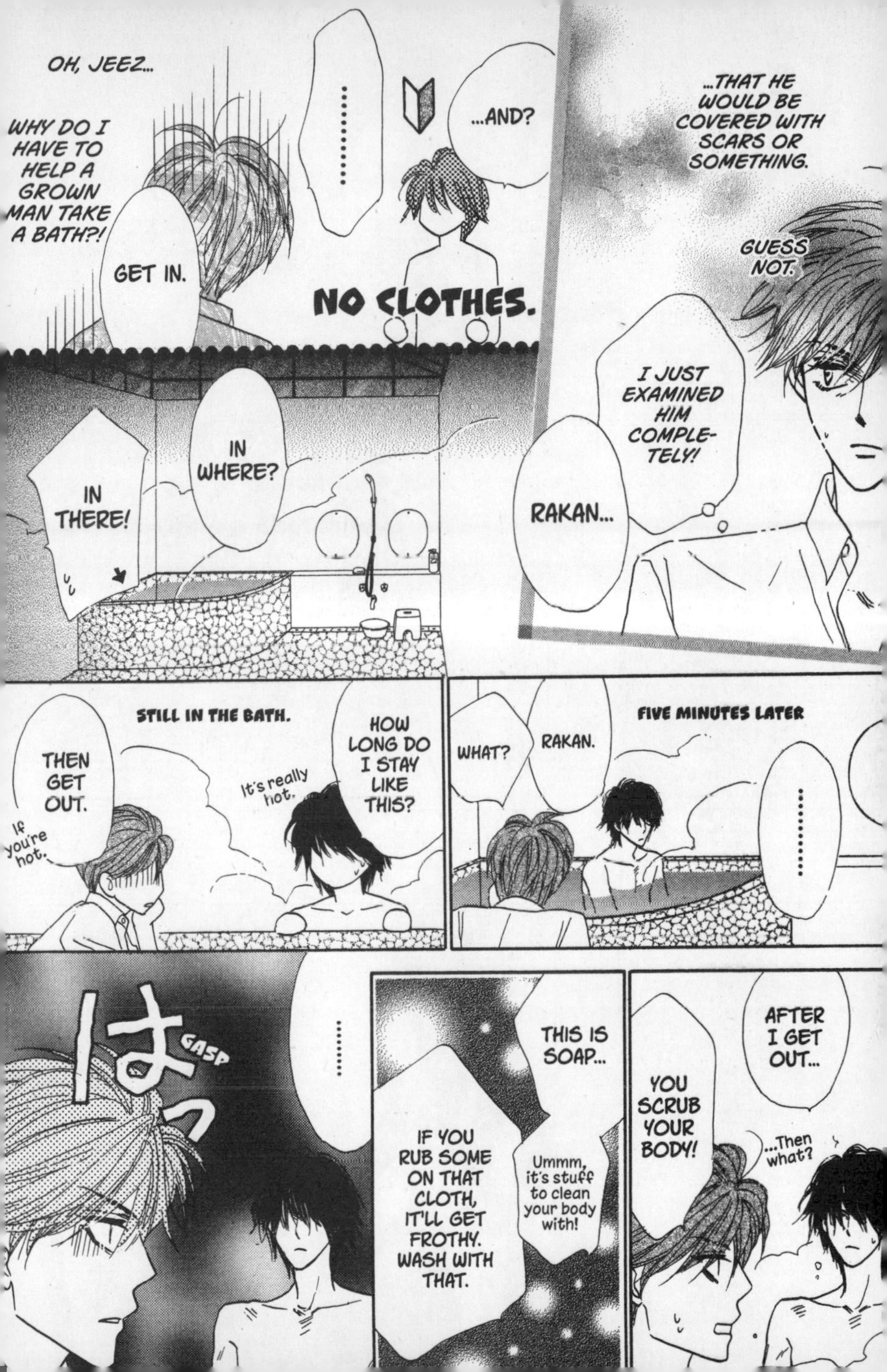
...THAT HE WOULD BE COVERED WITH SCARS OR SOMETHING.
GUESS NOT.
I JUST EXAMINED HIM COMPLETELY!
RAKAN...
...AND?
......
NO CLOTHES.
GET IN.
OH, JEEZ...
WHY DO I HAVE TO HELP A GROWN MAN TAKE A BATH?!
IN WHERE?
IN THERE!
FIVE MINUTES LATER
......
RAKAN.
WHAT?
HOW LONG DO I STAY LIKE THIS?
STILL IN THE BATH.
It's really hot.
THEN GET OUT.
If you're hot.
AFTER I GET OUT...
...Then what?
YOU SCRUB YOUR BODY!
THIS IS SOAP...
Ummm, it's stuff to clean your body with!
IF YOU RUB SOME ON THAT CLOTH, IT'LL GET FROTHY. WASH WITH THAT.
......
GASP
はっ

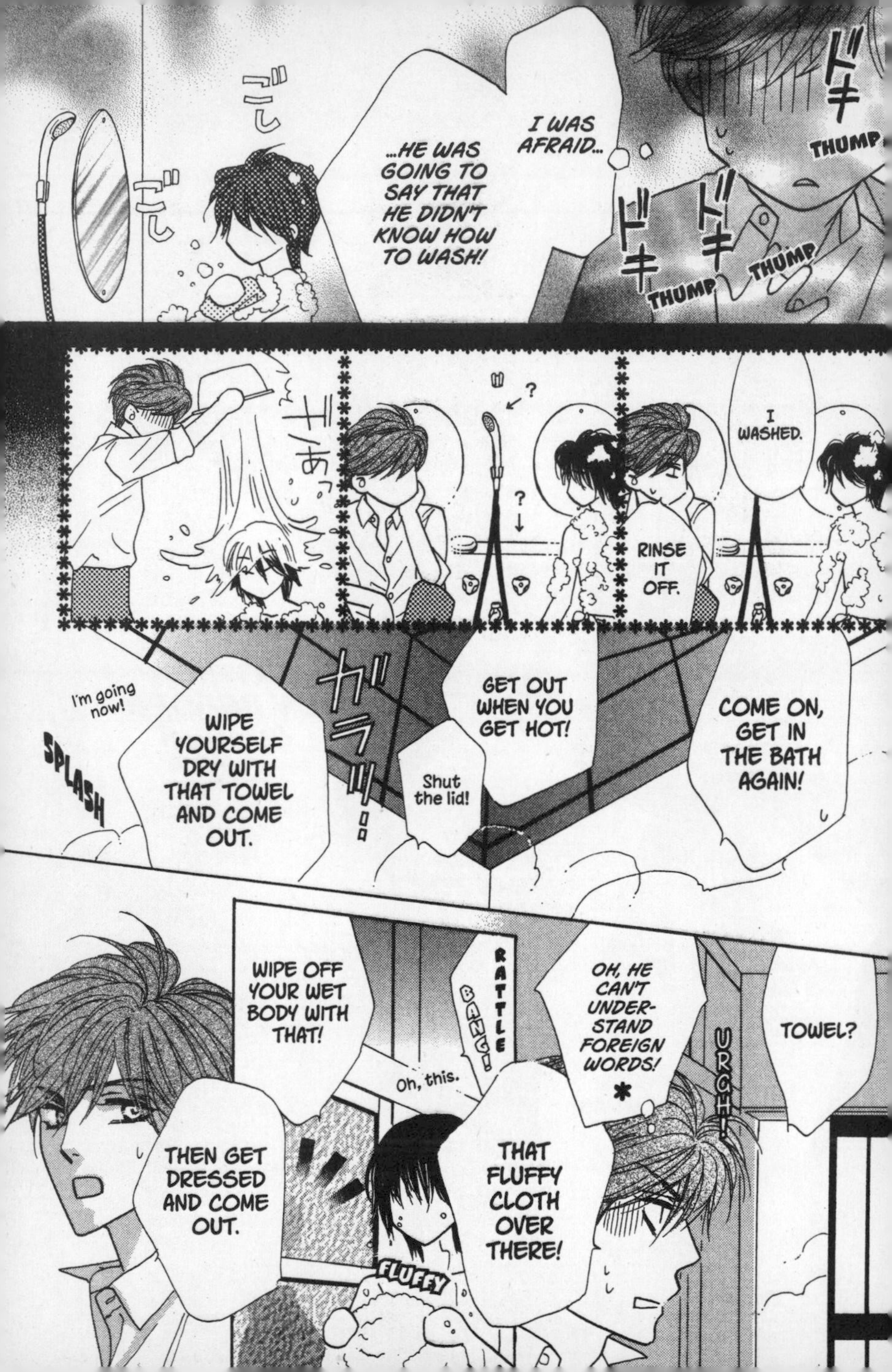
ドキ
THUMP
I WAS AFRAID...
...HE WAS GOING TO SAY THAT HE DIDN'T KNOW HOW TO WASH!
ドキ
ドキ
THUMP
THUMP
ごし
ごし
I WASHED.
RINSE IT OFF.
?
?
COME ON, GET IN THE BATH AGAIN!
GET OUT WHEN YOU GET HOT!
Shut the lid!
WIPE YOURSELF DRY WITH THAT TOWEL AND COME OUT.
I'm going now!
SPLASH
TOWEL?
URGH!
OH, HE CAN'T UNDER-STAND FOREIGN WORDS!
*
THAT FLUFFY CLOTH OVER THERE!
FLUFFY
RATTLE
BANG!
WIPE OFF YOUR WET BODY WITH THAT!
Oh, this.
THEN GET DRESSED AND COME OUT.

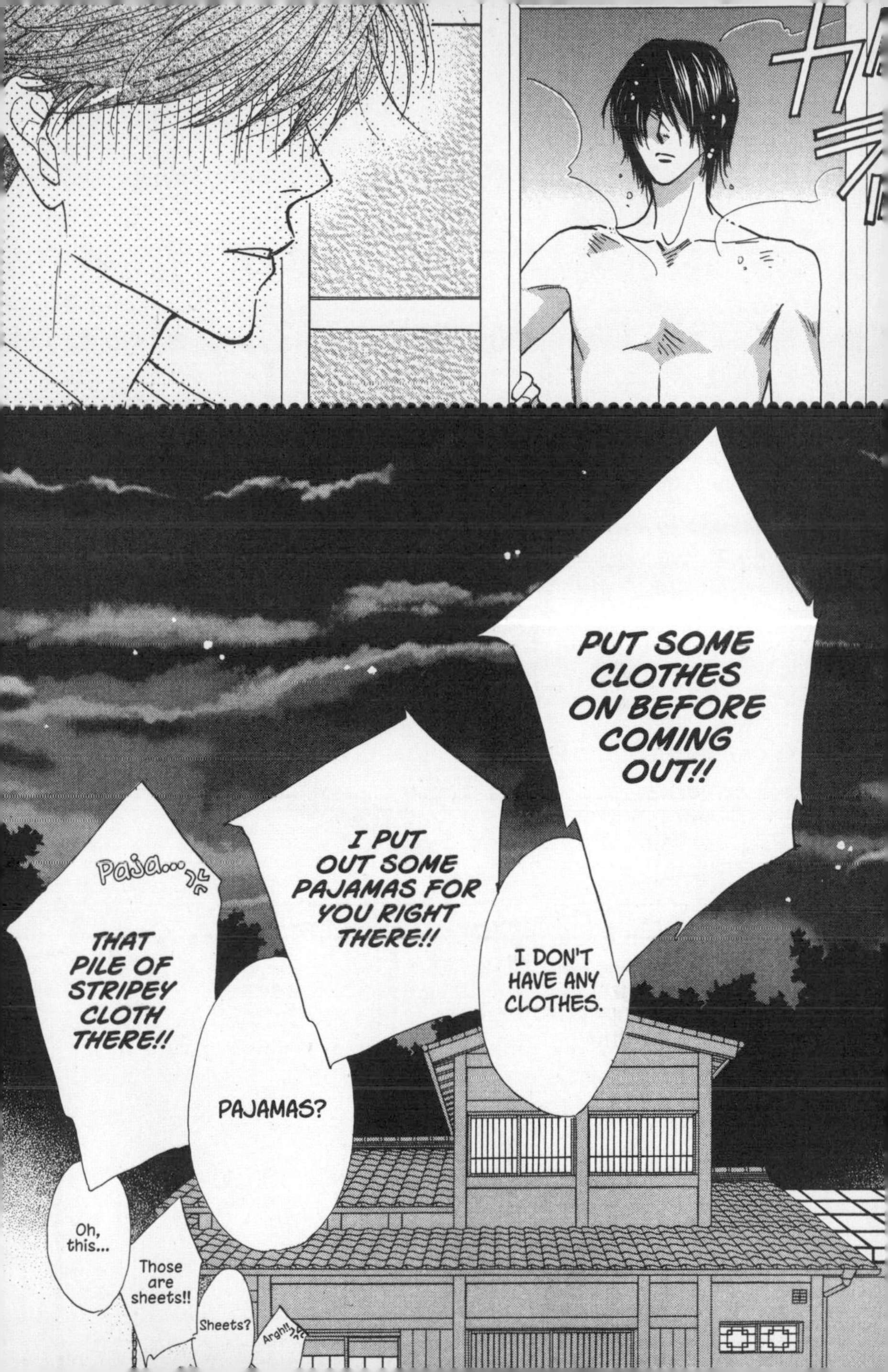
PUT SOME CLOTHES ON BEFORE COMING OUT!!
I DON'T HAVE ANY CLOTHES.
I PUT OUT SOME PAJAMAS FOR YOU RIGHT THERE!!
PAJAMAS?
Paja...
THAT PILE OF STRIPEY CLOTH THERE!!
Oh, this...
Those are sheets!!
Sheets?
Argh!!

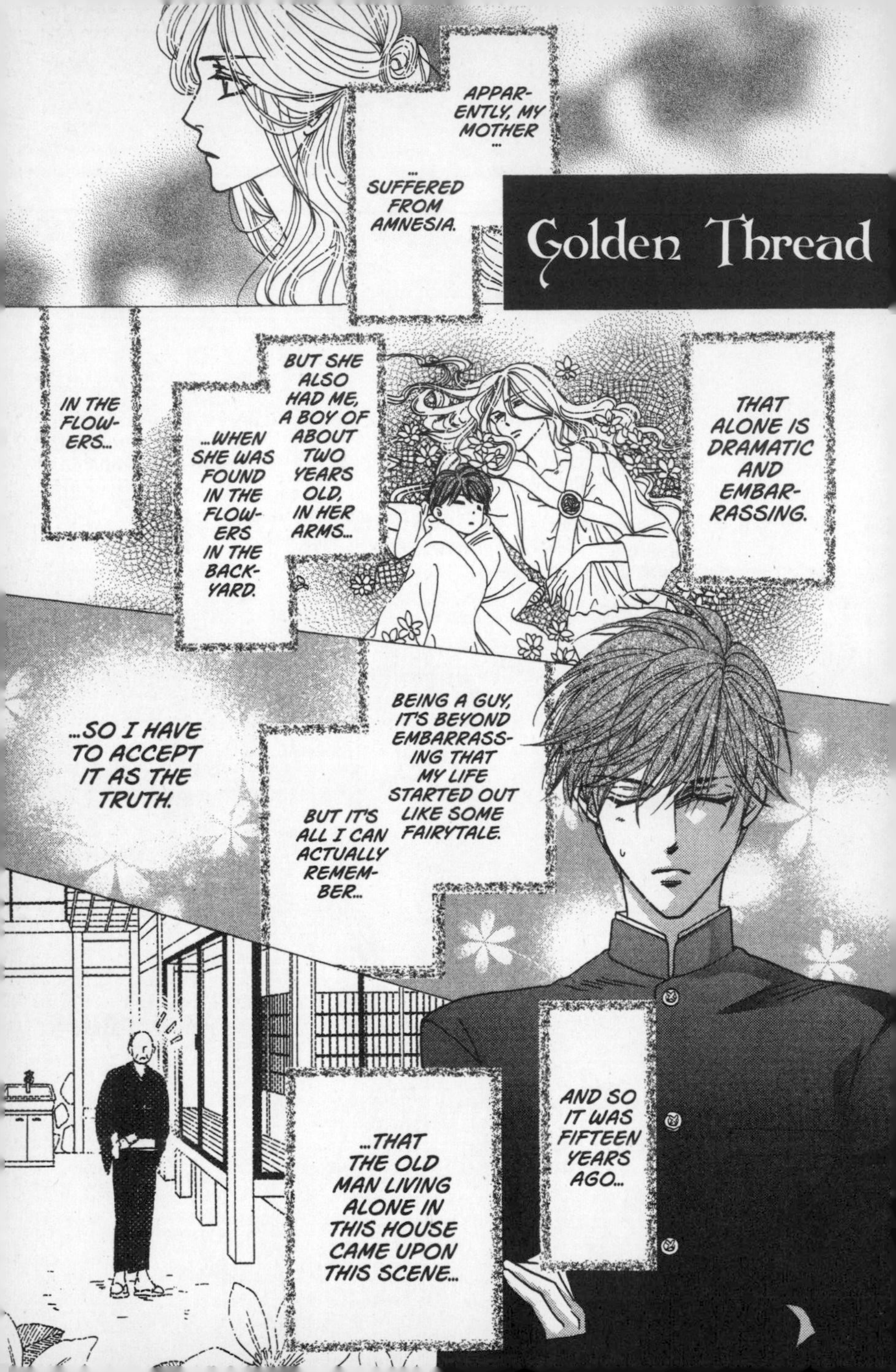
Golden Thread
APPARENTLY, MY MOTHER ...
... SUFFERED FROM AMNESIA.
THAT ALONE IS DRAMATIC AND EMBARRASSING.
BUT SHE ALSO HAD ME, A BOY OF ABOUT TWO YEARS OLD, IN HER ARMS...
...WHEN SHE WAS FOUND IN THE FLOWERS IN THE BACKYARD.
IN THE FLOWERS...
BEING A GUY, IT'S BEYOND EMBARRASSING THAT MY LIFE STARTED OUT LIKE SOME FAIRYTALE.
BUT IT'S ALL I CAN ACTUALLY REMEMBER...
...SO I HAVE TO ACCEPT IT AS THE TRUTH.
AND SO IT WAS FIFTEEN YEARS AGO...
...THAT THE OLD MAN LIVING ALONE IN THIS HOUSE CAME UPON THIS SCENE...

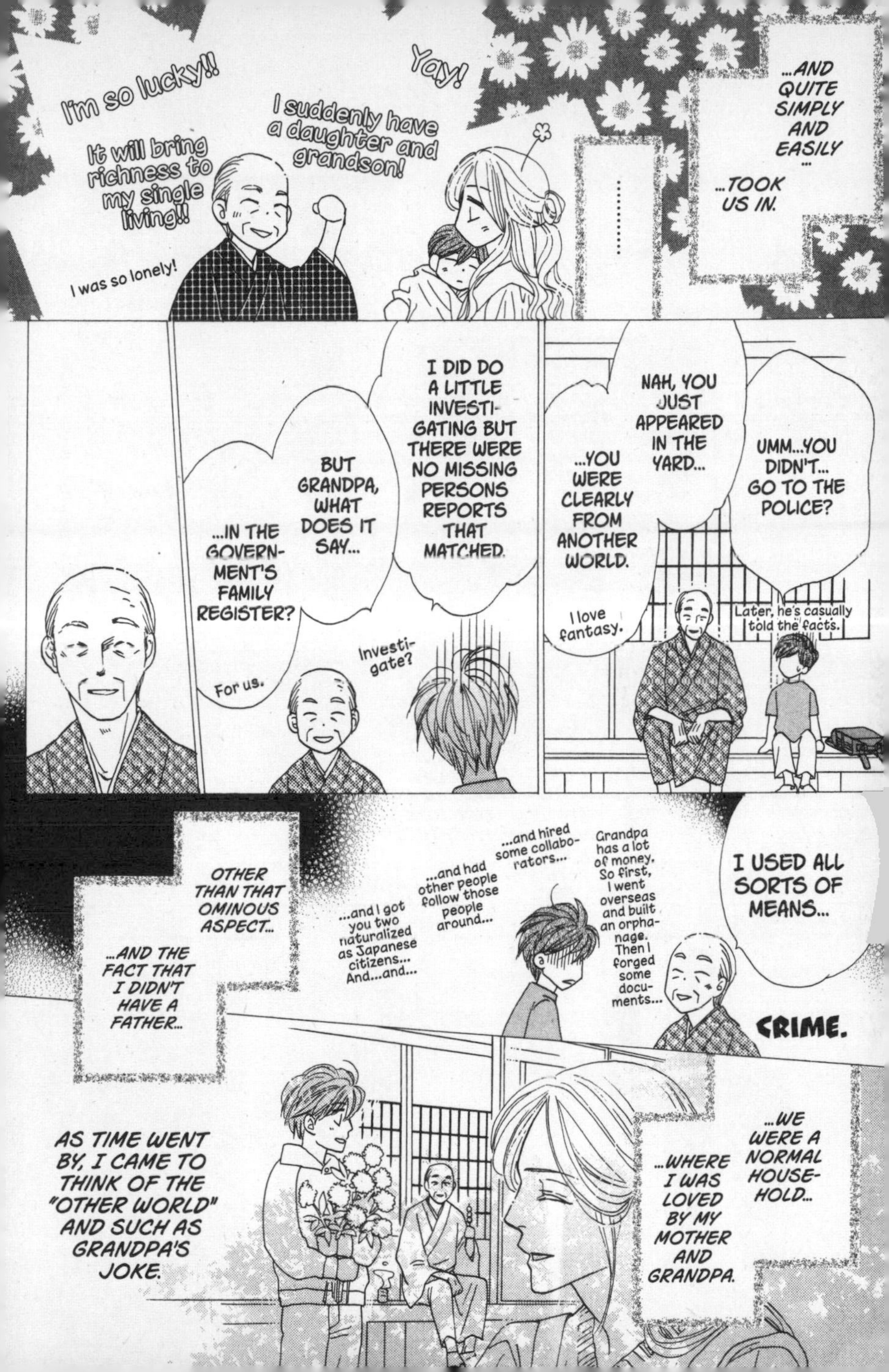
...AND QUITE SIMPLY AND EASILY ...
...TOOK US IN.
......
Yay!
I suddenly have a daughter and grandson!
I'm so lucky!!
It will bring richness to my single living!!
I was so lonely!
UMM...YOU DIDN'T... GO TO THE POLICE?
NAH, YOU JUST APPEARED IN THE YARD...
...YOU WERE CLEARLY FROM ANOTHER WORLD.
I love fantasy.
Later, he's casually told the facts.
I DID DO A LITTLE INVESTI-GATING BUT THERE WERE NO MISSING PERSONS REPORTS THAT MATCHED.
Investi-gate?
BUT GRANDPA, WHAT DOES IT SAY...
...IN THE GOVERN-MENT'S FAMILY REGISTER?
For us.
I USED ALL SORTS OF MEANS...
Grandpa has a lot of money. So first, I went overseas and built an orpha-nage. Then I forged some docu-ments...
...and hired some collabo-rators...
...and had other people follow those people around...
...and I got you two naturalized as Japanese citizens... And...and...
CRIME.
OTHER THAN THAT OMINOUS ASPECT...
...AND THE FACT THAT I DIDN'T HAVE A FATHER...
...WE WERE A NORMAL HOUSE-HOLD...
...WHERE I WAS LOVED BY MY MOTHER AND GRANDPA.
AS TIME WENT BY, I CAME TO THINK OF THE "OTHER WORLD" AND SUCH AS GRANDPA'S JOKE.

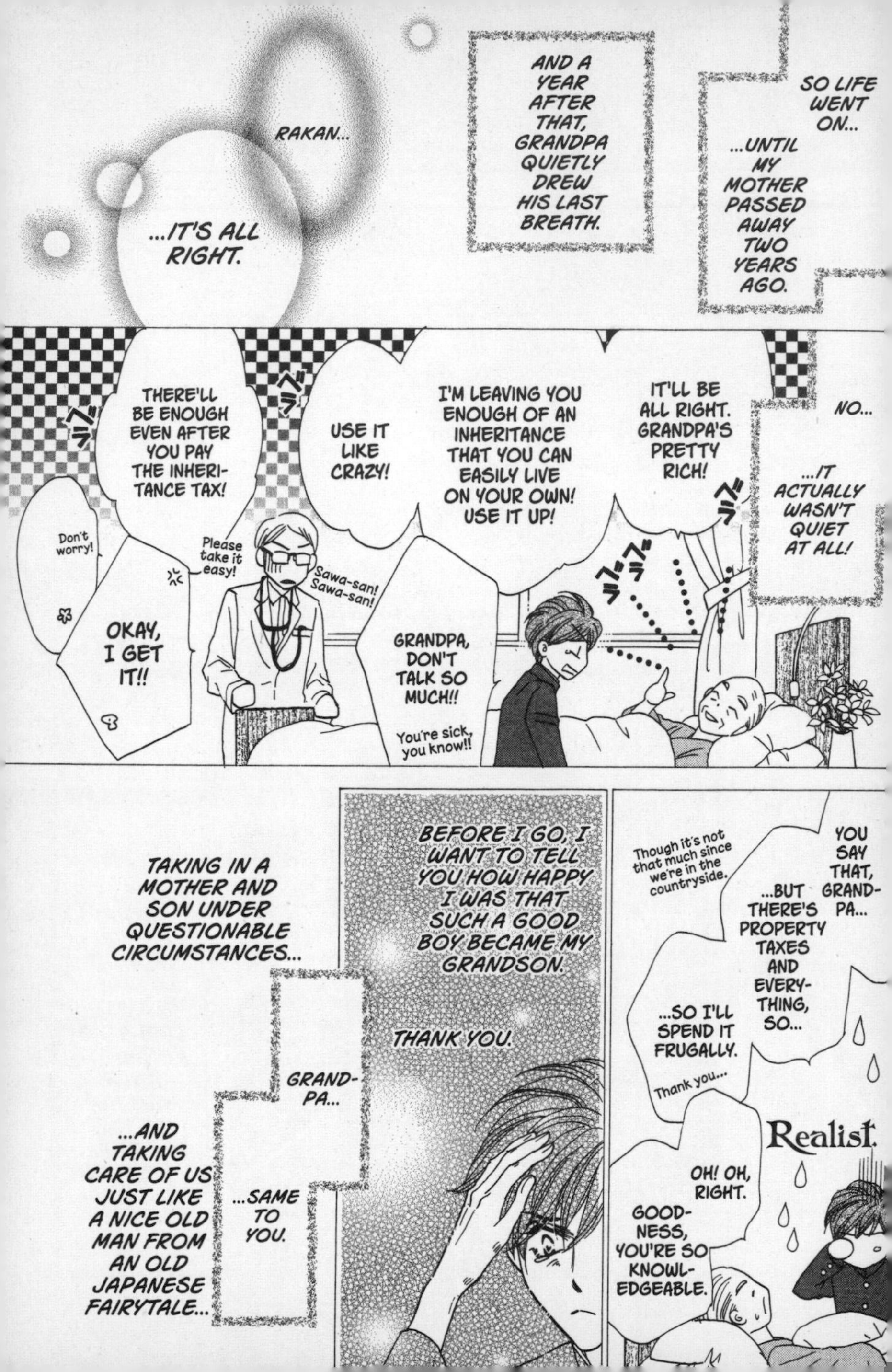
SO LIFE WENT ON...
...UNTIL MY MOTHER PASSED AWAY TWO YEARS AGO.
AND A YEAR AFTER THAT, GRANDPA QUIETLY DREW HIS LAST BREATH.
RAKAN...
...IT'S ALL RIGHT.
NO...
...IT ACTUALLY WASN'T QUIET AT ALL!
IT'LL BE ALL RIGHT. GRANDPA'S PRETTY RICH!
I'M LEAVING YOU ENOUGH OF AN INHERITANCE THAT YOU CAN EASILY LIVE ON YOUR OWN! USE IT UP!
USE IT LIKE CRAZY!
THERE'LL BE ENOUGH EVEN AFTER YOU PAY THE INHERITANCE TAX!
GRANDPA, DON'T TALK SO MUCH!!
You're sick, you know!!
Sawa-san! Sawa-san!
Please take it easy!
OKAY, I GET IT!!
Don't worry!
YOU SAY THAT, GRANDPA...
...BUT THERE'S PROPERTY TAXES AND EVERYTHING, SO...
Though it's not that much since we're in the countryside.
...SO I'LL SPEND IT FRUGALLY.
Thank you...
Realist.
OH! OH, RIGHT.
GOODNESS, YOU'RE SO KNOWLEDGEABLE.
BEFORE I GO, I WANT TO TELL YOU HOW HAPPY I WAS THAT SUCH A GOOD BOY BECAME MY GRANDSON.
THANK YOU.
TAKING IN A MOTHER AND SON UNDER QUESTIONABLE CIRCUMSTANCES...
GRANDPA...
...AND TAKING CARE OF US JUST LIKE A NICE OLD MAN FROM AN OLD JAPANESE FAIRYTALE...
...SAME TO YOU.

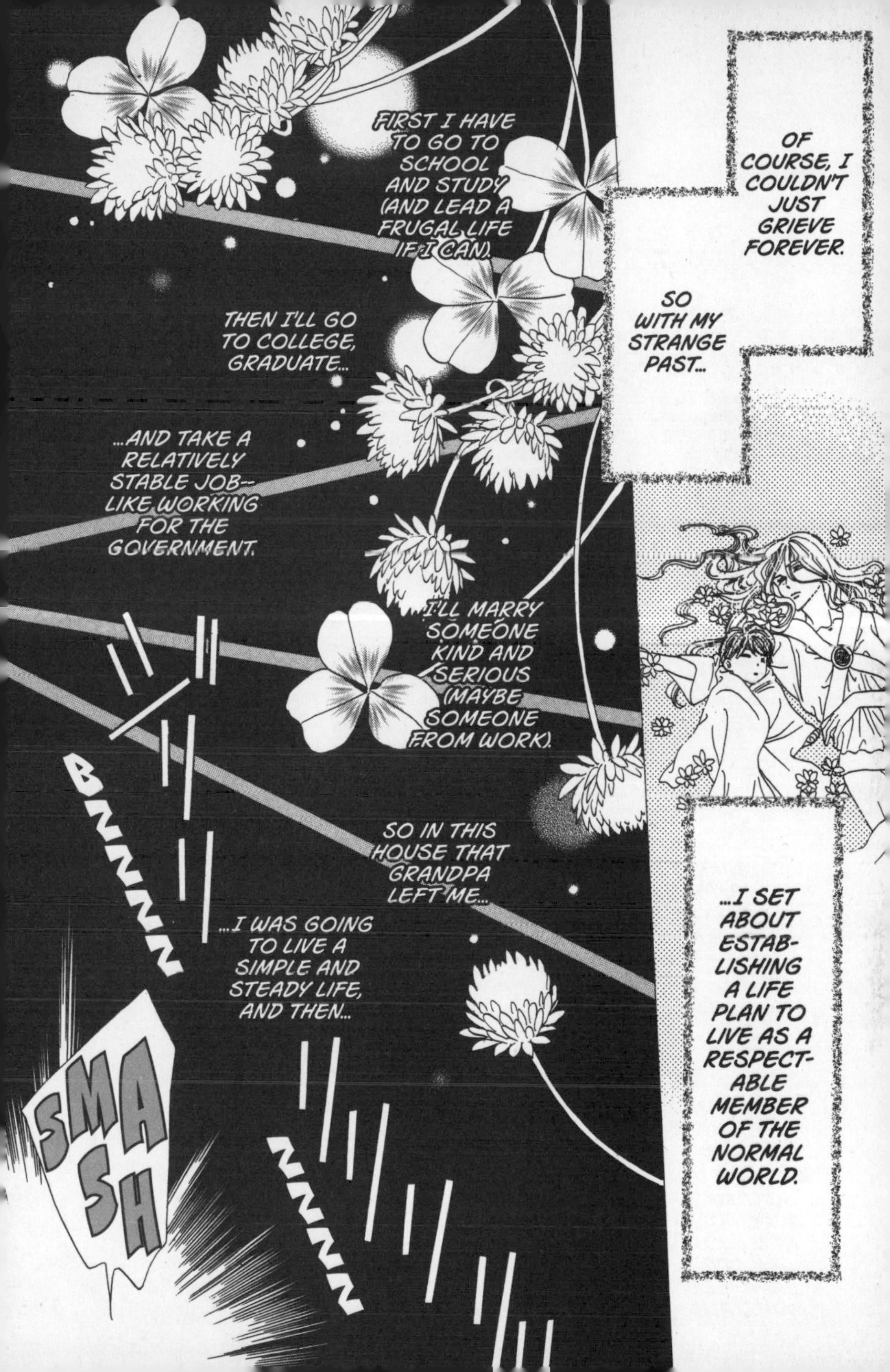
OF COURSE, I COULDN'T JUST GRIEVE FOREVER.
SO WITH MY STRANGE PAST...
...I SET ABOUT ESTABLISHING A LIFE PLAN TO LIVE AS A RESPECTABLE MEMBER OF THE NORMAL WORLD.
FIRST I HAVE TO GO TO SCHOOL AND STUDY (AND LEAD A FRUGAL LIFE IF I CAN).
THEN I'LL GO TO COLLEGE, GRADUATE...
...AND TAKE A RELATIVELY STABLE JOB-- LIKE WORKING FOR THE GOVERNMENT.
I'LL MARRY SOMEONE KIND AND SERIOUS (MAYBE SOMEONE FROM WORK).
SO IN THIS HOUSE THAT GRANDPA LEFT ME...
...I WAS GOING TO LIVE A SIMPLE AND STEADY LIFE, AND THEN...
BNNNNN
SMASH
NNNN

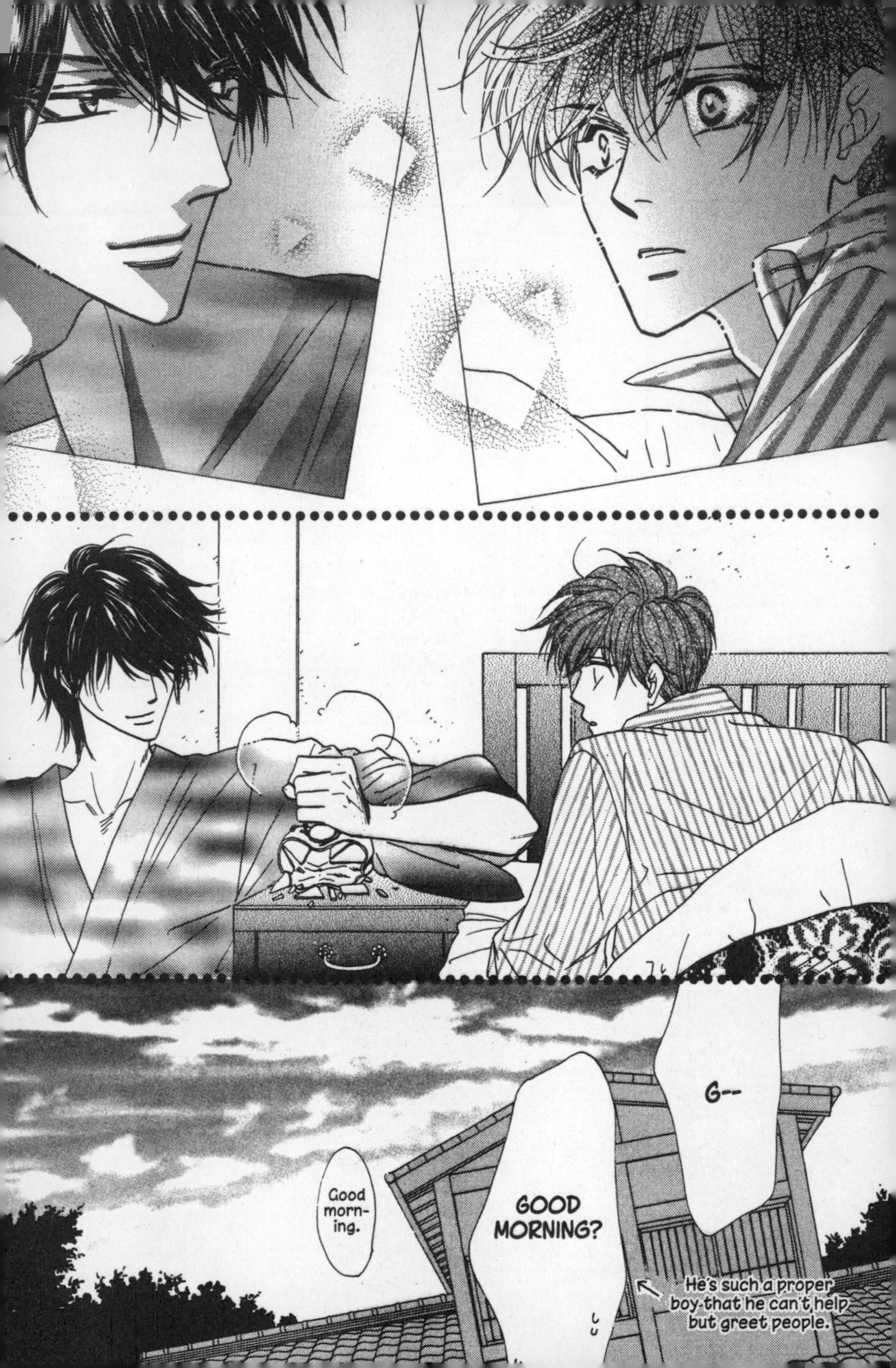
G--
GOOD MORNING?
Good morning.
He's such a proper boy that he can't help but greet people.

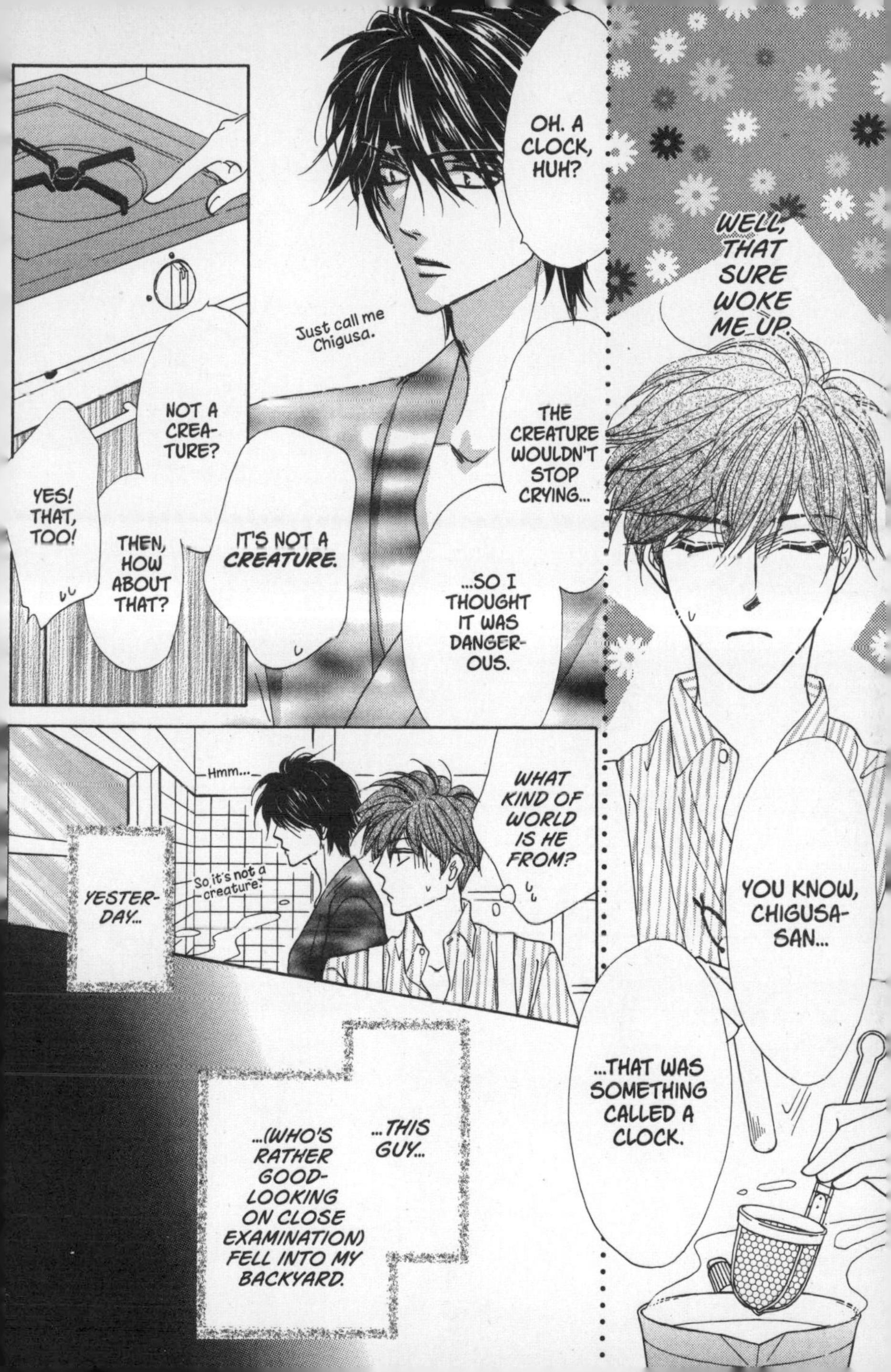
WELL, THAT SURE WOKE ME UP.
YOU KNOW, CHIGUSA-SAN...
...THAT WAS SOMETHING CALLED A CLOCK.
OH. A CLOCK, HUH?
Just call me Chigusa.
THE CREATURE WOULDN'T STOP CRYING...
...SO I THOUGHT IT WAS DANGER-OUS.
IT'S NOT A CREATURE.
NOT A CREA-TURE?
THEN, HOW ABOUT THAT?
YES! THAT, TOO!
WHAT KIND OF WORLD IS HE FROM?
Hmm...
So, it's not a creature.
YESTER-DAY...
...THIS GUY...
...(WHO'S RATHER GOOD-LOOKING ON CLOSE EXAMINATION) FELL INTO MY BACKYARD.

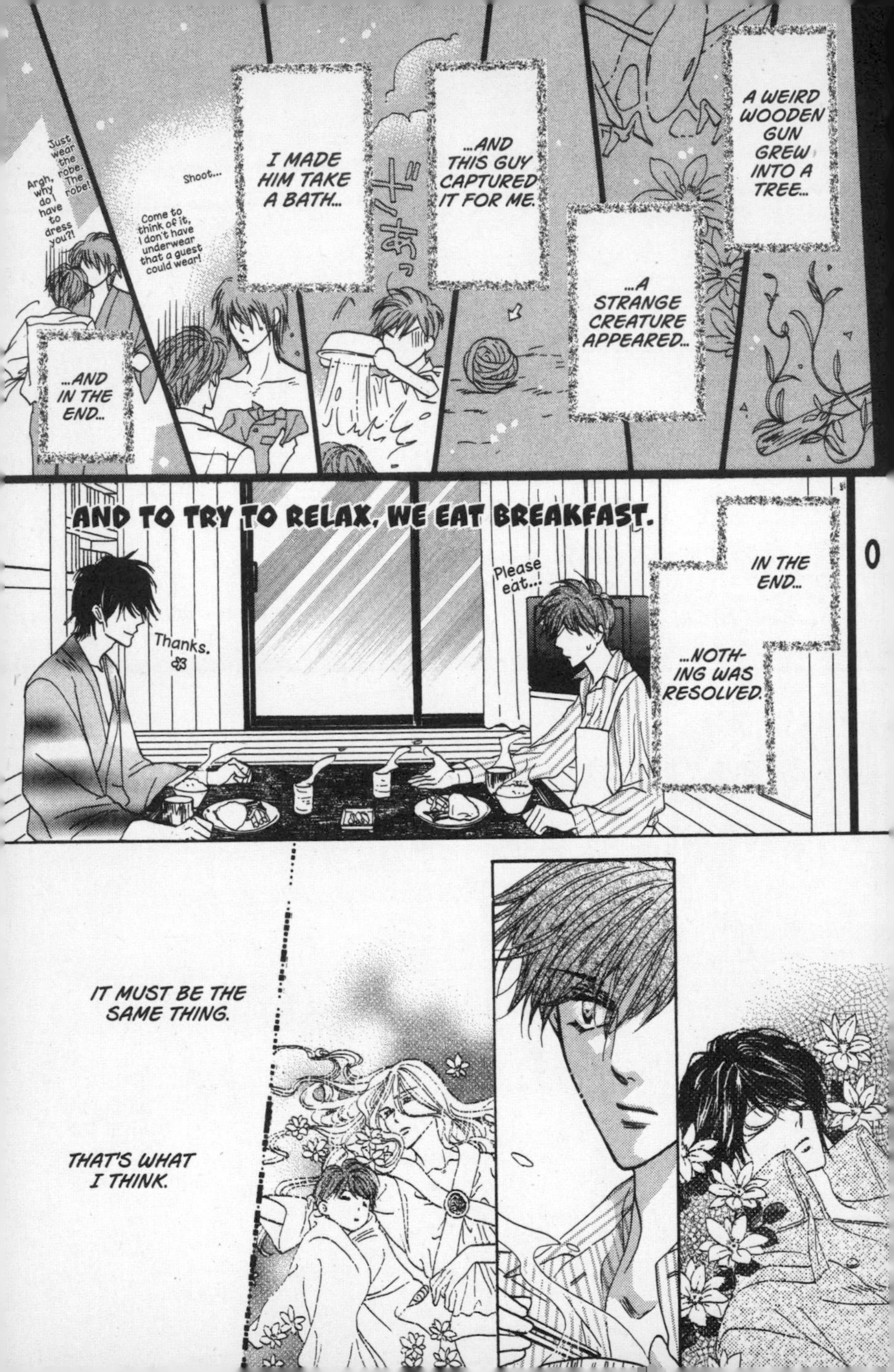
A WEIRD WOODEN GUN GREW INTO A TREE...
...A STRANGE CREATURE APPEARED...
...AND THIS GUY CAPTURED IT FOR ME.
I MADE HIM TAKE A BATH...
Shoot...
Come to think of it, I don't have underwear that a guest could wear!
Just wear the robe. The robe!
Argh, why do I have to dress you?!
...AND IN THE END...
IN THE END...
...NOTHING WAS RESOLVED.
AND TO TRY TO RELAX, WE EAT BREAKFAST.
Please eat...
Thanks.
IT MUST BE THE SAME THING.
THAT'S WHAT I THINK.

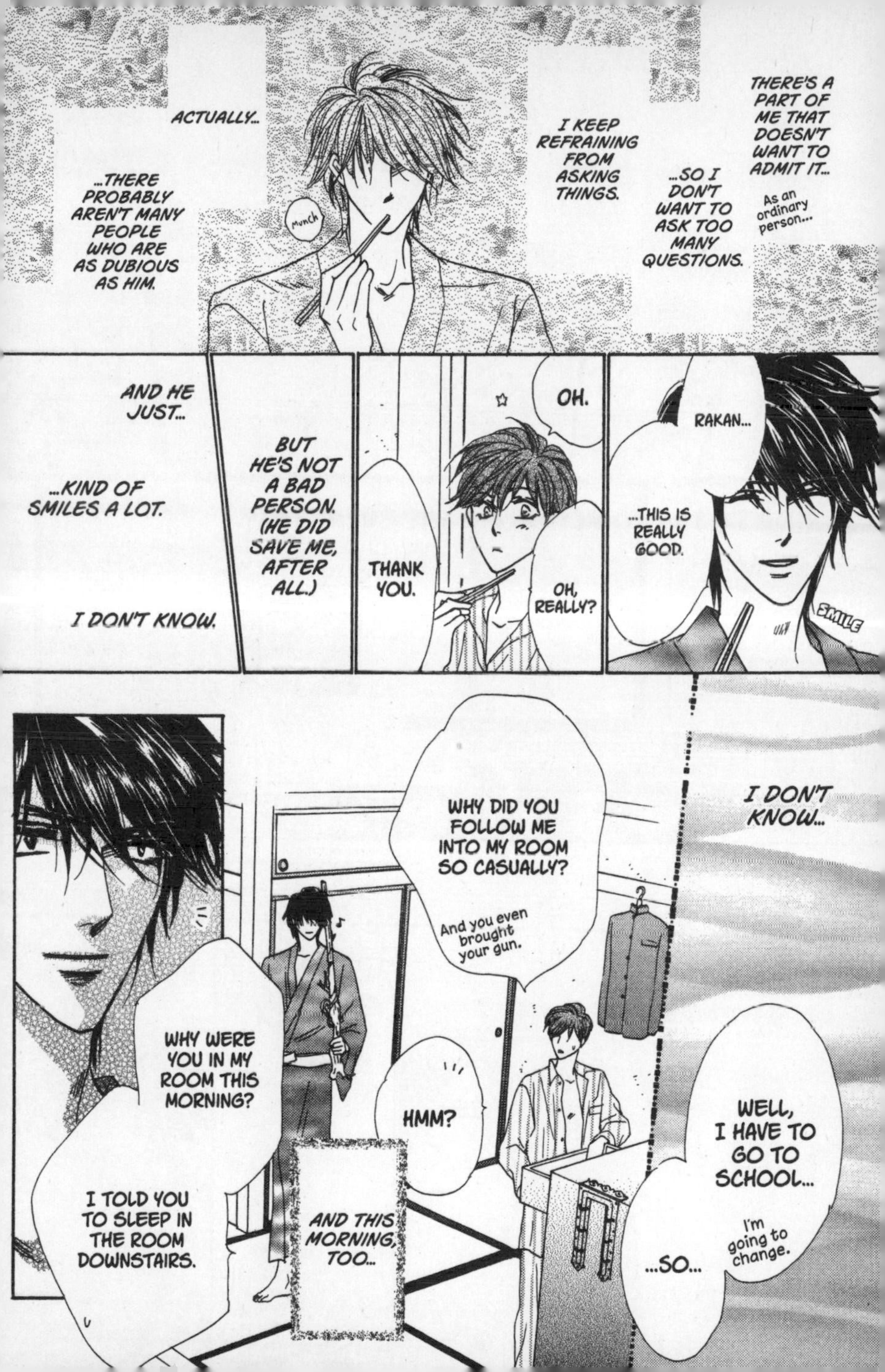

THERE'S A PART OF ME THAT DOESN'T WANT TO ADMIT IT...
As an ordinary person...
...SO I DON'T WANT TO ASK TOO MANY QUESTIONS.
I KEEP REFRAINING FROM ASKING THINGS.
Munch
ACTUALLY...
...THERE PROBABLY AREN'T MANY PEOPLE WHO ARE AS DUBIOUS AS HIM.
RAKAN...
...THIS IS REALLY GOOD.
SMILE
OH.
OH, REALLY?
THANK YOU.
BUT HE'S NOT A BAD PERSON. (HE DID SAVE ME, AFTER ALL.)
AND HE JUST...
...KIND OF SMILES A LOT.
I DON'T KNOW.
I DON'T KNOW...
WELL, I HAVE TO GO TO SCHOOL...
I'm going to change.
...SO...
WHY DID YOU FOLLOW ME INTO MY ROOM SO CASUALLY?
And you even brought your gun.
HMM?
AND THIS MORNING, TOO...
WHY WERE YOU IN MY ROOM THIS MORNING?
I TOLD YOU TO SLEEP IN THE ROOM DOWNSTAIRS.

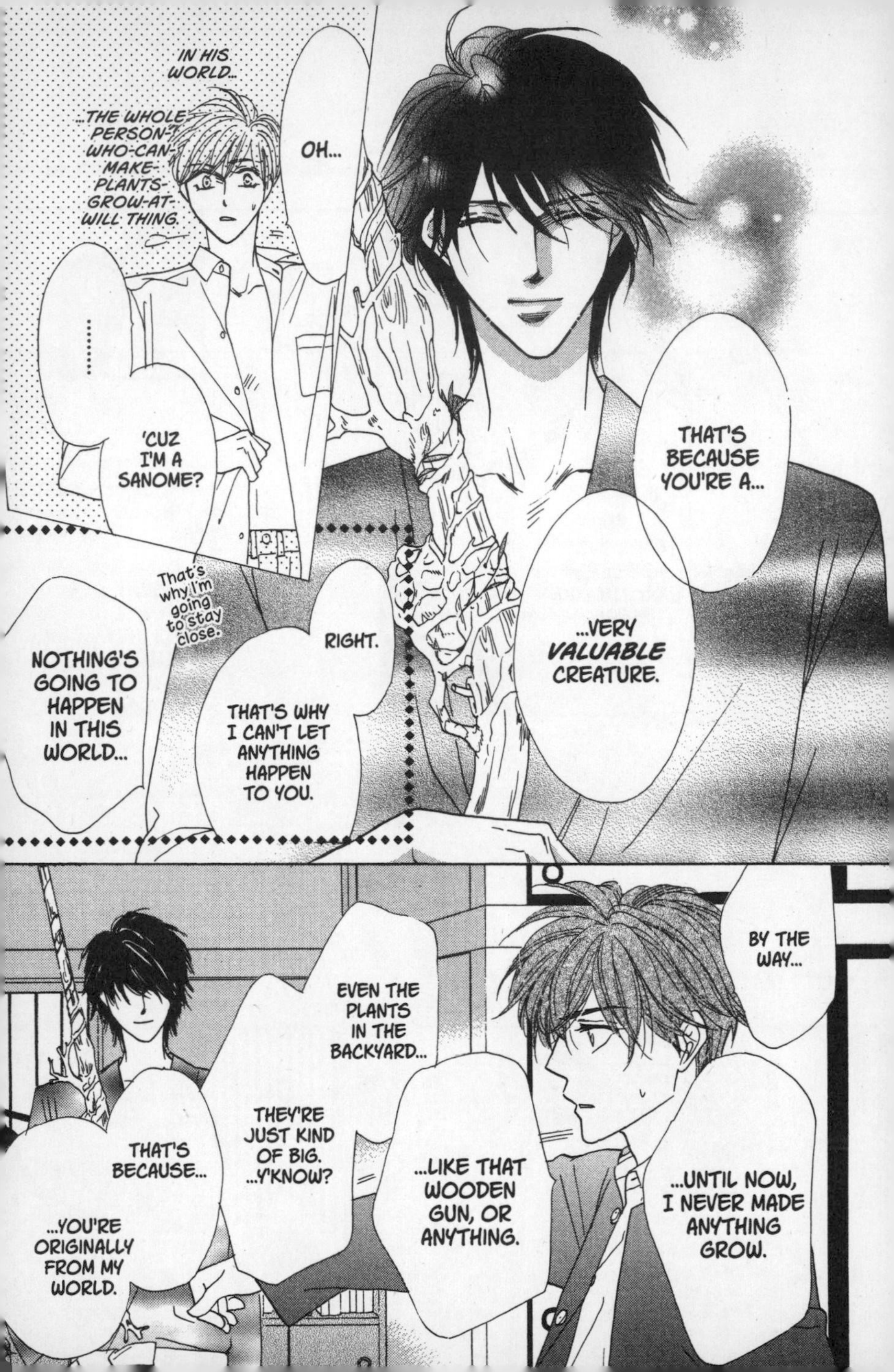
THAT'S BECAUSE YOU'RE A...
...VERY VALUABLE CREATURE.
OH...
IN HIS WORLD...
...THE WHOLE PERSON-WHO-CAN-MAKE-PLANTS-GROW-AT-WILL THING.
......
'CUZ I'M A SANOME?
RIGHT.
THAT'S WHY I CAN'T LET ANYTHING HAPPEN TO YOU.
NOTHING'S GOING TO HAPPEN IN THIS WORLD...
That's why I'm going to stay close.
BY THE WAY...
...UNTIL NOW, I NEVER MADE ANYTHING GROW.
...LIKE THAT WOODEN GUN, OR ANYTHING.
EVEN THE PLANTS IN THE BACKYARD...
THEY'RE JUST KIND OF BIG. ...Y'KNOW?
THAT'S BECAUSE...
...YOU'RE ORIGINALLY FROM MY WORLD.

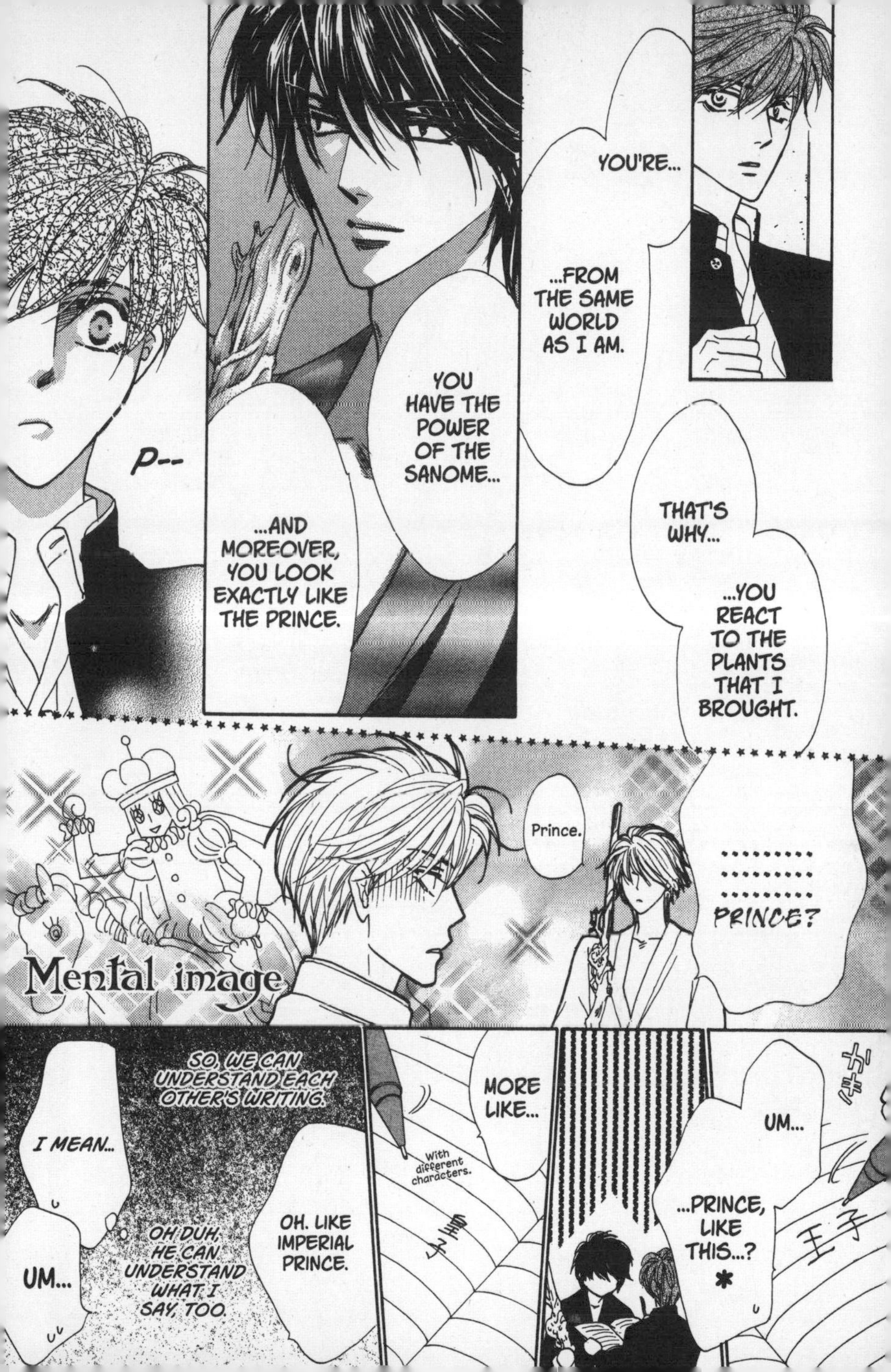
YOU'RE...
...FROM THE SAME WORLD AS I AM.
THAT'S WHY...
...YOU REACT TO THE PLANTS THAT I BROUGHT.
YOU HAVE THE POWER OF THE SANOME...
...AND MOREOVER, YOU LOOK EXACTLY LIKE THE PRINCE.
P--
....
....
....
PRINCE?
Prince.
Mental image
UM...
...PRINCE, LIKE THIS...?
*
王子
MORE LIKE...
OH. LIKE IMPERIAL PRINCE.
With different characters.
SO, WE CAN UNDERSTAND EACH OTHER'S WRITING.
I MEAN...
UM...
OH DUH, HE CAN UNDERSTAND WHAT I SAY, TOO.

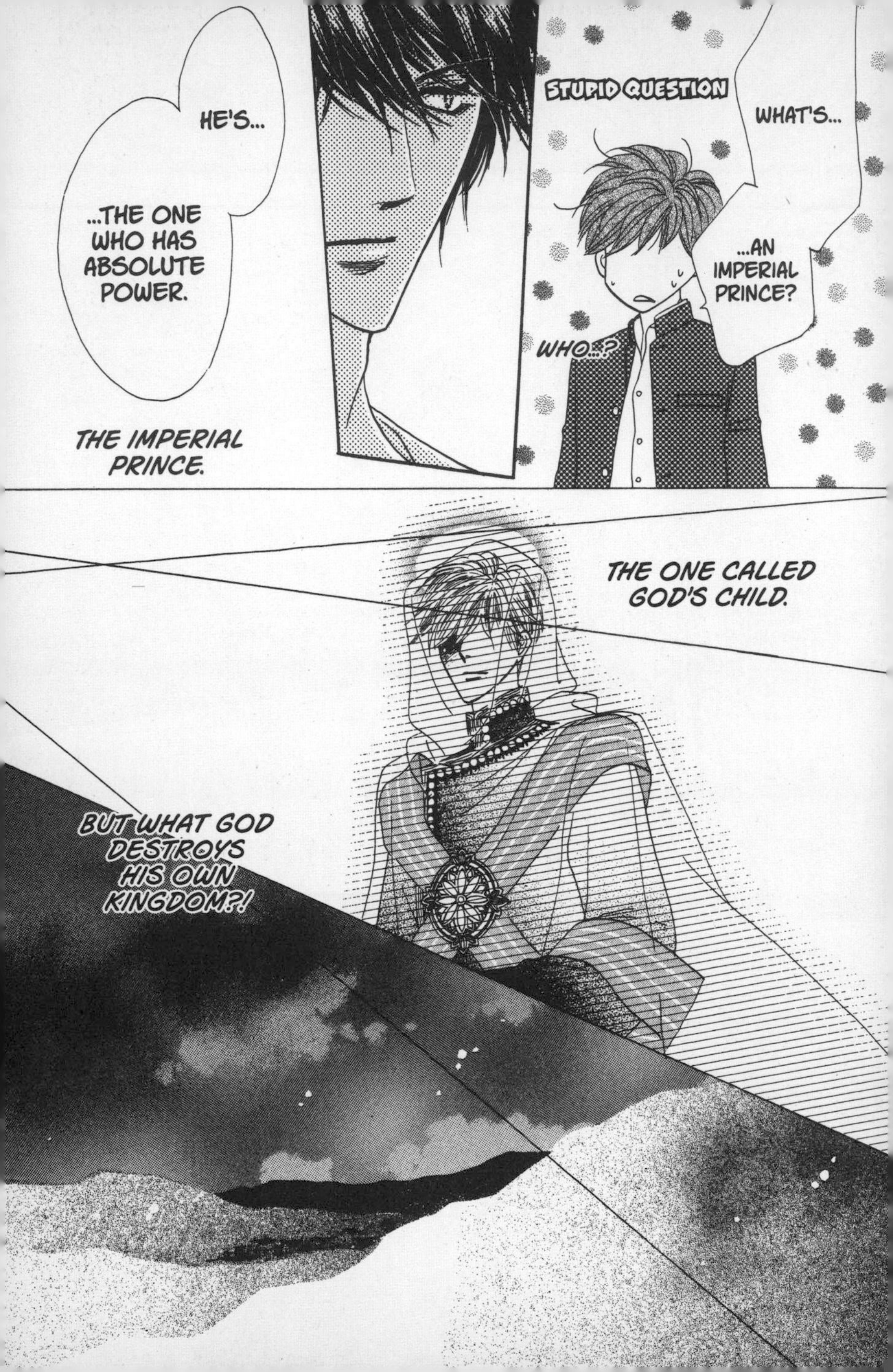
STUPID QUESTION
WHAT'S...
...AN IMPERIAL PRINCE?
WHO...?
HE'S...
...THE ONE WHO HAS ABSOLUTE POWER.
THE IMPERIAL PRINCE.
THE ONE CALLED GOD'S CHILD.
BUT WHAT GOD DESTROYS HIS OWN KINGDOM?!

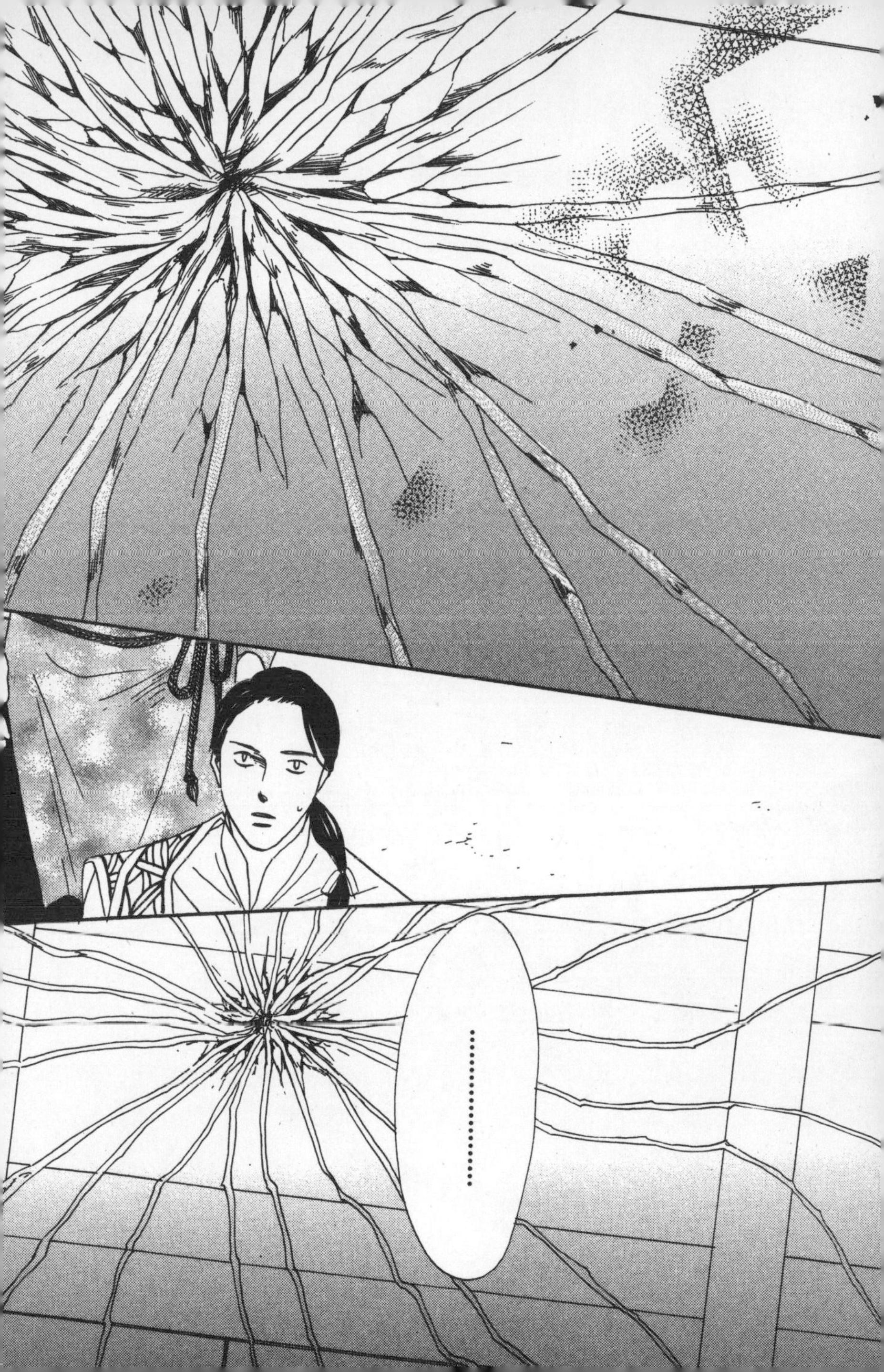
……

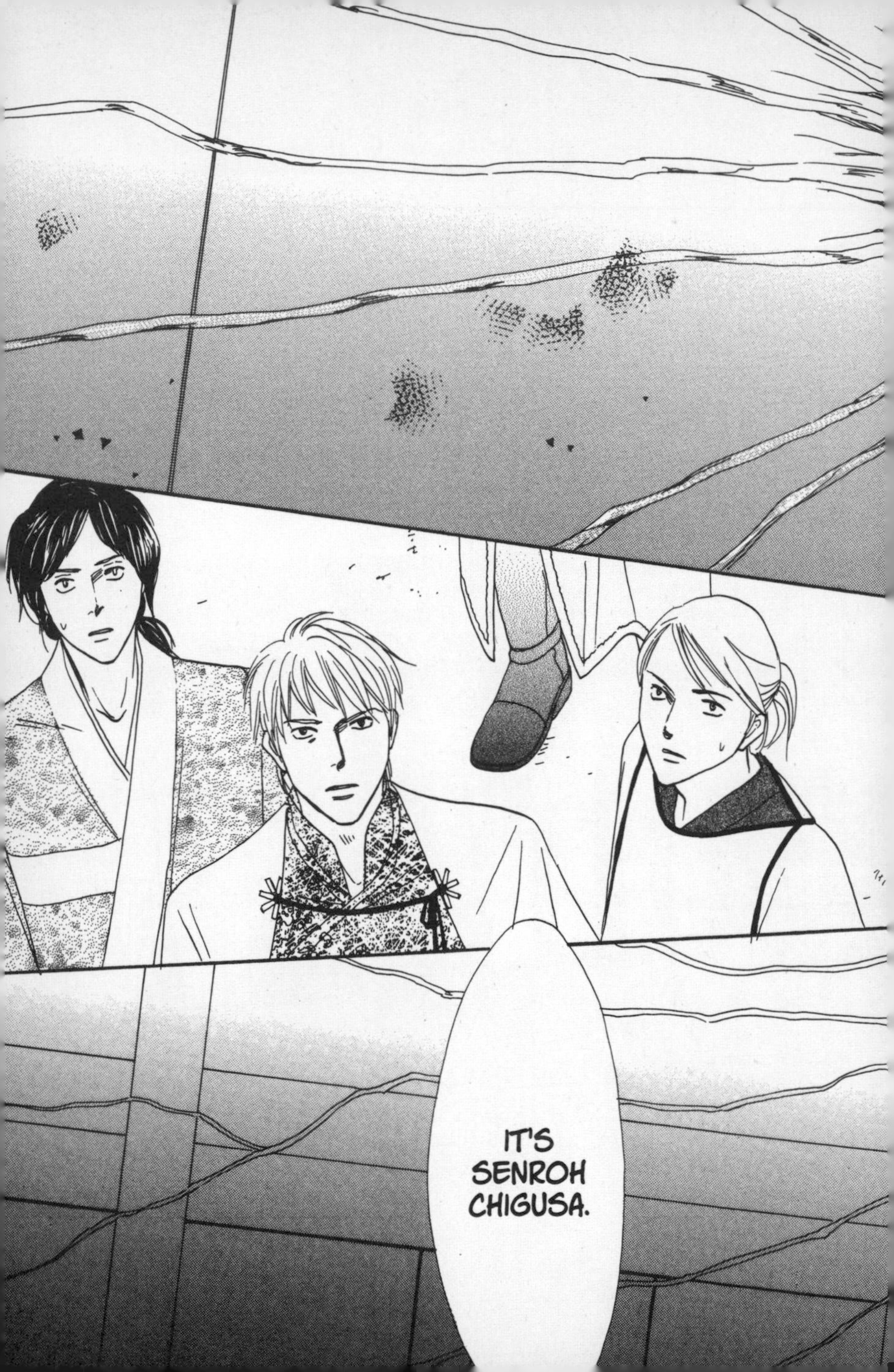
IT'S SENROH CHIGUSA.

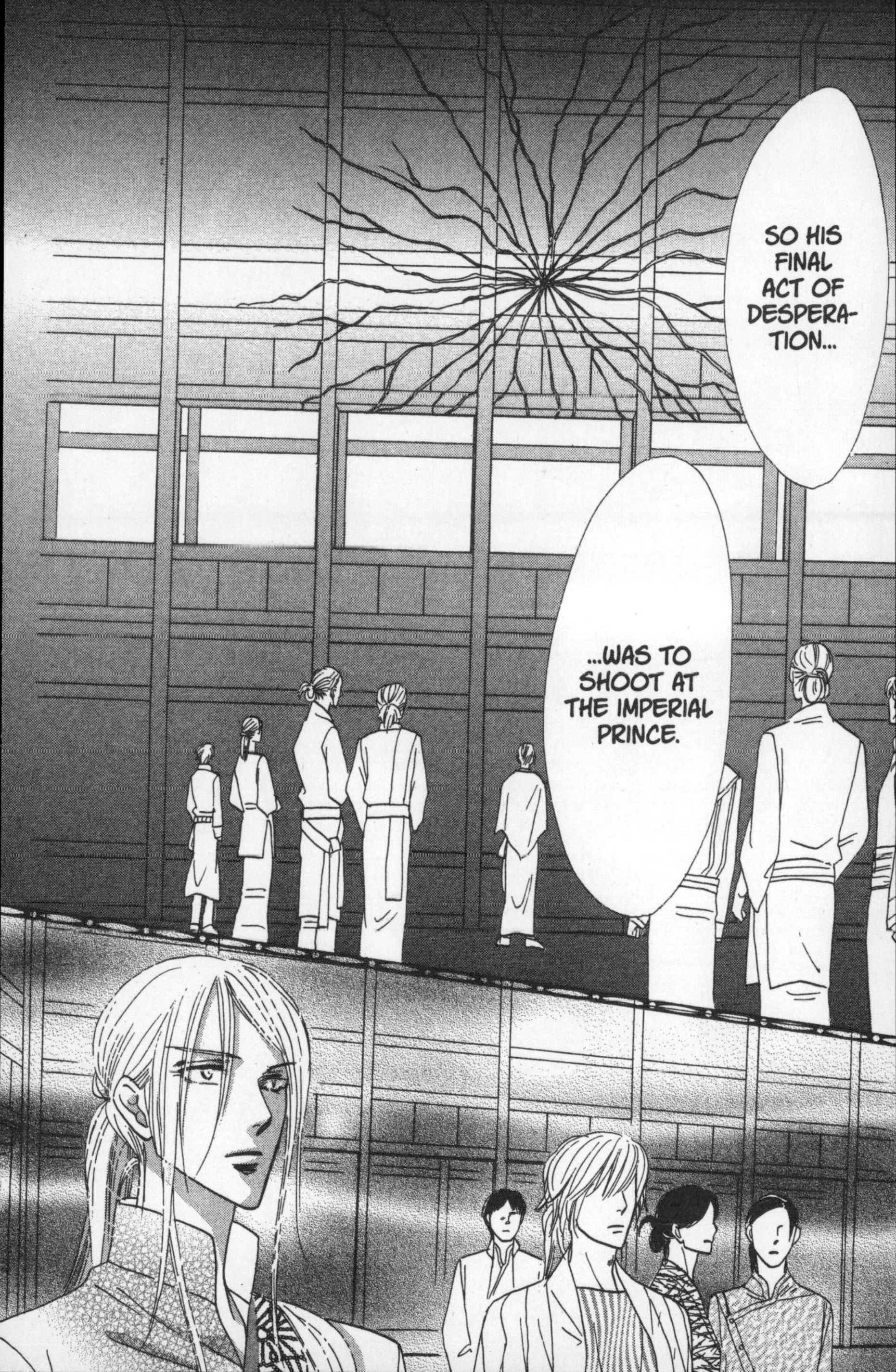
SO HIS FINAL ACT OF DESPERA- TION...
...WAS TO SHOOT AT THE IMPERIAL PRINCE.

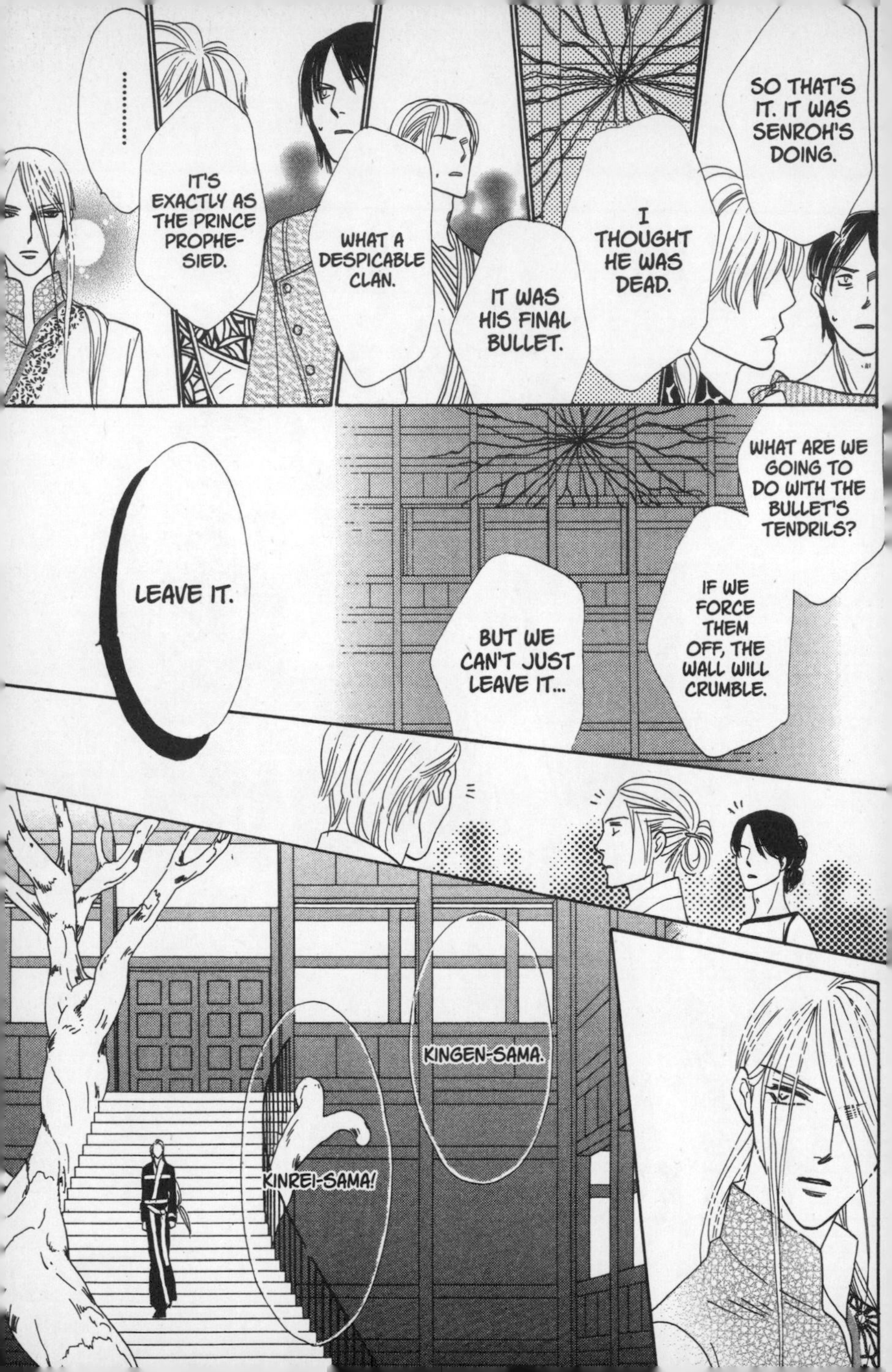
SO THAT'S IT. IT WAS SENROH'S DOING.
I THOUGHT HE WAS DEAD.
IT WAS HIS FINAL BULLET.
WHAT A DESPICABLE CLAN.
IT'S EXACTLY AS THE PRINCE PROPHESIED.
......
WHAT ARE WE GOING TO DO WITH THE BULLET'S TENDRILS?
IF WE FORCE THEM OFF, THE WALL WILL CRUMBLE.
BUT WE CAN'T JUST LEAVE IT...
LEAVE IT.
KINGEN-SAMA.
KINREI-SAMA!

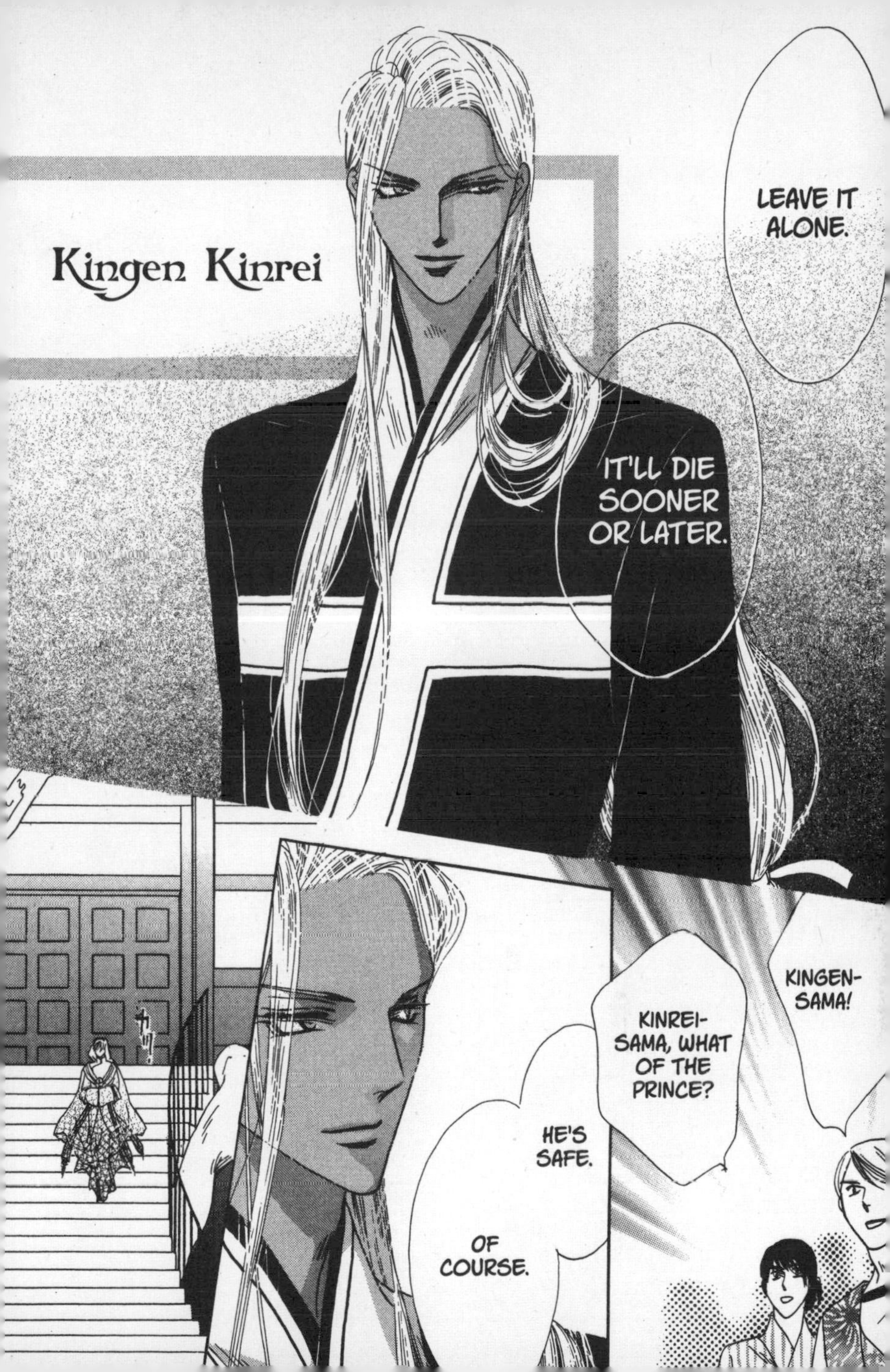
LEAVE IT ALONE.
IT'LL DIE SOONER OR LATER.
Kingen Kinrei
KINGEN-SAMA!
KINREI-SAMA, WHAT OF THE PRINCE?
HE'S SAFE.
OF COURSE.

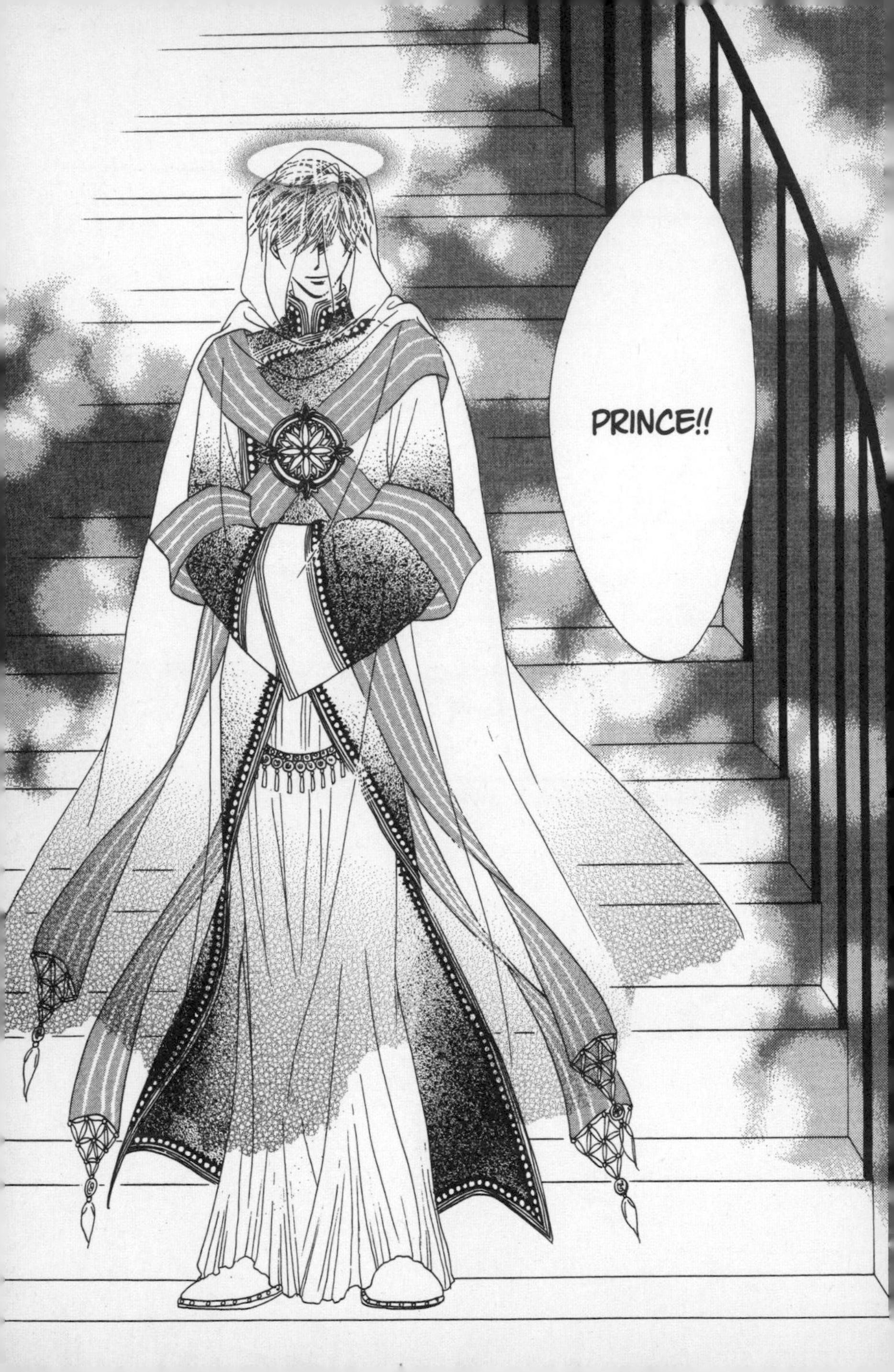
PRINCE!!

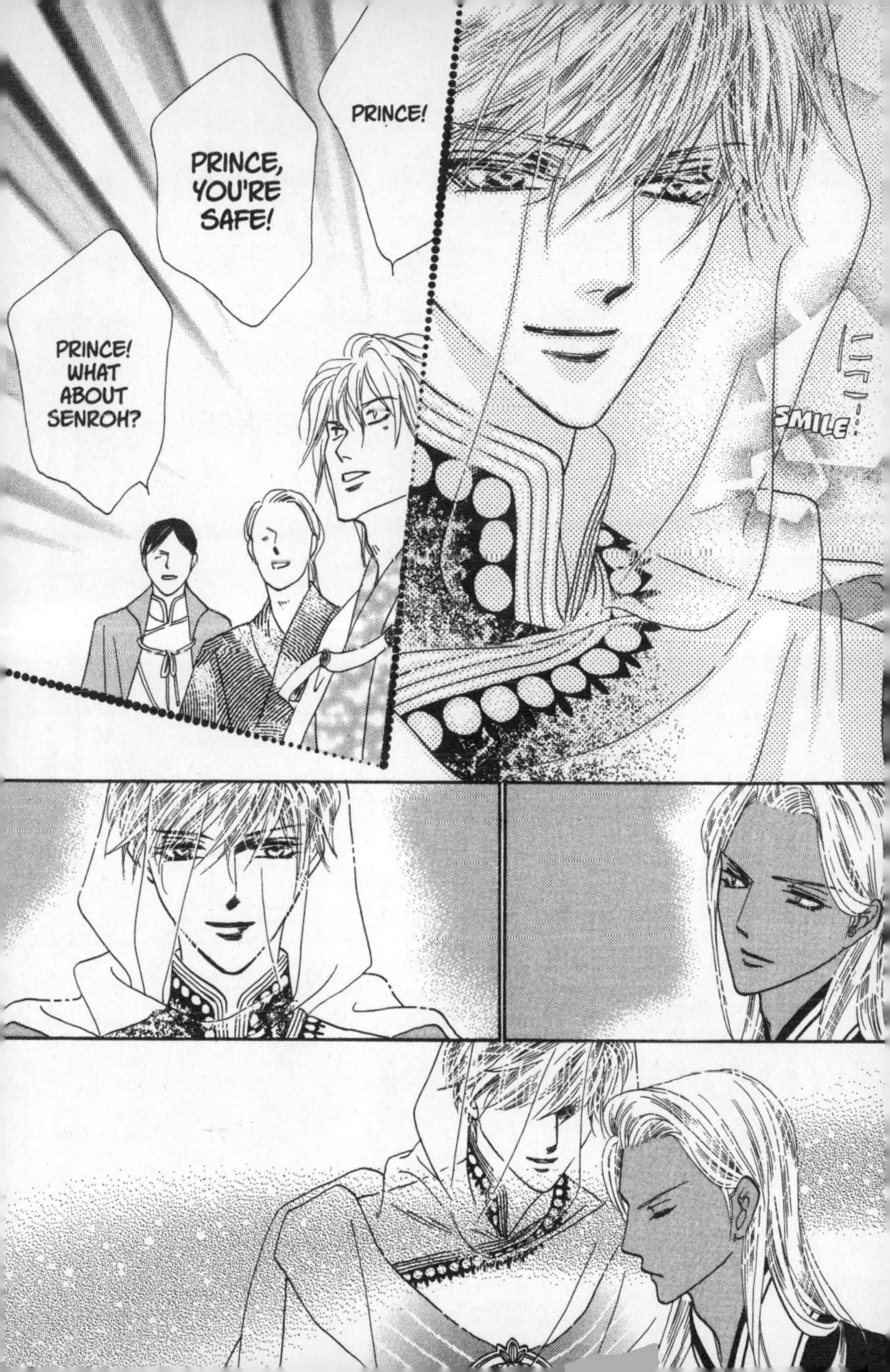
SMILE
PRINCE!
PRINCE, YOU'RE SAFE!
PRINCE! WHAT ABOUT SENROH?

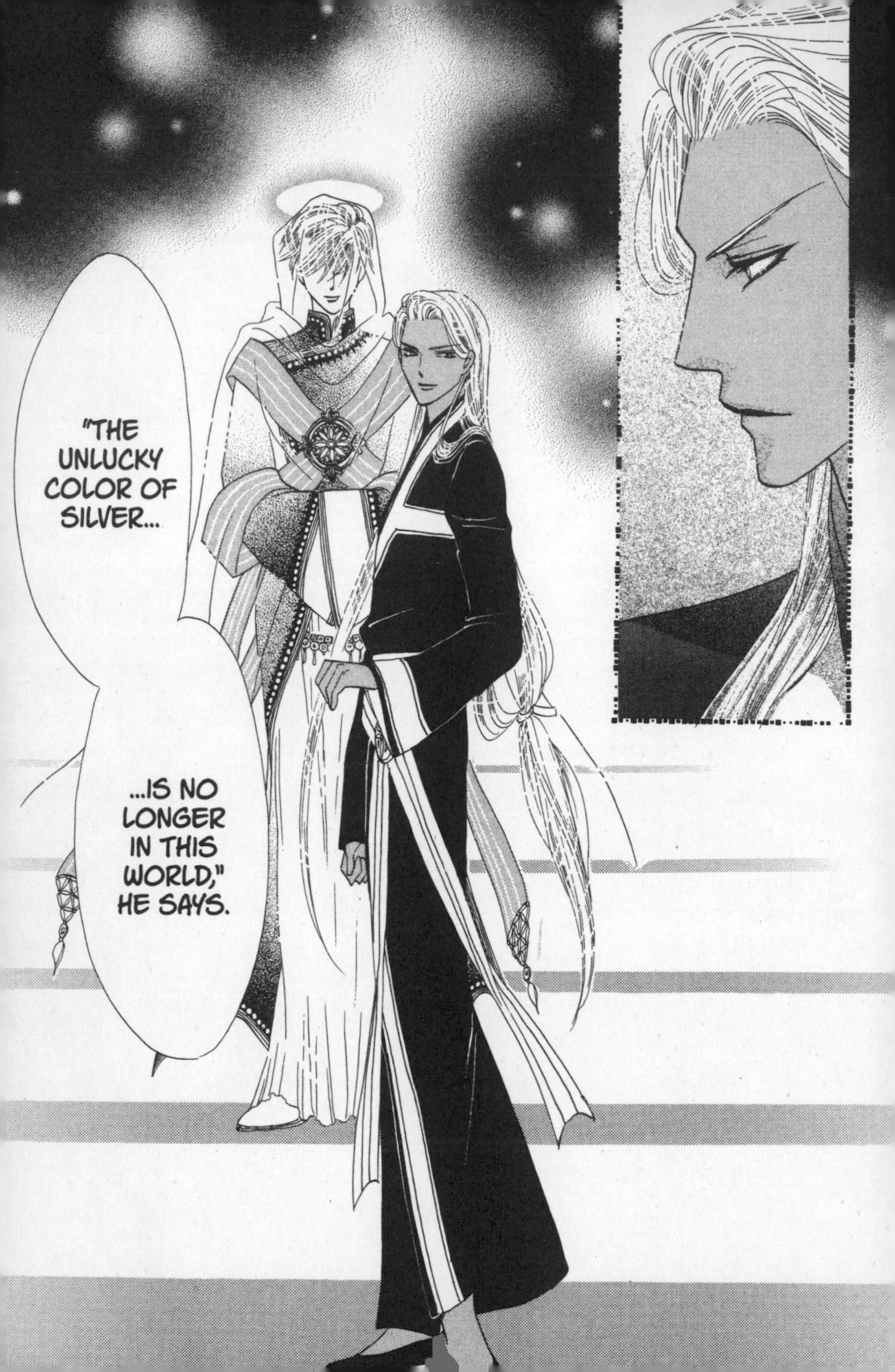
"THE UNLUCKY COLOR OF SILVER...
...IS NO LONGER IN THIS WORLD," HE SAYS.

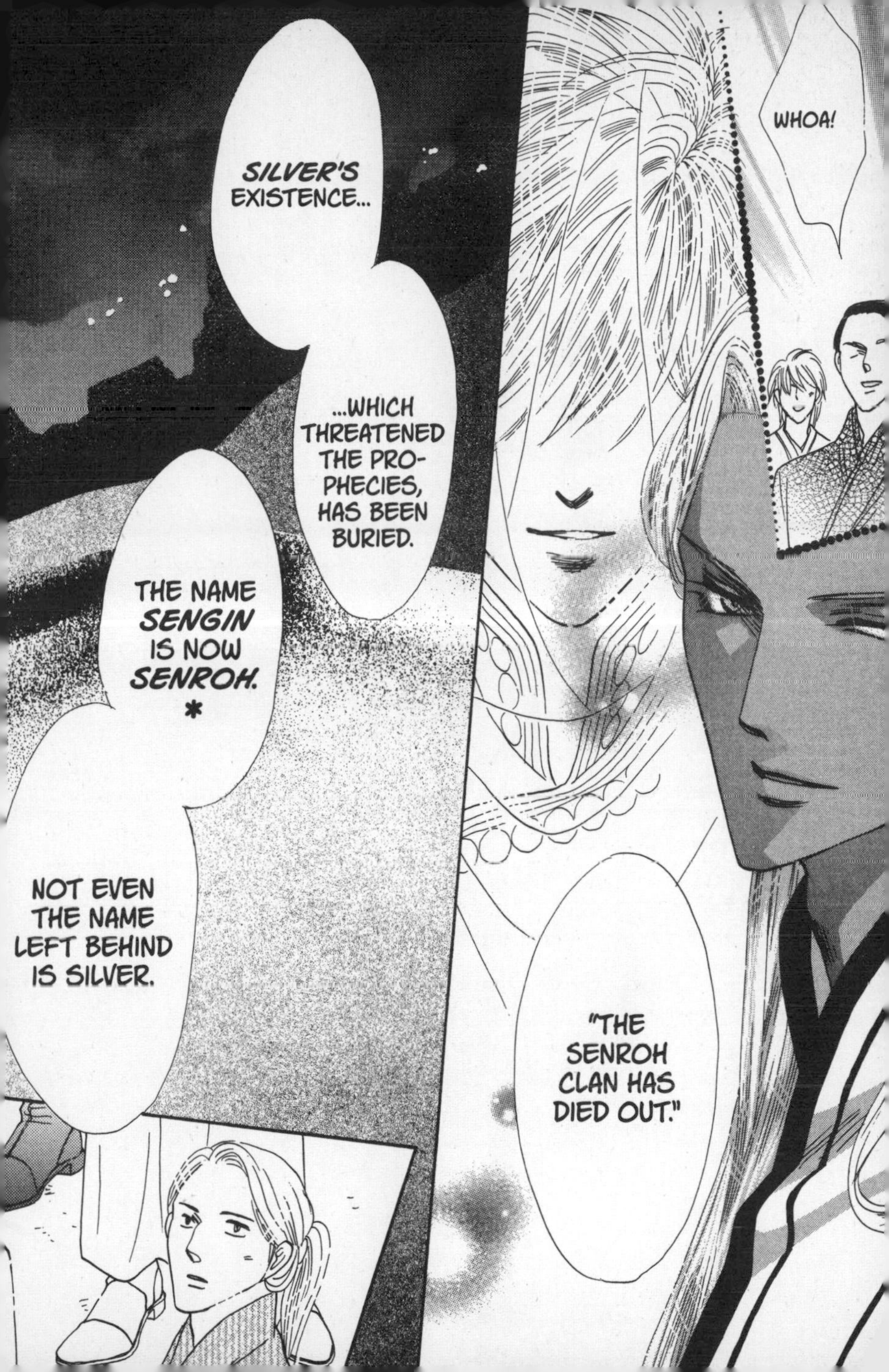
WHOA!
"THE SENROH CLAN HAS DIED OUT."
SILVER'S EXISTENCE...
...WHICH THREATENED THE PRO-PHECIES, HAS BEEN BURIED.
THE NAME SENGIN IS NOW SENROH. *
NOT EVEN THE NAME LEFT BEHIND IS SILVER.

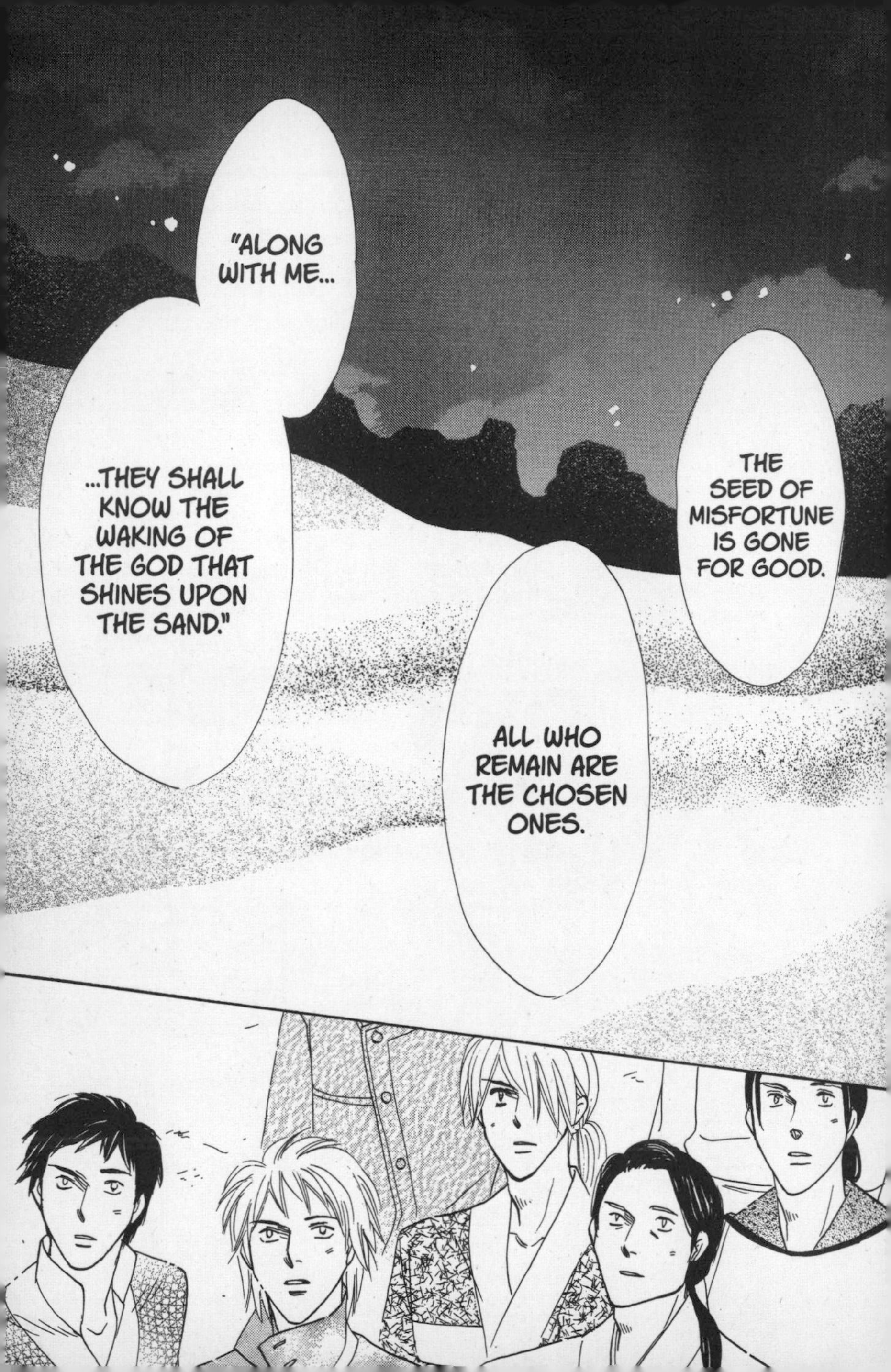
THE SEED OF MISFORTUNE IS GONE FOR GOOD.
ALL WHO REMAIN ARE THE CHOSEN ONES.
"ALONG WITH ME...
...THEY SHALL KNOW THE WAKING OF THE GOD THAT SHINES UPON THE SAND."

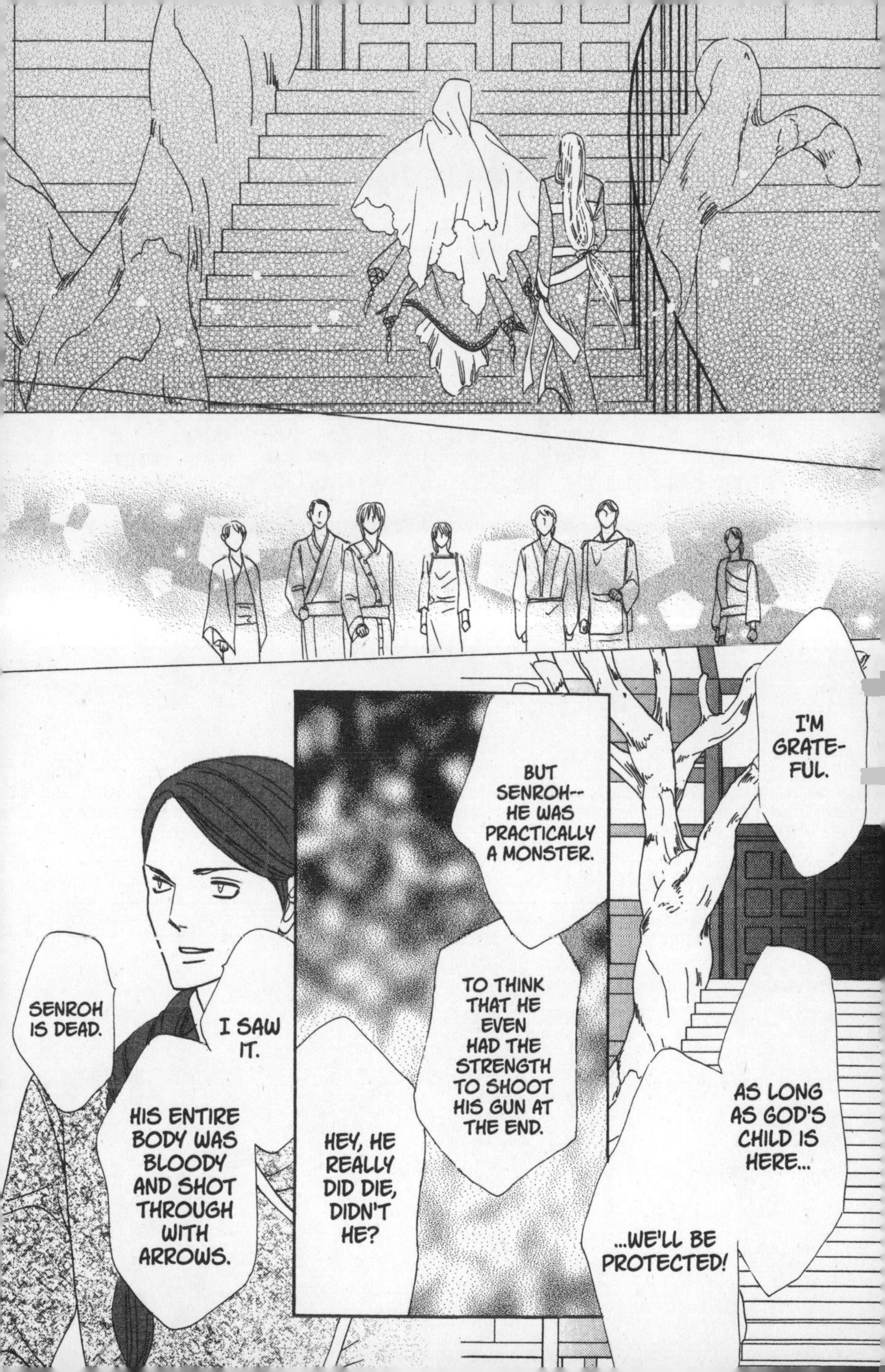
I'M GRATE-FUL.
AS LONG AS GOD'S CHILD IS HERE...
...WE'LL BE PROTECTED!
BUT SENROH-- HE WAS PRACTICALLY A MONSTER.
TO THINK THAT HE EVEN HAD THE STRENGTH TO SHOOT HIS GUN AT THE END.
HEY, HE REALLY DID DIE, DIDN'T HE?
SENROH IS DEAD.
I SAW IT.
HIS ENTIRE BODY WAS BLOODY AND SHOT THROUGH WITH ARROWS.

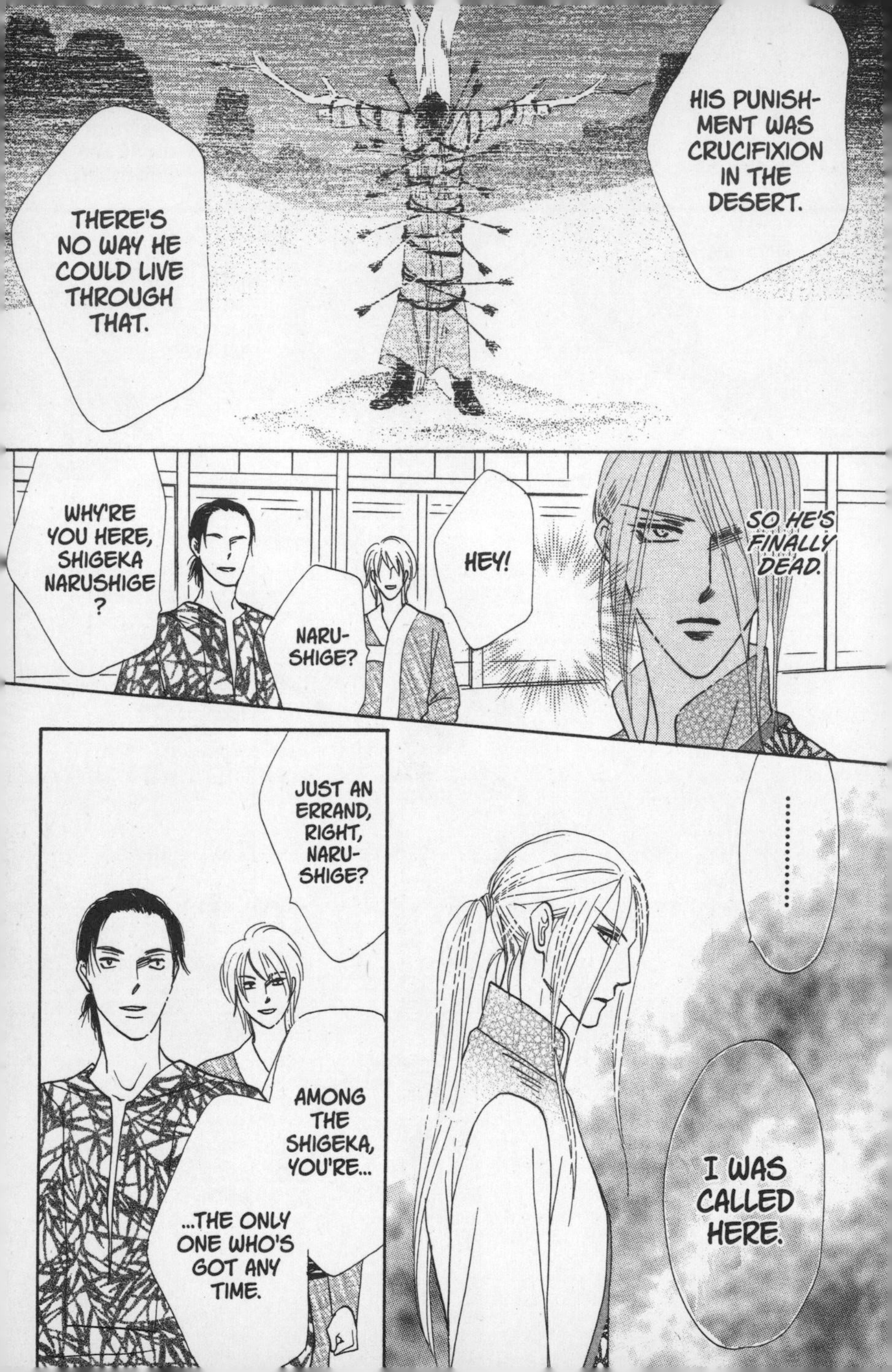
HIS PUNISHMENT WAS CRUCIFIXION IN THE DESERT.
THERE'S NO WAY HE COULD LIVE THROUGH THAT.
SO HE'S FINALLY DEAD.
HEY!
NARU-SHIGE?
WHY'RE YOU HERE, SHIGEKA NARUSHIGE?
......
I WAS CALLED HERE.
JUST AN ERRAND, RIGHT, NARU-SHIGE?
AMONG THE SHIGEKA, YOU'RE...
...THE ONLY ONE WHO'S GOT ANY TIME.

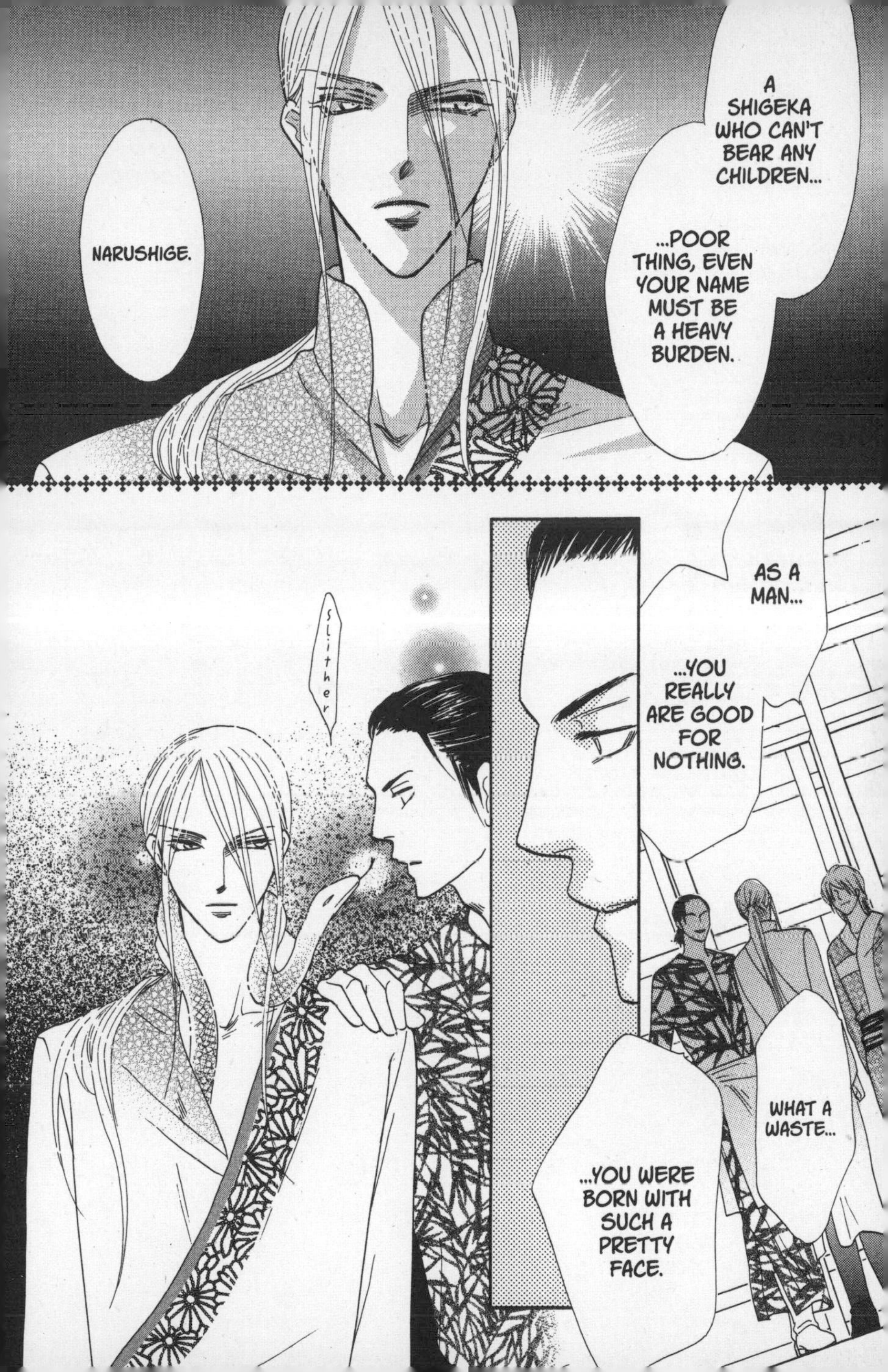
A SHIGEKA WHO CAN'T BEAR ANY CHILDREN...
...POOR THING, EVEN YOUR NAME MUST BE A HEAVY BURDEN.
NARUSHIGE.
AS A MAN...
...YOU REALLY ARE GOOD FOR NOTHING.
WHAT A WASTE...
...YOU WERE BORN WITH SUCH A PRETTY FACE.
Slither

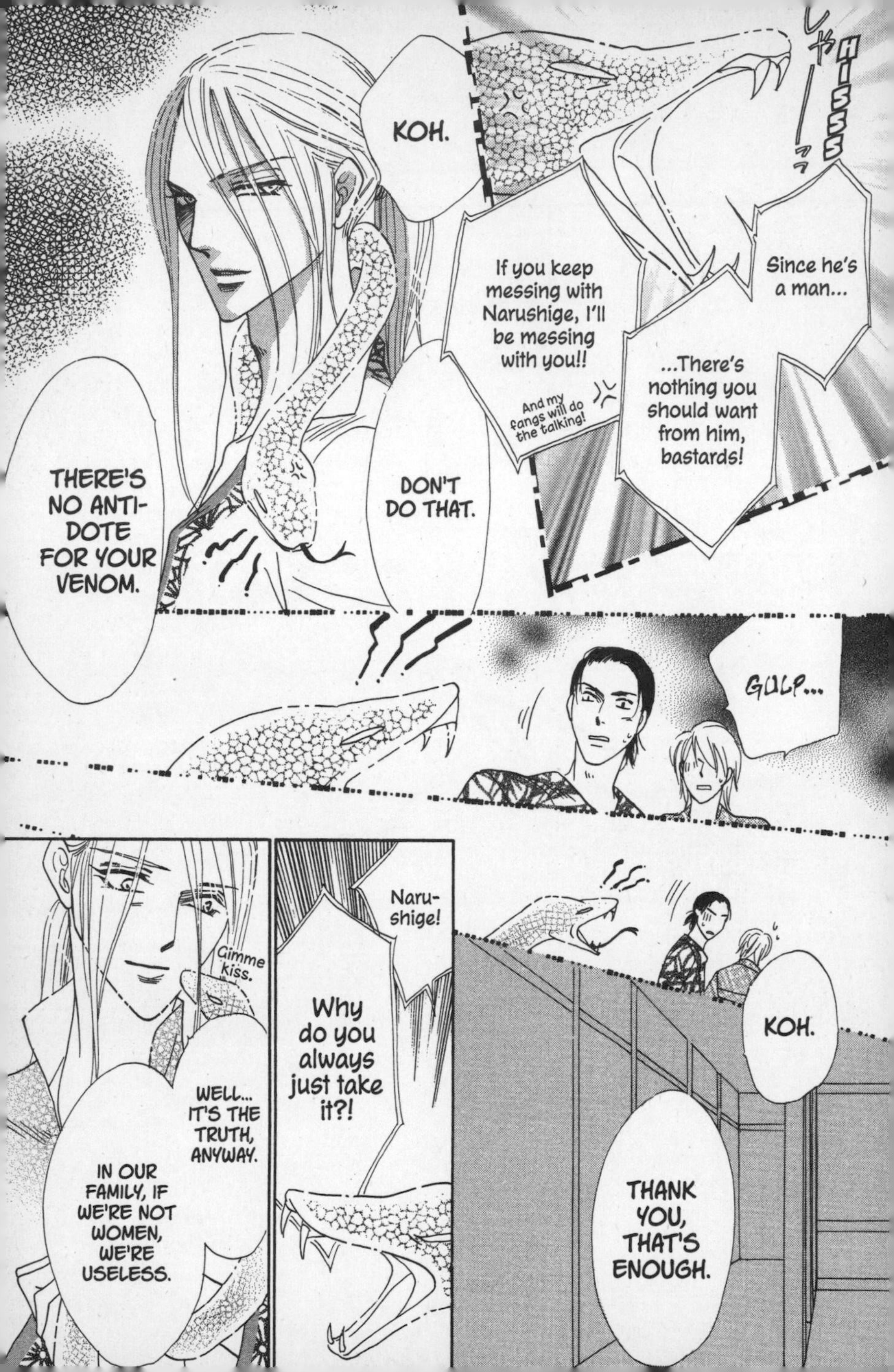
HISS
Since he's a man...
...There's nothing you should want from him, bastards!
If you keep messing with Narushige, I'll be messing with you!!
And my fangs will do the talking!
KOH.
DON'T DO THAT.
THERE'S NO ANTI-DOTE FOR YOUR VENOM.
GULP...
KOH.
THANK YOU, THAT'S ENOUGH.
Naru-shige!
Why do you always just take it?!
Gimme kiss.
WELL... IT'S THE TRUTH, ANYWAY.
IN OUR FAMILY, IF WE'RE NOT WOMEN, WE'RE USELESS.

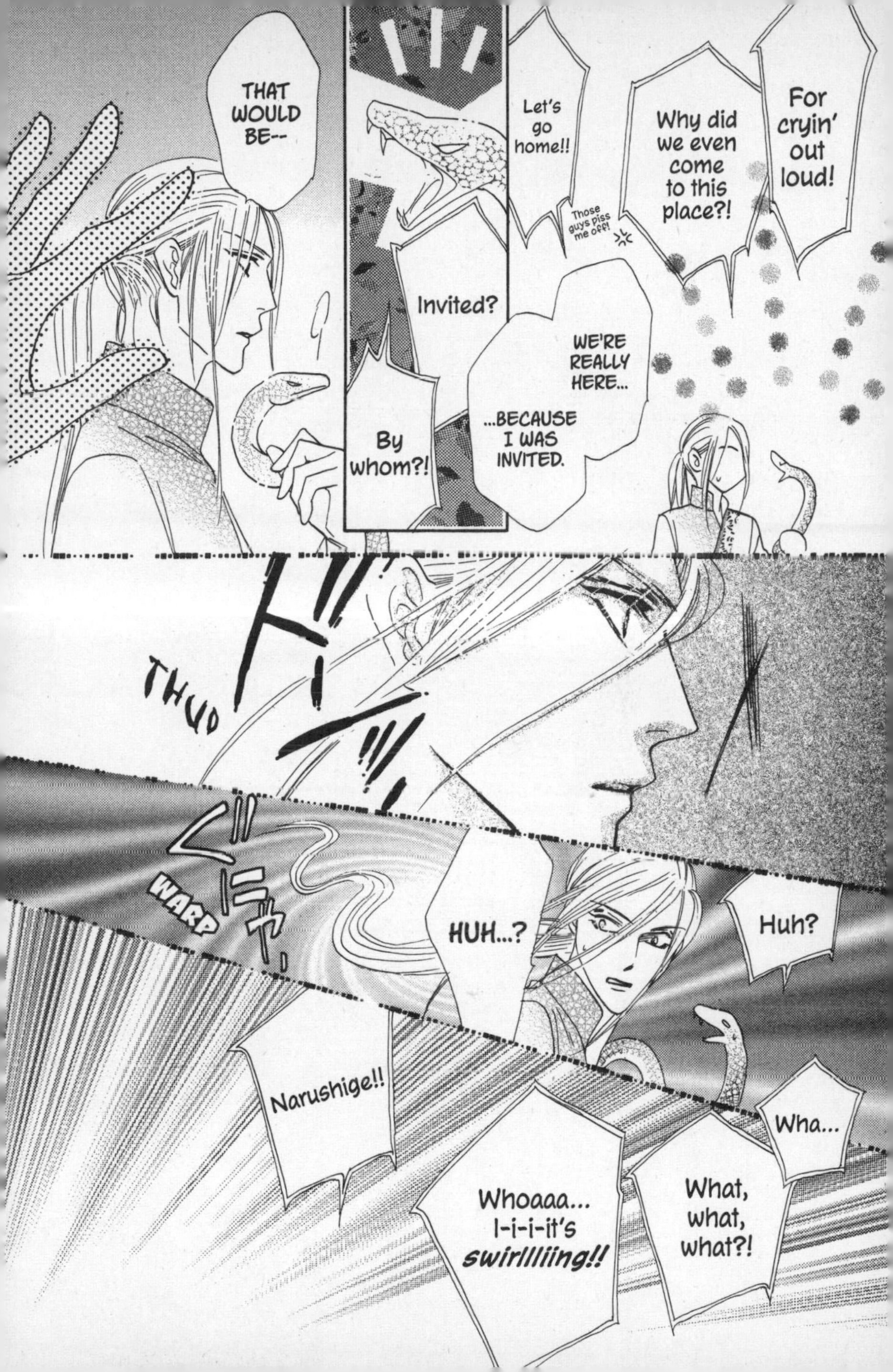
For cryin' out loud!
Why did we even come to this place?!
Let's go home!!
Those guys piss me off!
WE'RE REALLY HERE...
...BECAUSE I WAS INVITED.
Invited?
By whom?!
THAT WOULD BE--
THUD
Huh?
HUH...?
WARP
Wha...
What, what, what?!
Whoaaa... I-i-i-it's *swirlllliing!!*
Narushige!!

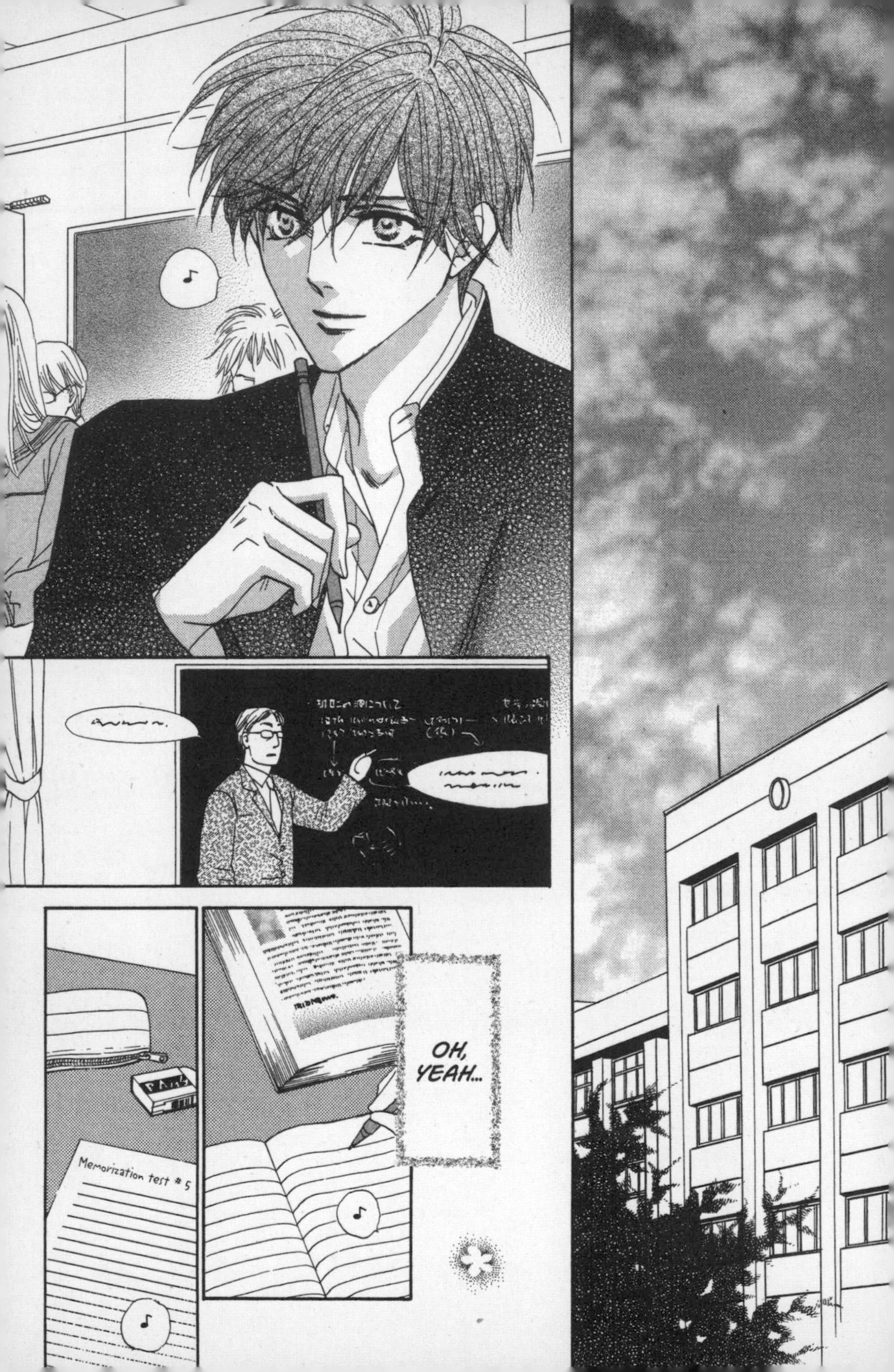
OH, YEAH...
Memorization test # 5

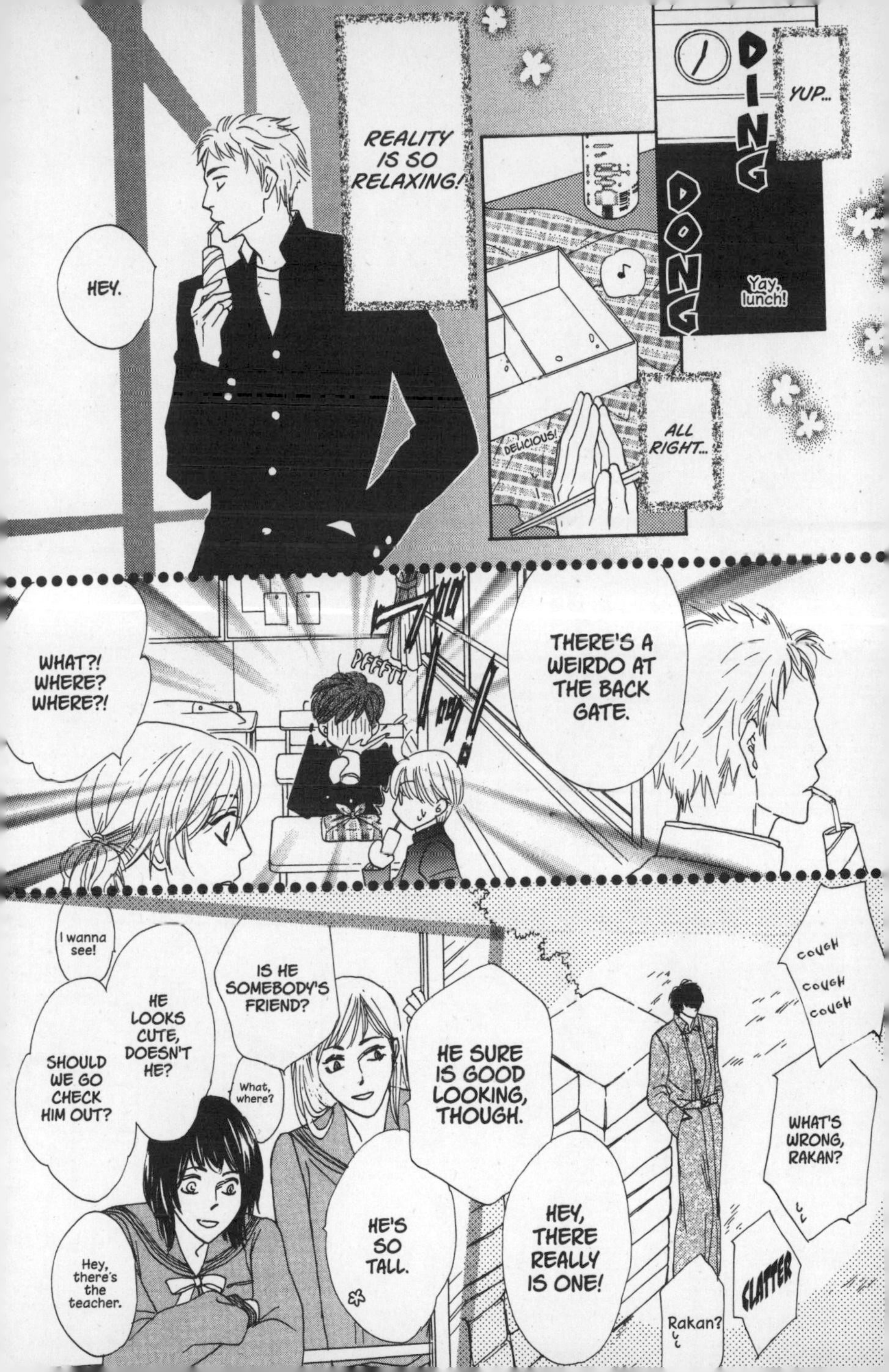
YUP...
DING DONG
Yay, lunch!
ALL RIGHT...
DELICIOUS!
REALITY IS SO RELAXING!
HEY.
THERE'S A WEIRDO AT THE BACK GATE.
PFFFT!
WHAT?! WHERE? WHERE?!
COUGH COUGH COUGH
WHAT'S WRONG, RAKAN?
CLATTER
Rakan?
HEY, THERE REALLY IS ONE!
HE SURE IS GOOD LOOKING, THOUGH.
HE'S SO TALL.
IS HE SOMEBODY'S FRIEND?
What, where?
HE LOOKS CUTE, DOESN'T HE?
I wanna see!
SHOULD WE GO CHECK HIM OUT?
Hey, there's the teacher.

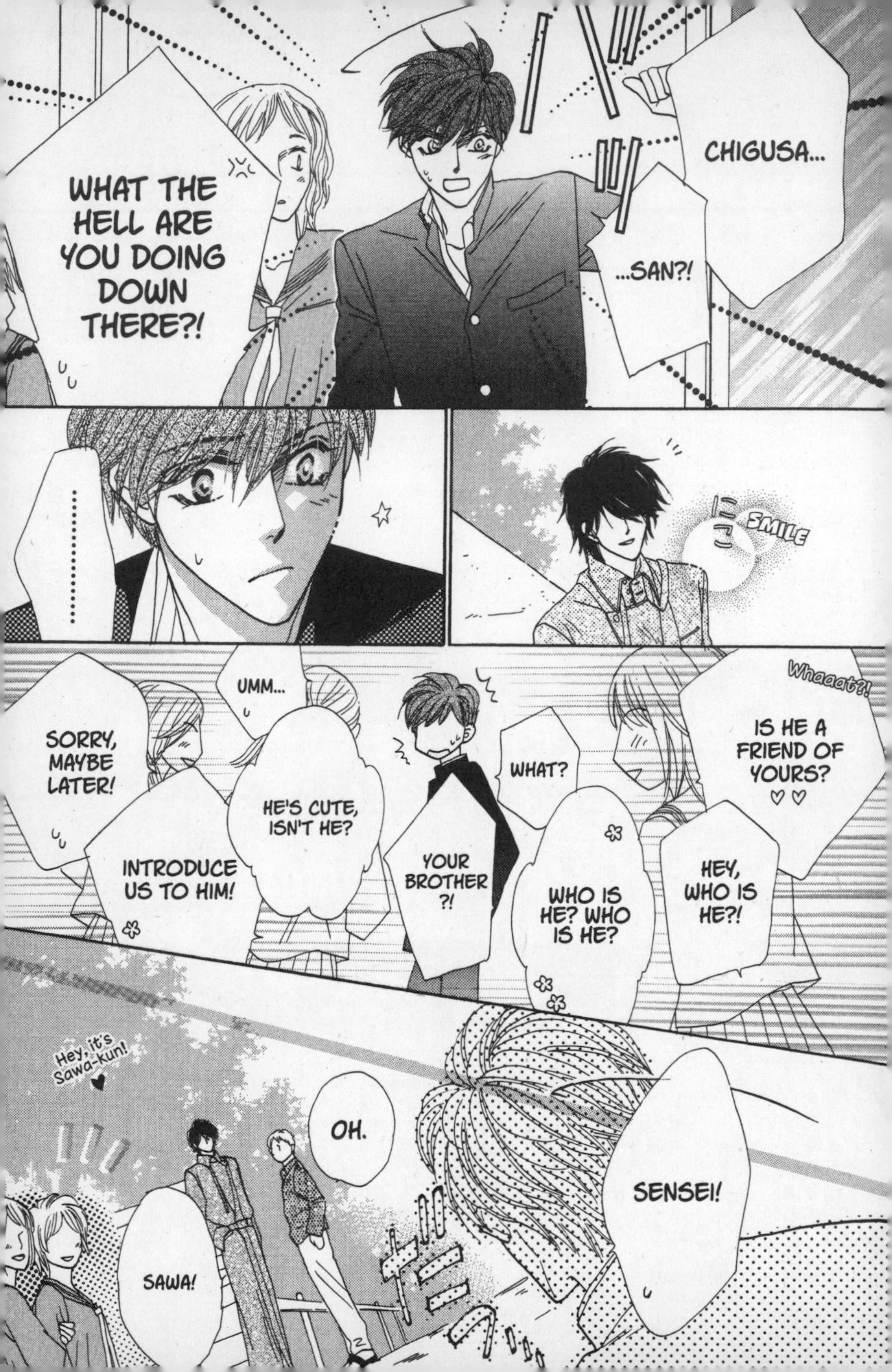
CHIGUSA...
...SAN?!
WHAT THE HELL ARE YOU DOING DOWN THERE?!
SMILE
......
Whaaat?!
IS HE A FRIEND OF YOURS? ♡ ♡
HEY, WHO IS HE?!
WHO IS HE? WHO IS HE?
WHAT?
YOUR BROTHER ?!
UMM...
HE'S CUTE, ISN'T HE?
SORRY, MAYBE LATER!
INTRODUCE US TO HIM!
SENSEI!
OH.
Hey, it's Sawa-kun! ♥
SAWA!

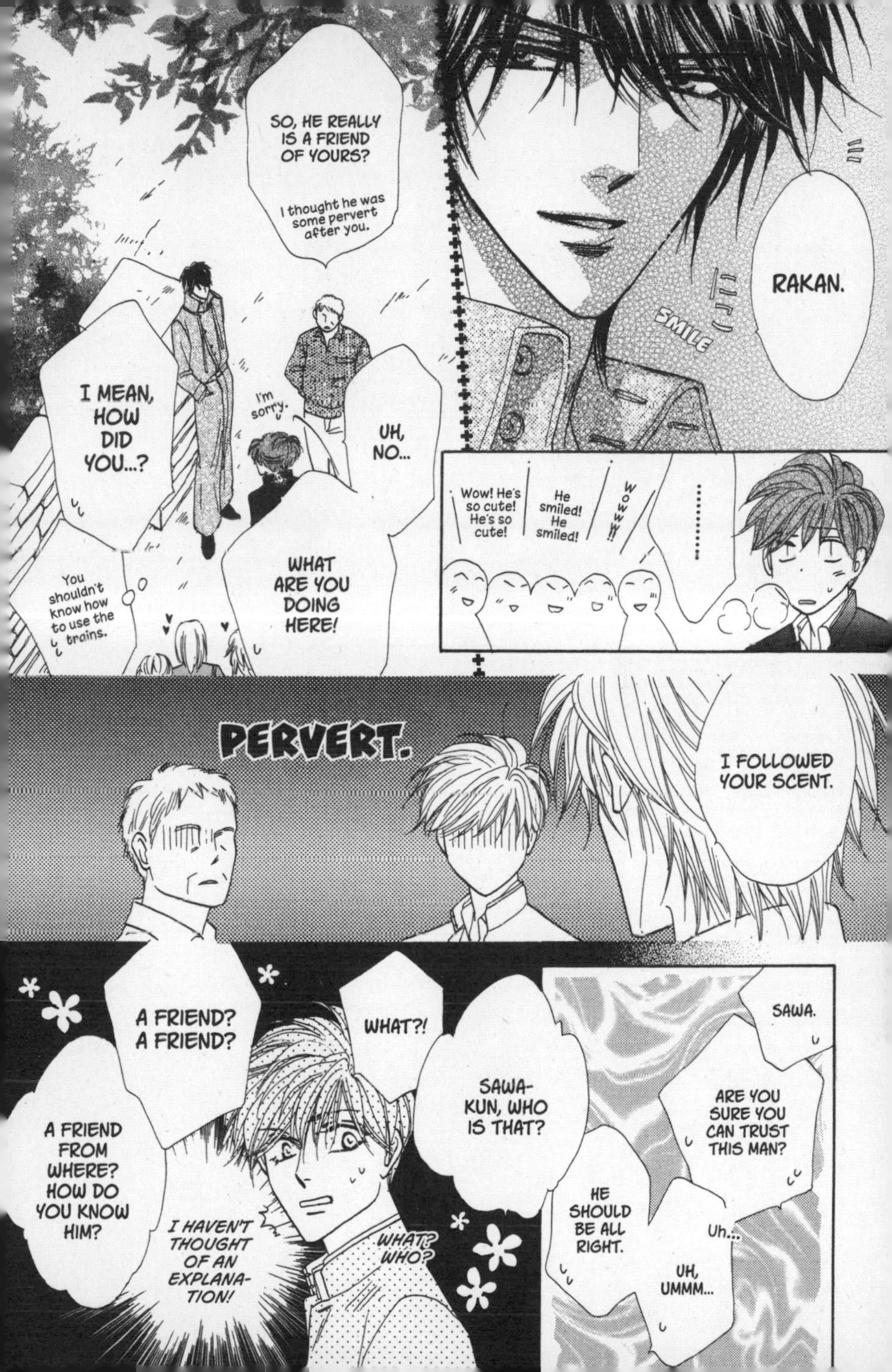
RAKAN.
SMILE
......
Wowww!!
He smiled! He smiled!
Wow! He's so cute! He's so cute!
SO, HE REALLY IS A FRIEND OF YOURS?
I thought he was some pervert after you.
UH, NO...
I'm sorry.
I MEAN, HOW DID YOU...?
WHAT ARE YOU DOING HERE!
You shouldn't know how to use the trains.
I FOLLOWED YOUR SCENT.
PERVERT.
SAWA.
ARE YOU SURE YOU CAN TRUST THIS MAN?
Uh...
HE SHOULD BE ALL RIGHT.
UH, UMMM...
WHAT?!
SAWA-KUN, WHO IS THAT?
A FRIEND? A FRIEND?
A FRIEND FROM WHERE? HOW DO YOU KNOW HIM?
WHAT? WHO?
I HAVEN'T THOUGHT OF AN EXPLANATION!

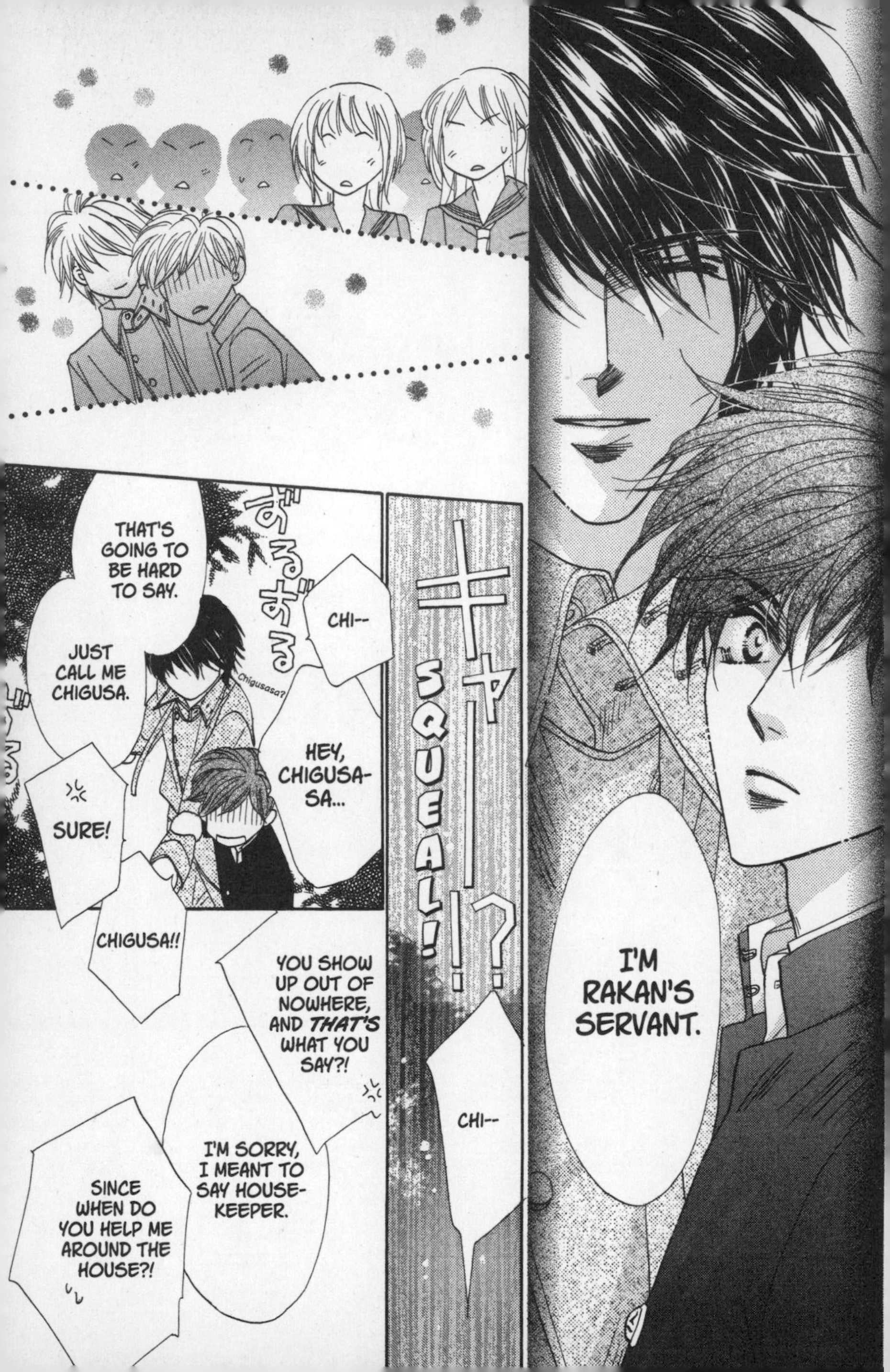
I'M RAKAN'S SERVANT.
キャー!?
SQUEAL!!
CHI--
CHI--
HEY, CHIGUSA-SA...
Chigusasa?
THAT'S GOING TO BE HARD TO SAY.
JUST CALL ME CHIGUSA.
SURE!
CHIGUSA!!
YOU SHOW UP OUT OF NOWHERE, AND *THAT'S* WHAT YOU SAY?!
I'M SORRY, I MEANT TO SAY HOUSE-KEEPER.
SINCE WHEN DO YOU HELP ME AROUND THE HOUSE?!

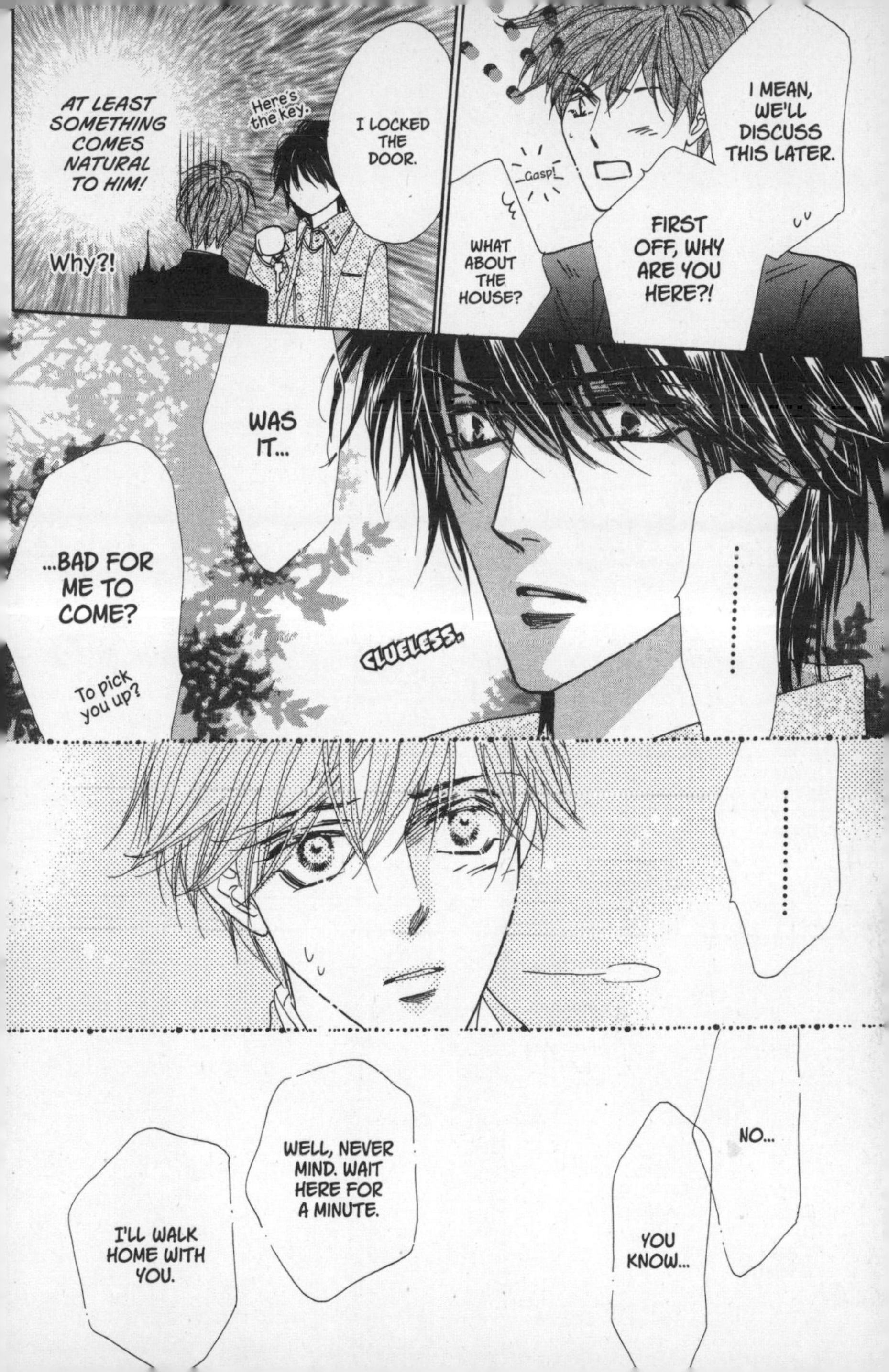
I MEAN, WE'LL DISCUSS THIS LATER.
Gasp!
FIRST OFF, WHY ARE YOU HERE?!
WHAT ABOUT THE HOUSE?
I LOCKED THE DOOR.
Here's the key.
AT LEAST SOMETHING COMES NATURAL TO HIM!
Why?!
......
WAS IT...
...BAD FOR ME TO COME?
CLUELESS.
To pick you up?
......
NO...
YOU KNOW...
WELL, NEVER MIND. WAIT HERE FOR A MINUTE.
I'LL WALK HOME WITH YOU.

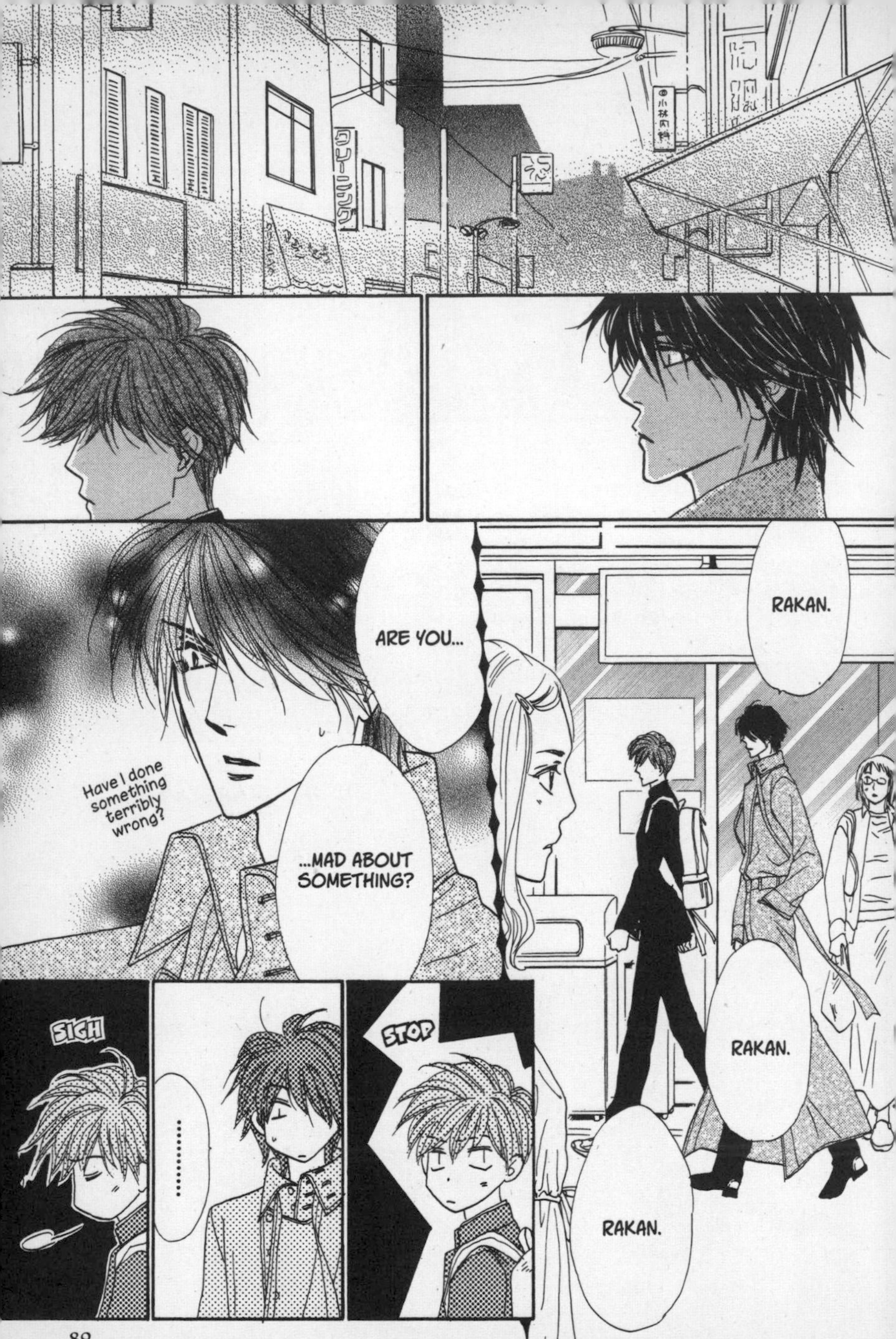
クリーニング
RAKAN.
RAKAN.
RAKAN.
ARE YOU...
...MAD ABOUT SOMETHING?
Have I done something terribly wrong?
STOP
......
SIGH

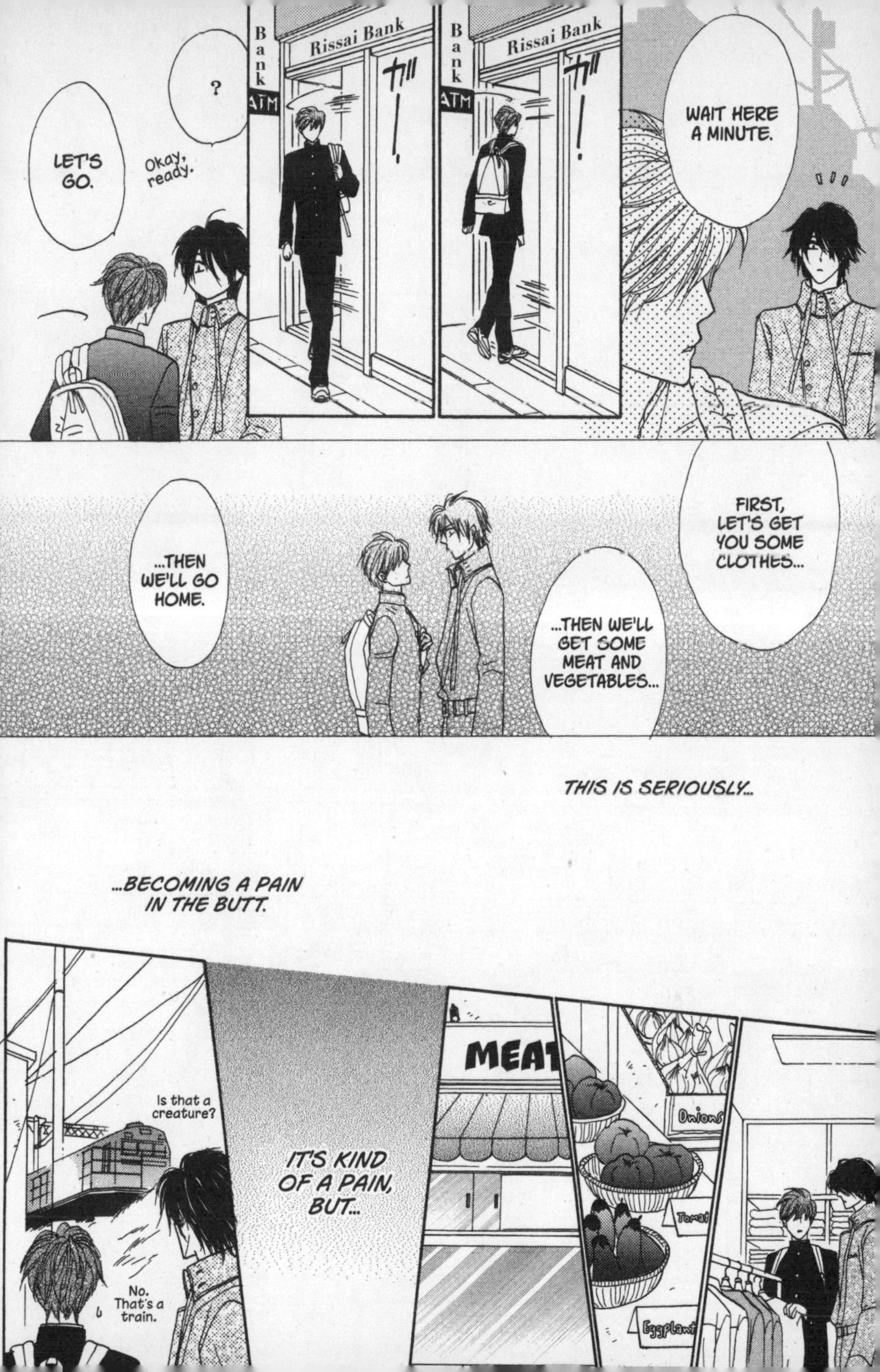
WAIT HERE A MINUTE.
Rissai Bank
Bank
ATM
Rissai Bank
Bank
ATM
?
LET'S GO.
Okay, ready.
FIRST, LET'S GET YOU SOME CLOTHES...
...THEN WE'LL GET SOME MEAT AND VEGETABLES...
...THEN WE'LL GO HOME.
THIS IS SERIOUSLY...
...BECOMING A PAIN IN THE BUTT.
Onions
Tomat
Eggplant
MEAT
IT'S KIND OF A PAIN, BUT...
Is that a creature?
No. That's a train.

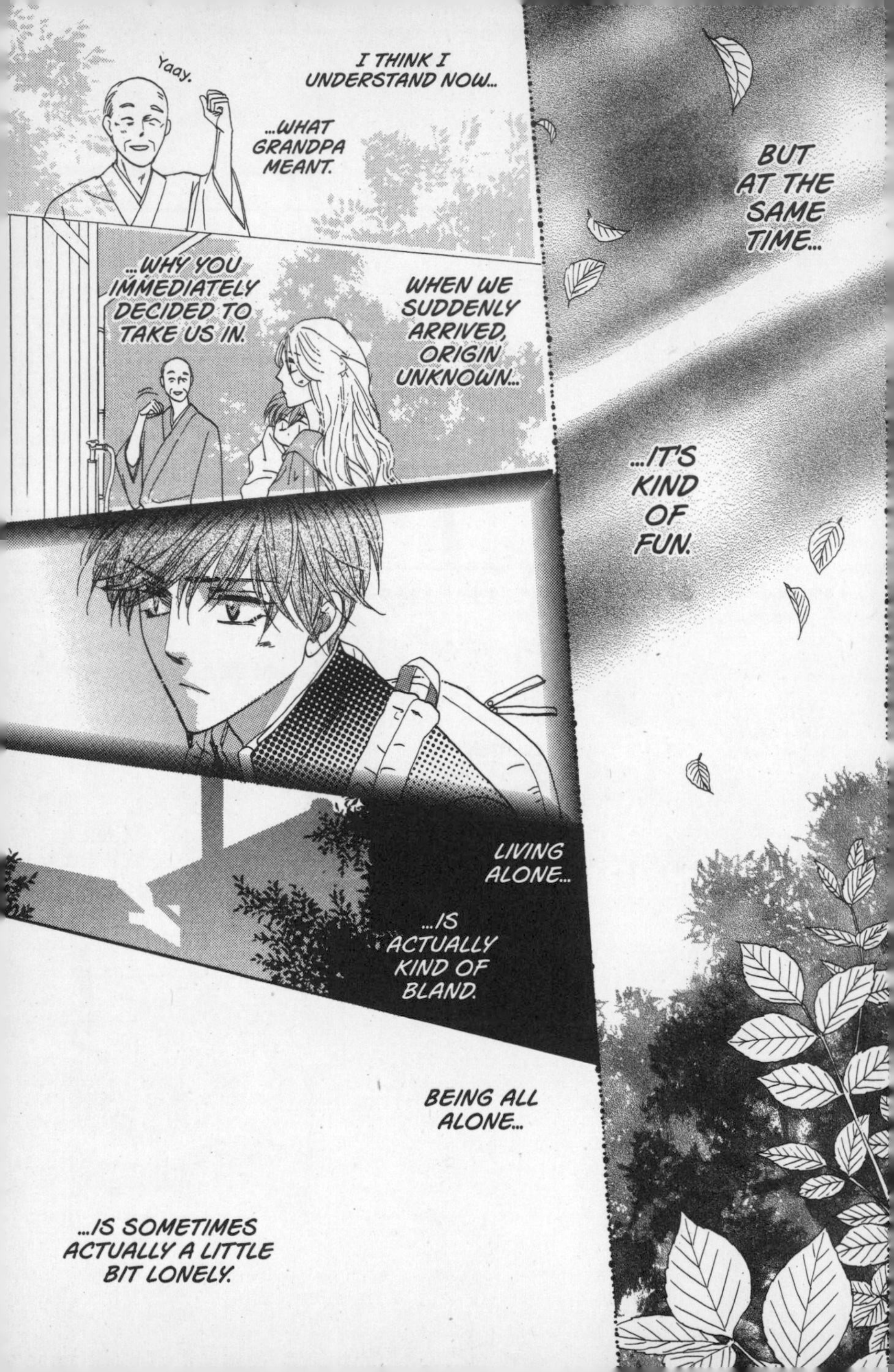
I THINK I UNDERSTAND NOW...
Yaay.
...WHAT GRANDPA MEANT.
WHEN WE SUDDENLY ARRIVED, ORIGIN UNKNOWN...
...WHY YOU IMMEDIATELY DECIDED TO TAKE US IN.
LIVING ALONE...
...IS ACTUALLY KIND OF BLAND.
BEING ALL ALONE...
...IS SOMETIMES ACTUALLY A LITTLE BIT LONELY.
BUT AT THE SAME TIME...
...IT'S KIND OF FUN.

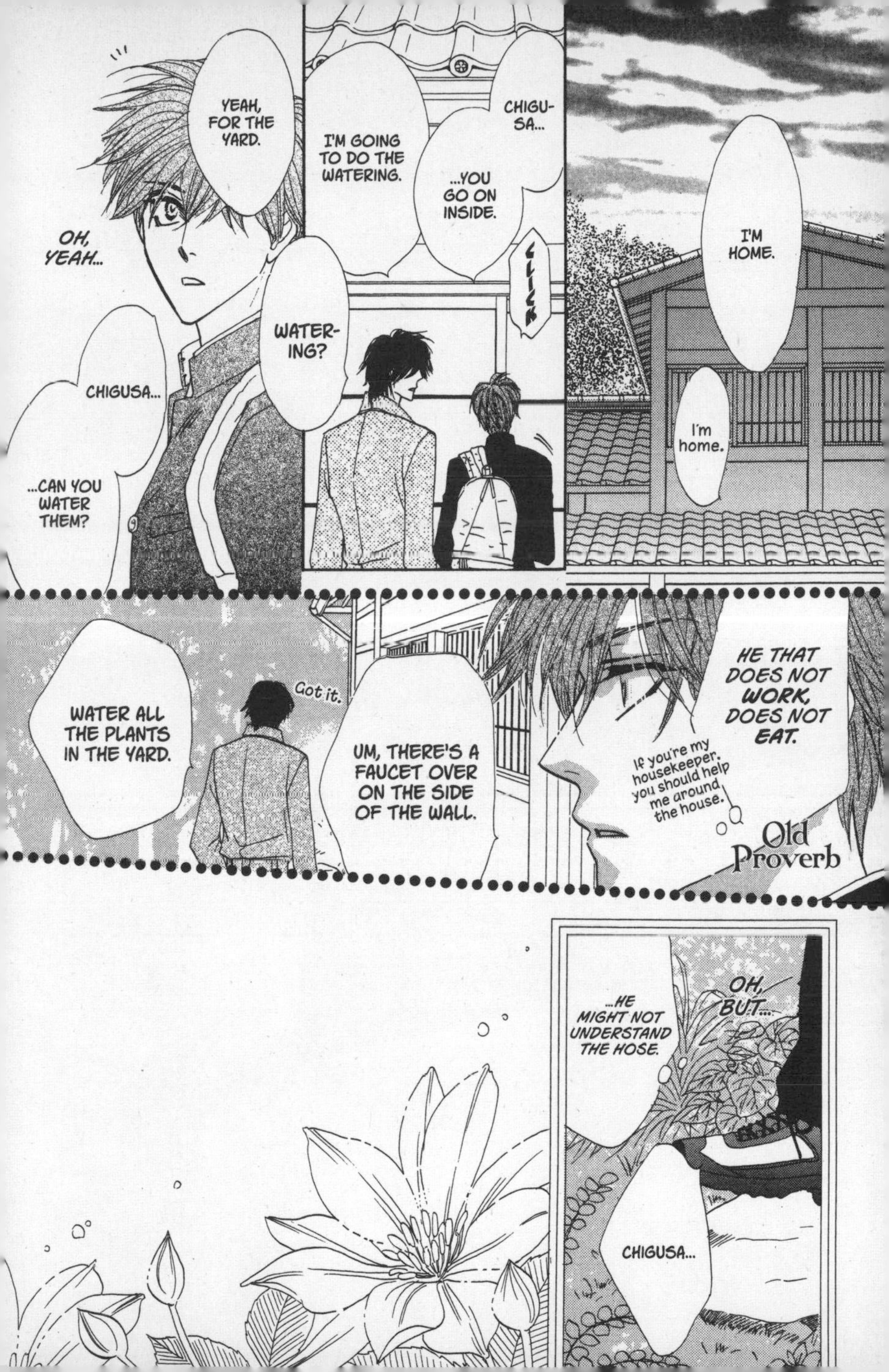
I'M HOME.
I'm home.
CHIGUSA...
...YOU GO ON INSIDE.
CLICK
I'M GOING TO DO THE WATERING.
WATERING?
YEAH, FOR THE YARD.
OH, YEAH...
CHIGUSA...
...CAN YOU WATER THEM?
HE THAT DOES NOT WORK, DOES NOT EAT.
If you're my housekeeper, you should help me around the house.
Old Proverb
UM, THERE'S A FAUCET OVER ON THE SIDE OF THE WALL.
Got it.
WATER ALL THE PLANTS IN THE YARD.
OH, BUT...
...HE MIGHT NOT UNDERSTAND THE HOSE.
CHIGUSA...

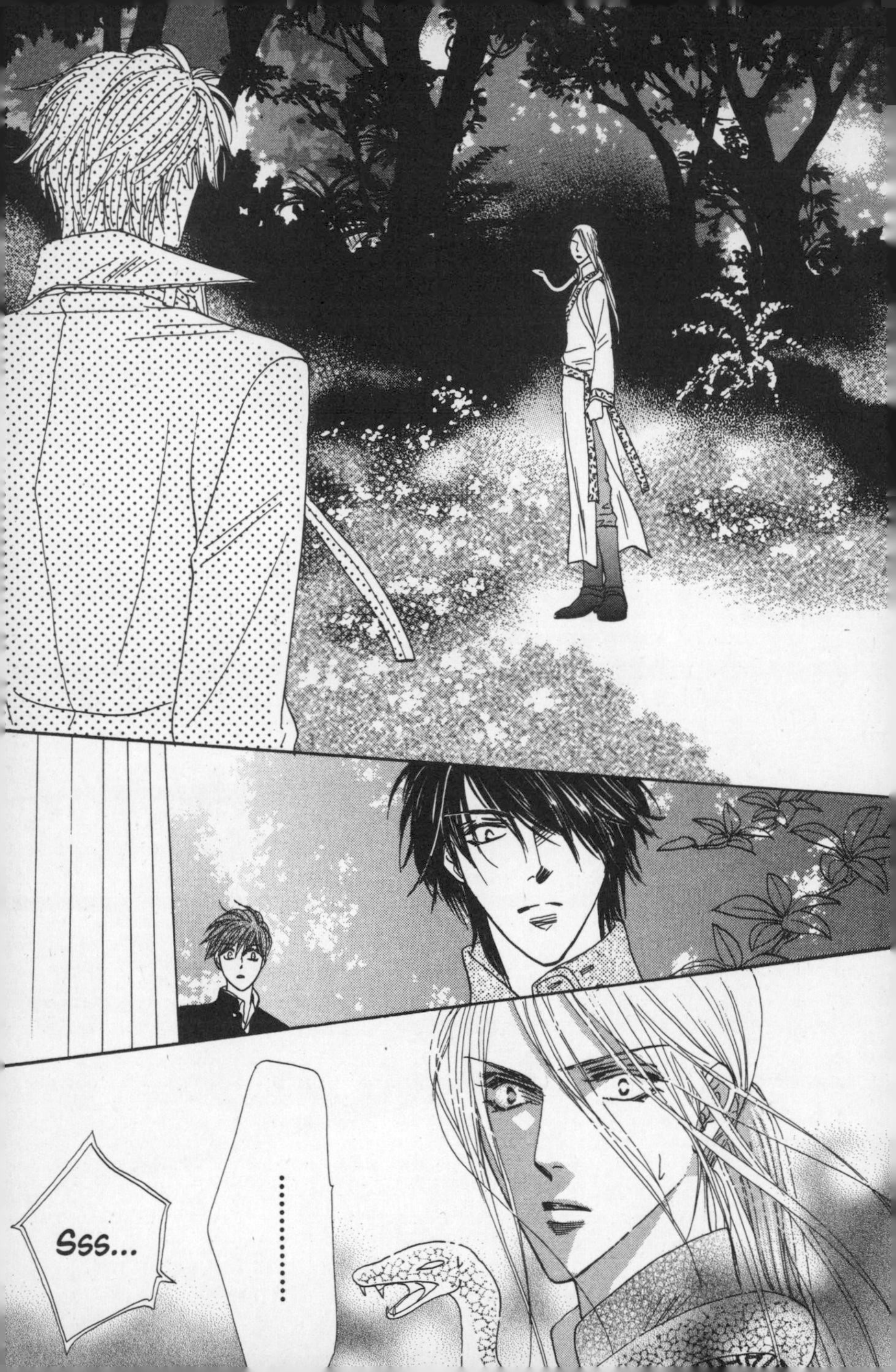

......
Sss...

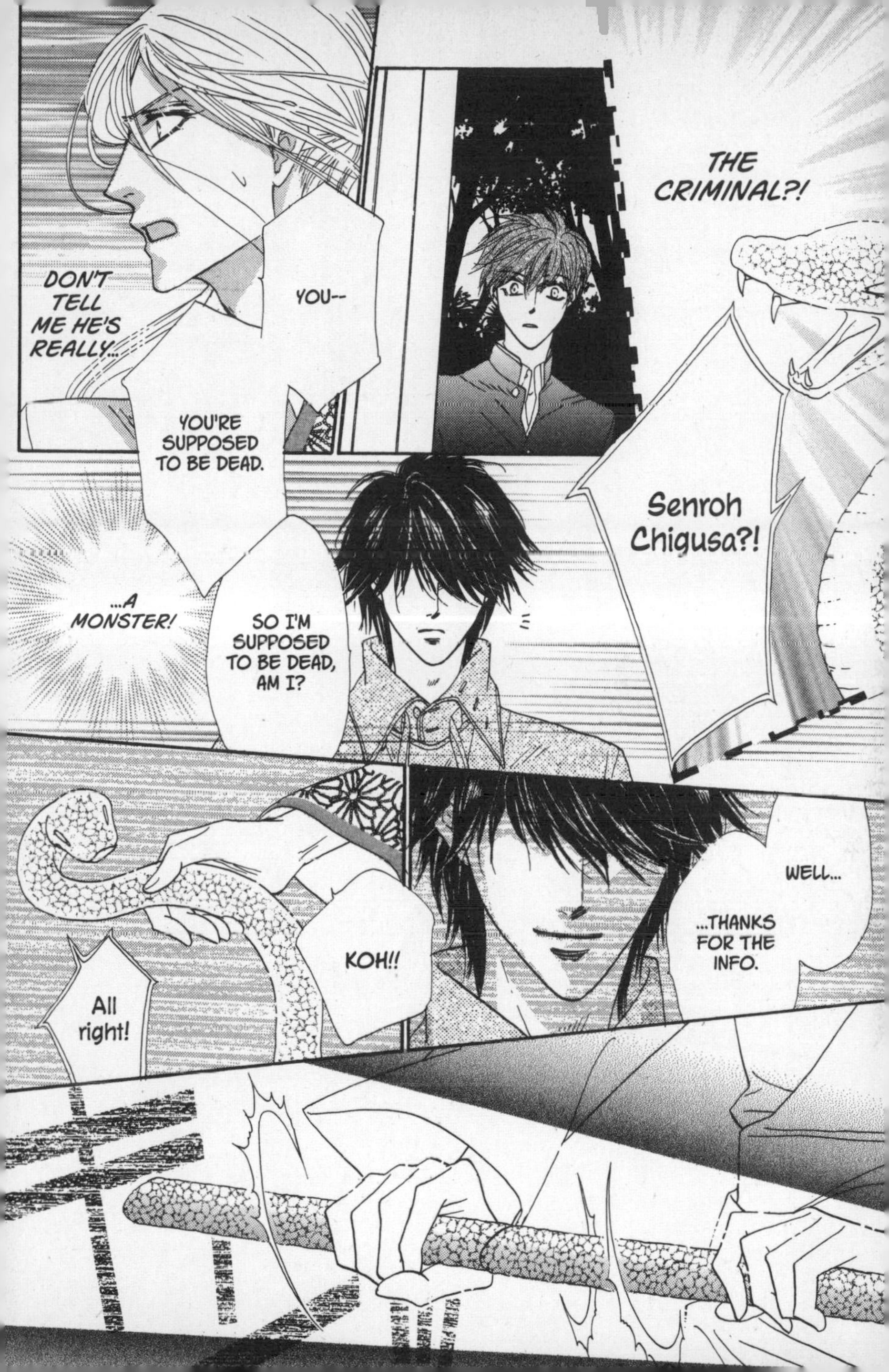
THE CRIMINAL?!
YOU--
DON'T TELL ME HE'S REALLY...
YOU'RE SUPPOSED TO BE DEAD.
Senroh Chigusa?!
SO I'M SUPPOSED TO BE DEAD, AM I?
...A MONSTER!
WELL...
...THANKS FOR THE INFO.
KOH!!
All right!

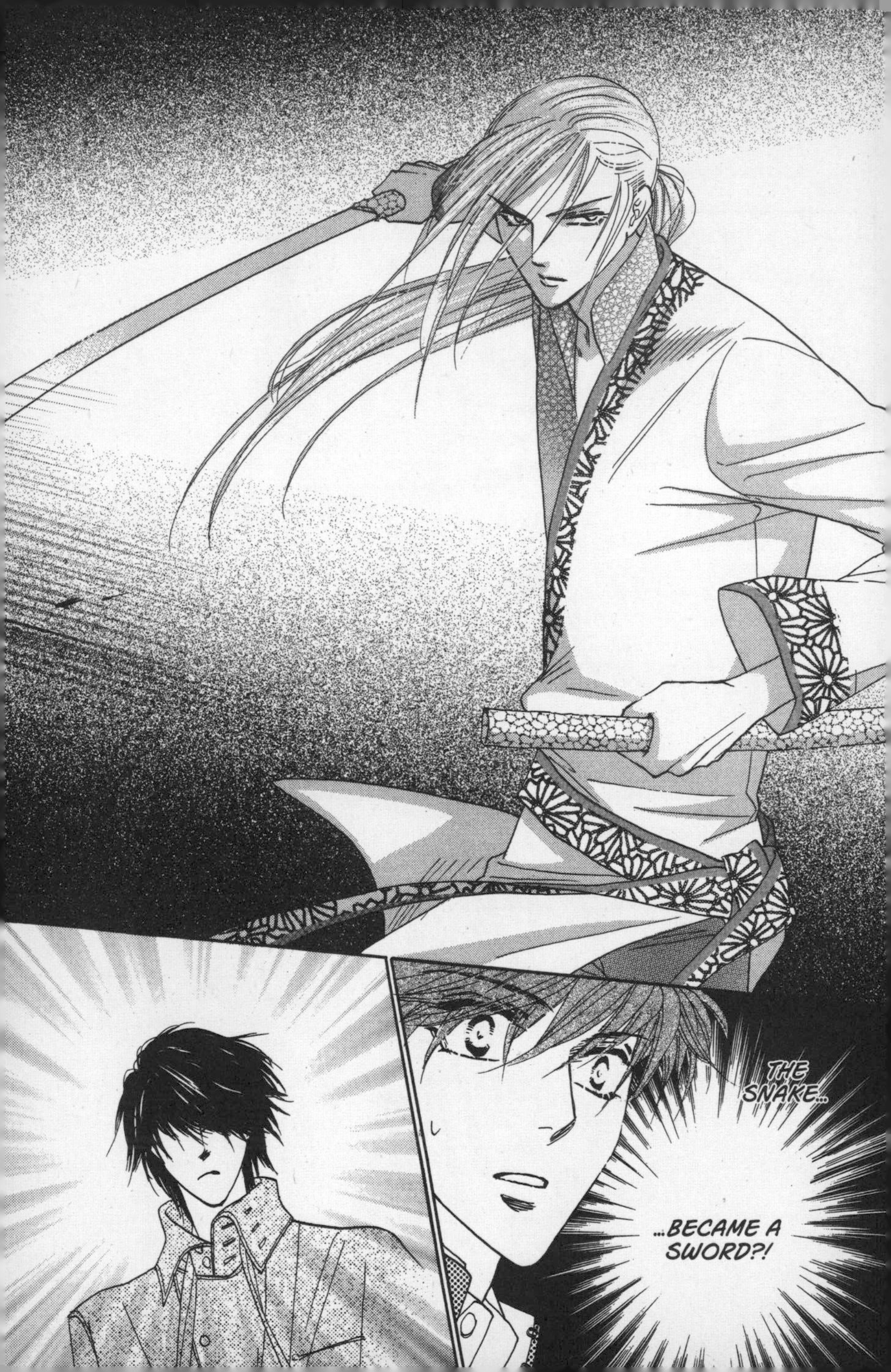
THE SNAKE...
...BECAME A SWORD?!

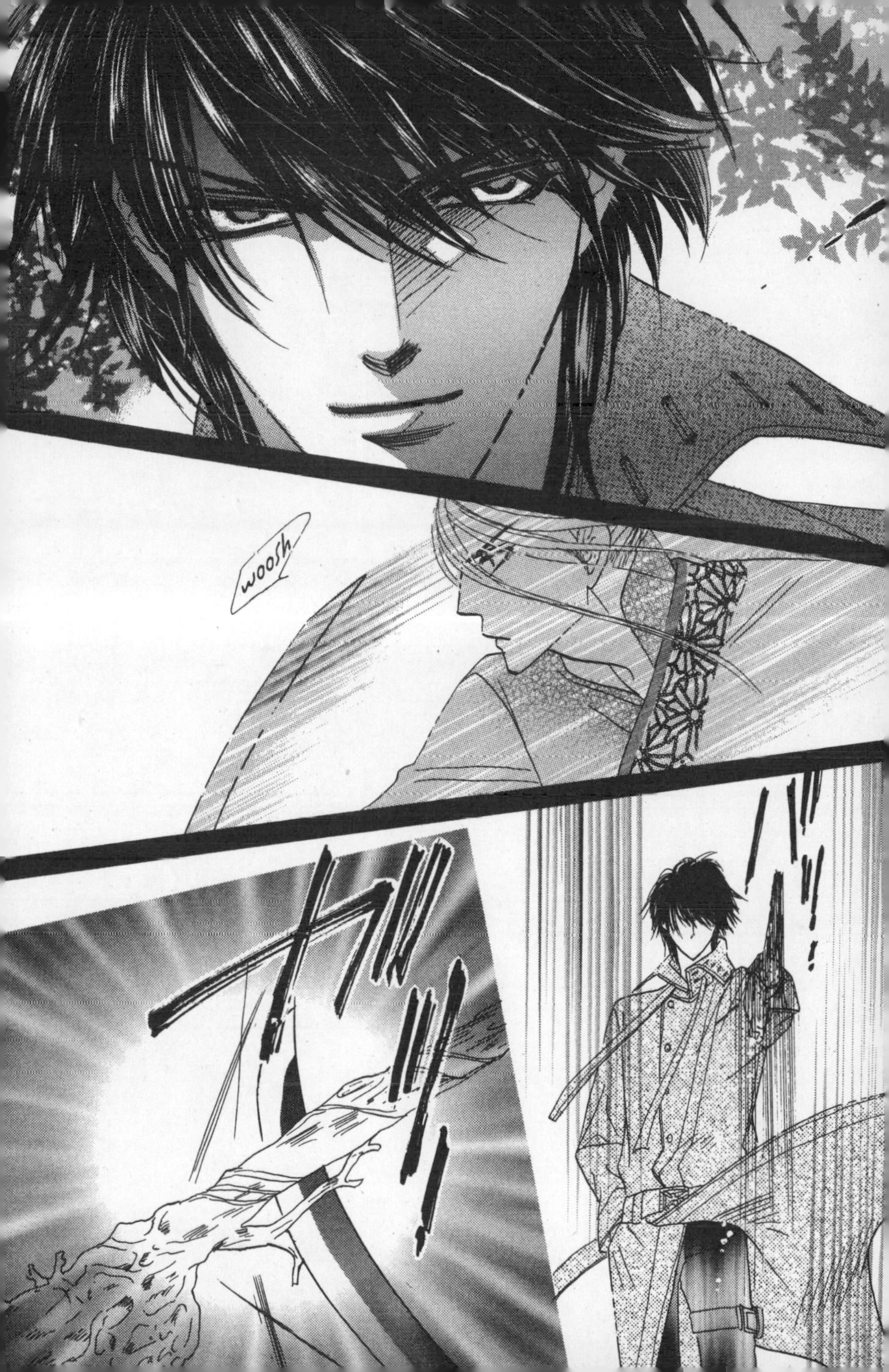
woosh

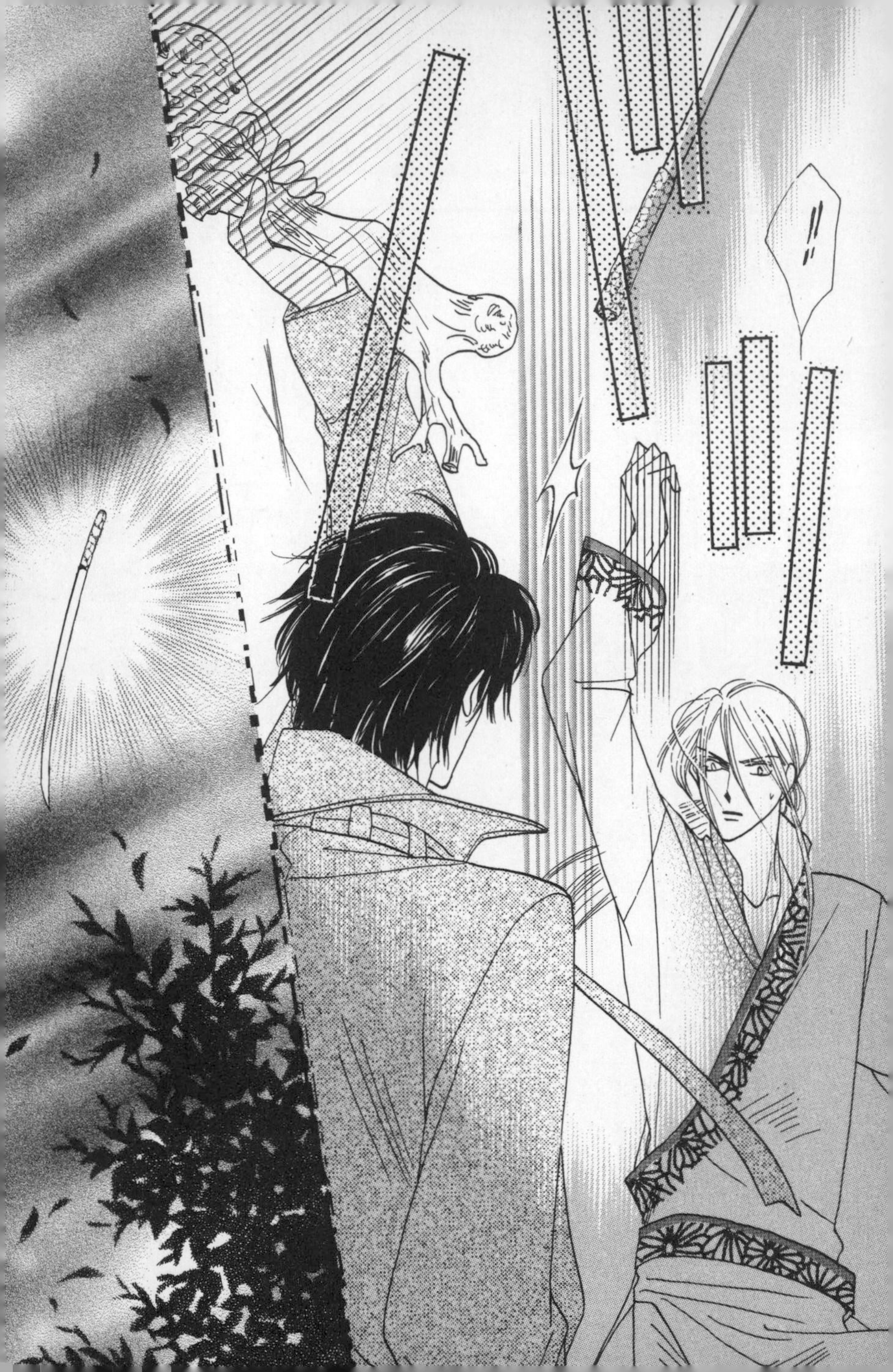
!!

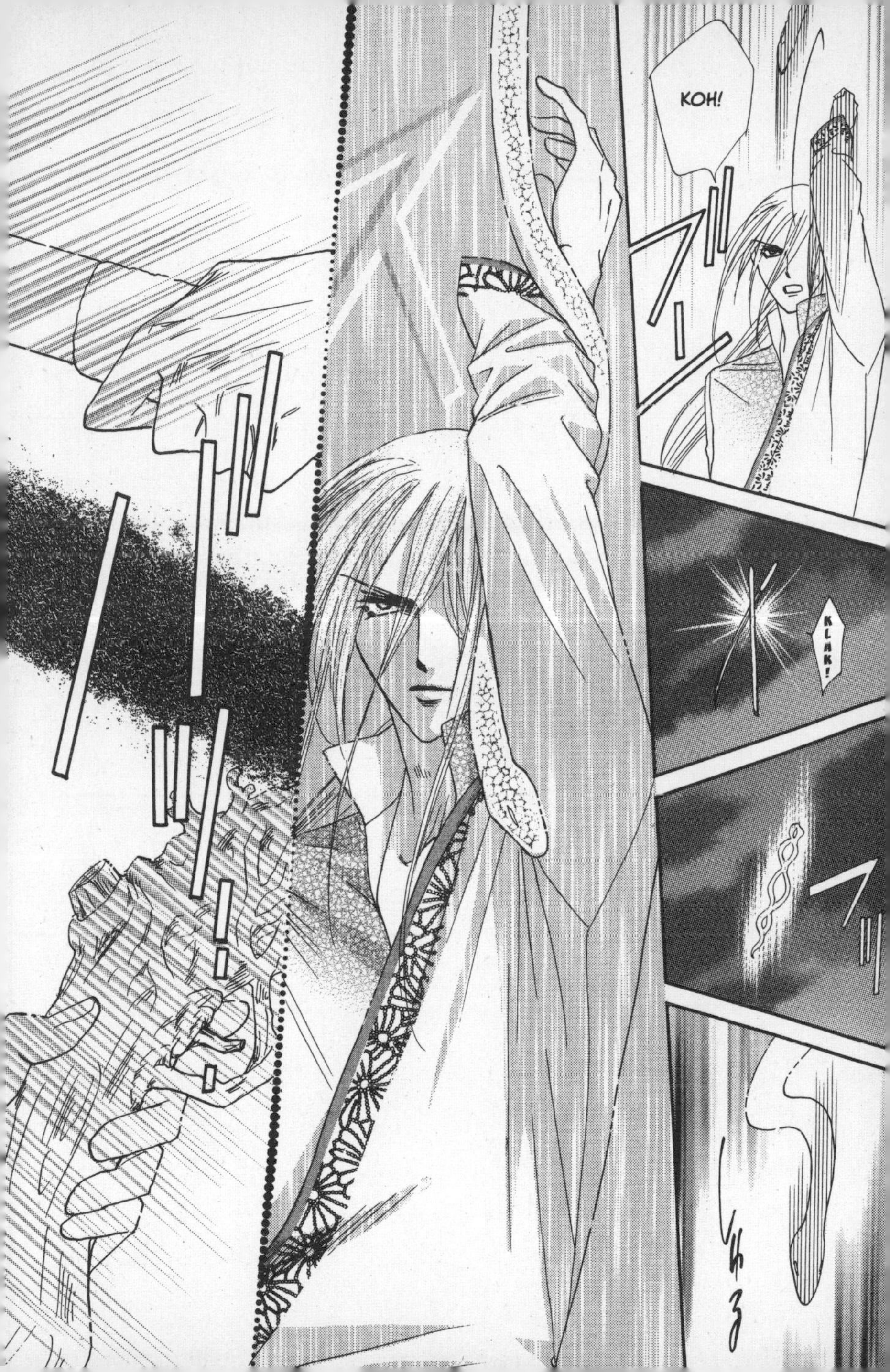
KOH!
KLAK!

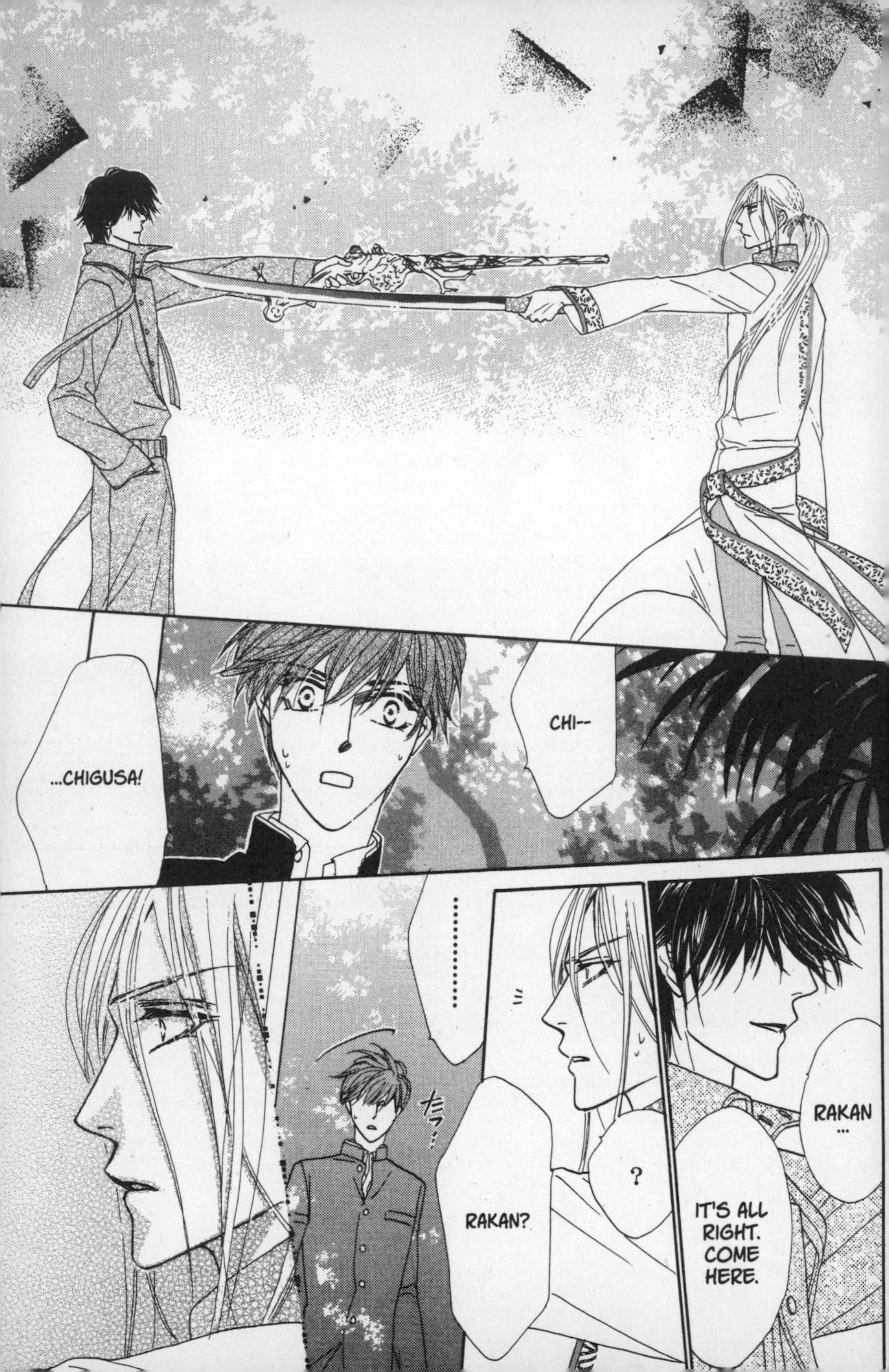
CHI--
...CHIGUSA!
RAKAN ...
?
IT'S ALL RIGHT. COME HERE.
......
RAKAN?

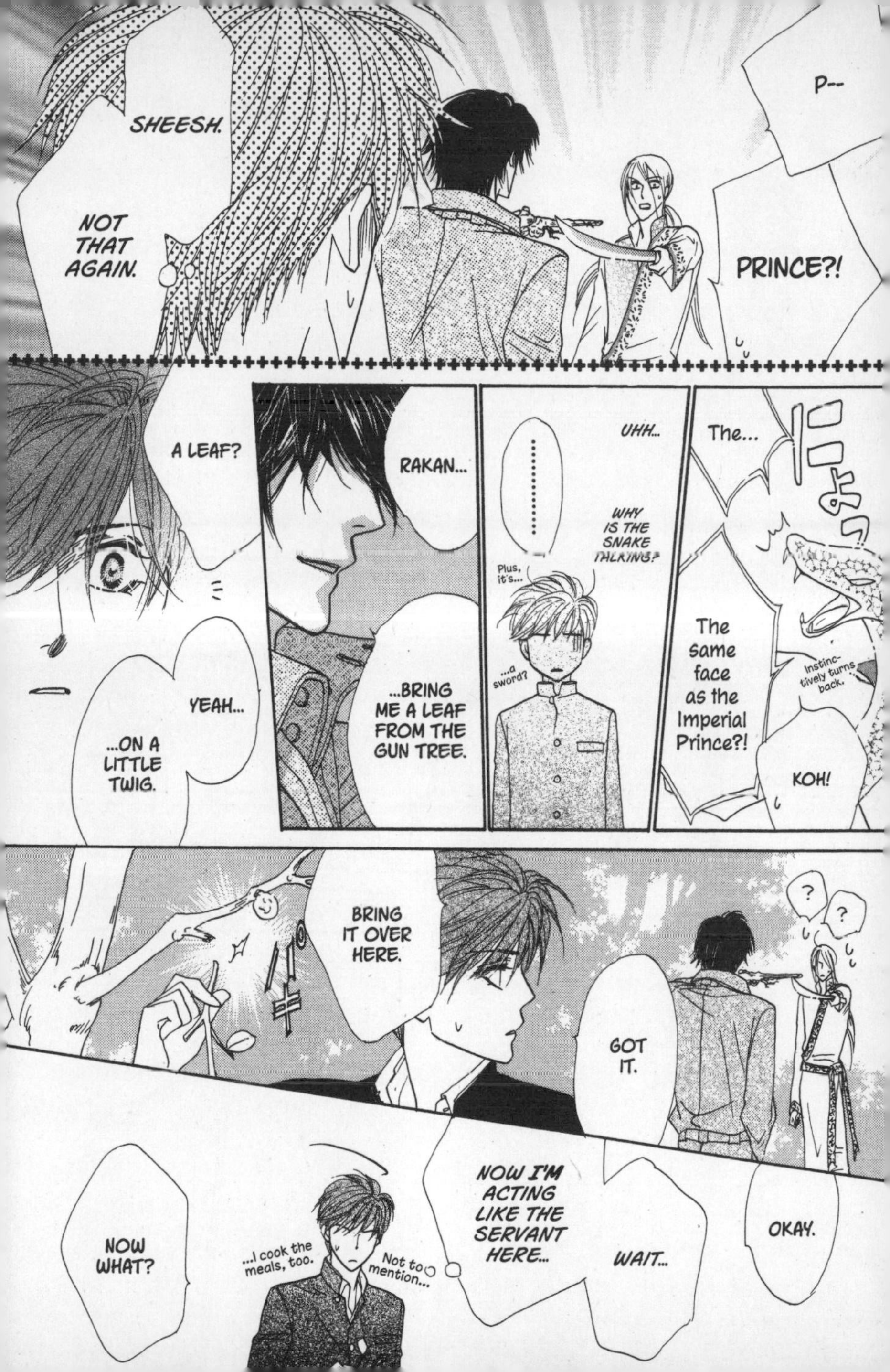
P--
PRINCE?!
SHEESH.
NOT THAT AGAIN.
The...
にょっ
The same face as the Imperial Prince?!
Instinctively turns back.
KOH!
UHH...
WHY IS THE SNAKE TALKING?
......
Plus, it's...
...a sword?
RAKAN...
...BRING ME A LEAF FROM THE GUN TREE.
A LEAF?
YEAH...
...ON A LITTLE TWIG.
?
?
GOT IT.
BRING IT OVER HERE.
OKAY.
WAIT...
NOW I'M ACTING LIKE THE SERVANT HERE...
Not to mention...
...I cook the meals, too.
NOW WHAT?

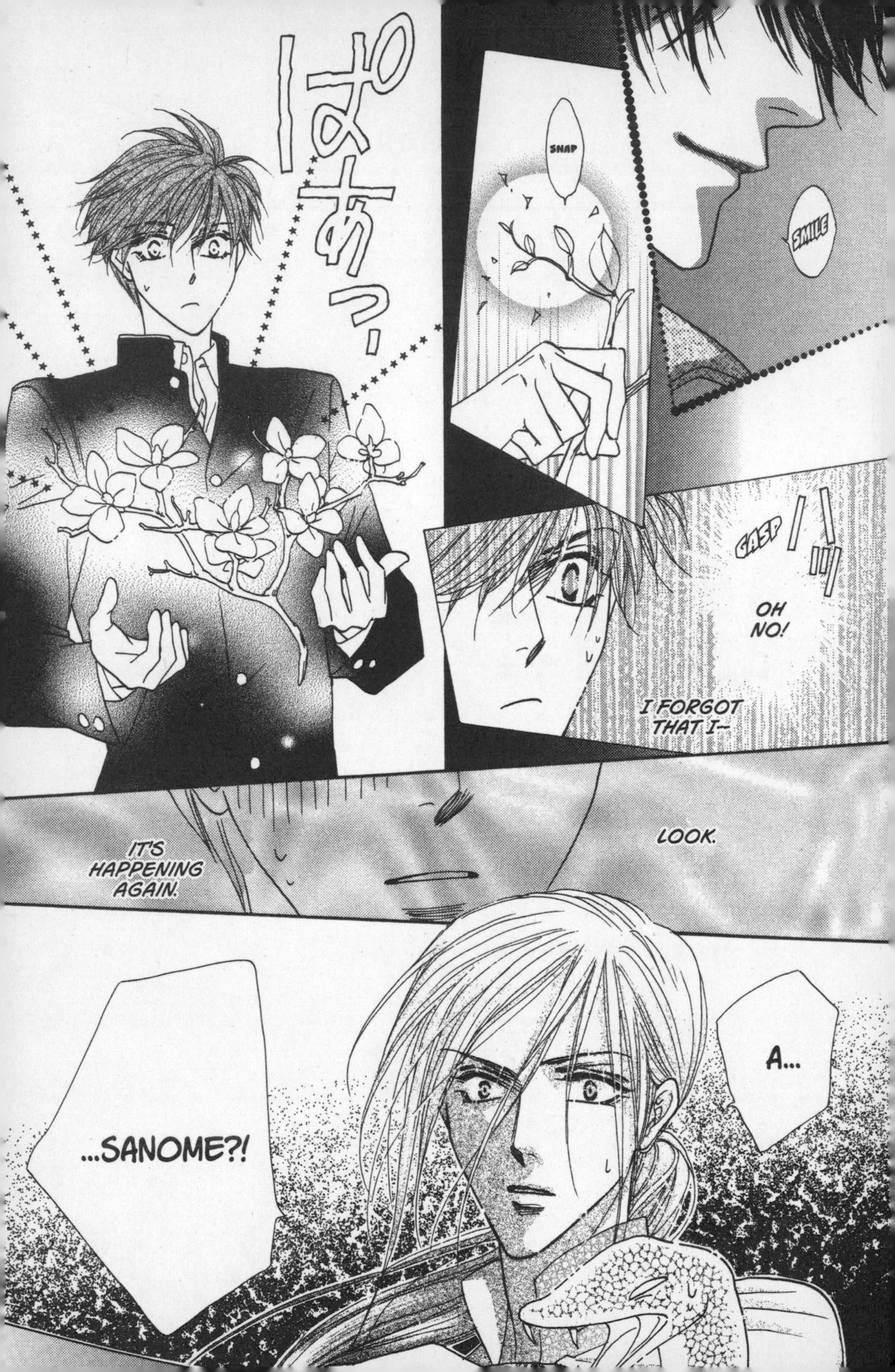
SMILE
SNAP
GASP
OH NO!
I FORGOT THAT I--
ぱあっ
LOOK.
IT'S HAPPENING AGAIN.
A...
...SANOME?!

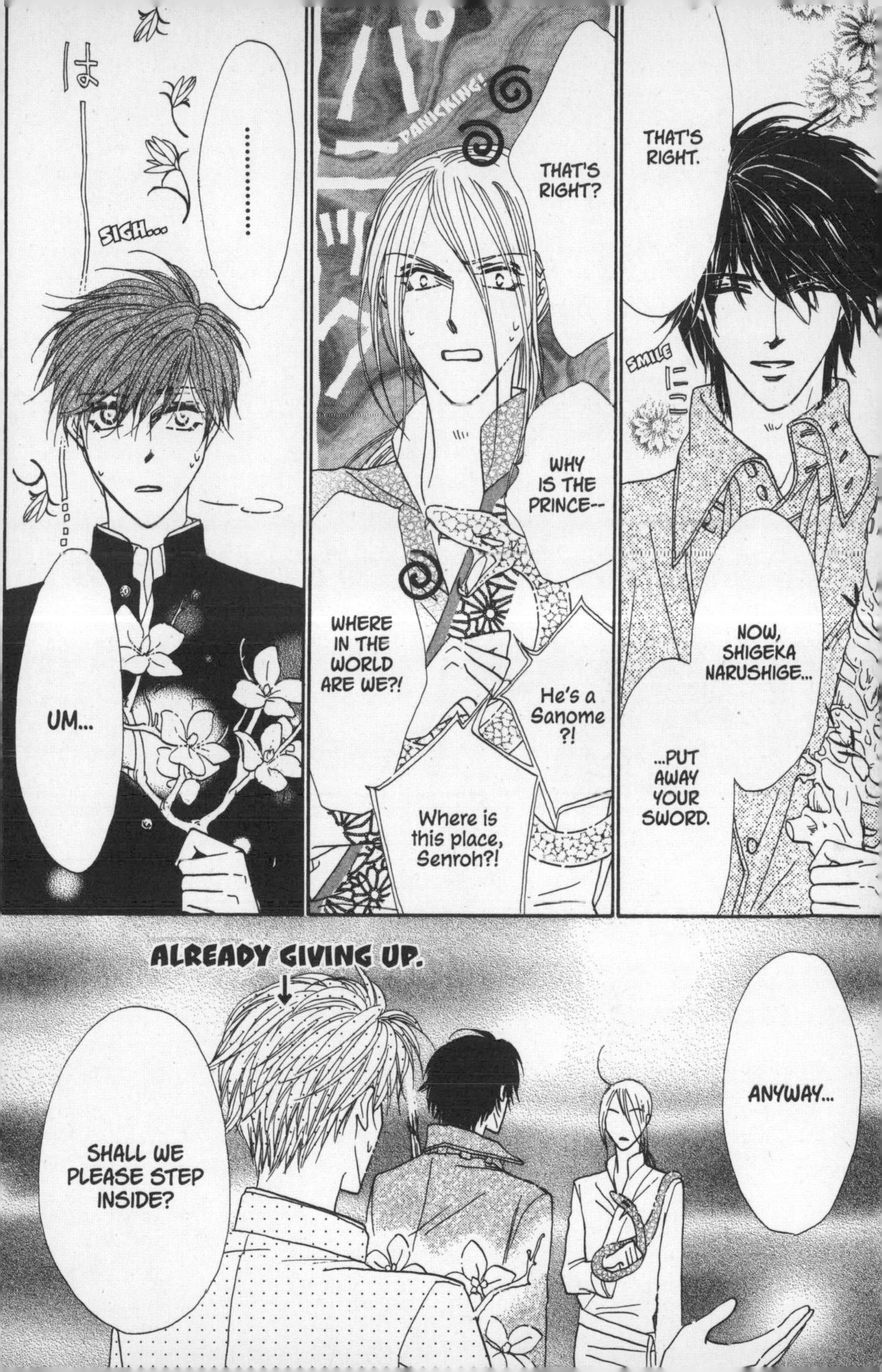
THAT'S RIGHT.
SMILE
ニコ
NOW, SHIGEKA NARUSHIGE...
...PUT AWAY YOUR SWORD.
PANICKING!
THAT'S RIGHT?
WHY IS THE PRINCE--
He's a Sanome ?!
WHERE IN THE WORLD ARE WE?!
Where is this place, Senroh?!
SIGH...
はー
......
UM...
ALREADY GIVING UP.
ANYWAY...
SHALL WE PLEASE STEP INSIDE?

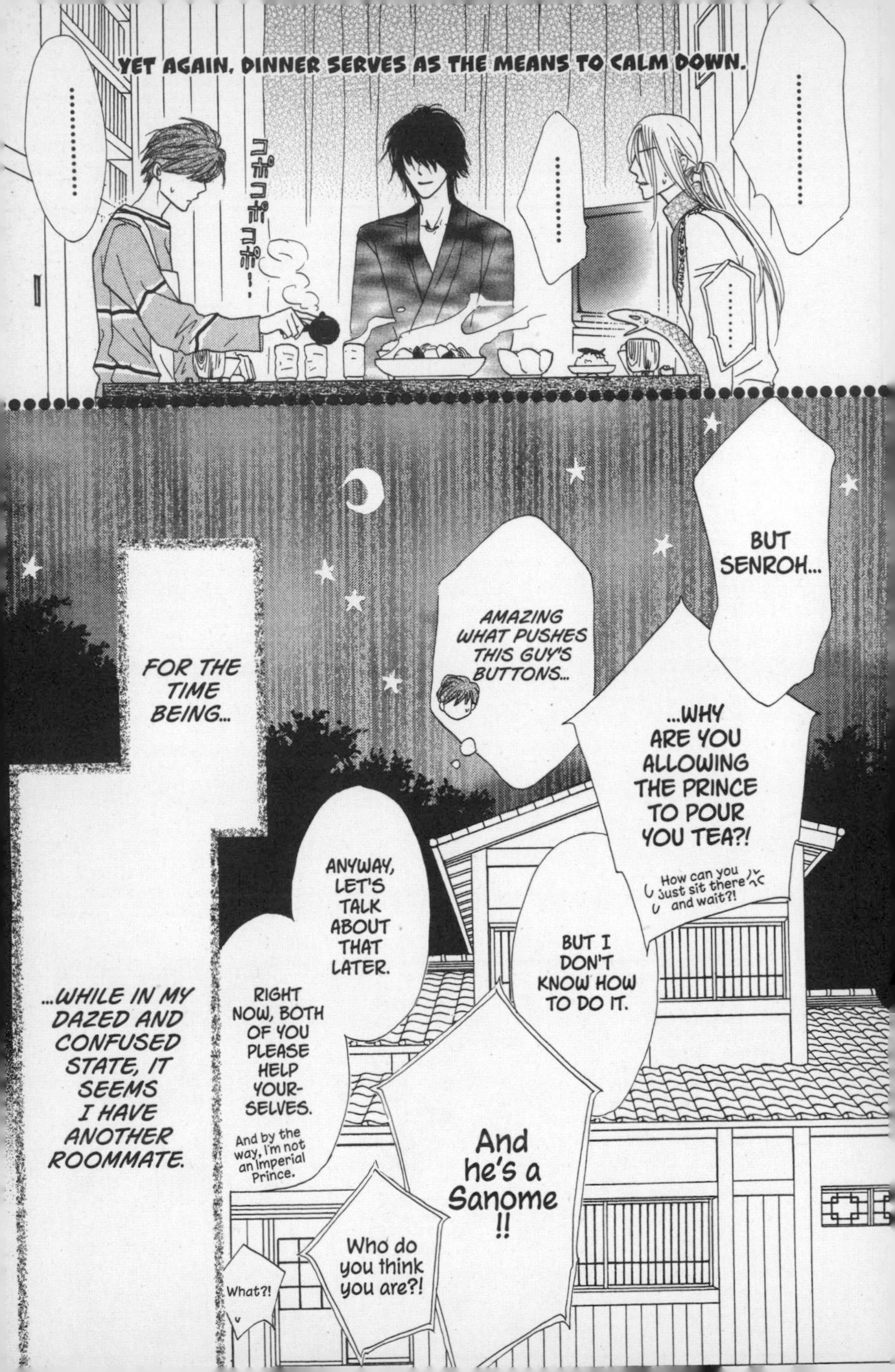
YET AGAIN, DINNER SERVES AS THE MEANS TO CALM DOWN.
……
……
……
コポコポコポ…
……
BUT SENROH...
...WHY ARE YOU ALLOWING THE PRINCE TO POUR YOU TEA?!
How can you just sit there and wait?!
AMAZING WHAT PUSHES THIS GUY'S BUTTONS...
BUT I DON'T KNOW HOW TO DO IT.
ANYWAY, LET'S TALK ABOUT THAT LATER.
RIGHT NOW, BOTH OF YOU PLEASE HELP YOURSELVES.
And by the way, I'm not an Imperial Prince.
And he's a Sanome!!
Who do you think you are?!
What?!
FOR THE TIME BEING...
...WHILE IN MY DAZED AND CONFUSED STATE, IT SEEMS I HAVE ANOTHER ROOMMATE.

♣ I don't have much time for this page, so this'll be mostly writing. Sorry. During the run in the original magazine, Ichiraci, the pages were crammed together so I was adding pages and making corrections so much that I was in danger of missing my deadline for the graphic novel release. (↑ The additions were to pages 29-31 of the third chapter) The people who were reading the original probably thought, "Now why would this scene be crammed into so many tiny panels"? It was really just my mistake dividing the pages. Heh heh.

Okay, what else should I write? Oh, the main characters are recycled from something I used to draw for the manga club bulletin back in high school. ✿ When I was younger, I used to think "I want to draw manga like this when I become a manga-ka, ✿" and now I've realized my dream. My friend Maki-chan used to say "I'll even wait 10 years for you!" Maki-chan continued to say it, and Maki-chan really did have to wait 10 years...

The power of language is frightening, isn't it?

(I'm kidding, Maki-san. It's not your fault!) Anyway, I'm glad I was finally able to fulfill my promise.

Of course the storyline is completely different... (Though only Maki-san would notice...)

♣ Incidentally, there is a photography studio named "Rakan" on a floor above my publisher, Tosuisha. I didn't get Rakan's name from that though, it's just an odd coincidence.

↓ Okay, I'll leave you with a final goodie from my other series, Koori no Mamono Monogatari. (I'm sorry to those who don't get it).

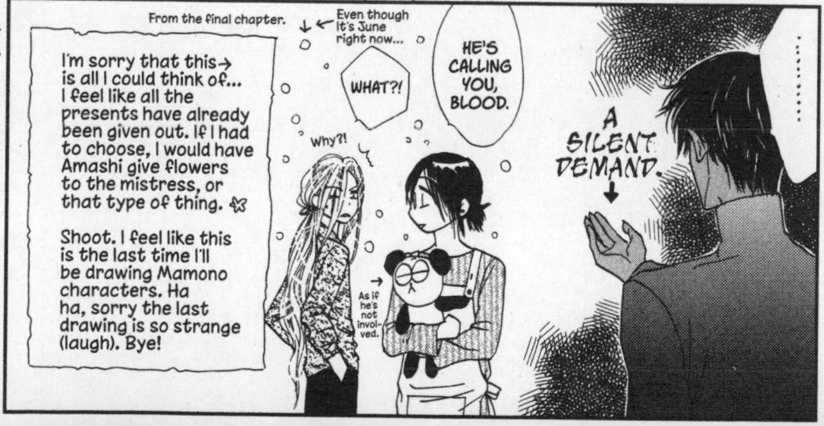

......
A SILENT DEMAND. ↓
HE'S CALLING YOU, BLOOD.
Even though it's June right now...
From the final chapter.
WHAT?!
Why?!
As if he's not involved.
I'm sorry that this→ is all I could think of... I feel like all the presents have already been given out. If I had to choose, I would have Amashi give flowers to the mistress, or that type of thing. ✿
Shoot. I feel like this is the last time I'll be drawing Mamono characters. Ha ha, sorry the last drawing is so strange (laugh). Bye!

◇ A present to my characters. ◇

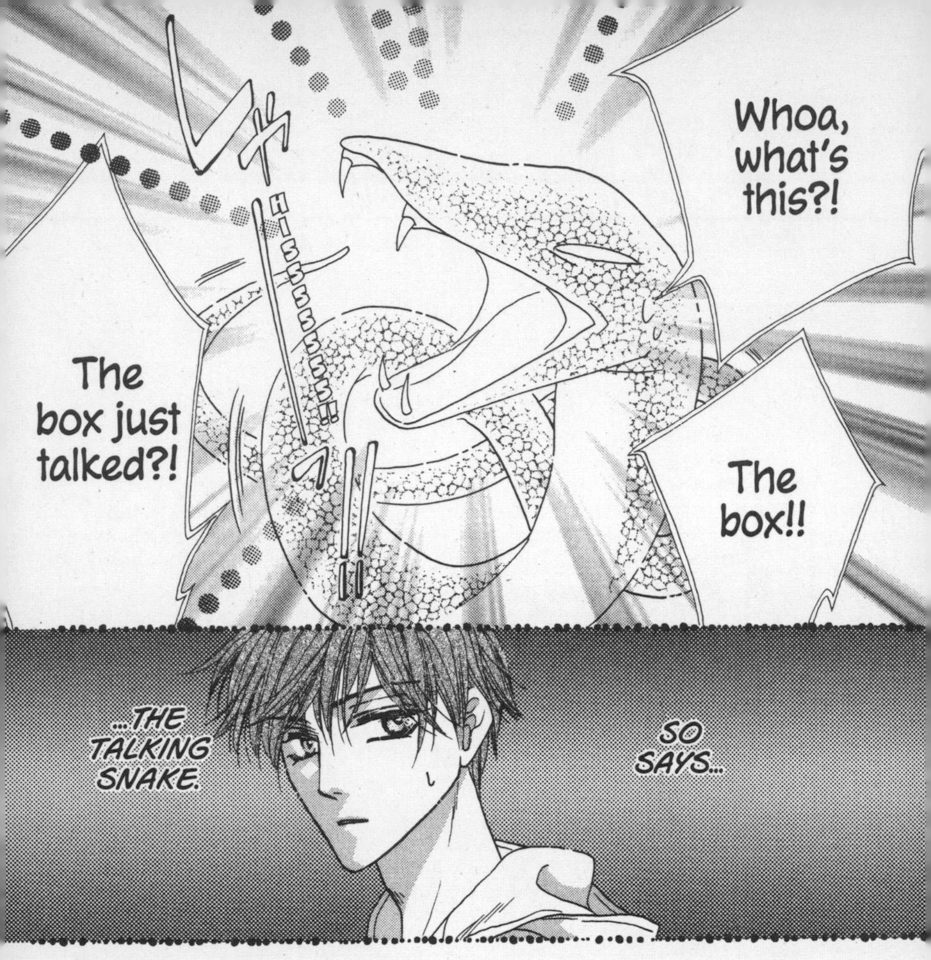
Whoa, what's this?!
The box!!
HISSSSSSS!!
The box just talked?!
SO SAYS...
...THE TALKING SNAKE.

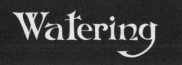

Watering

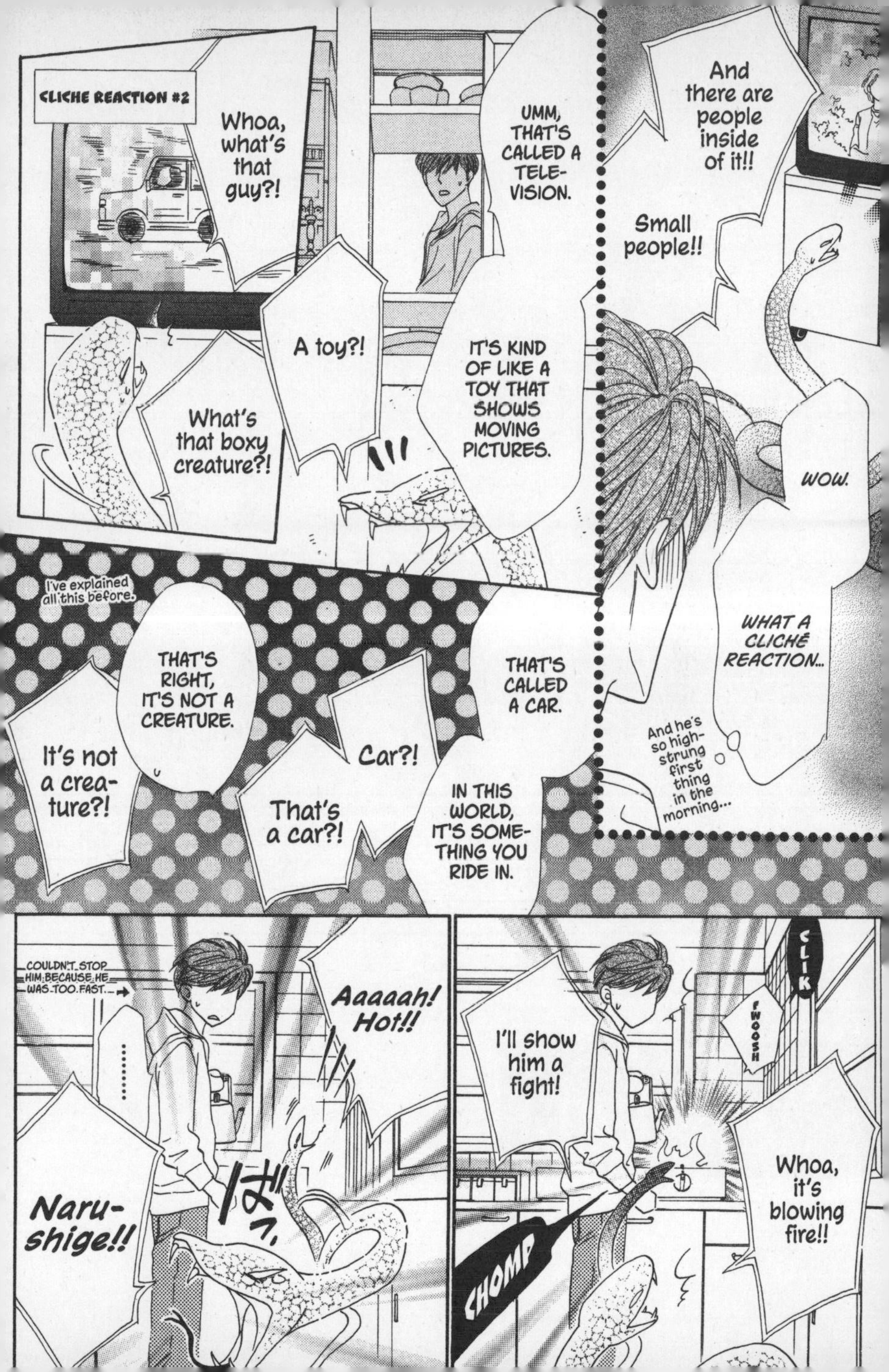
And there are people inside of it!!
Small people!!
WOW.
WHAT A CLICHÉ REACTION...
And he's so high-strung first thing in the morning...
CLICHE REACTION #2
UMM, THAT'S CALLED A TELE-VISION.
Whoa, what's that guy?!
IT'S KIND OF LIKE A TOY THAT SHOWS MOVING PICTURES.
A toy?!
What's that boxy creature?!
THAT'S CALLED A CAR.
Car?!
That's a car?!
IN THIS WORLD, IT'S SOME-THING YOU RIDE IN.
THAT'S RIGHT, IT'S NOT A CREATURE.
It's not a crea-ture?!
I've explained all this before.
CLIK
FWOOSH
I'll show him a fight!
Whoa, it's blowing fire!!
CHOMP
Aaaaah! Hot!!
COULDN'T STOP HIM BECAUSE HE WAS TOO FAST. →
....
Naru-shige!!

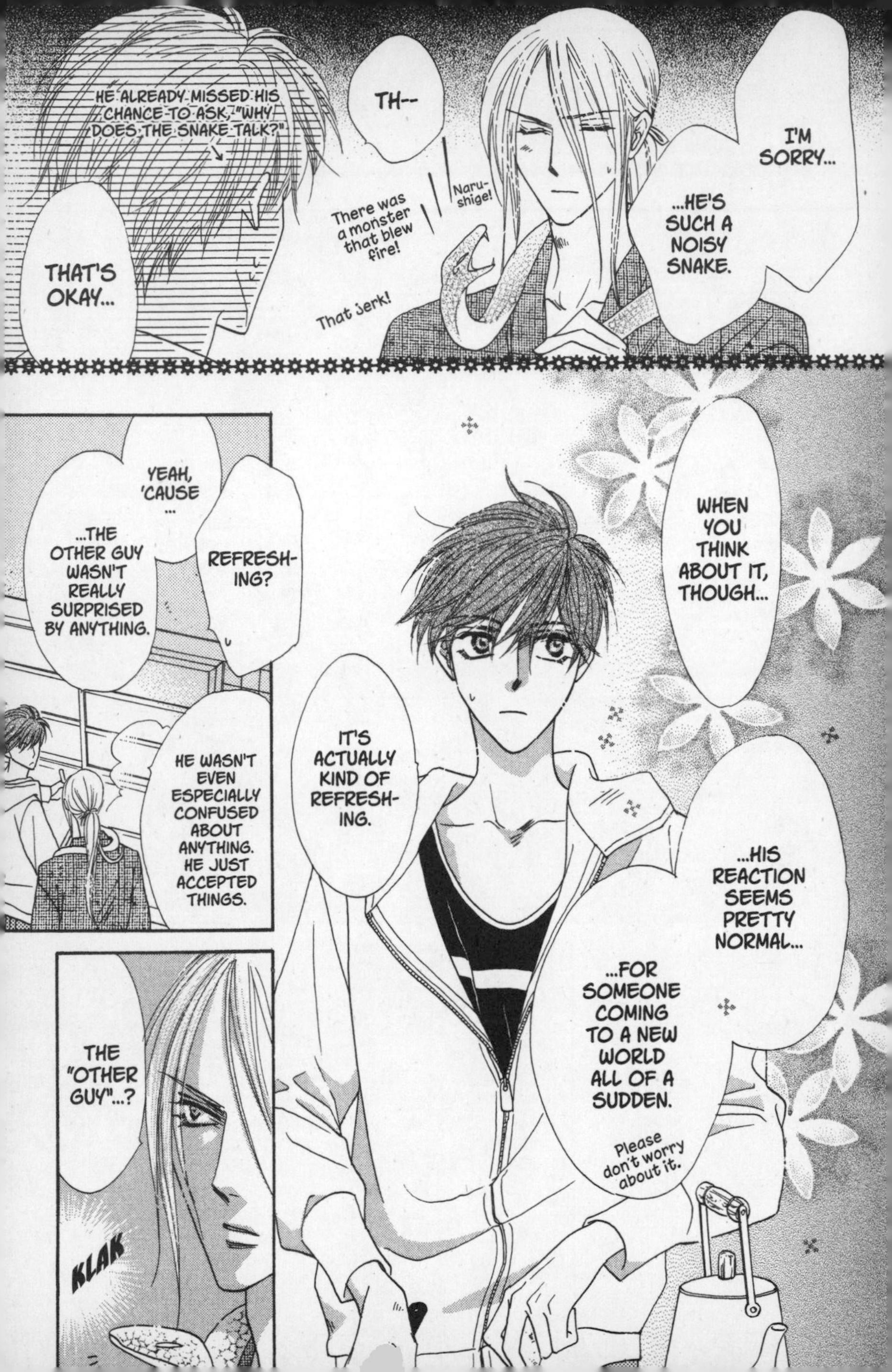
I'M SORRY...
...HE'S SUCH A NOISY SNAKE.
Naru-shige!
There was a monster that blew fire!
That jerk!
TH--
HE ALREADY MISSED HIS CHANCE TO ASK, "WHY DOES THE SNAKE TALK?"
THAT'S OKAY...
WHEN YOU THINK ABOUT IT, THOUGH...
...HIS REACTION SEEMS PRETTY NORMAL...
...FOR SOMEONE COMING TO A NEW WORLD ALL OF A SUDDEN.
Please don't worry about it.
IT'S ACTUALLY KIND OF REFRESHING.
REFRESHING?
YEAH, 'CAUSE...
...THE OTHER GUY WASN'T REALLY SURPRISED BY ANYTHING.
HE WASN'T EVEN ESPECIALLY CONFUSED ABOUT ANYTHING. HE JUST ACCEPTED THINGS.
THE "OTHER GUY"...?
KLAK

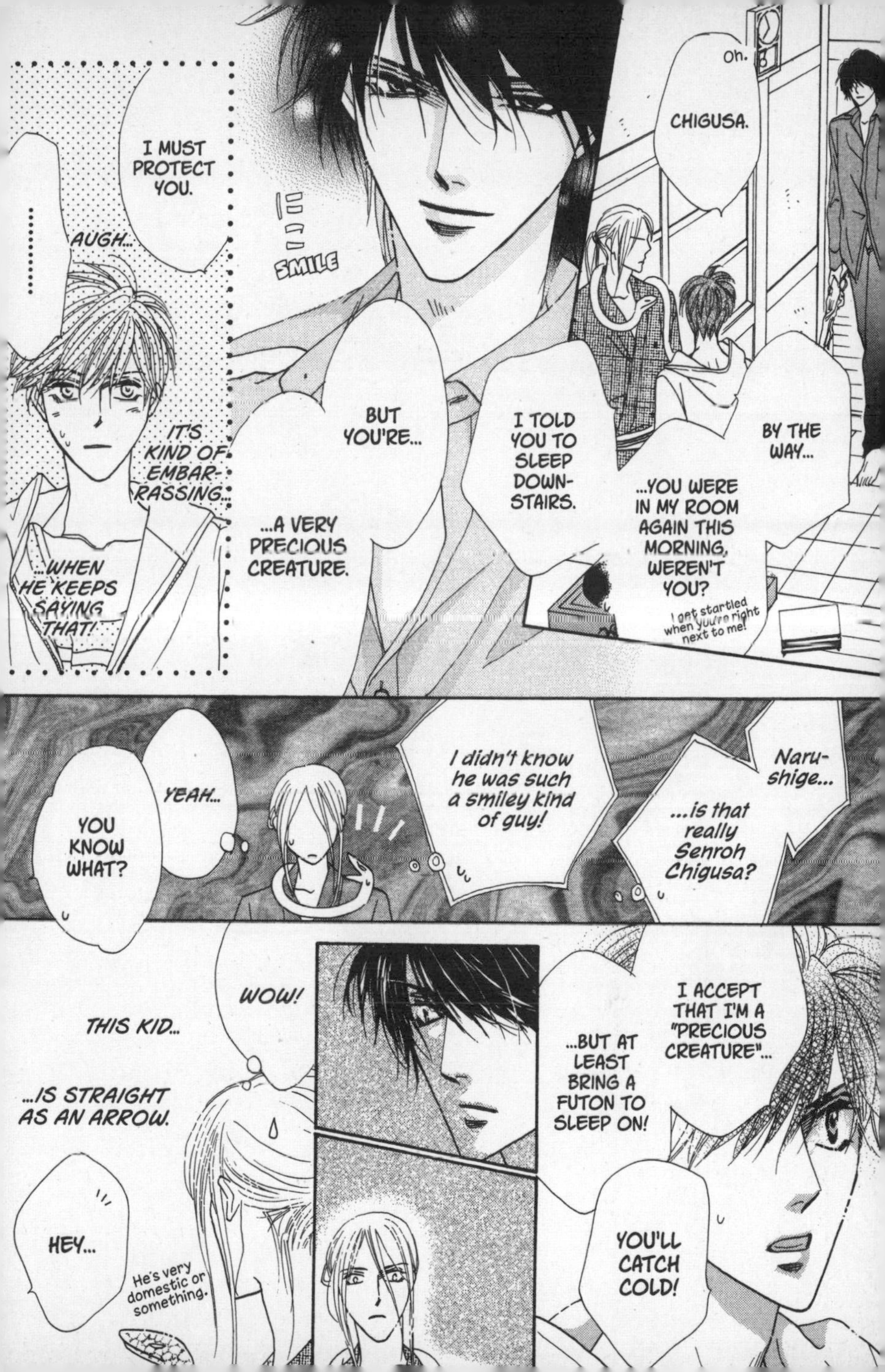
Oh.
CHIGUSA.
BY THE WAY...
...YOU WERE IN MY ROOM AGAIN THIS MORNING, WEREN'T YOU?
I get startled when you're right next to me!
I TOLD YOU TO SLEEP DOWN-STAIRS.
BUT YOU'RE...
...A VERY PRECIOUS CREATURE.
SMILE
I MUST PROTECT YOU.
AUGH...
IT'S KIND OF EMBAR-RASSING...
...WHEN HE KEEPS SAYING THAT!
Naru-shige...
...is that really Senroh Chigusa?
I didn't know he was such a smiley kind of guy!
YEAH...
YOU KNOW WHAT?
I ACCEPT THAT I'M A "PRECIOUS CREATURE"...
...BUT AT LEAST BRING A FUTON TO SLEEP ON!
YOU'LL CATCH COLD!
WOW!
THIS KID...
...IS STRAIGHT AS AN ARROW.
HEY...
He's very domestic or something.

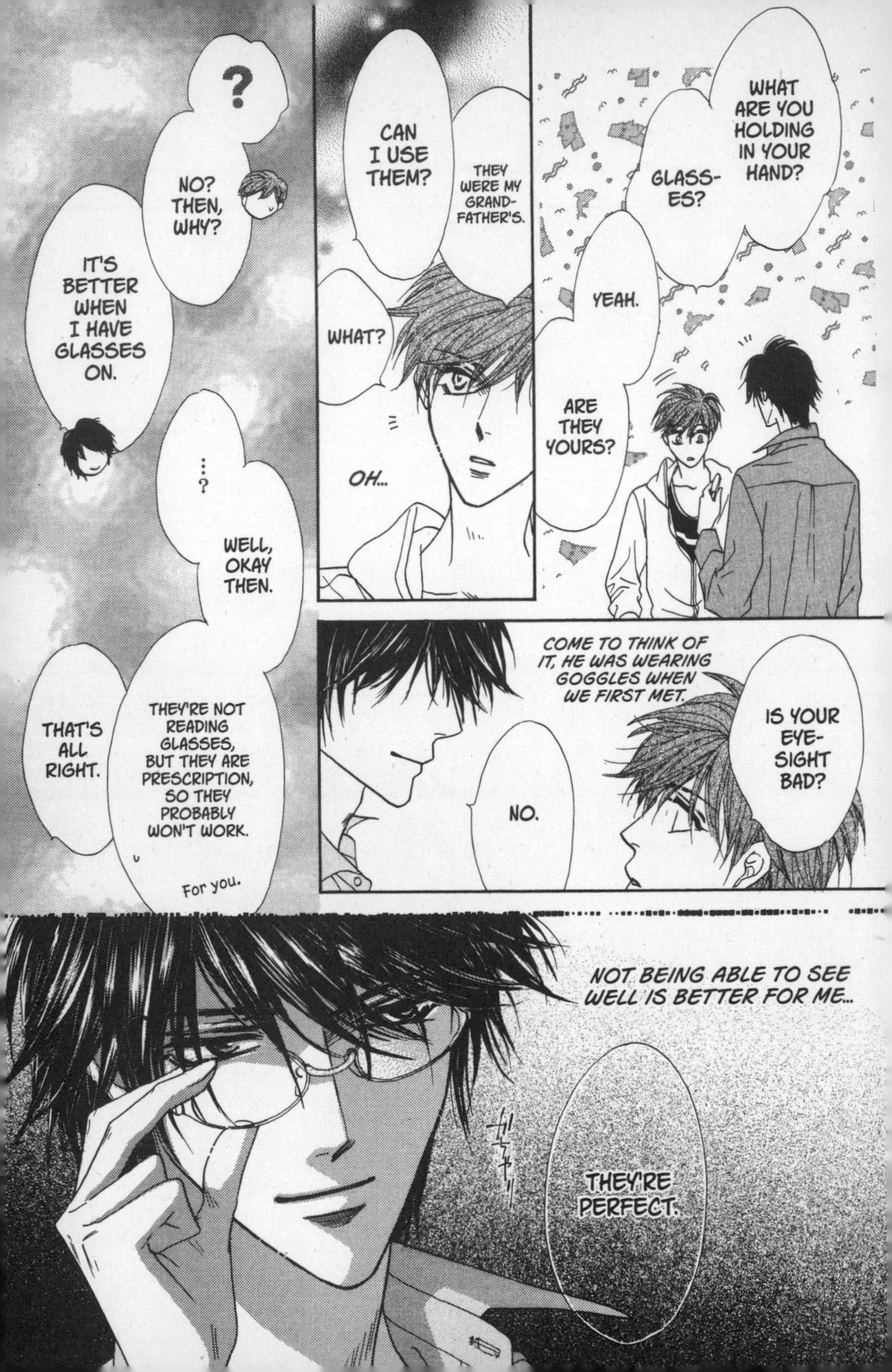
WHAT ARE YOU HOLDING IN YOUR HAND?
GLASSES?
YEAH.
ARE THEY YOURS?
THEY WERE MY GRANDFATHER'S.
CAN I USE THEM?
WHAT?
OH...
COME TO THINK OF IT, HE WAS WEARING GOGGLES WHEN WE FIRST MET.
IS YOUR EYESIGHT BAD?
NO.
?
NO? THEN, WHY?
IT'S BETTER WHEN I HAVE GLASSES ON.
...?
WELL, OKAY THEN.
THEY'RE NOT READING GLASSES, BUT THEY ARE PRESCRIPTION, SO THEY PROBABLY WON'T WORK.
For you.
THAT'S ALL RIGHT.
NOT BEING ABLE TO SEE WELL IS BETTER FOR ME...
THEY'RE PERFECT.

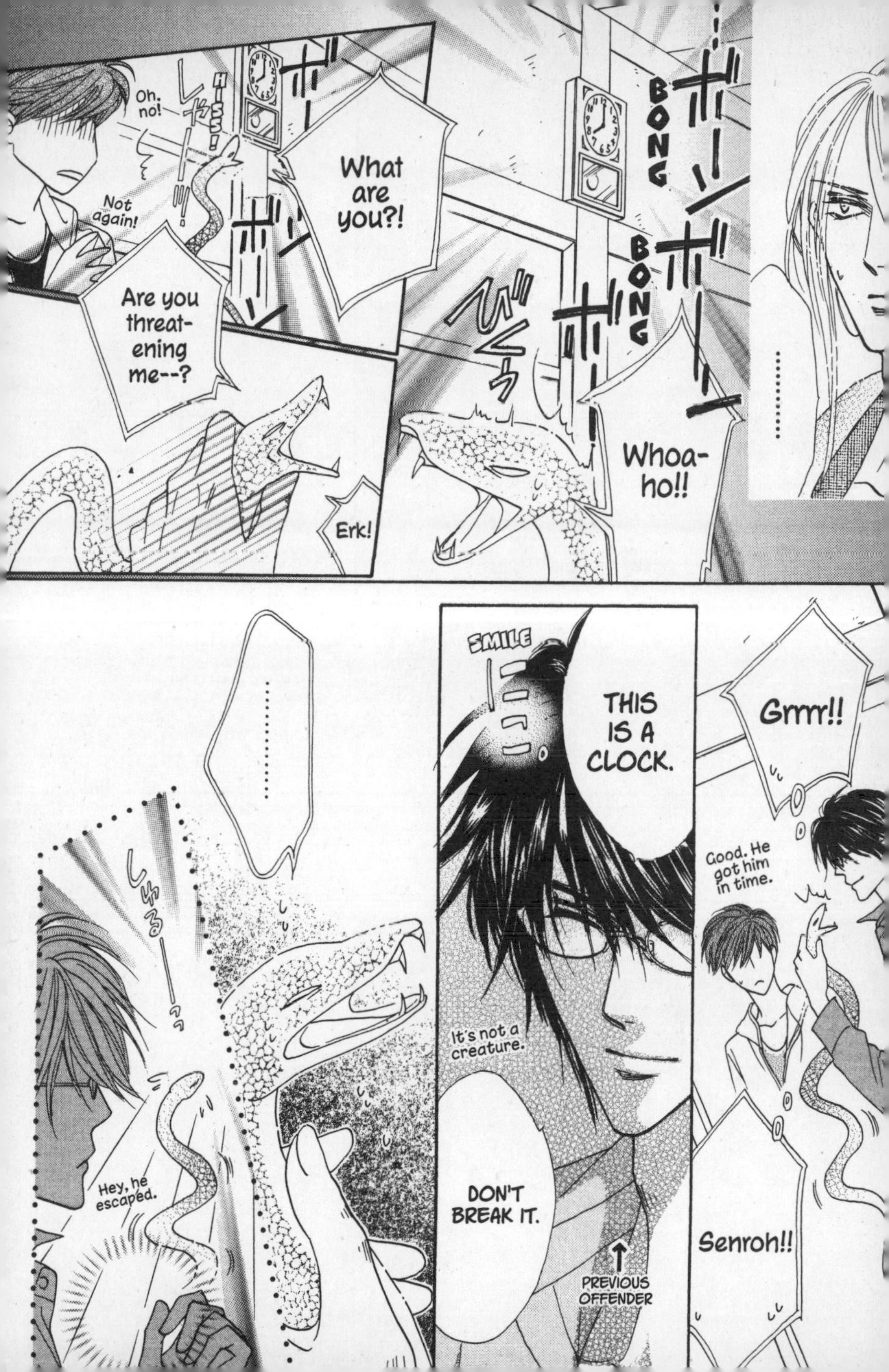
......
BONG
BONG
Whoa-ho!!
What are you?!
Oh. no!
HISS!
Not again!
Are you threatening me--?
Erk!
Grrr!!
Good. He got him in time.
Senroh!!
SMILE
THIS IS A CLOCK.
It's not a creature.
DON'T BREAK IT.
↑ PREVIOUS OFFENDER
......
Hey, he escaped.

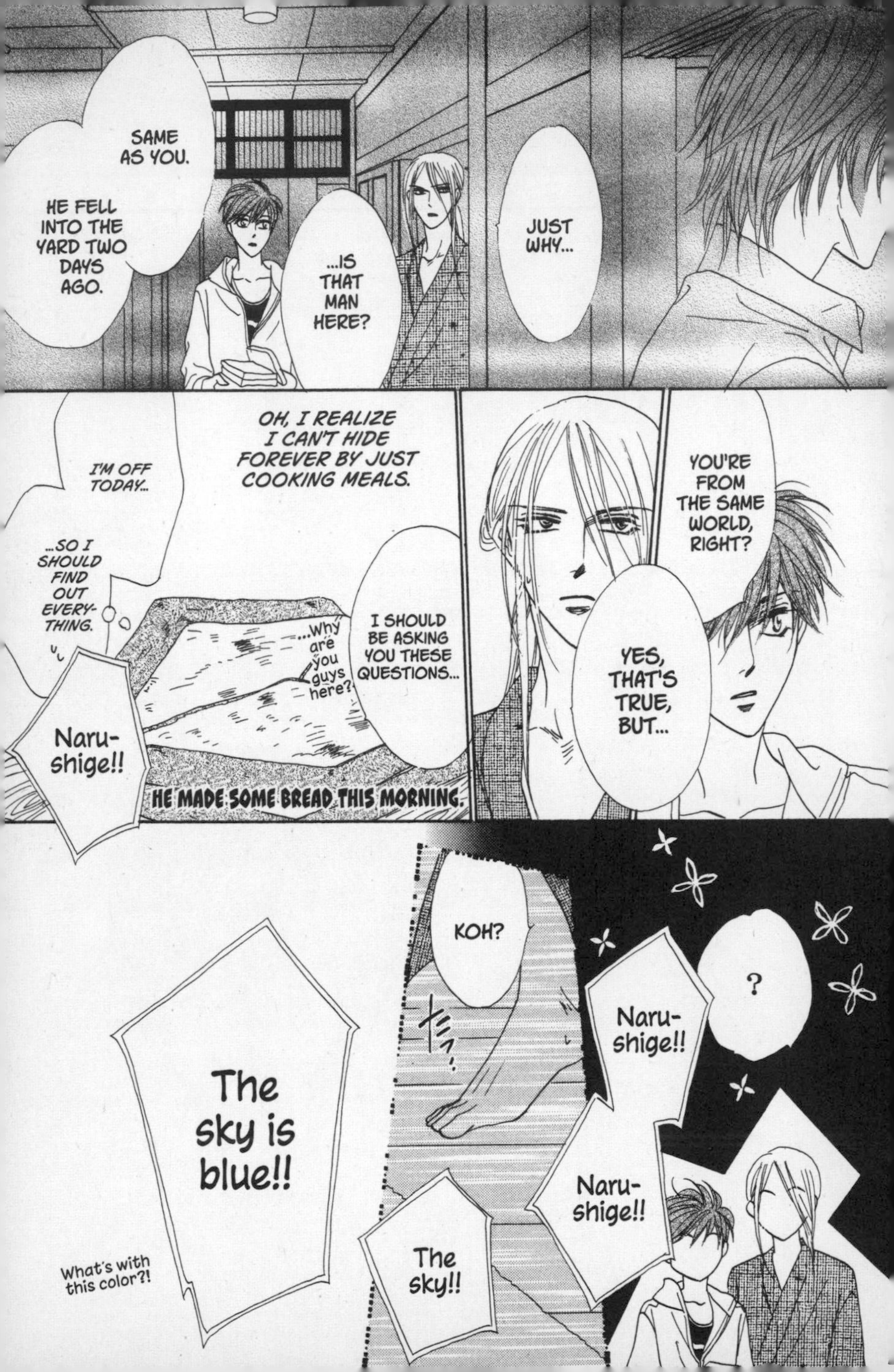
JUST WHY...
...IS THAT MAN HERE?
SAME AS YOU.
HE FELL INTO THE YARD TWO DAYS AGO.
YOU'RE FROM THE SAME WORLD, RIGHT?
YES, THAT'S TRUE, BUT...
I SHOULD BE ASKING YOU THESE QUESTIONS...
...Why are you guys here?
OH, I REALIZE I CAN'T HIDE FOREVER BY JUST COOKING MEALS.
I'M OFF TODAY...
...SO I SHOULD FIND OUT EVERYTHING.
Naru-shige!!
HE MADE SOME BREAD THIS MORNING.
?
Naru-shige!!
Naru-shige!!
KOH?
The sky!!
The sky is blue!!
What's with this color?!

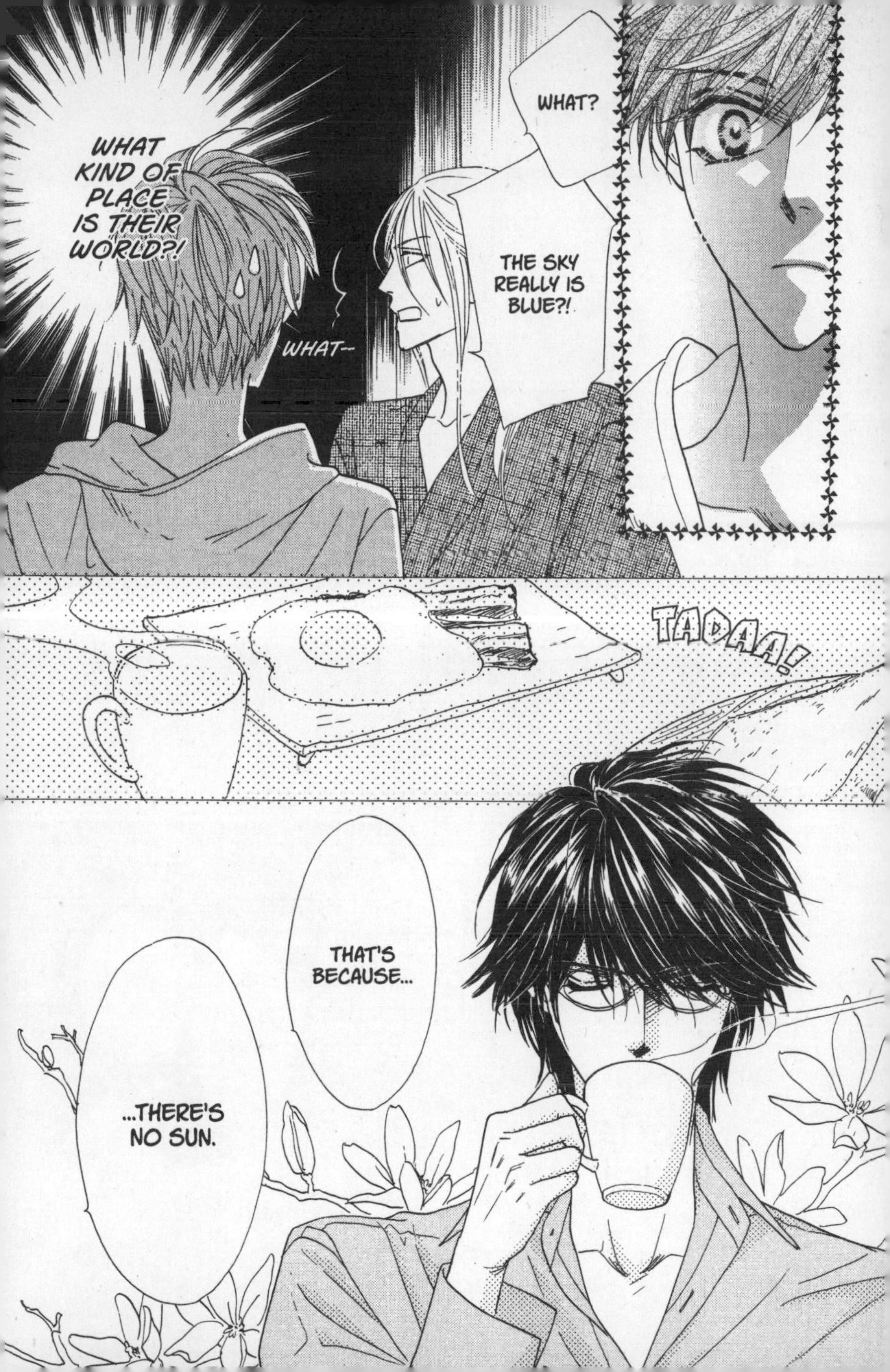
WHAT?
THE SKY REALLY IS BLUE?!
WHAT--
WHAT KIND OF PLACE IS THEIR WORLD?!
TADAA!
THAT'S BECAUSE...
...THERE'S NO SUN.

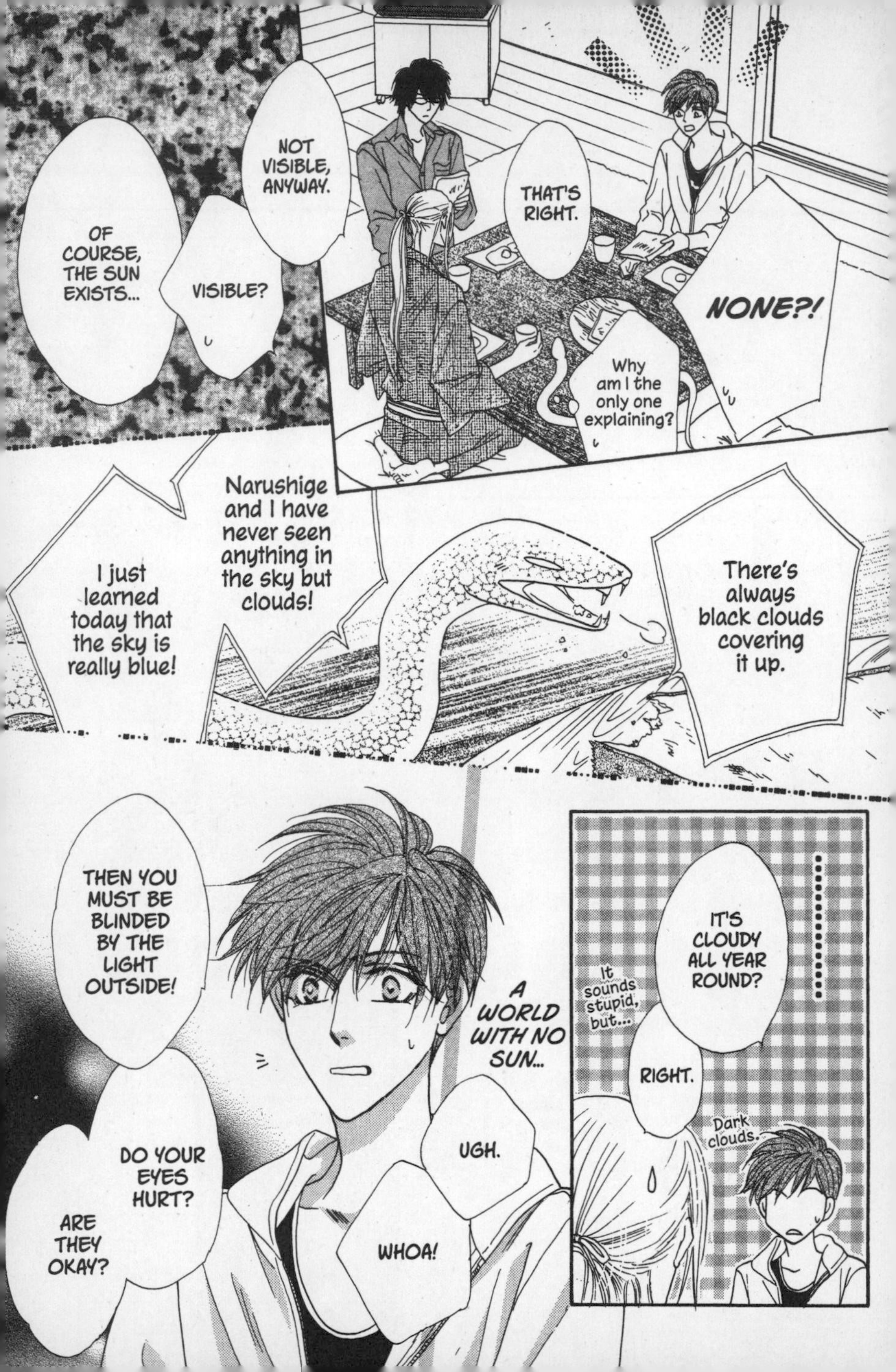
NONE?!
Why am I the only one explaining?
THAT'S RIGHT.
NOT VISIBLE, ANYWAY.
VISIBLE?
OF COURSE, THE SUN EXISTS...
There's always black clouds covering it up.
Narushige and I have never seen anything in the sky but clouds!
I just learned today that the sky is really blue!
....
IT'S CLOUDY ALL YEAR ROUND?
It sounds stupid, but...
RIGHT.
Dark clouds.
A WORLD WITH NO SUN...
THEN YOU MUST BE BLINDED BY THE LIGHT OUTSIDE!
UGH.
WHOA!
DO YOUR EYES HURT?
ARE THEY OKAY?

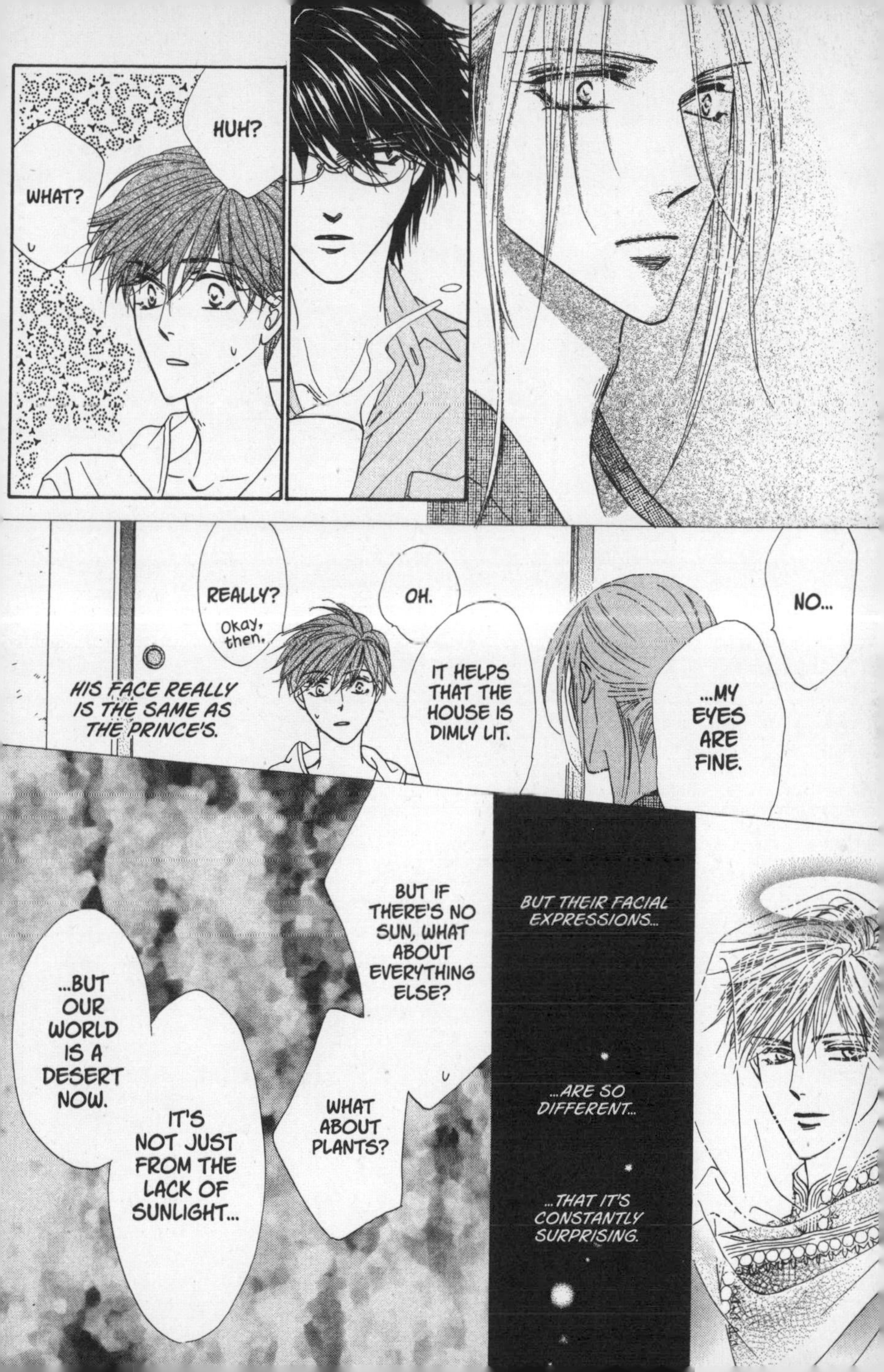

HUH?
WHAT?
NO...
...MY EYES ARE FINE.
IT HELPS THAT THE HOUSE IS DIMLY LIT.
OH.
REALLY?
Okay, then.
HIS FACE REALLY IS THE SAME AS THE PRINCE'S.
BUT THEIR FACIAL EXPRESSIONS...
...ARE SO DIFFERENT...
...THAT IT'S CONSTANTLY SURPRISING.
BUT IF THERE'S NO SUN, WHAT ABOUT EVERYTHING ELSE?
WHAT ABOUT PLANTS?
...BUT OUR WORLD IS A DESERT NOW.
IT'S NOT JUST FROM THE LACK OF SUNLIGHT...

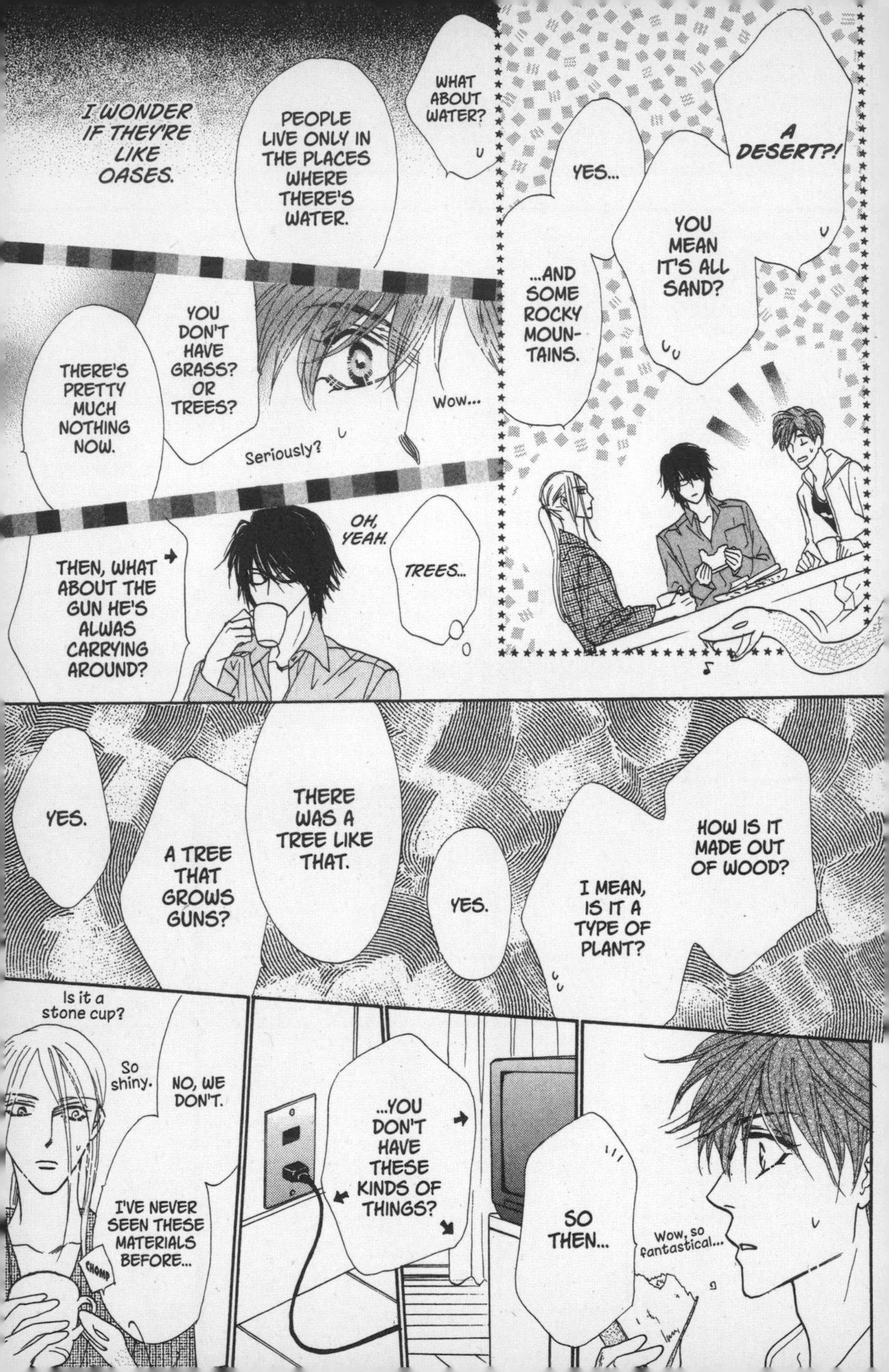
A DESERT?!
YOU MEAN IT'S ALL SAND?
YES...
...AND SOME ROCKY MOUNTAINS.
WHAT ABOUT WATER?
PEOPLE LIVE ONLY IN THE PLACES WHERE THERE'S WATER.
I WONDER IF THEY'RE LIKE OASES.
Wow...
YOU DON'T HAVE GRASS? OR TREES?
Seriously?
THERE'S PRETTY MUCH NOTHING NOW.
OH, YEAH.
TREES...
THEN, WHAT ABOUT THE GUN HE'S ALWAS CARRYING AROUND?
HOW IS IT MADE OUT OF WOOD?
I MEAN, IS IT A TYPE OF PLANT?
YES.
THERE WAS A TREE LIKE THAT.
A TREE THAT GROWS GUNS?
YES.
SO THEN...
Wow, so fantastical...
...YOU DON'T HAVE THESE KINDS OF THINGS?
NO, WE DON'T.
Is it a stone cup?
So shiny.
I'VE NEVER SEEN THESE MATERIALS BEFORE...
CHOMP

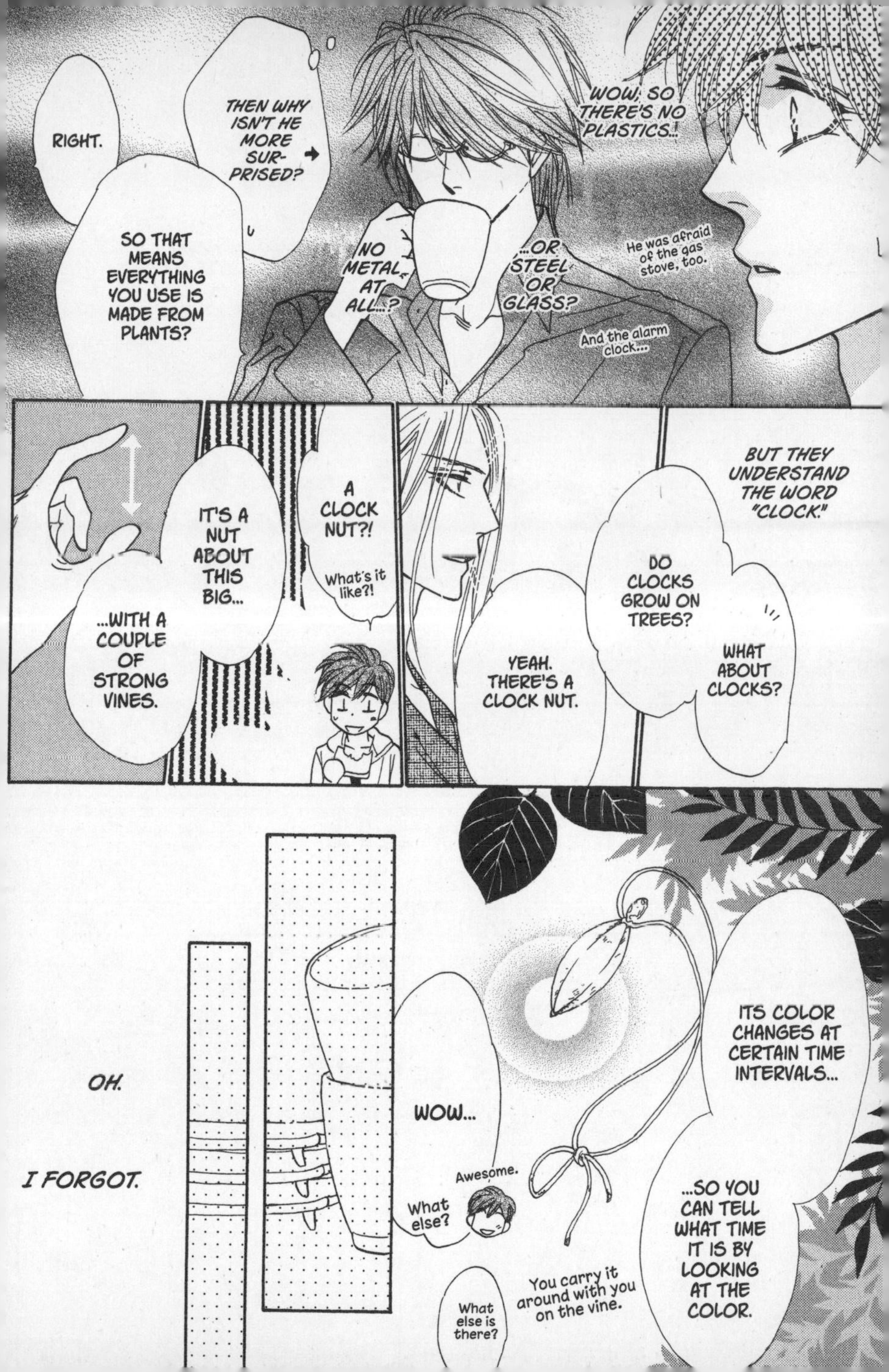
WOW, SO THERE'S NO PLASTICS...
He was afraid of the gas stove, too.
...OR STEEL OR GLASS?
NO METAL AT ALL...?
And the alarm clock...
THEN WHY ISN'T HE MORE SUR-PRISED?
RIGHT.
SO THAT MEANS EVERYTHING YOU USE IS MADE FROM PLANTS?
BUT THEY UNDERSTAND THE WORD "CLOCK."
WHAT ABOUT CLOCKS?
DO CLOCKS GROW ON TREES?
YEAH. THERE'S A CLOCK NUT.
A CLOCK NUT?!
What's it like?!
IT'S A NUT ABOUT THIS BIG...
...WITH A COUPLE OF STRONG VINES.
ITS COLOR CHANGES AT CERTAIN TIME INTERVALS...
...SO YOU CAN TELL WHAT TIME IT IS BY LOOKING AT THE COLOR.
You carry it around with you on the vine.
WOW...
Awesome.
What else?
What else is there?
OH.
I FORGOT.

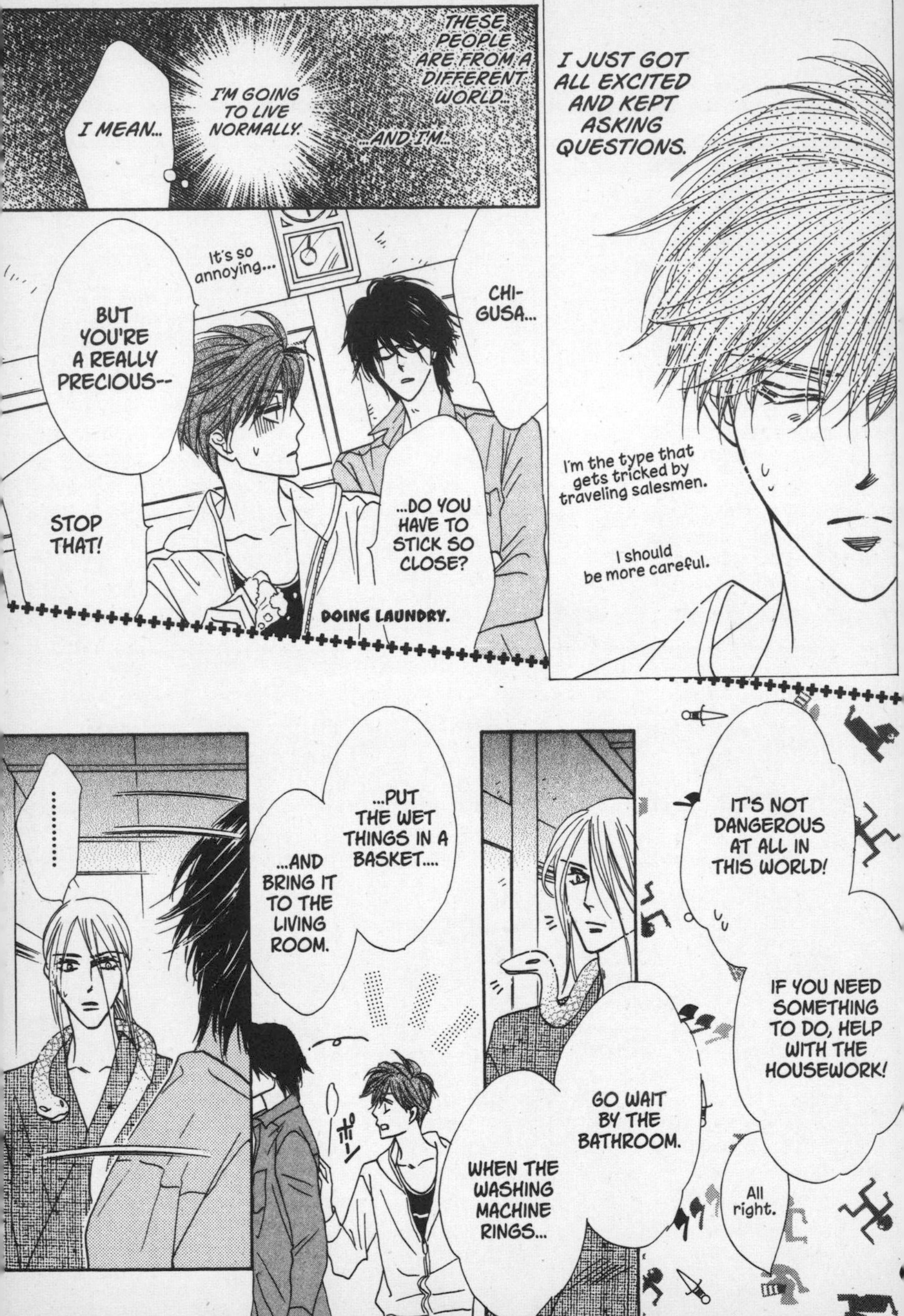
I JUST GOT ALL EXCITED AND KEPT ASKING QUESTIONS.
I'm the type that gets tricked by traveling salesmen.
I should be more careful.
THESE PEOPLE ARE FROM A DIFFERENT WORLD...
...AND I'M...
I'M GOING TO LIVE NORMALLY.
I MEAN...
CHI-GUSA...
...DO YOU HAVE TO STICK SO CLOSE?
It's so annoying...
BUT YOU'RE A REALLY PRECIOUS--
STOP THAT!
DOING LAUNDRY.
IT'S NOT DANGEROUS AT ALL IN THIS WORLD!
IF YOU NEED SOMETHING TO DO, HELP WITH THE HOUSEWORK!
All right.
GO WAIT BY THE BATHROOM.
WHEN THE WASHING MACHINE RINGS...
...PUT THE WET THINGS IN A BASKET....
...AND BRING IT TO THE LIVING ROOM.
....

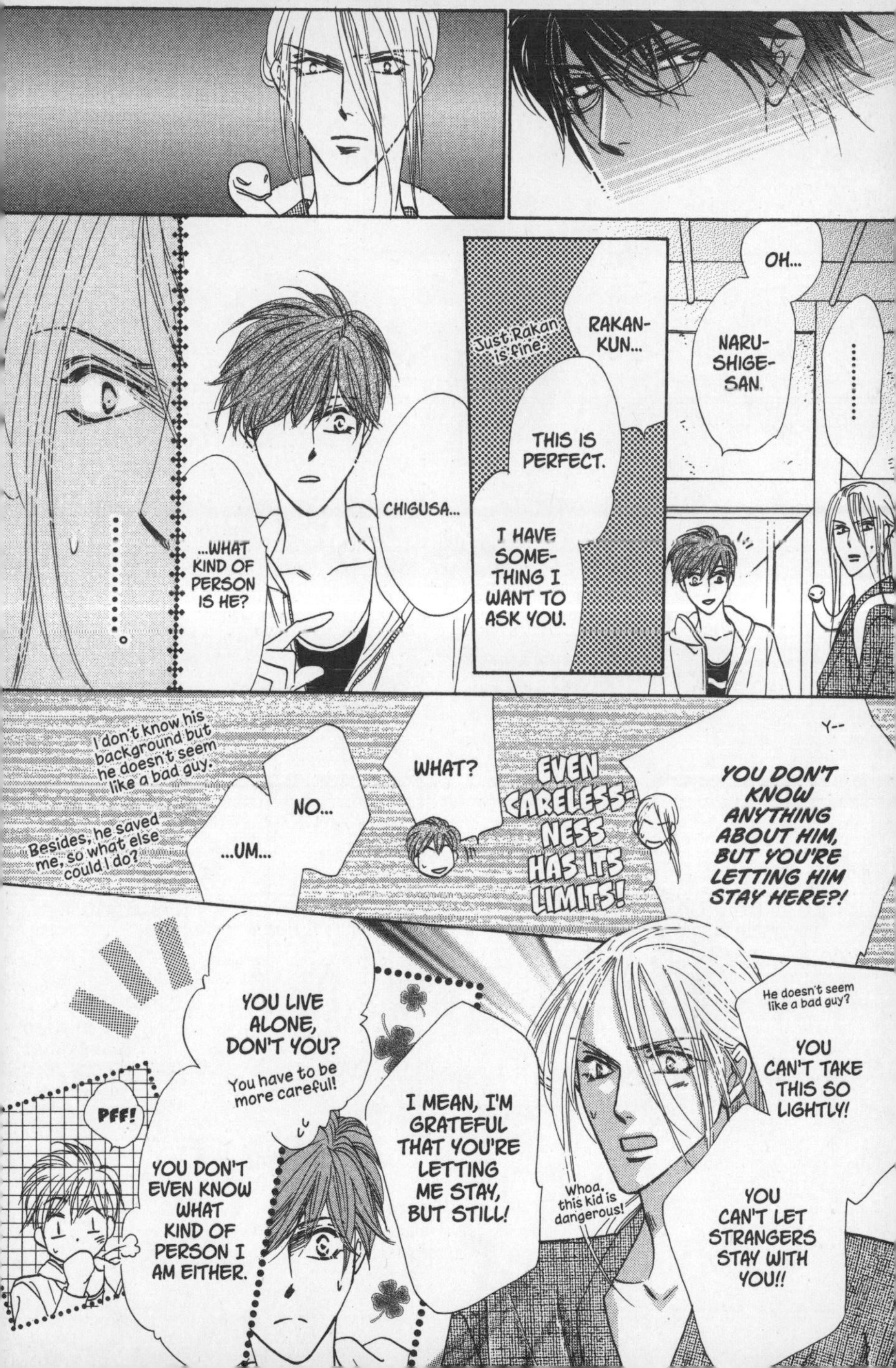
OH...
NARU-SHIGE-SAN.
......
RAKAN-KUN...
Just Rakan is fine.
THIS IS PERFECT.
I HAVE SOME-THING I WANT TO ASK YOU.
CHIGUSA...
...WHAT KIND OF PERSON IS HE?
....
Y--
YOU DON'T KNOW ANYTHING ABOUT HIM, BUT YOU'RE LETTING HIM STAY HERE?!
EVEN CARELESS-NESS HAS ITS LIMITS!
WHAT?
NO...
...UM...
I don't know his background but he doesn't seem like a bad guy.
Besides, he saved me, so what else could I do?
He doesn't seem like a bad guy?
YOU CAN'T TAKE THIS SO LIGHTLY!
YOU CAN'T LET STRANGERS STAY WITH YOU!!
Whoa, this kid is dangerous!
I MEAN, I'M GRATEFUL THAT YOU'RE LETTING ME STAY, BUT STILL!
YOU LIVE ALONE, DON'T YOU?
You have to be more careful!
YOU DON'T EVEN KNOW WHAT KIND OF PERSON I AM EITHER.
PFF!

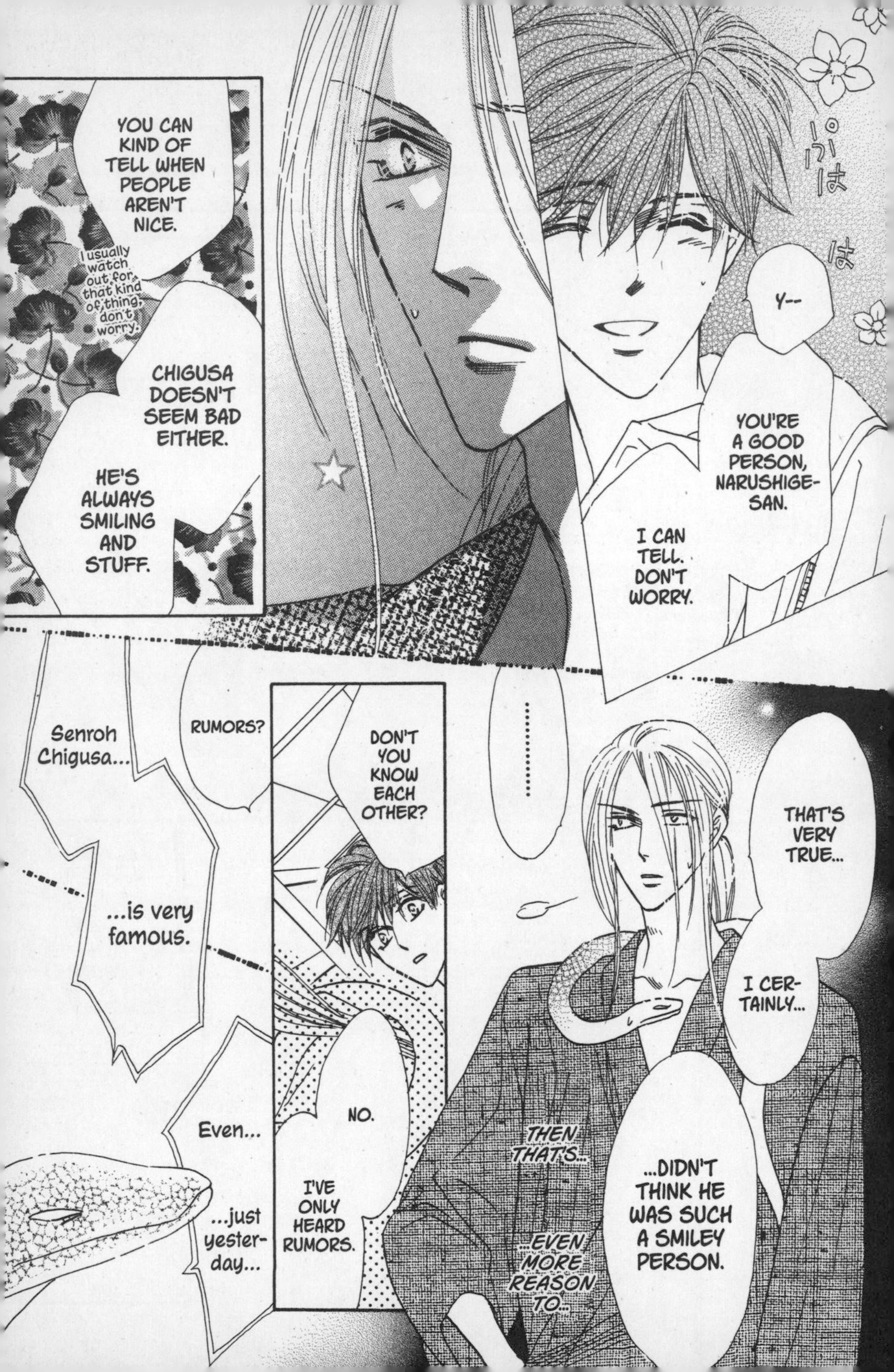
ぷはは
Y--
YOU'RE A GOOD PERSON, NARUSHIGE-SAN.
I CAN TELL. DON'T WORRY.
YOU CAN KIND OF TELL WHEN PEOPLE AREN'T NICE.
I usually watch out for that kind of thing, don't worry.
CHIGUSA DOESN'T SEEM BAD EITHER.
HE'S ALWAYS SMILING AND STUFF.
......
THAT'S VERY TRUE...
I CERTAINLY...
...DIDN'T THINK HE WAS SUCH A SMILEY PERSON.
THEN THAT'S...
...EVEN MORE REASON TO...
DON'T YOU KNOW EACH OTHER?
NO.
I'VE ONLY HEARD RUMORS.
RUMORS?
Senroh Chigusa...
...is very famous.
Even...
...just yesterday...

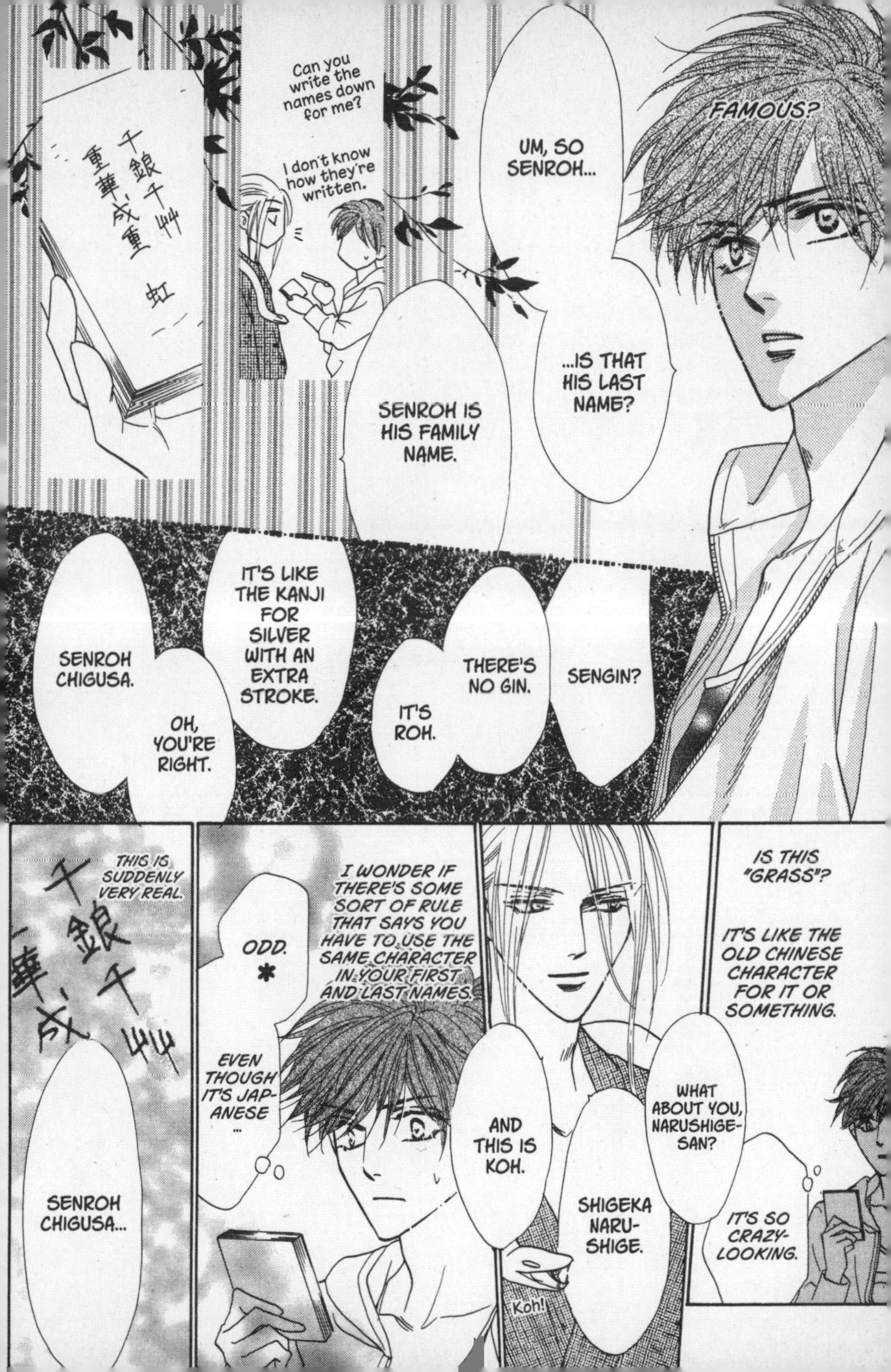
FAMOUS?
UM, SO SENROH...
...IS THAT HIS LAST NAME?
SENROH IS HIS FAMILY NAME.
Can you write the names down for me?
I don't know how they're written.
千銀千艸
重華成重
虹
SENGIN?
THERE'S NO GIN.
IT'S ROH.
IT'S LIKE THE KANJI FOR SILVER WITH AN EXTRA STROKE.
OH, YOU'RE RIGHT.
SENROH CHIGUSA.
IS THIS "GRASS"?
IT'S LIKE THE OLD CHINESE CHARACTER FOR IT OR SOMETHING.
IT'S SO CRAZY-LOOKING.
WHAT ABOUT YOU, NARUSHIGE-SAN?
SHIGEKA NARUSHIGE.
AND THIS IS KOH.
Koh!
I WONDER IF THERE'S SOME SORT OF RULE THAT SAYS YOU HAVE TO USE THE SAME CHARACTER IN YOUR FIRST AND LAST NAMES.
ODD. *
EVEN THOUGH IT'S JAPANESE...
THIS IS SUDDENLY VERY REAL.
千銀千艸
華成
SENROH CHIGUSA...

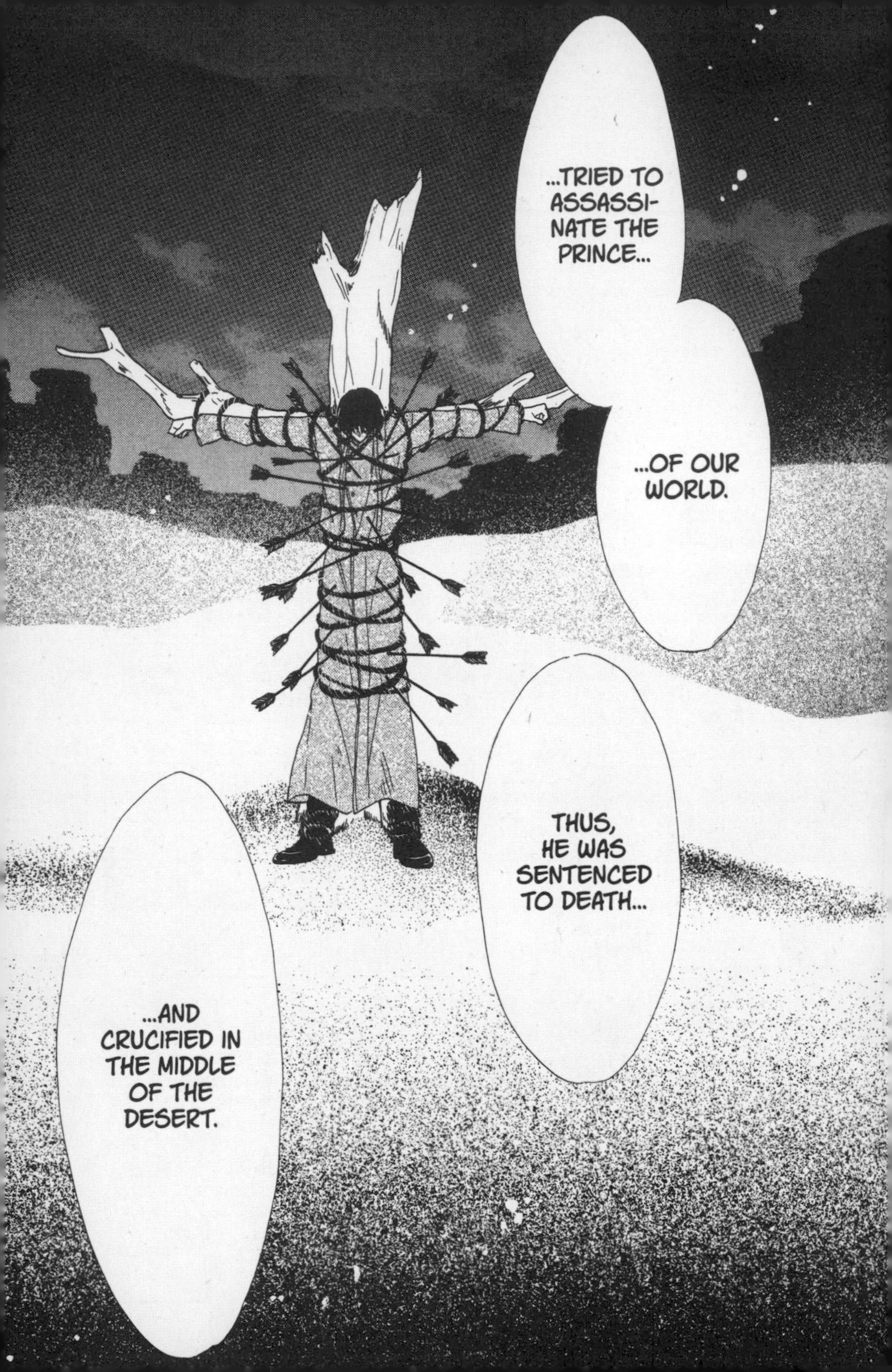
...TRIED TO ASSASSI-NATE THE PRINCE...
...OF OUR WORLD.
THUS, HE WAS SENTENCED TO DEATH...
...AND CRUCIFIED IN THE MIDDLE OF THE DESERT.

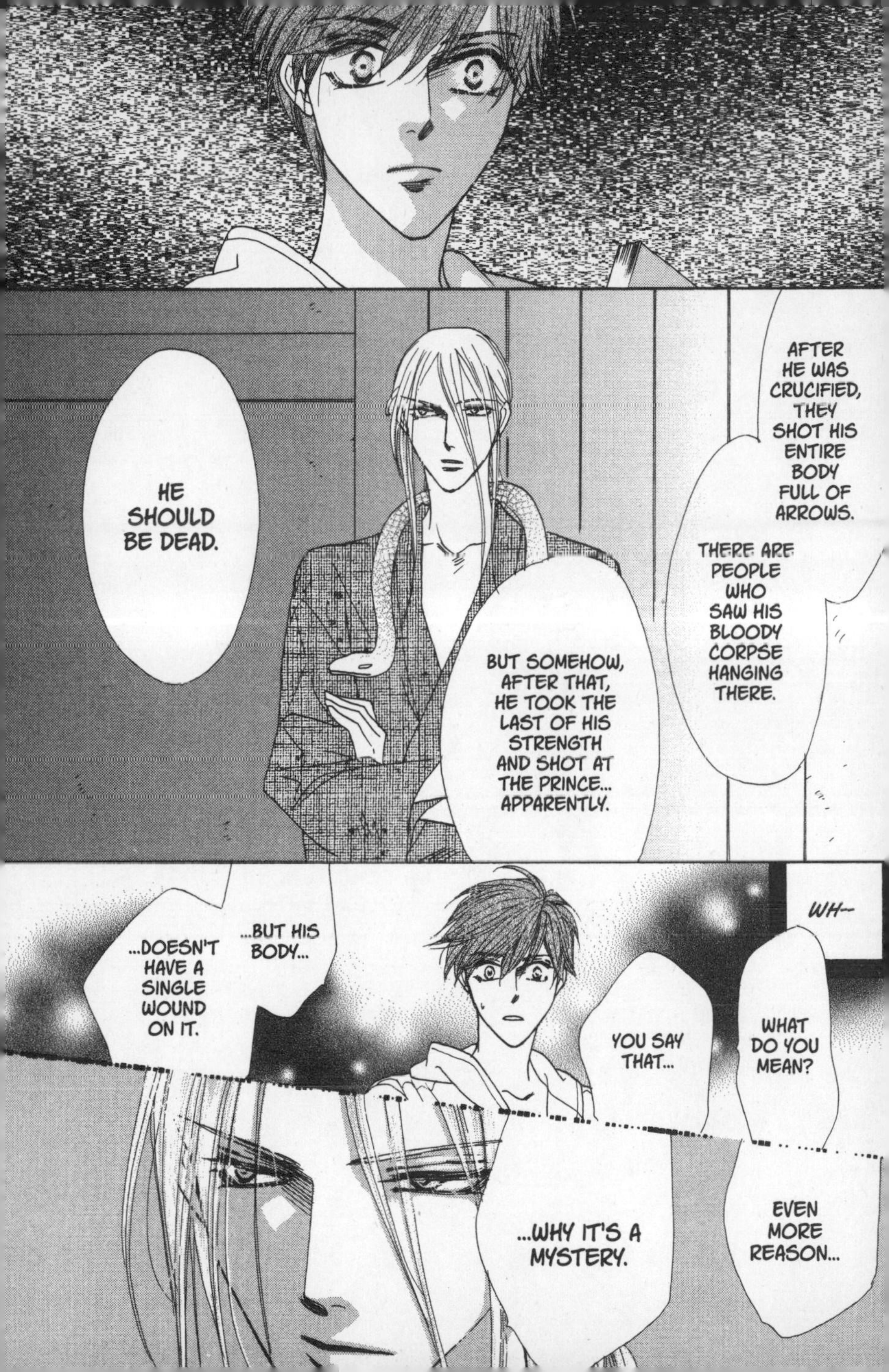
AFTER HE WAS CRUCIFIED, THEY SHOT HIS ENTIRE BODY FULL OF ARROWS.
THERE ARE PEOPLE WHO SAW HIS BLOODY CORPSE HANGING THERE.
BUT SOMEHOW, AFTER THAT, HE TOOK THE LAST OF HIS STRENGTH AND SHOT AT THE PRINCE... APPARENTLY.
HE SHOULD BE DEAD.
WH--
WHAT DO YOU MEAN?
YOU SAY THAT...
...BUT HIS BODY...
...DOESN'T HAVE A SINGLE WOUND ON IT.
EVEN MORE REASON...
...WHY IT'S A MYSTERY.

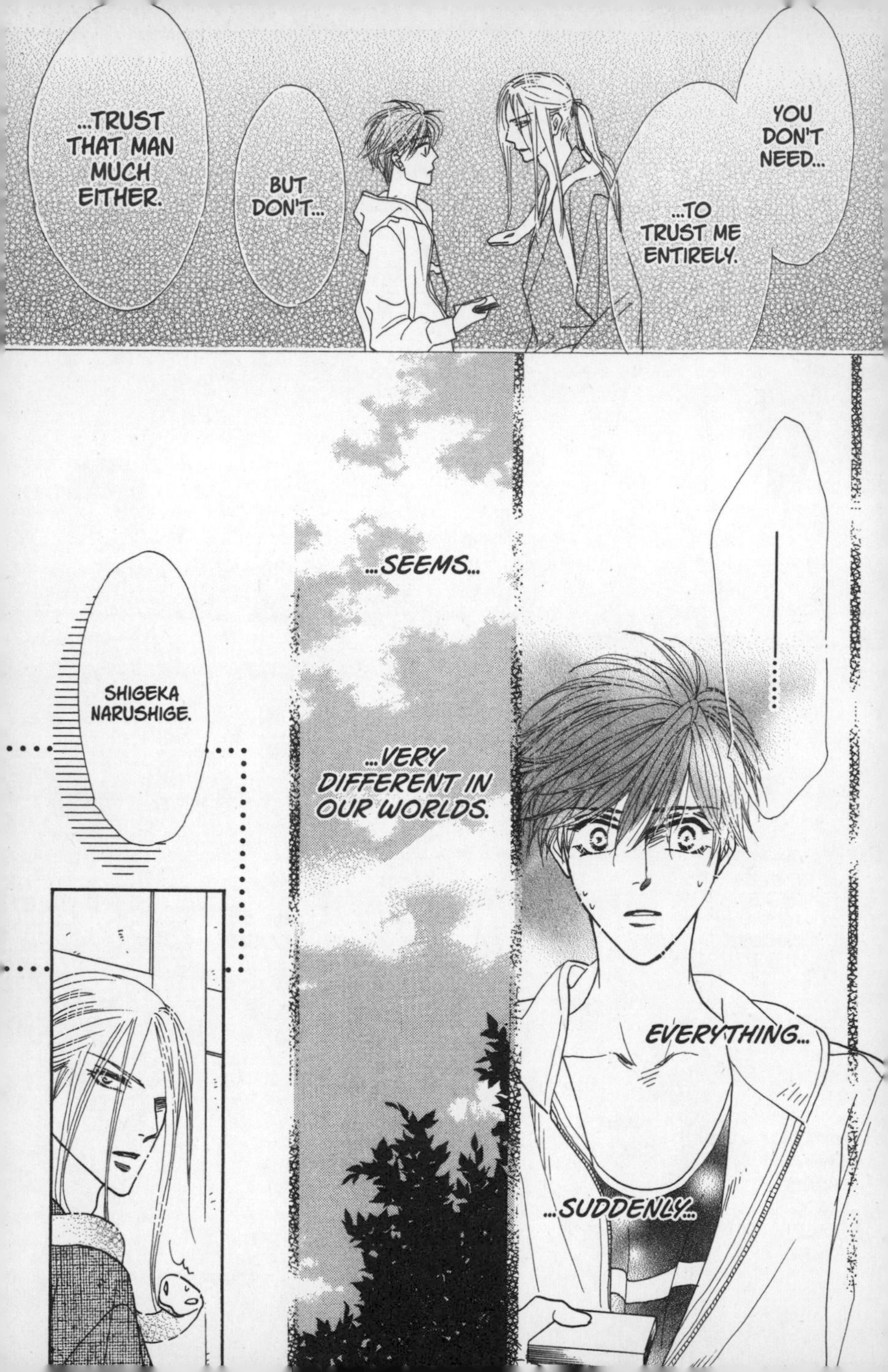

YOU DON'T NEED...
...TO TRUST ME ENTIRELY.
BUT DON'T...
...TRUST THAT MAN MUCH EITHER.
EVERYTHING...
...SUDDENLY...
...SEEMS...
...VERY DIFFERENT IN OUR WORLDS.
SHIGEKA NARUSHIGE.

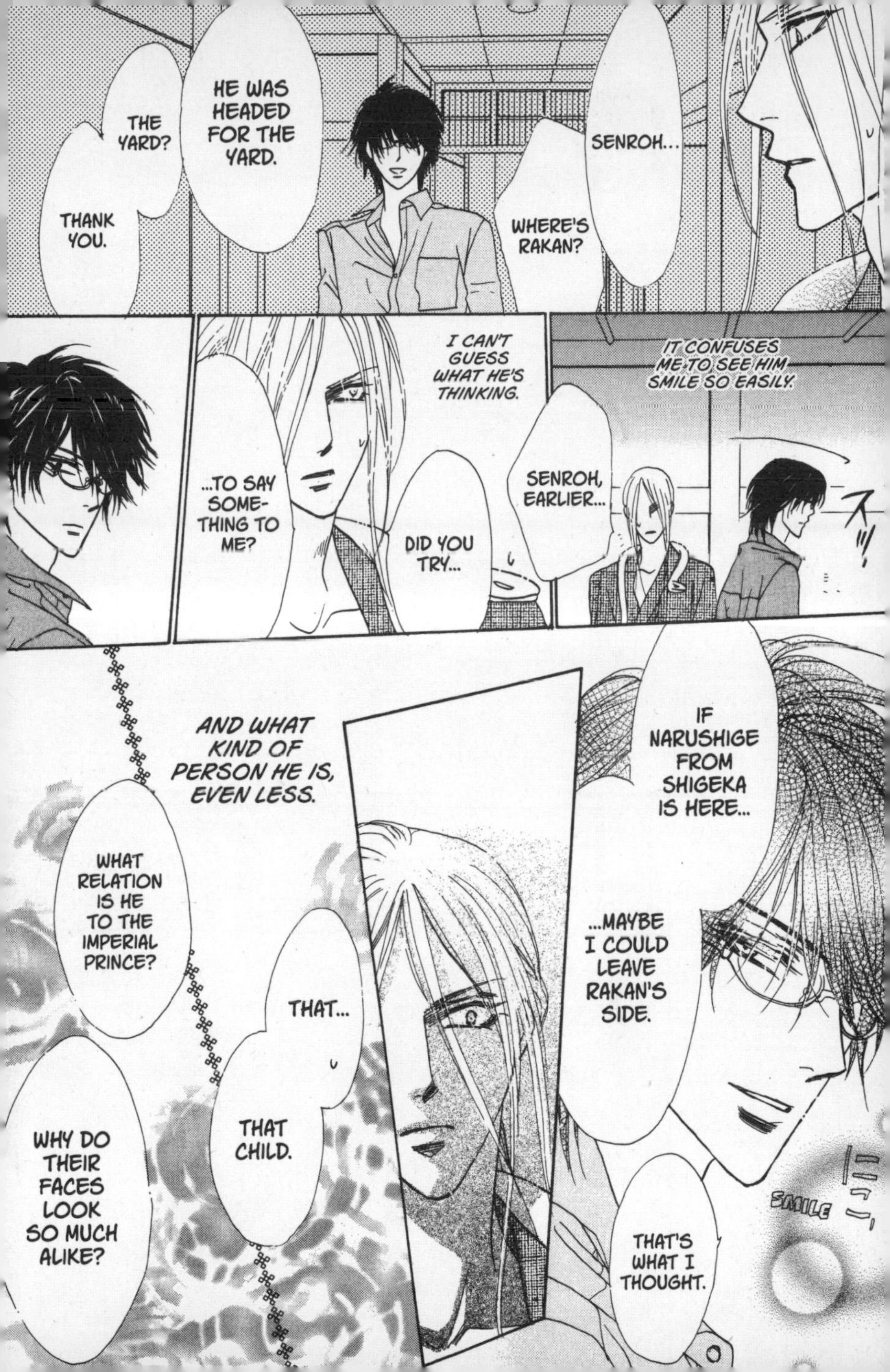
SENROH...
WHERE'S RAKAN?
HE WAS HEADED FOR THE YARD.
THE YARD?
THANK YOU.
IT CONFUSES ME TO SEE HIM SMILE SO EASILY.
SENROH, EARLIER...
I CAN'T GUESS WHAT HE'S THINKING.
DID YOU TRY...
...TO SAY SOME-THING TO ME?
IF NARUSHIGE FROM SHIGEKA IS HERE...
...MAYBE I COULD LEAVE RAKAN'S SIDE.
SMILE
THAT'S WHAT I THOUGHT.
AND WHAT KIND OF PERSON HE IS, EVEN LESS.
THAT...
THAT CHILD.
WHAT RELATION IS HE TO THE IMPERIAL PRINCE?
WHY DO THEIR FACES LOOK SO MUCH ALIKE?

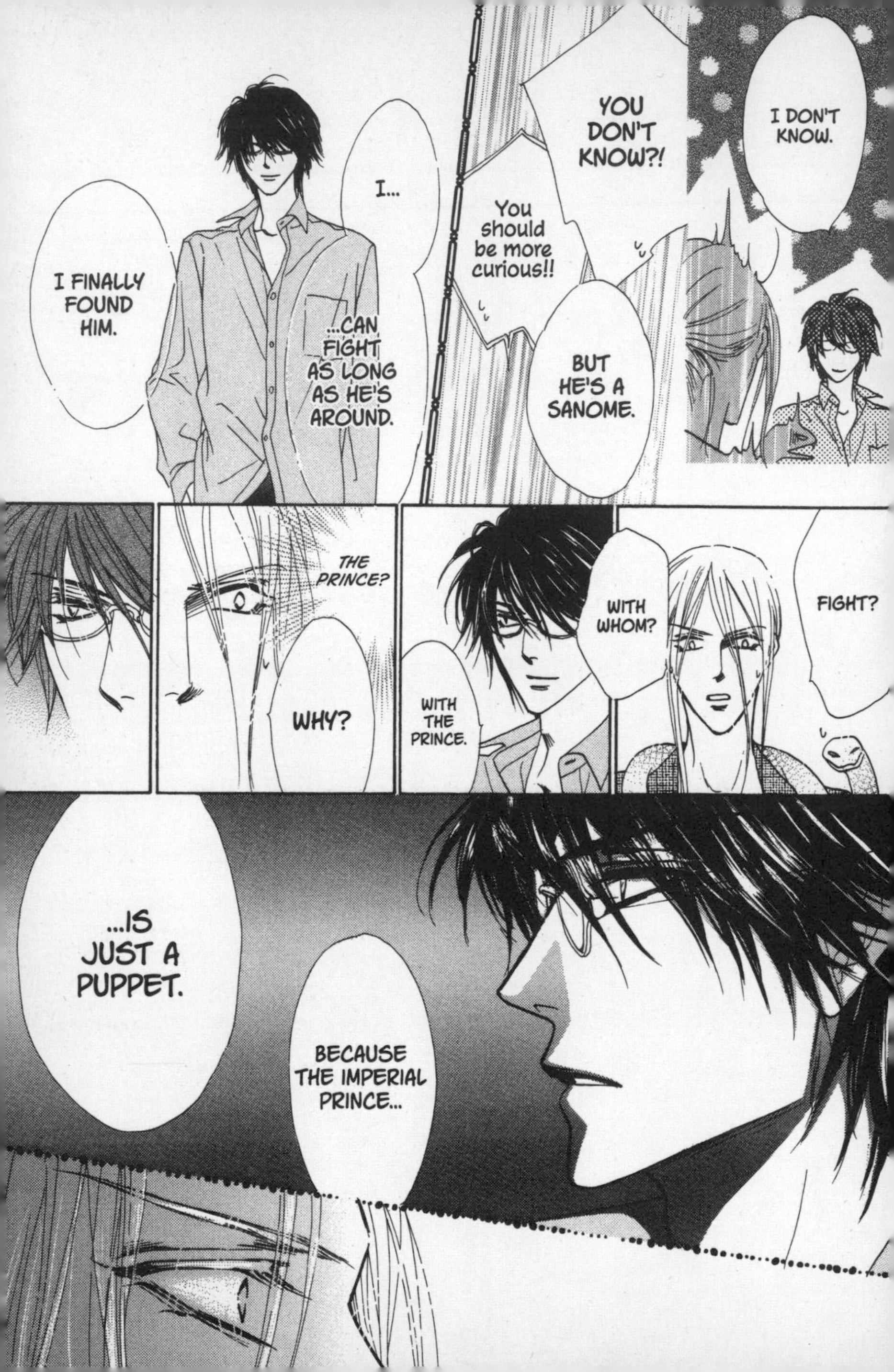
I DON'T KNOW.
YOU DON'T KNOW?!
You should be more curious!!
BUT HE'S A SANOME.
I...
...CAN FIGHT AS LONG AS HE'S AROUND.
I FINALLY FOUND HIM.
FIGHT?
WITH WHOM?
WITH THE PRINCE.
THE PRINCE?
WHY?
BECAUSE THE IMPERIAL PRINCE...
...IS JUST A PUPPET.

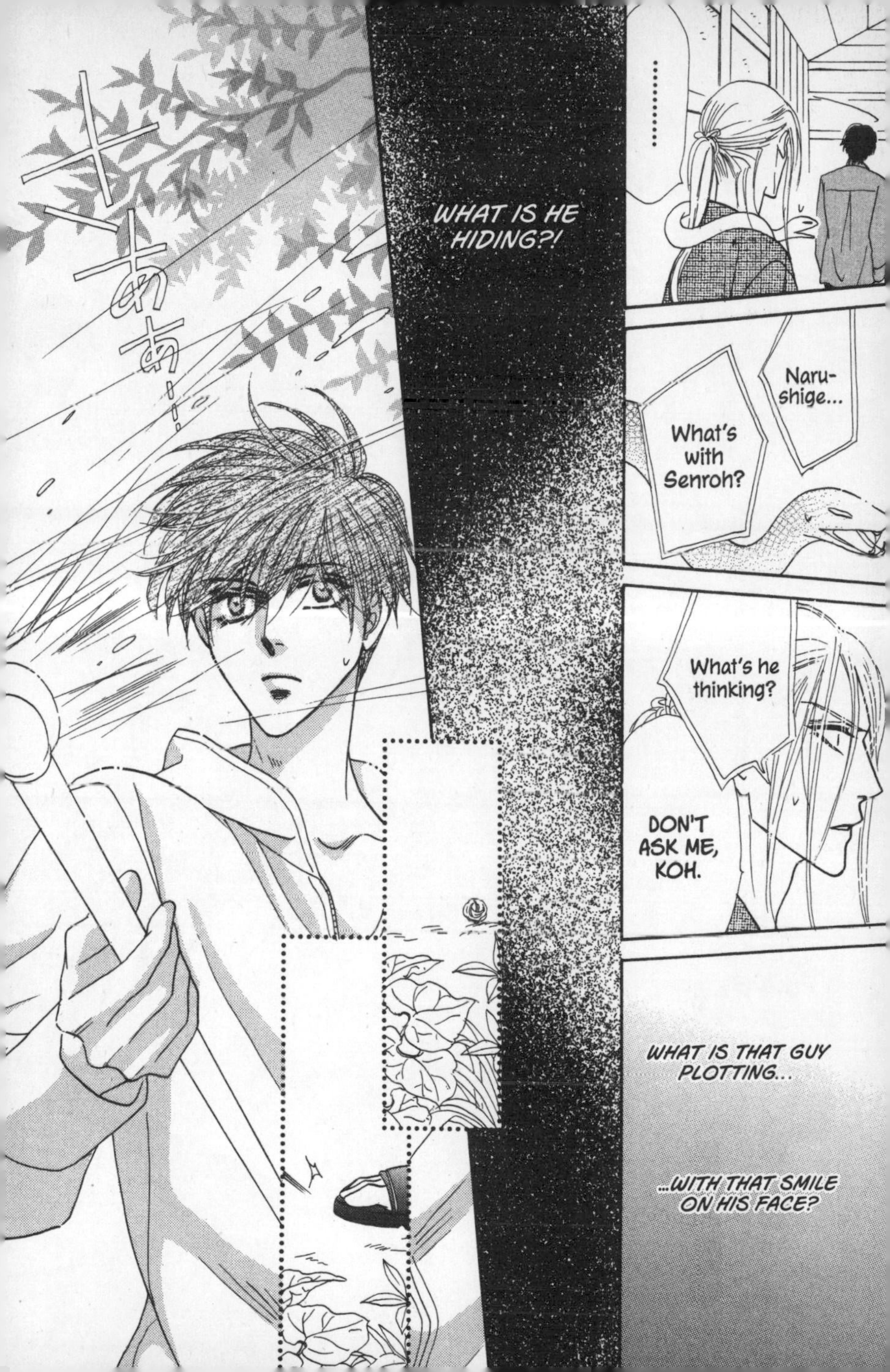
......
Naru-shige...
What's with Senroh?
What's he thinking?
DON'T ASK ME, KOH.
WHAT IS THAT GUY PLOTTING...
...WITH THAT SMILE ON HIS FACE?
WHAT IS HE HIDING?!
キャああ!!

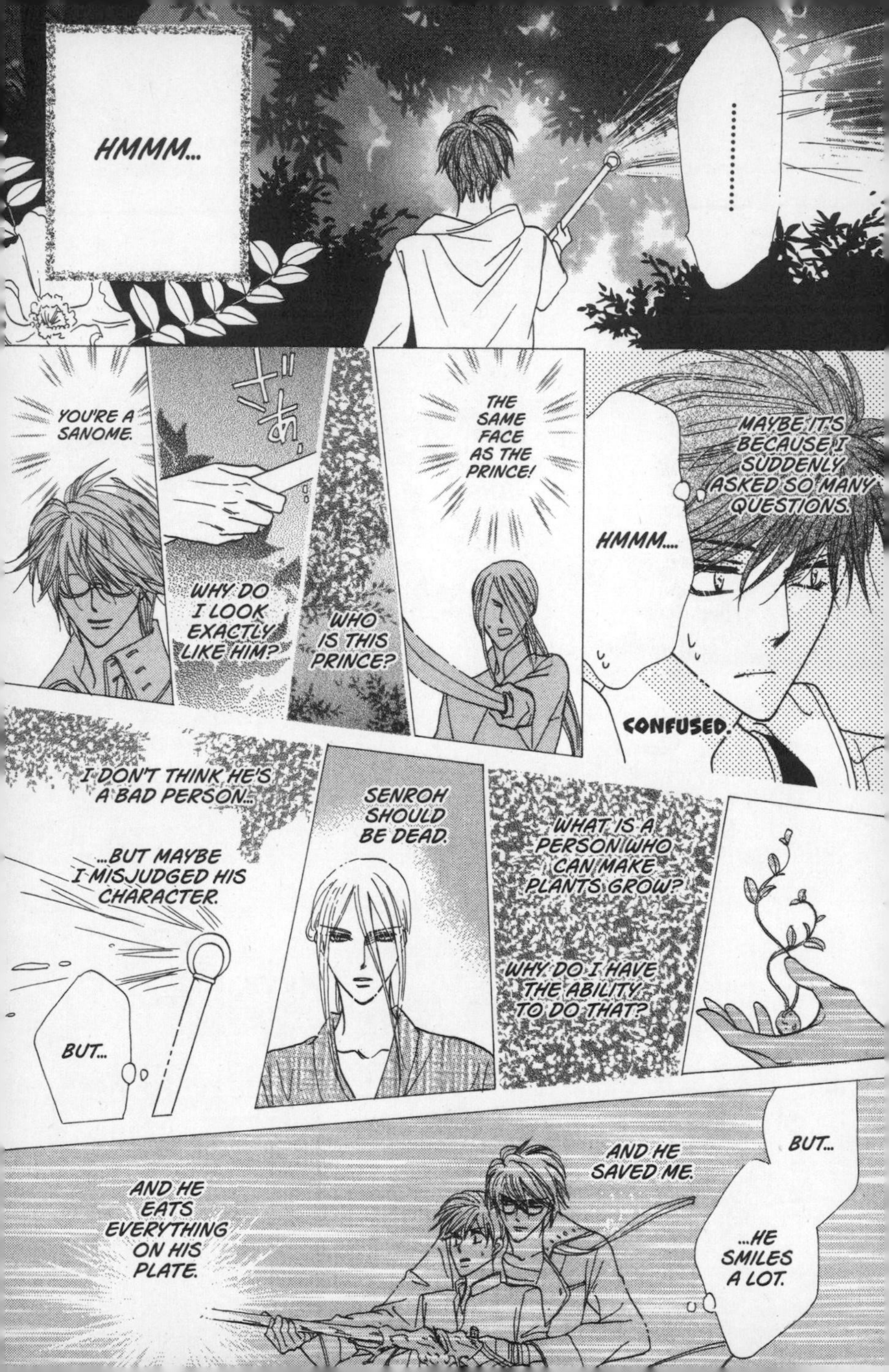

......
HMMM...
MAYBE IT'S BECAUSE I SUDDENLY ASKED SO MANY QUESTIONS.
HMMM....
CONFUSED.
THE SAME FACE AS THE PRINCE!
WHO IS THIS PRINCE?
ざあ
WHY DO I LOOK EXACTLY LIKE HIM?
YOU'RE A SANOME.
WHAT IS A PERSON WHO CAN MAKE PLANTS GROW?
WHY DO I HAVE THE ABILITY TO DO THAT?
SENROH SHOULD BE DEAD.
I DON'T THINK HE'S A BAD PERSON...
...BUT MAYBE I MISJUDGED HIS CHARACTER.
BUT...
BUT...
...HE SMILES A LOT.
AND HE SAVED ME.
AND HE EATS EVERYTHING ON HIS PLATE.

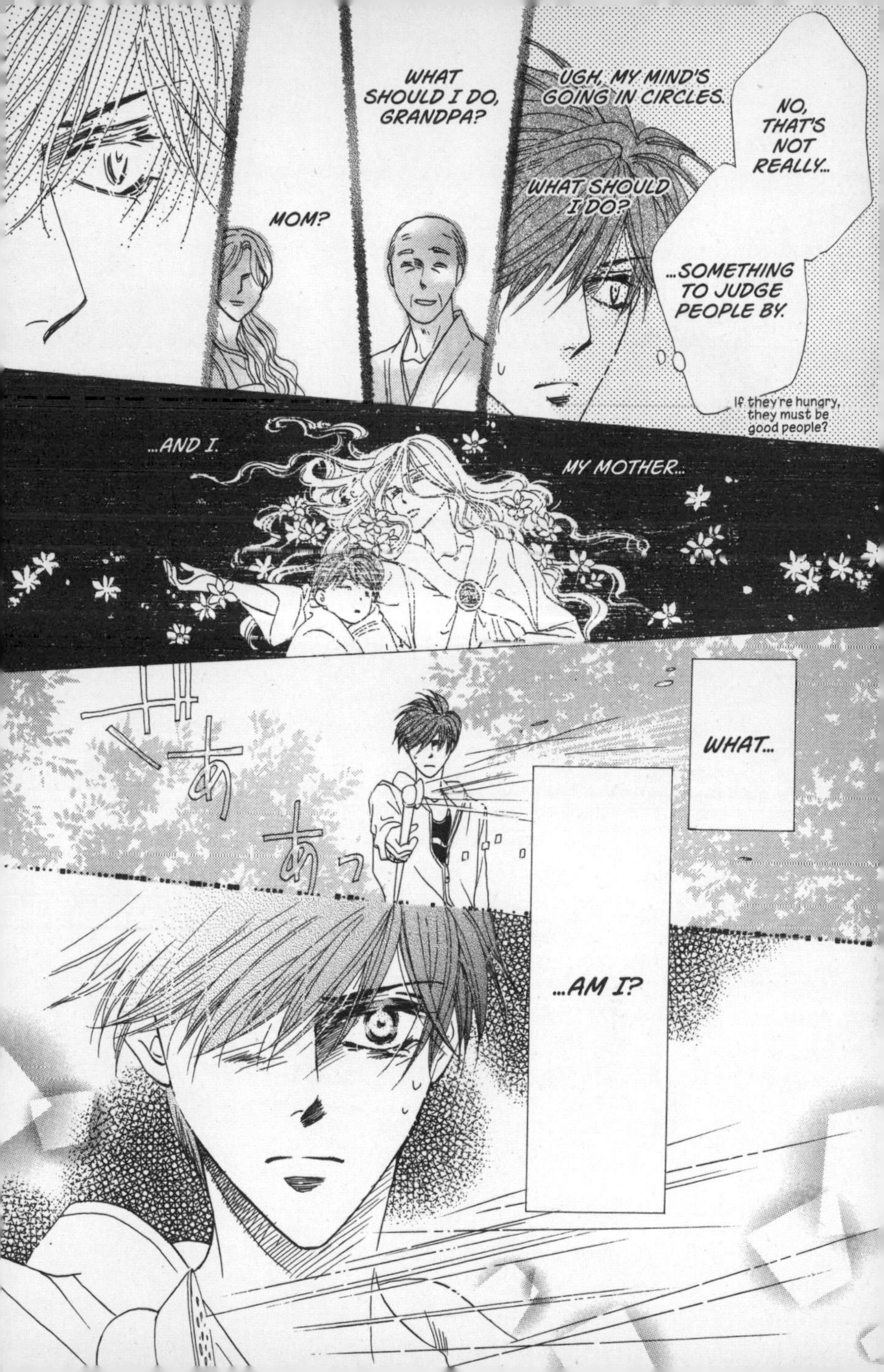

UGH, MY MIND'S GOING IN CIRCLES.
WHAT SHOULD I DO?
NO, THAT'S NOT REALLY...
...SOMETHING TO JUDGE PEOPLE BY.
If they're hungry, they must be good people?
WHAT SHOULD I DO, GRANDPA?
MOM?
MY MOTHER...
...AND I.
WHAT...
あ
あっ
...AM I?

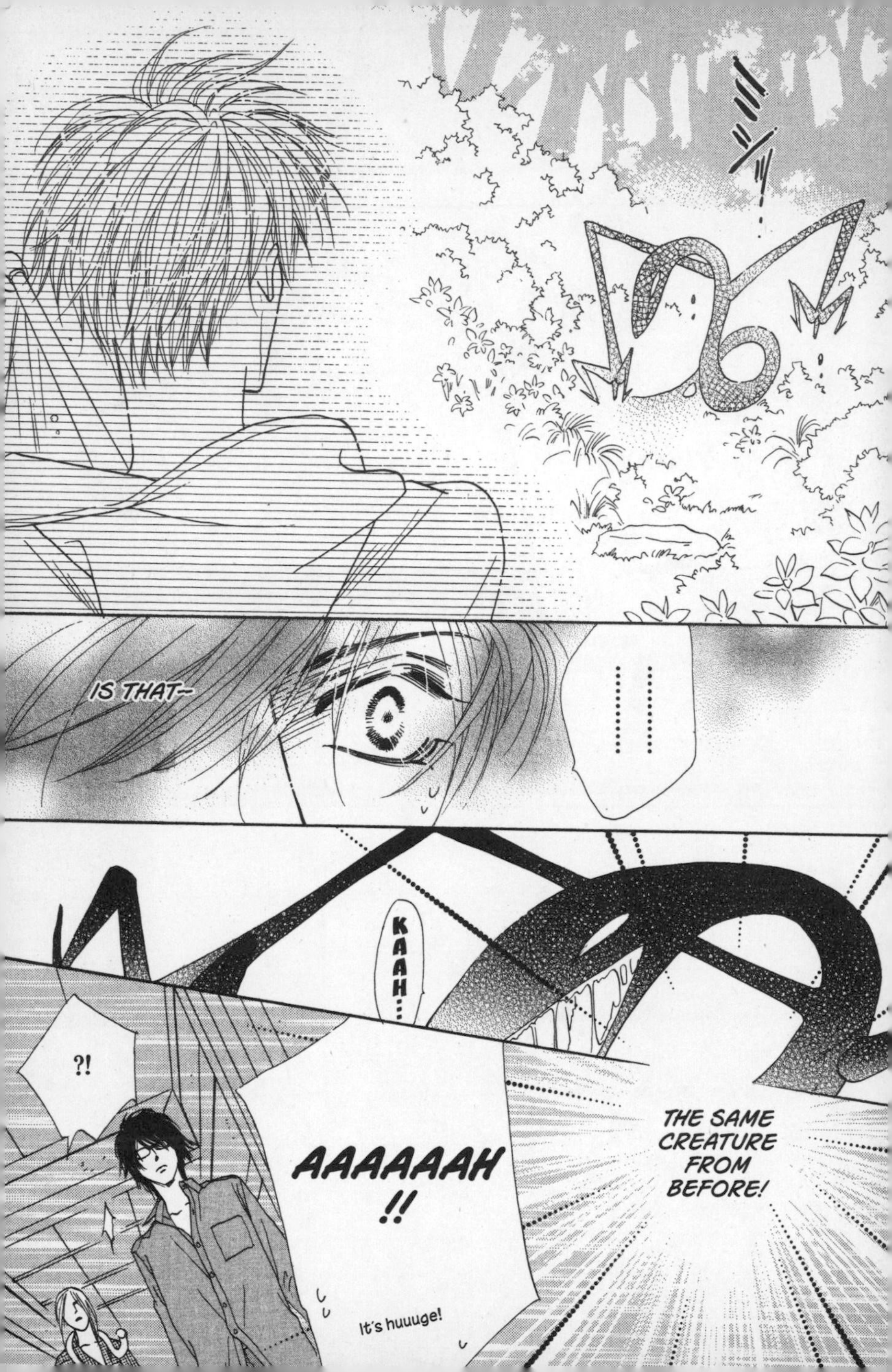
!!
IS THAT--
KAAH...
THE SAME CREATURE FROM BEFORE!
AAAAAAH!!
?!
It's huuuge!

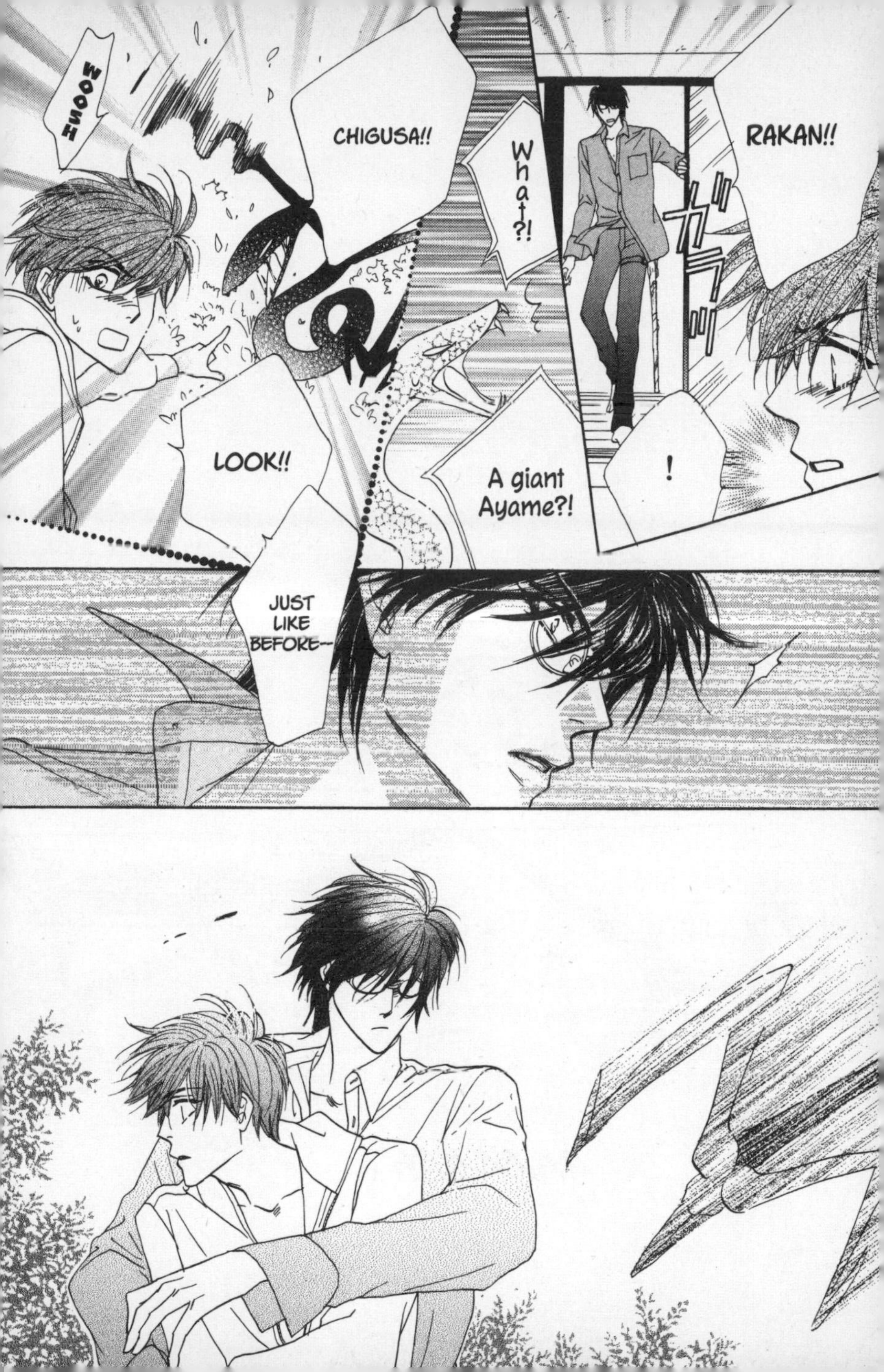
RAKAN!!
ガラッ
!
What?!
A giant Ayame?!
WOOSH
CHIGUSA!!
LOOK!!
JUST LIKE BEFORE--

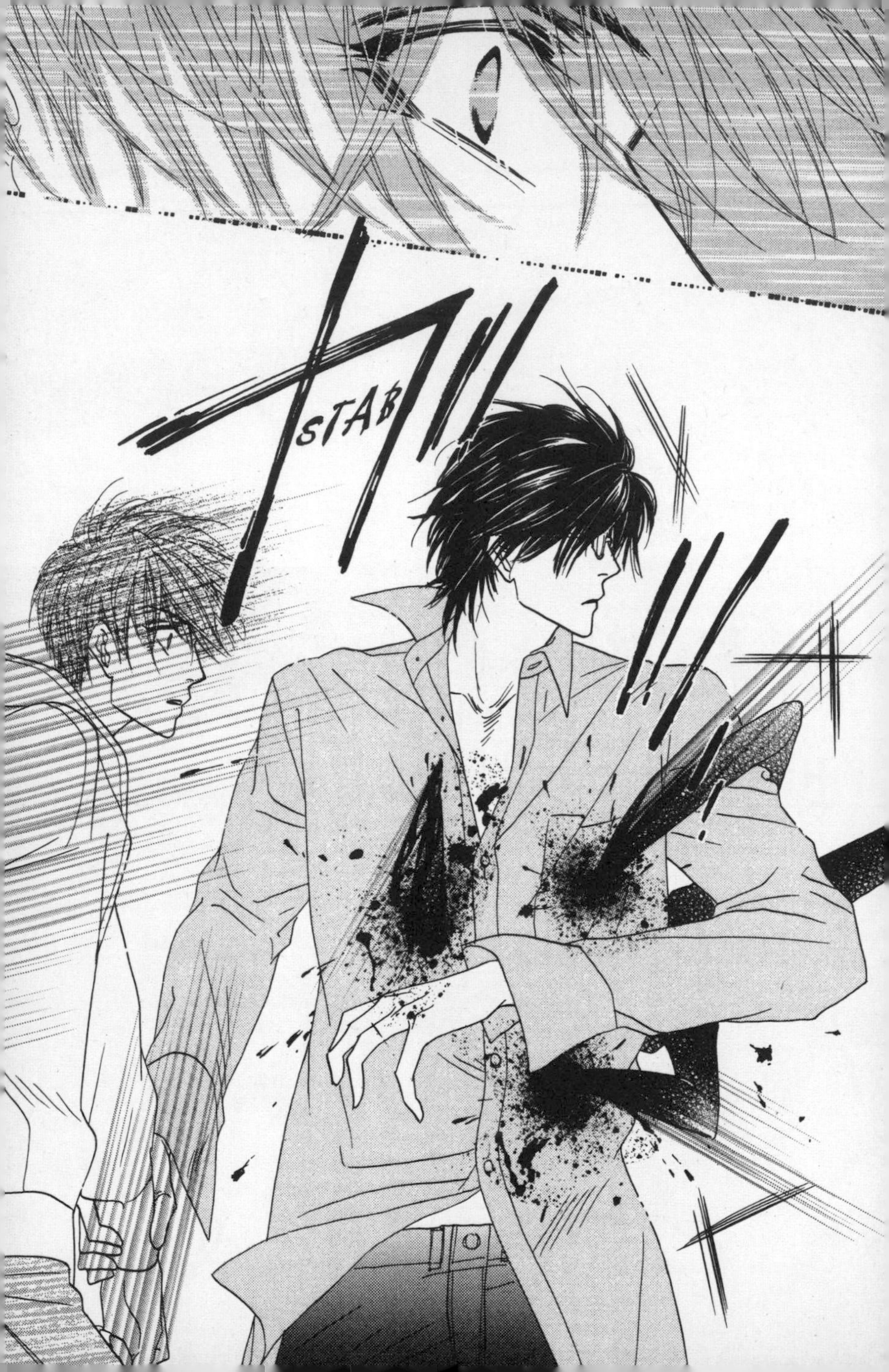
STAB

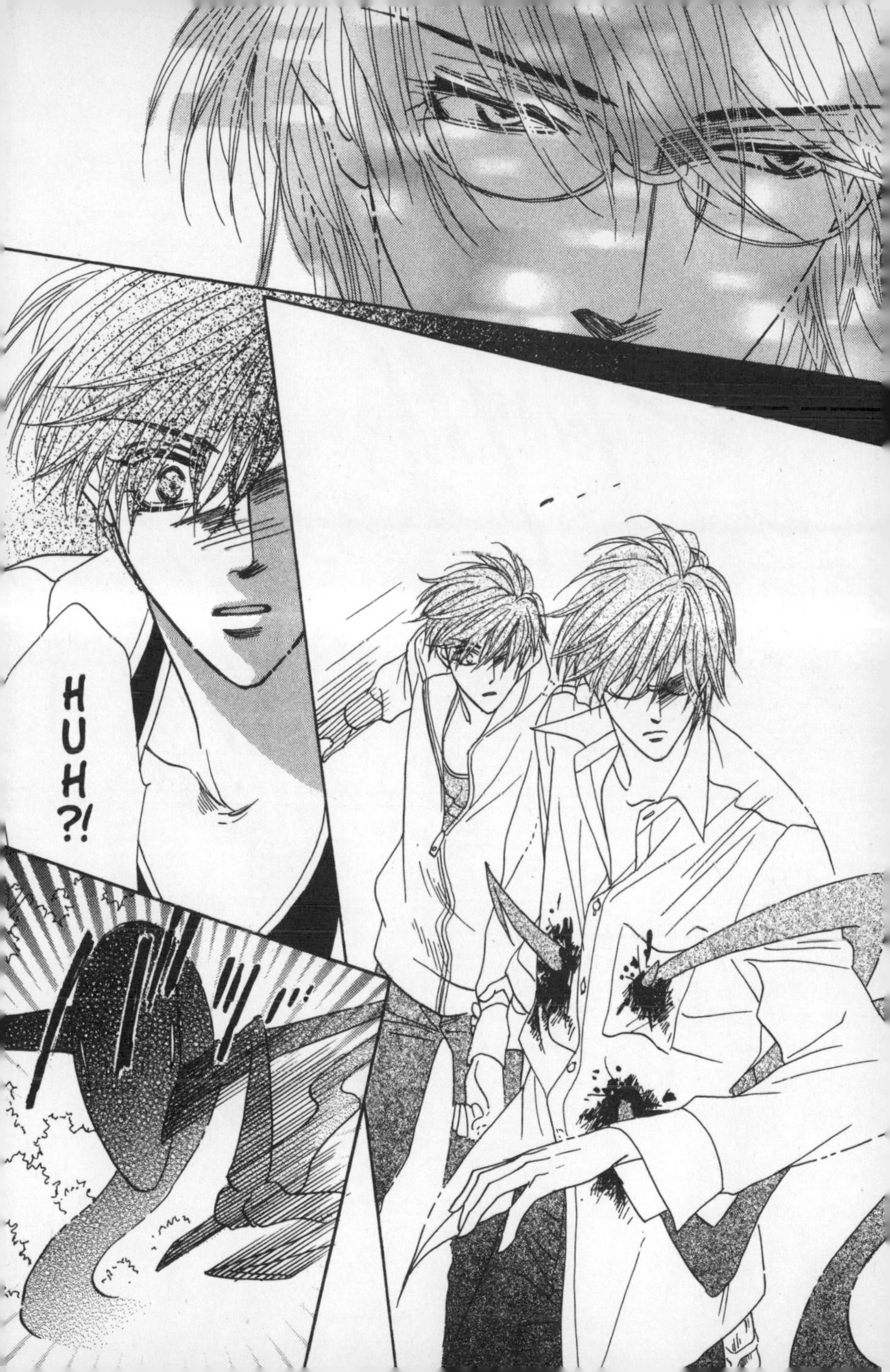
HUH?!

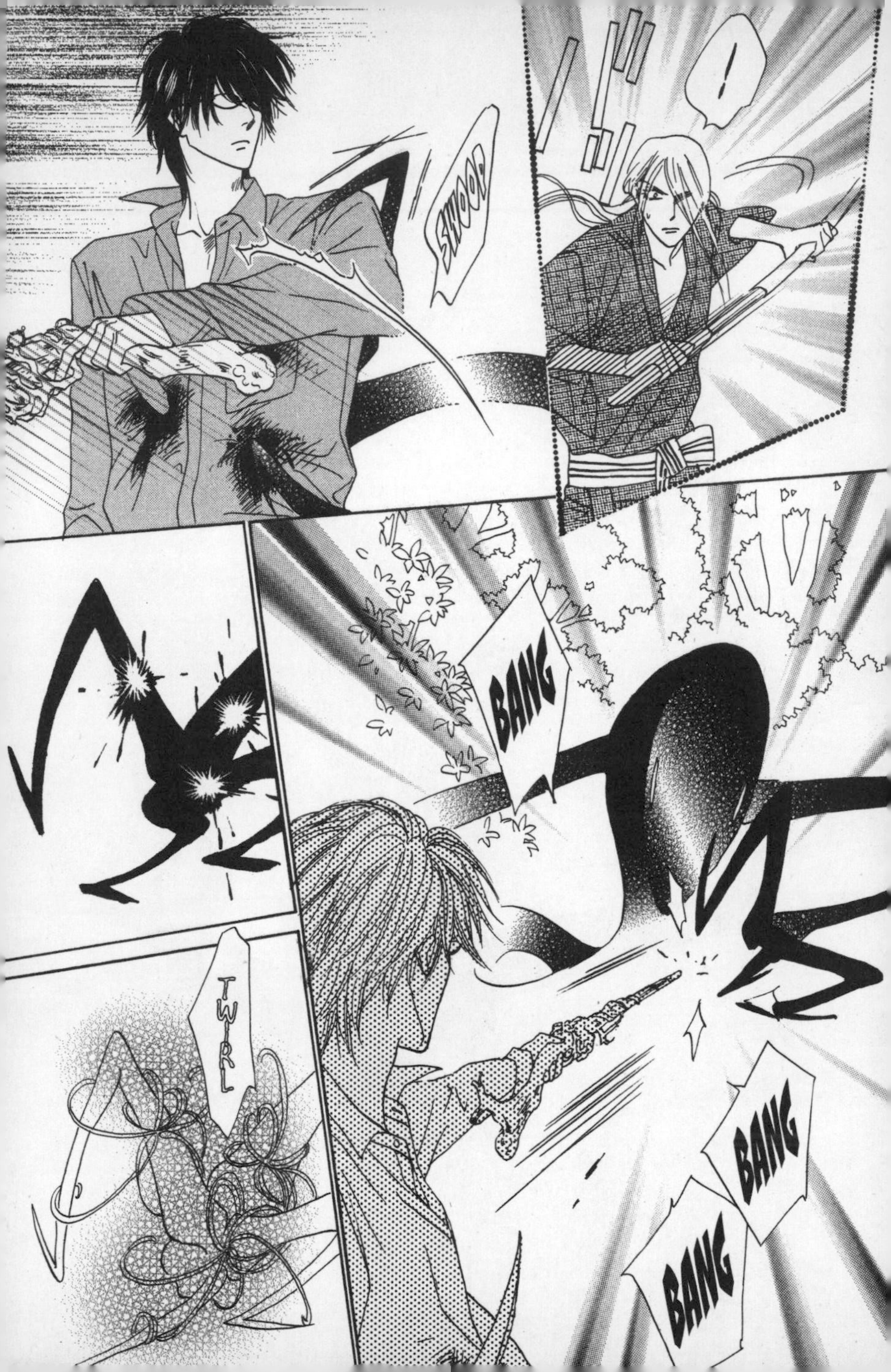
!
SHOOP
BANG
BANG
BANG
BANG
TWIRL

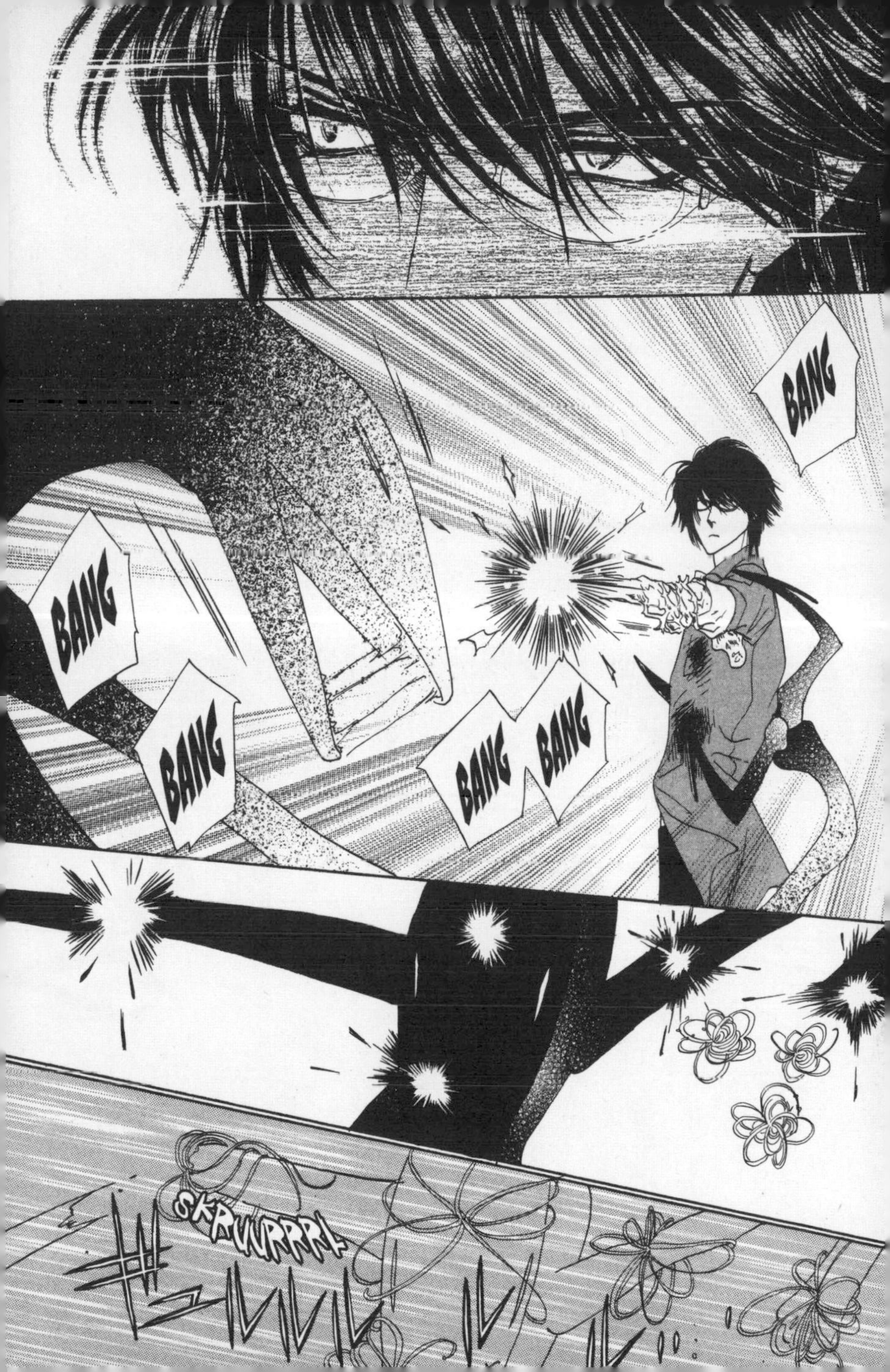
BANG
BANG
BANG
BANG
BANG
SKRUURRRL

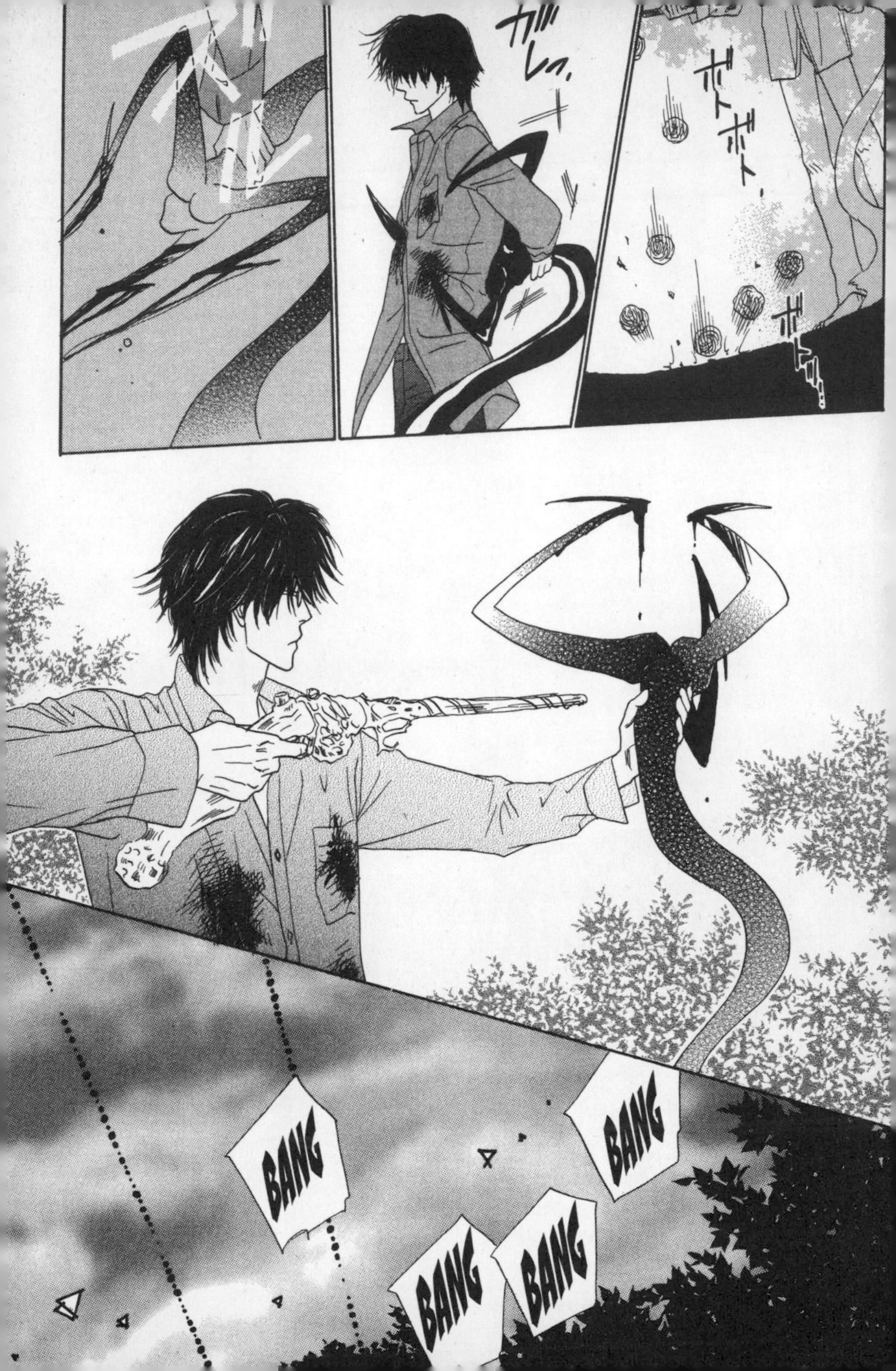
ボトボト、
ボト…
BANG
BANG
BANG
BANG

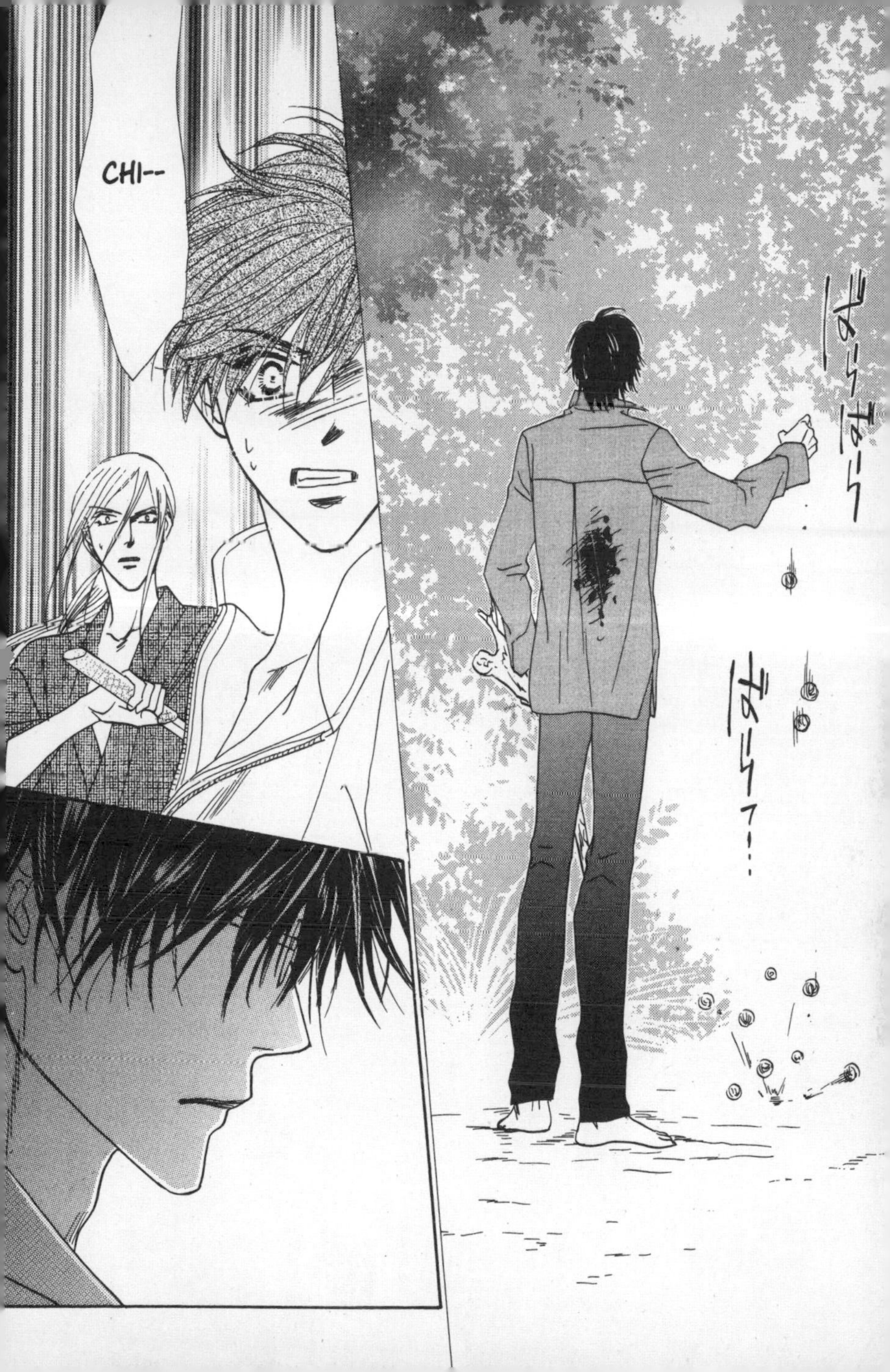
CHI--

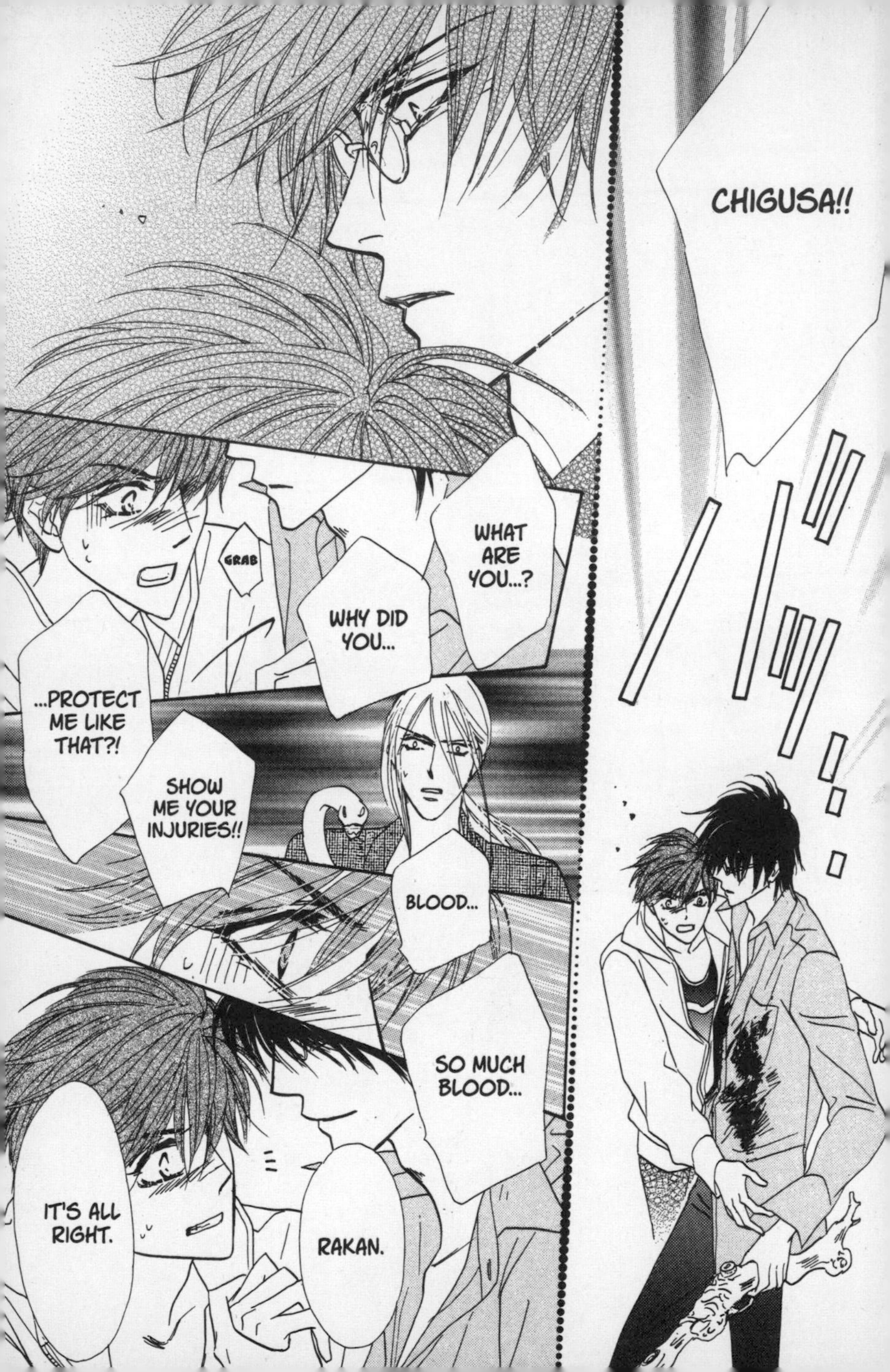
CHIGUSA!!
WHAT ARE YOU...?
GRAB
WHY DID YOU...
...PROTECT ME LIKE THAT?!
SHOW ME YOUR INJURIES!!
BLOOD...
SO MUCH BLOOD...
RAKAN.
IT'S ALL RIGHT.

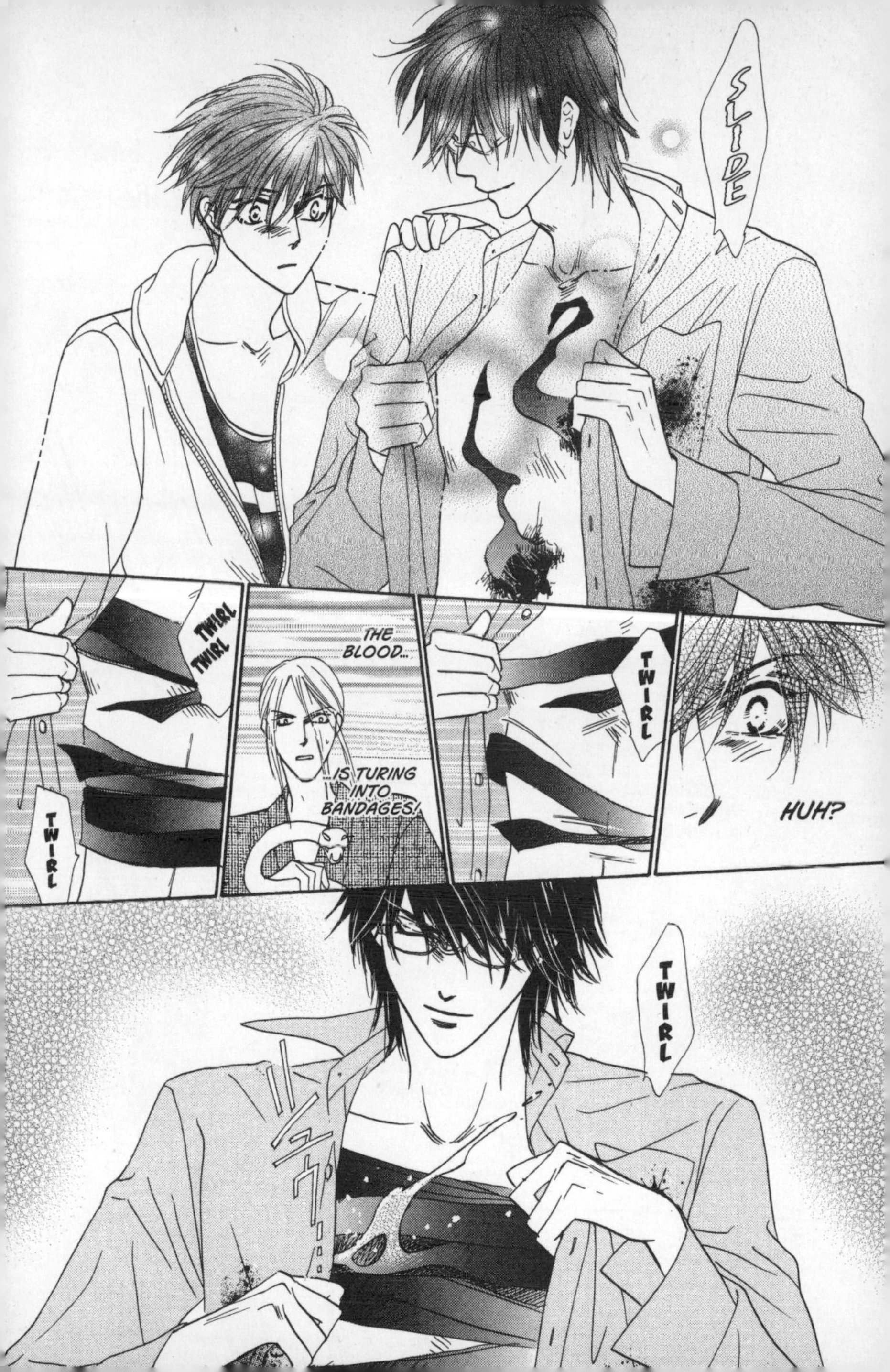
SLIDE
HUH?
TWIRL
THE BLOOD...
...IS TURING INTO BANDAGES!
TWIRL TWIRL
TWIRL
TWIRL

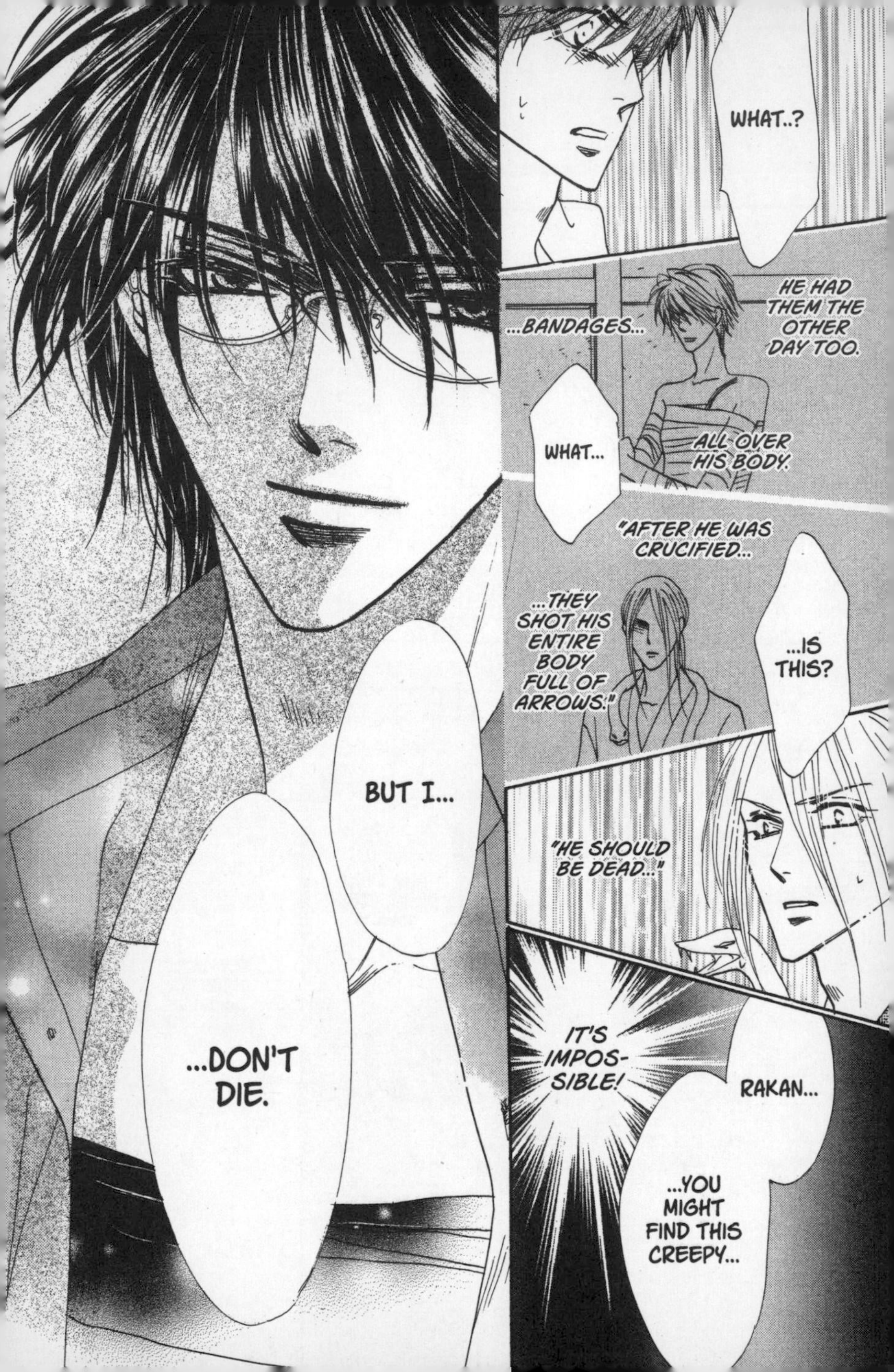
WHAT..?
HE HAD THEM THE OTHER DAY TOO.
...BANDAGES...
ALL OVER HIS BODY.
WHAT...
...IS THIS?
"AFTER HE WAS CRUCIFIED...
...THEY SHOT HIS ENTIRE BODY FULL OF ARROWS."
"HE SHOULD BE DEAD..."
RAKAN...
IT'S IMPOSSIBLE!
...YOU MIGHT FIND THIS CREEPY...
BUT I...
...DON'T DIE.

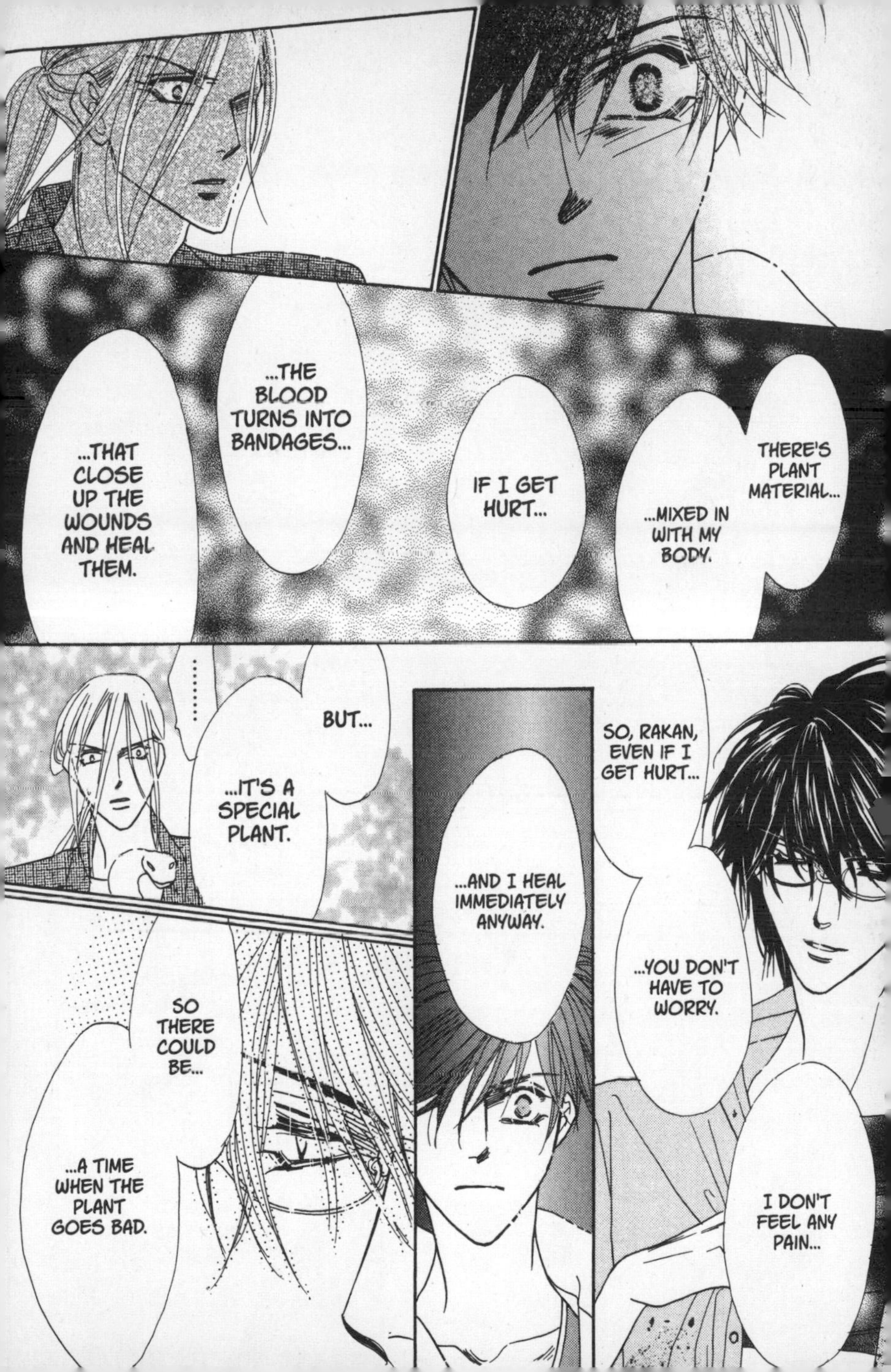
THERE'S PLANT MATERIAL...
...MIXED IN WITH MY BODY.
IF I GET HURT...
...THE BLOOD TURNS INTO BANDAGES...
...THAT CLOSE UP THE WOUNDS AND HEAL THEM.
SO, RAKAN, EVEN IF I GET HURT...
...YOU DON'T HAVE TO WORRY.
I DON'T FEEL ANY PAIN...
...AND I HEAL IMMEDIATELY ANYWAY.
......
BUT...
...IT'S A SPECIAL PLANT.
SO THERE COULD BE...
...A TIME WHEN THE PLANT GOES BAD.

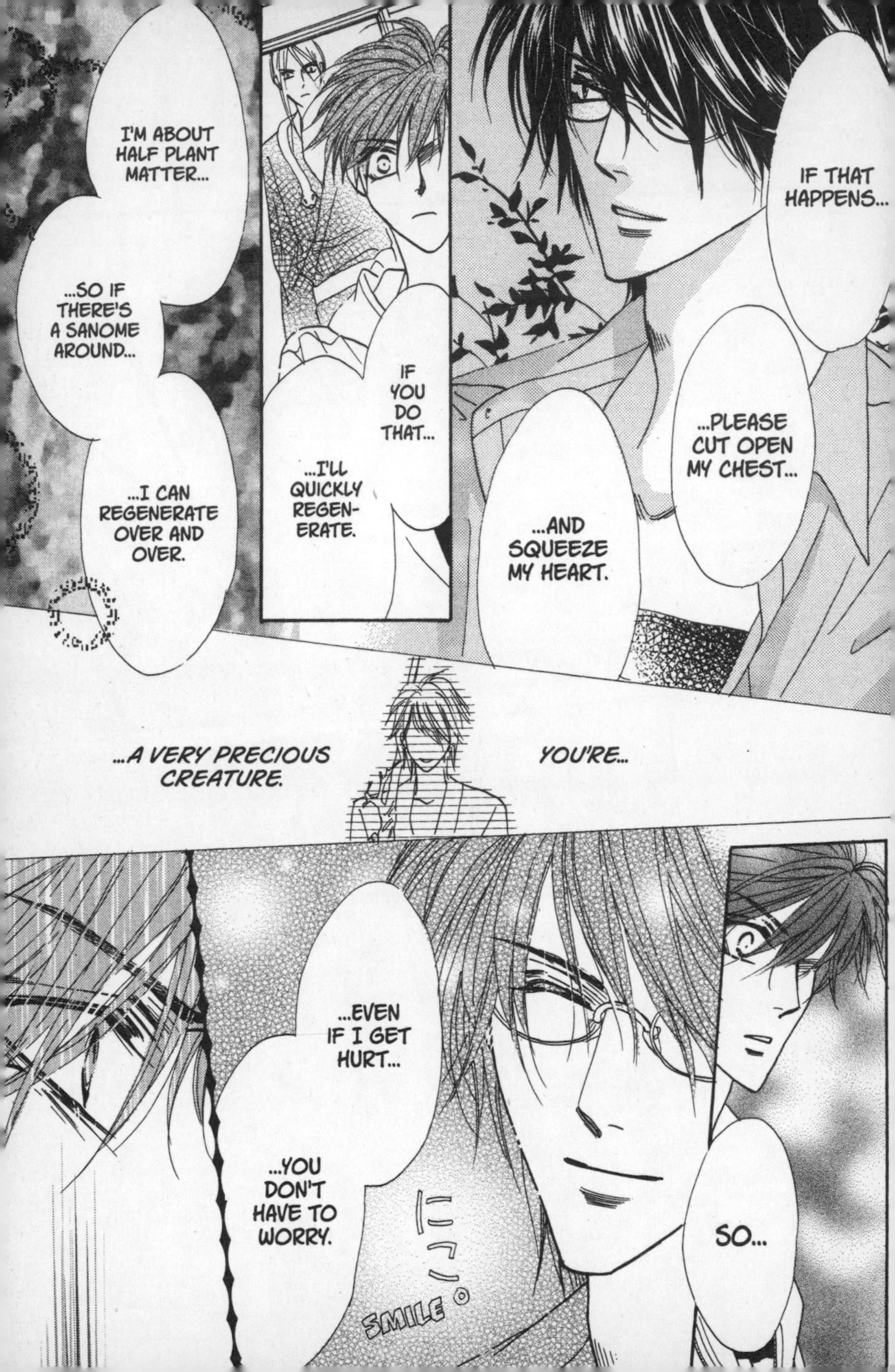
IF THAT HAPPENS...
...PLEASE CUT OPEN MY CHEST...
...AND SQUEEZE MY HEART.
IF YOU DO THAT...
...I'LL QUICKLY REGENERATE.
I'M ABOUT HALF PLANT MATTER...
...SO IF THERE'S A SANOME AROUND...
...I CAN REGENERATE OVER AND OVER.
YOU'RE...
...A VERY PRECIOUS CREATURE.
SO...
...EVEN IF I GET HURT...
...YOU DON'T HAVE TO WORRY.
SMILE

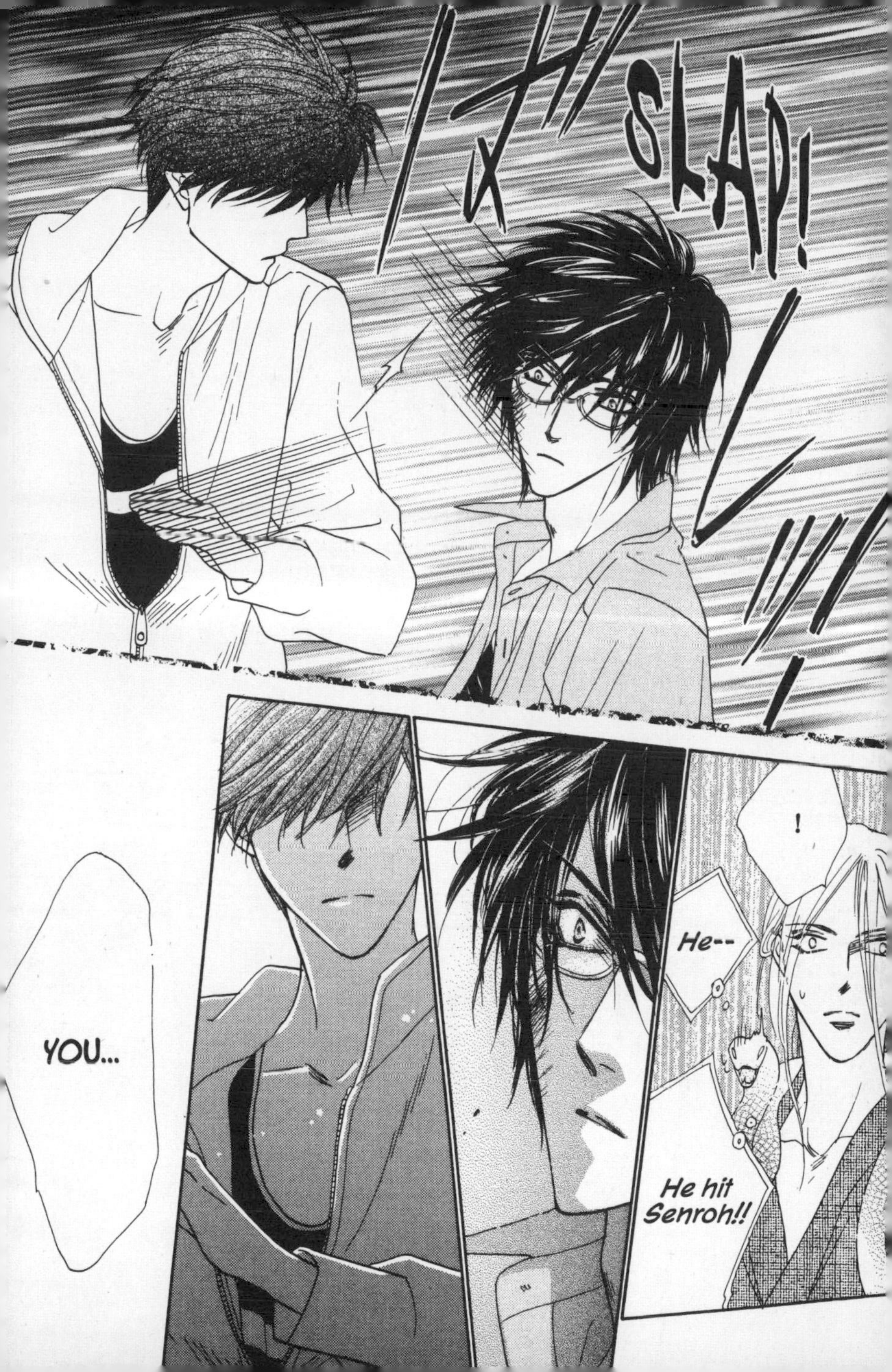
SLAP!
!
He--
He hit Senroh!!
YOU...

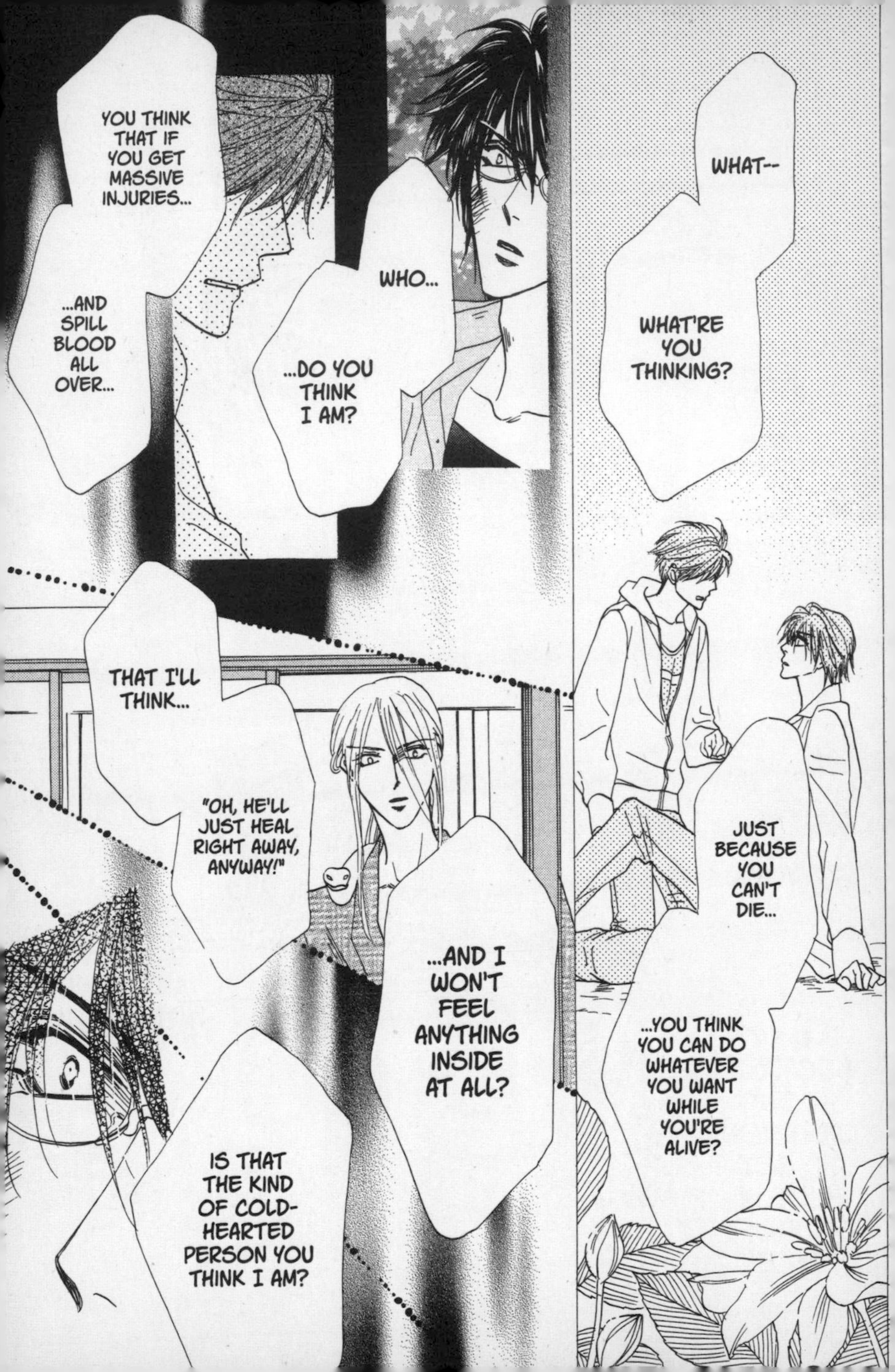
WHAT--
WHAT'RE YOU THINKING?
JUST BECAUSE YOU CAN'T DIE...
...YOU THINK YOU CAN DO WHATEVER YOU WANT WHILE YOU'RE ALIVE?
WHO...
...DO YOU THINK I AM?
YOU THINK THAT IF YOU GET MASSIVE INJURIES...
...AND SPILL BLOOD ALL OVER...
THAT I'LL THINK...
"OH, HE'LL JUST HEAL RIGHT AWAY, ANYWAY!"
...AND I WON'T FEEL ANYTHING INSIDE AT ALL?
IS THAT THE KIND OF COLD-HEARTED PERSON YOU THINK I AM?

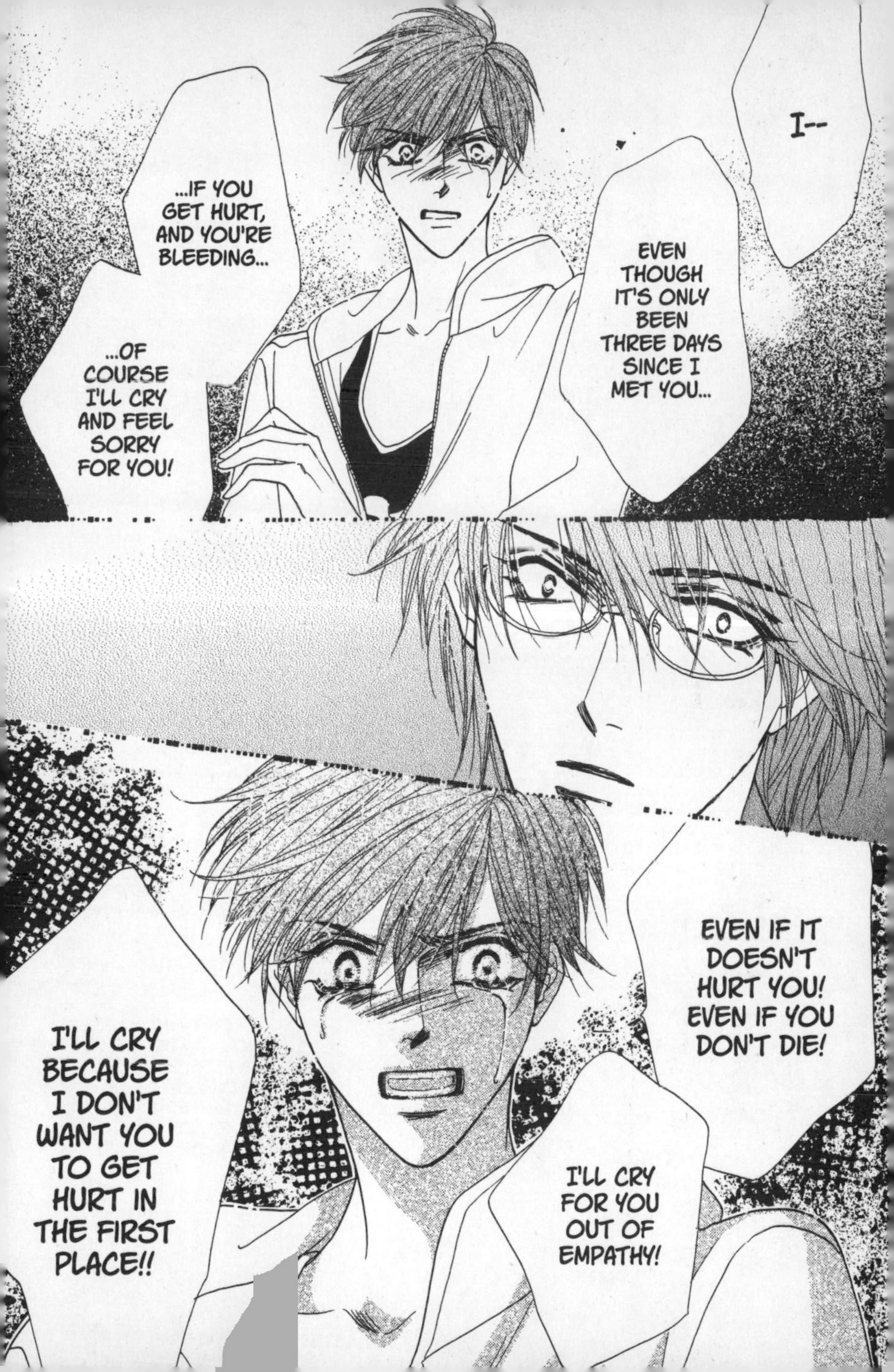
I--
EVEN THOUGH IT'S ONLY BEEN THREE DAYS SINCE I MET YOU...
...IF YOU GET HURT, AND YOU'RE BLEEDING...
...OF COURSE I'LL CRY AND FEEL SORRY FOR YOU!
EVEN IF IT DOESN'T HURT YOU! EVEN IF YOU DON'T DIE!
I'LL CRY FOR YOU OUT OF EMPATHY!
I'LL CRY BECAUSE I DON'T WANT YOU TO GET HURT IN THE FIRST PLACE!!

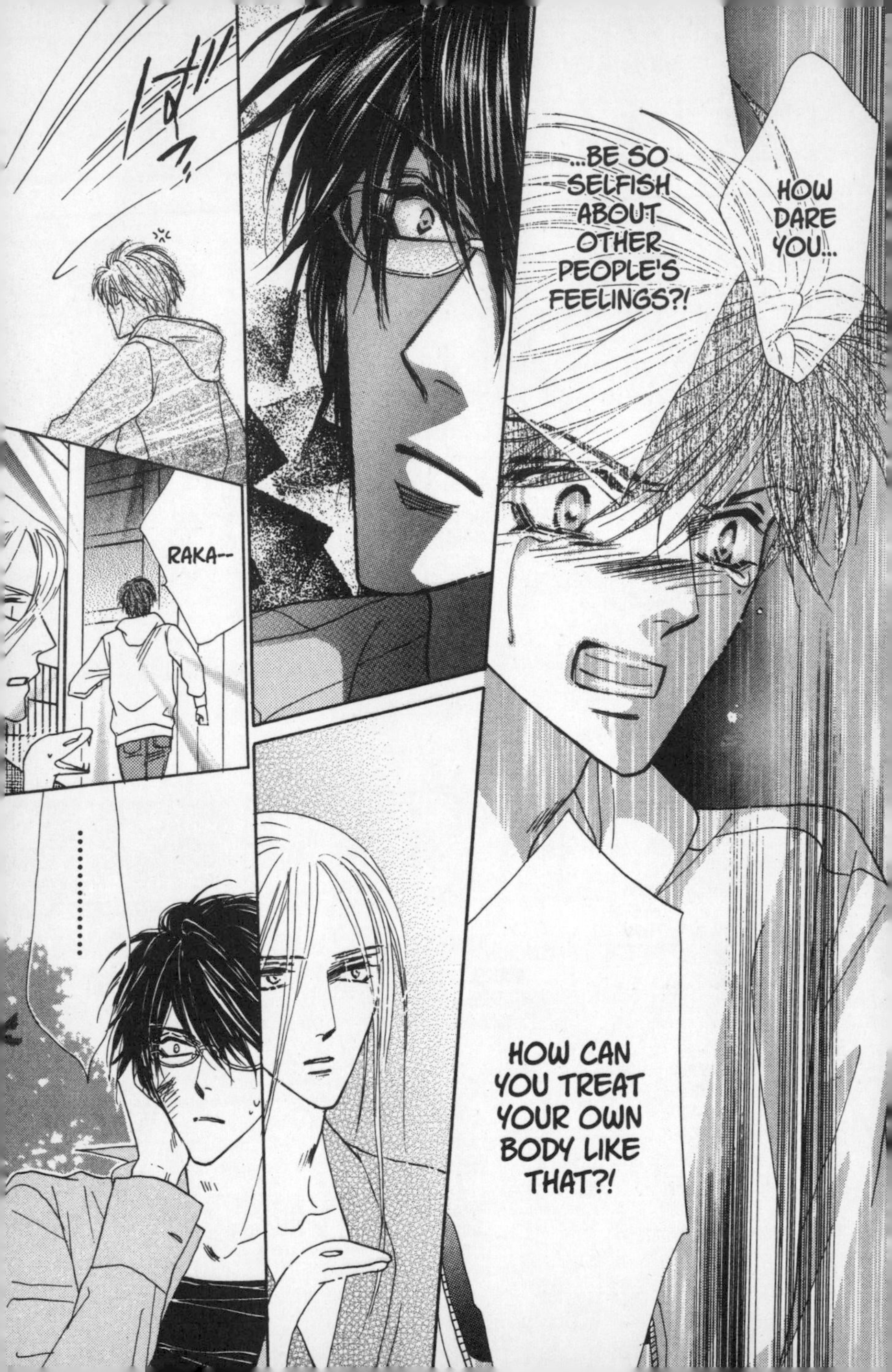
HOW DARE YOU...
...BE SO SELFISH ABOUT OTHER PEOPLE'S FEELINGS?!
HOW CAN YOU TREAT YOUR OWN BODY LIKE THAT?!
RAKA--
....

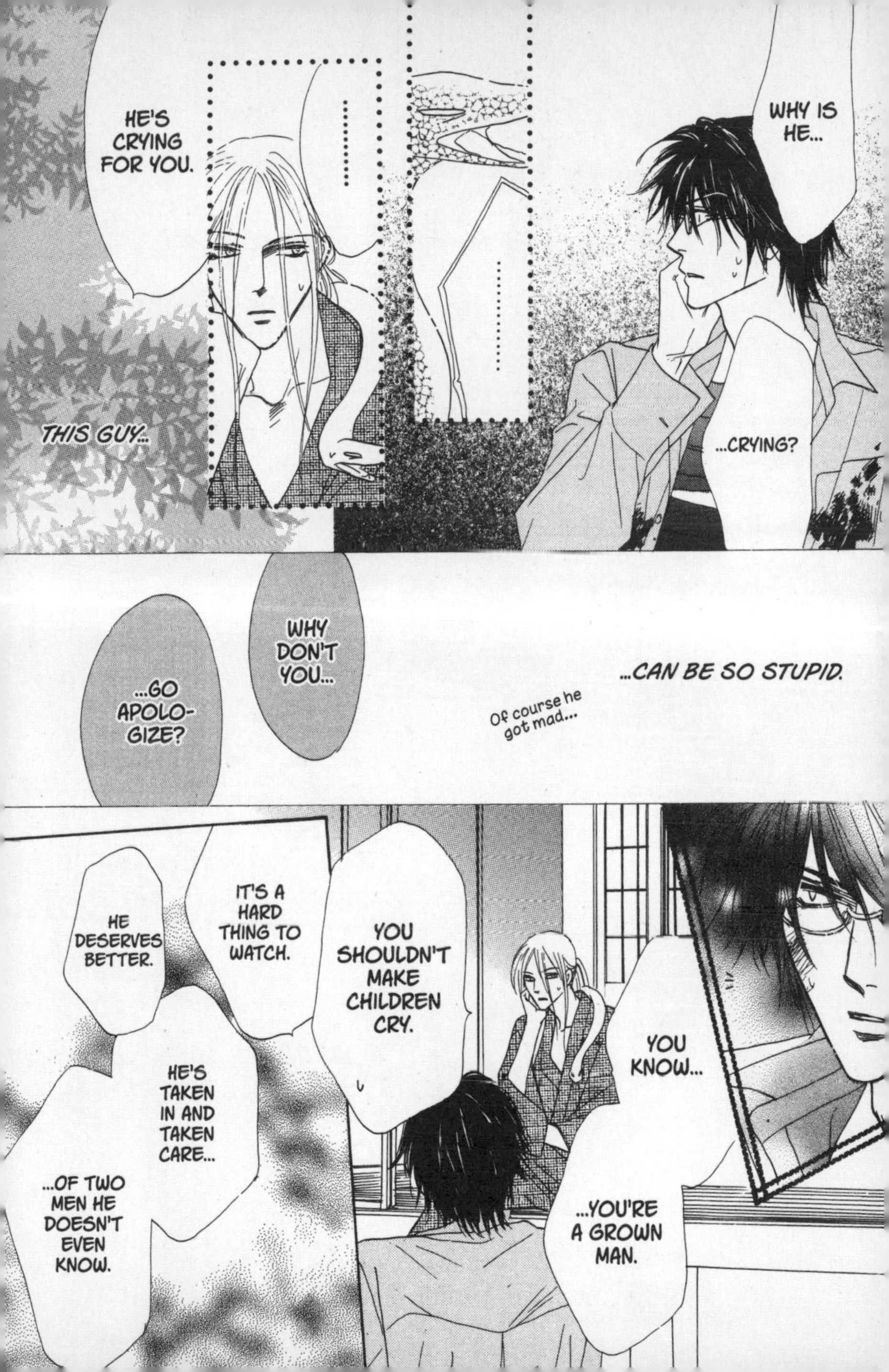
WHY IS HE...
...CRYING?
HE'S CRYING FOR YOU.
THIS GUY...
...CAN BE SO STUPID.
Of course he got mad...
WHY DON'T YOU...
...GO APOLOGIZE?
YOU KNOW...
...YOU'RE A GROWN MAN.
YOU SHOULDN'T MAKE CHILDREN CRY.
IT'S A HARD THING TO WATCH.
HE DESERVES BETTER.
HE'S TAKEN IN AND TAKEN CARE...
...OF TWO MEN HE DOESN'T EVEN KNOW.

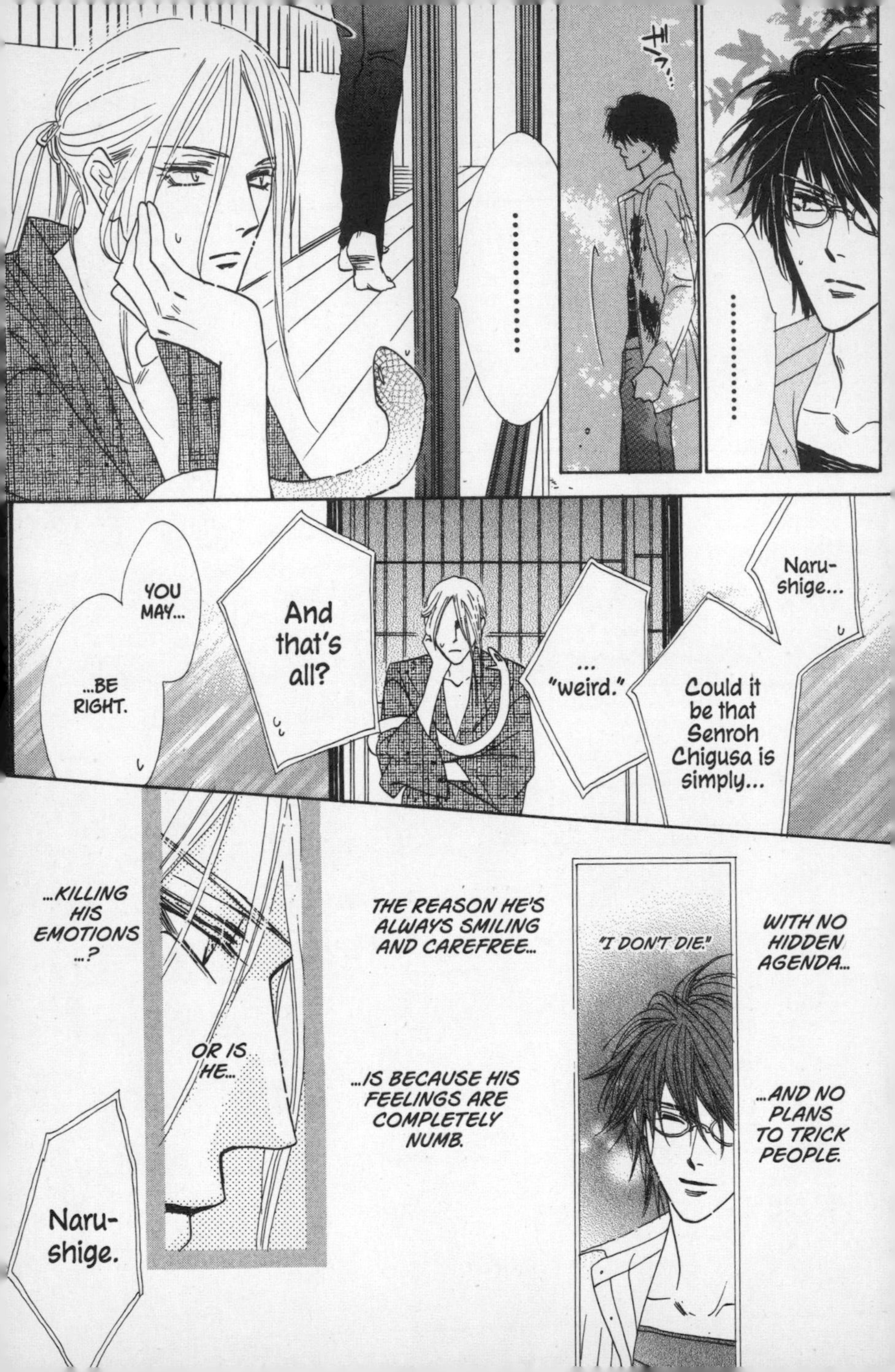

......
....
Naru-shige...
Could it be that Senroh Chigusa is simply...
... "weird."
And that's all?
YOU MAY...
...BE RIGHT.
WITH NO HIDDEN AGENDA...
...AND NO PLANS TO TRICK PEOPLE.
"I DON'T DIE."
THE REASON HE'S ALWAYS SMILING AND CAREFREE...
...IS BECAUSE HIS FEELINGS ARE COMPLETELY NUMB.
OR IS HE...
...KILLING HIS EMOTIONS ...?
Naru-shige.

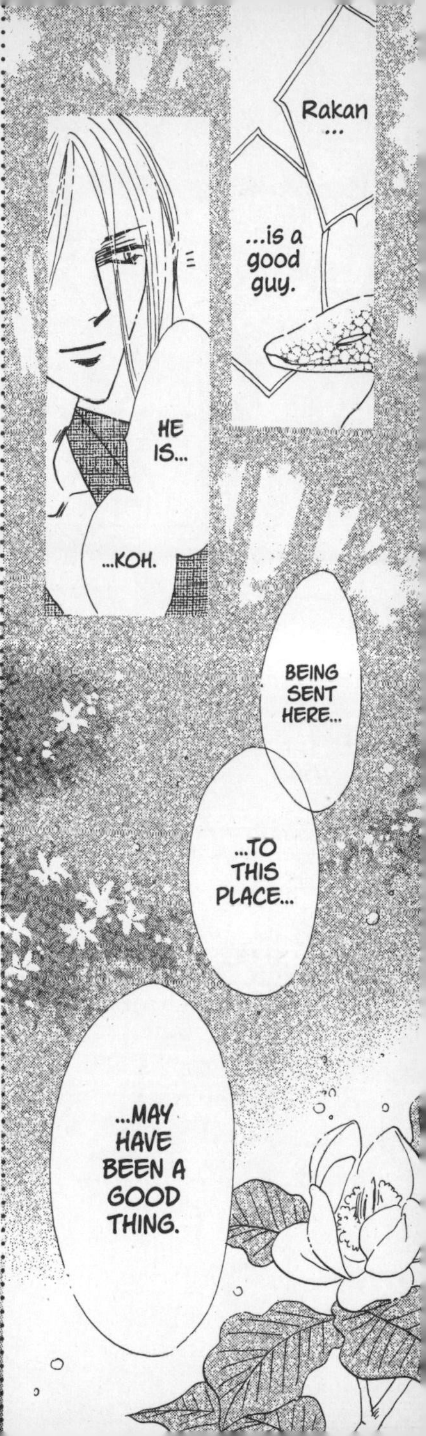
Rakan ...
...is a good guy.
HE IS...
...KOH.
BEING SENT HERE...
...TO THIS PLACE...
...MAY HAVE BEEN A GOOD THING.

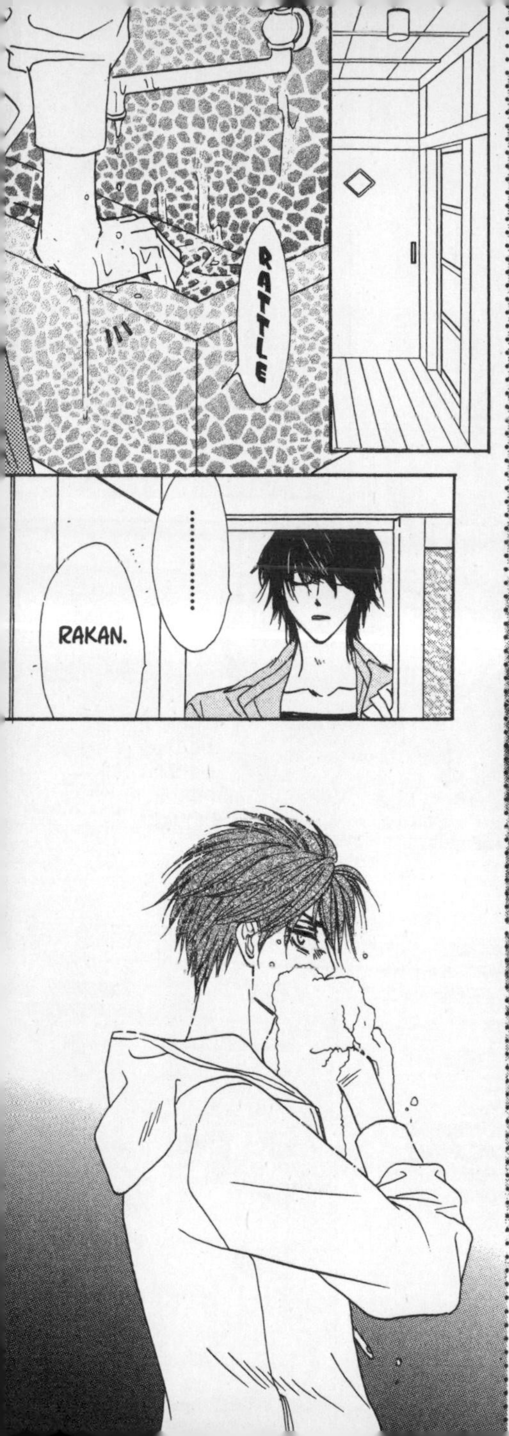
RATTLE
......
RAKAN.

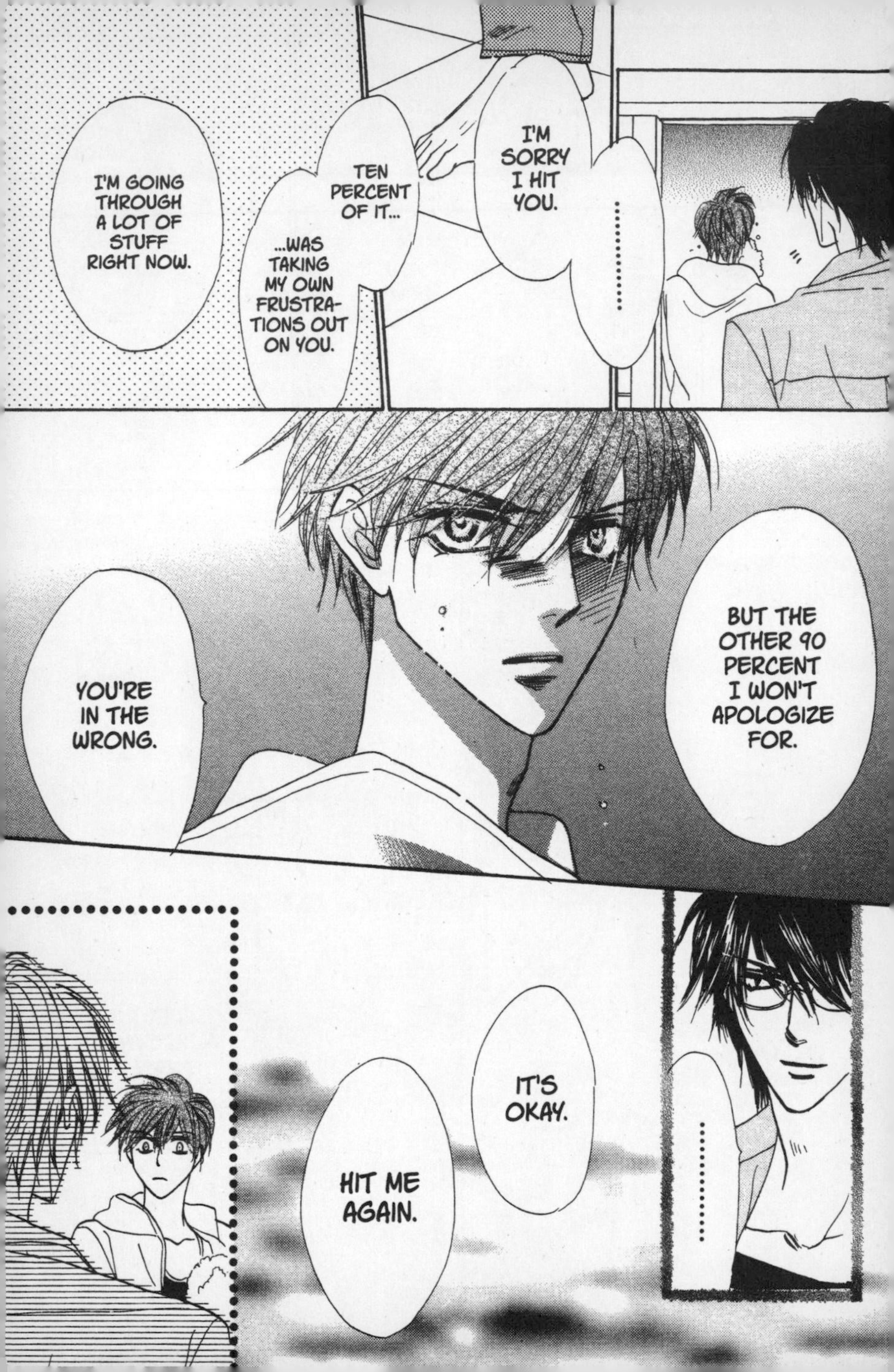
......
I'M SORRY I HIT YOU.
TEN PERCENT OF IT...
...WAS TAKING MY OWN FRUSTRATIONS OUT ON YOU.
I'M GOING THROUGH A LOT OF STUFF RIGHT NOW.
BUT THE OTHER 90 PERCENT I WON'T APOLOGIZE FOR.
YOU'RE IN THE WRONG.
......
IT'S OKAY.
HIT ME AGAIN.

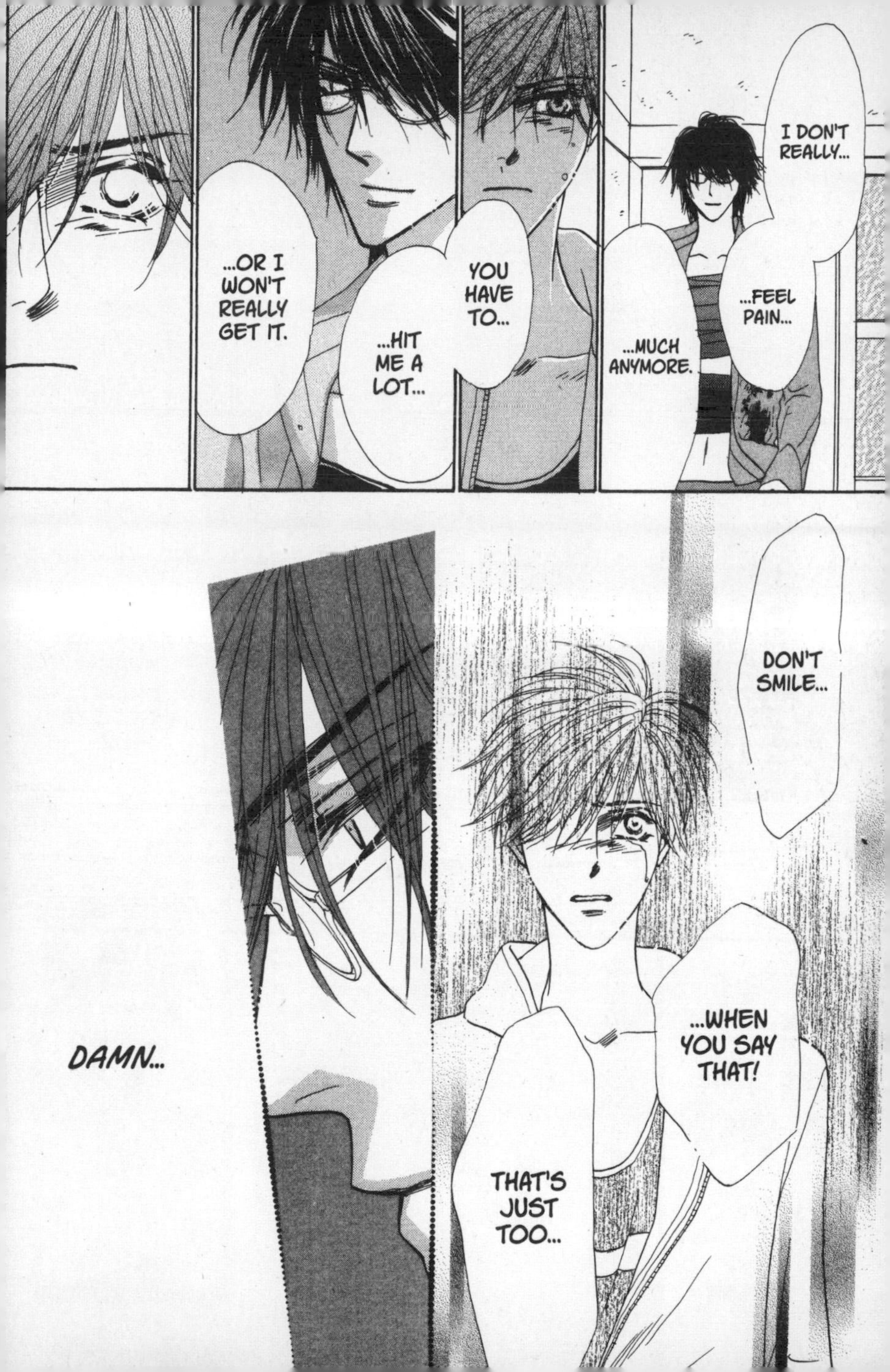
I DON'T REALLY...
...FEEL PAIN...
...MUCH ANYMORE.
YOU HAVE TO...
...HIT ME A LOT...
...OR I WON'T REALLY GET IT.
DON'T SMILE...
...WHEN YOU SAY THAT!
THAT'S JUST TOO...
DAMN...

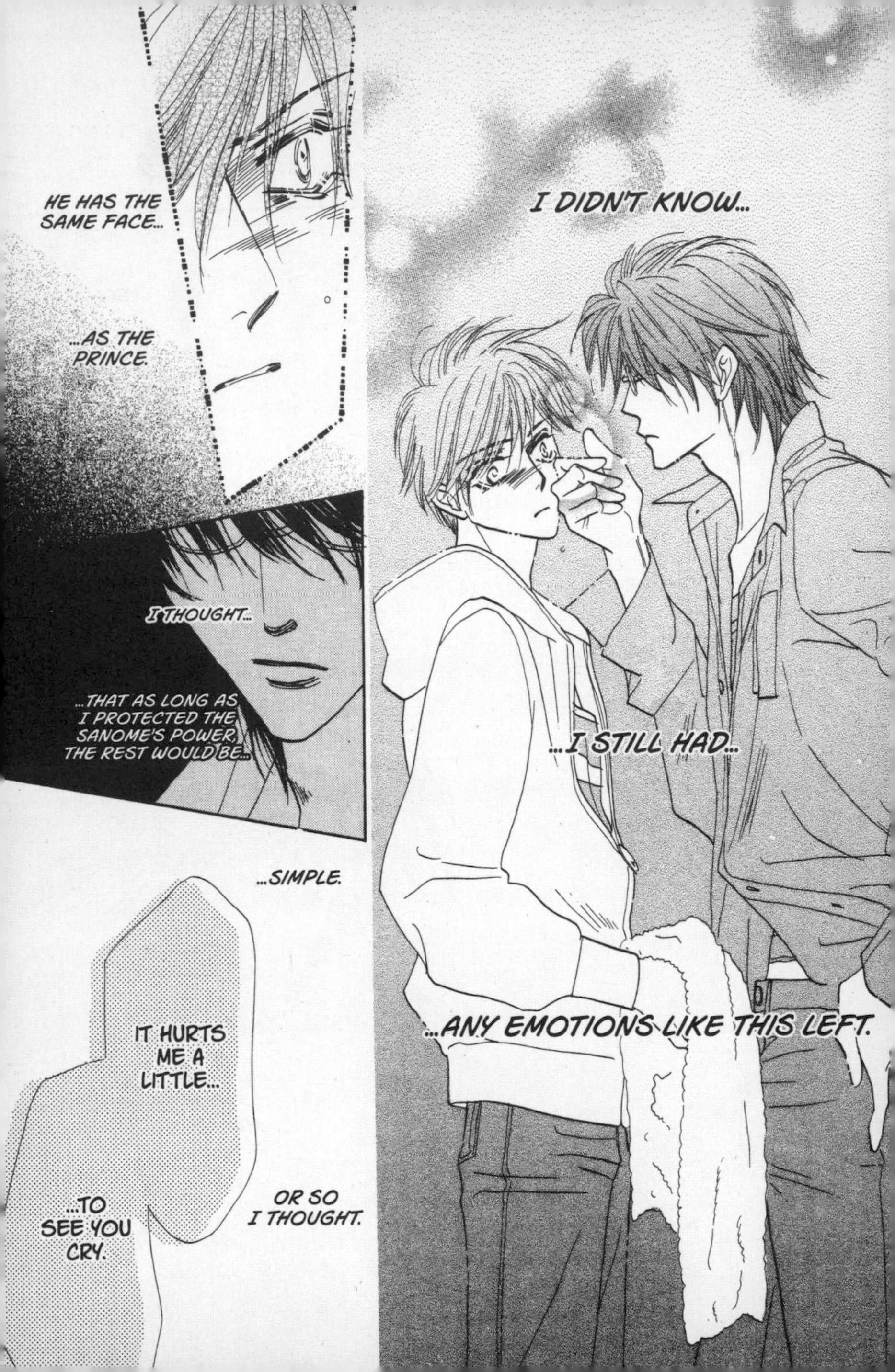
I DIDN'T KNOW...
...I STILL HAD...
...ANY EMOTIONS LIKE THIS LEFT.
HE HAS THE SAME FACE...
...AS THE PRINCE.
I THOUGHT...
...THAT AS LONG AS I PROTECTED THE SANOME'S POWER, THE REST WOULD BE...
...SIMPLE.
OR SO I THOUGHT.
IT HURTS ME A LITTLE...
...TO SEE YOU CRY.

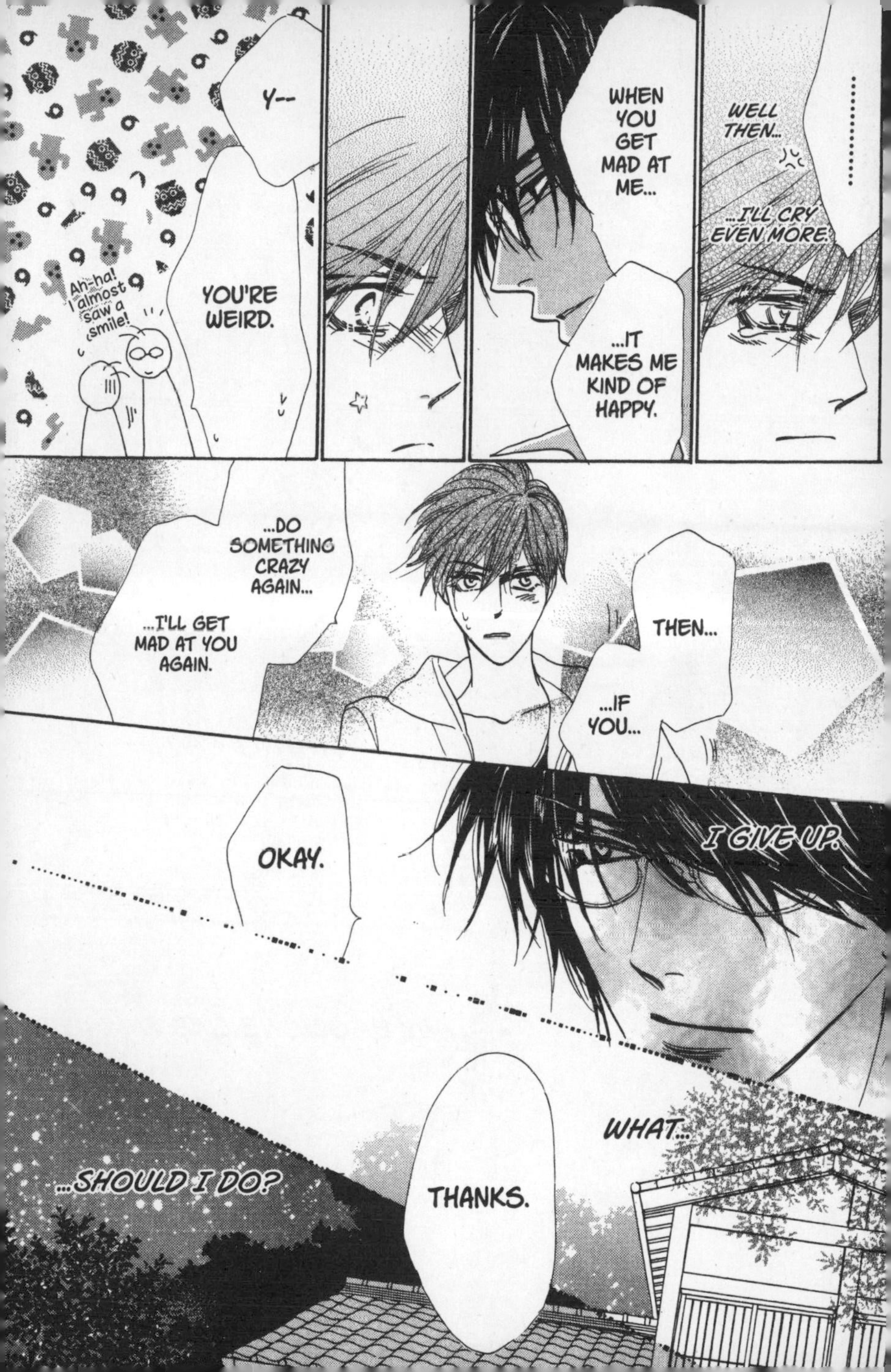

......
WELL THEN...
...I'LL CRY EVEN MORE.
WHEN YOU GET MAD AT ME...
...IT MAKES ME KIND OF HAPPY.
Y--
YOU'RE WEIRD.
Ah-ha! I almost saw a smile!
THEN...
...IF YOU...
...DO SOMETHING CRAZY AGAIN...
...I'LL GET MAD AT YOU AGAIN.
I GIVE UP.
OKAY.
WHAT...
THANKS.
...SHOULD I DO?

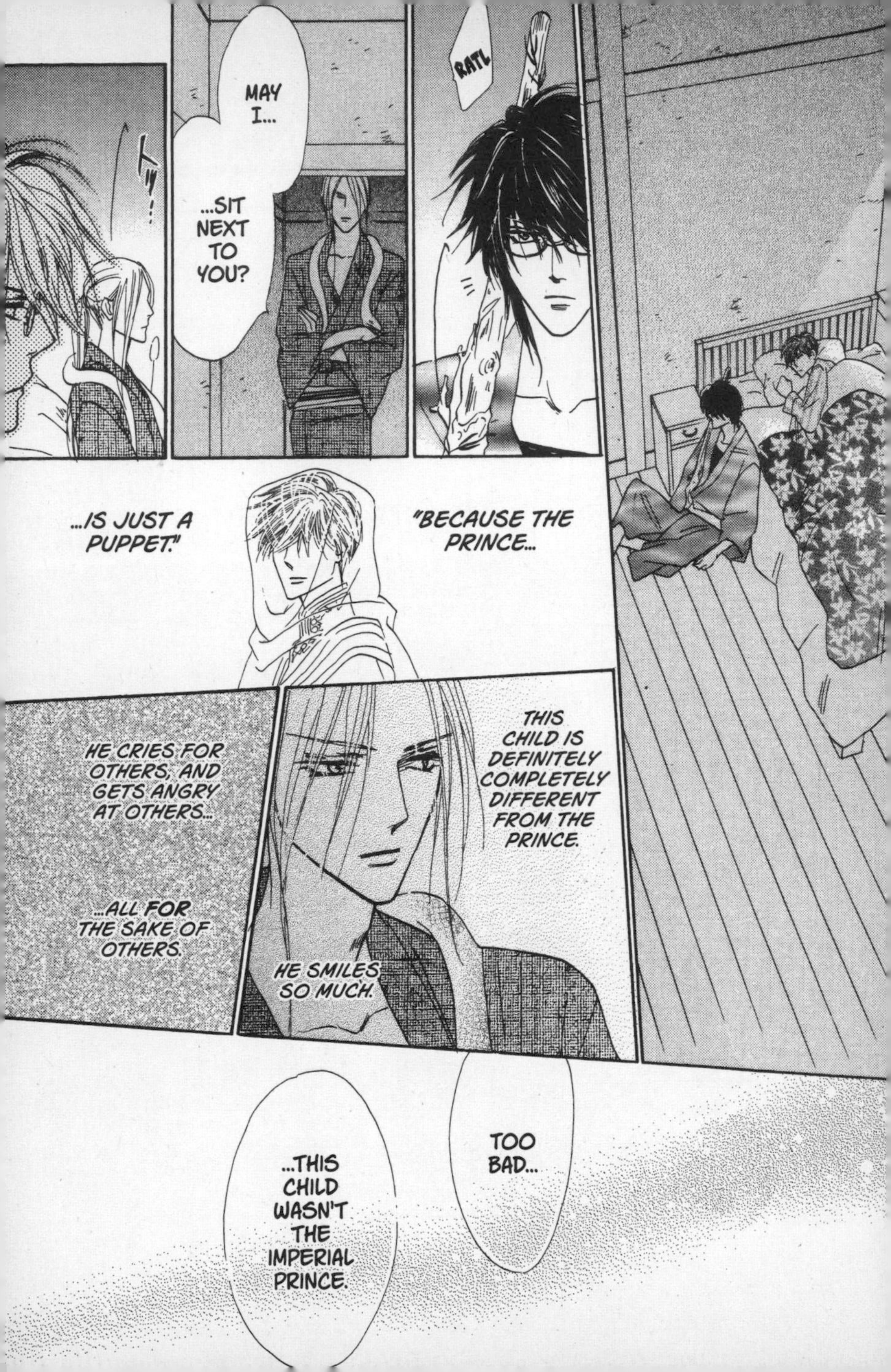
RATL
MAY I...
...SIT NEXT TO YOU?
"BECAUSE THE PRINCE...
...IS JUST A PUPPET."
THIS CHILD IS DEFINITELY COMPLETELY DIFFERENT FROM THE PRINCE.
HE SMILES SO MUCH.
HE CRIES FOR OTHERS, AND GETS ANGRY AT OTHERS...
...ALL FOR THE SAKE OF OTHERS.
TOO BAD...
...THIS CHILD WASN'T THE IMPERIAL PRINCE.

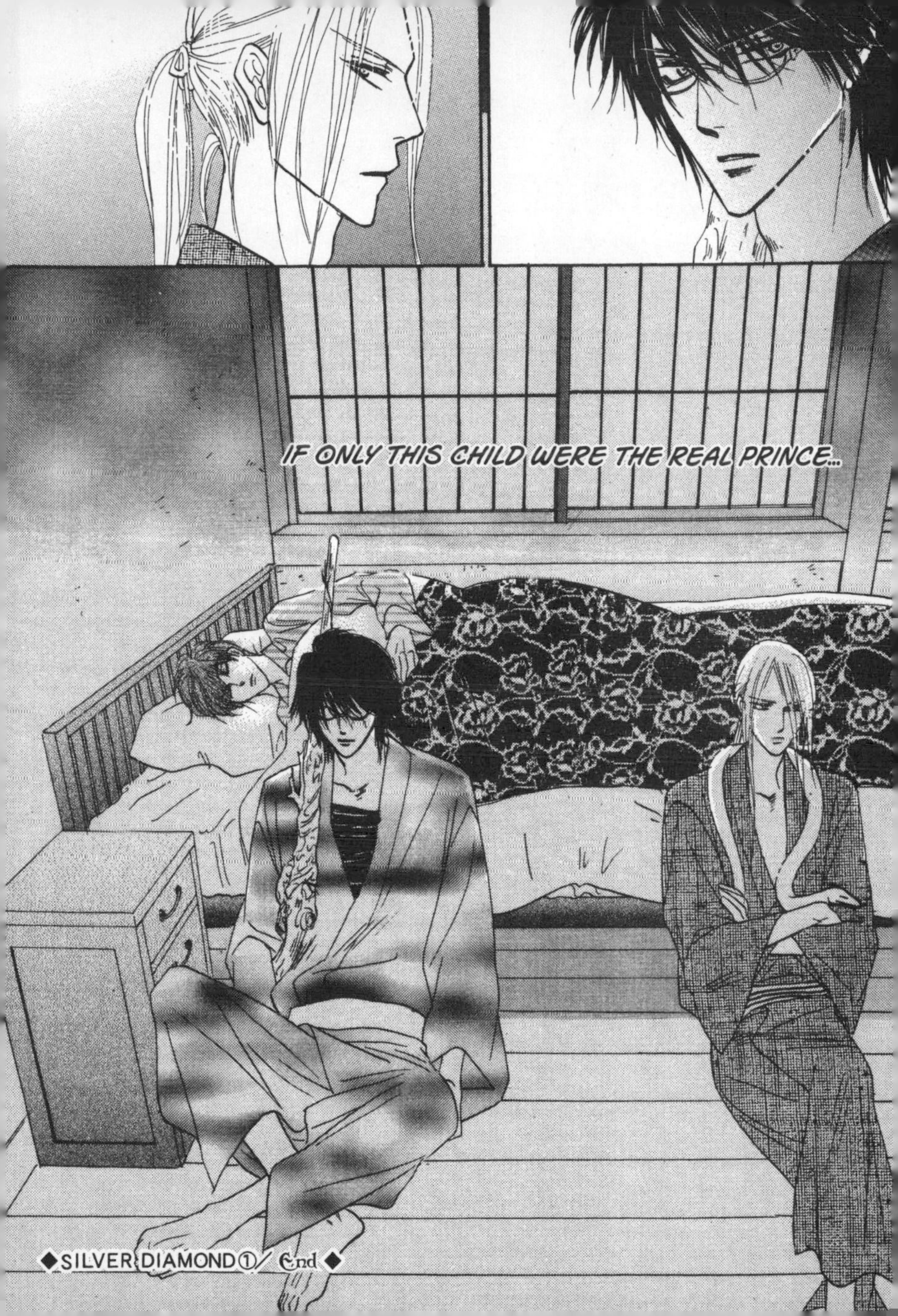
IF ONLY THIS CHILD WERE THE REAL PRINCE...
◆SILVER DIAMOND ①/ End◆

Umm, let's see, thank you for all of your thoughts through letters, email, fax, etc. ❀ (Oh, emails and faxes should be addressed to Tosuisha, my publisher. It's not like I have a public email address). I can't really respond (I'm sorry!!), but I gladly read them all. I hate to talk about Mamono again (I'm sorry I keep bringing it up. This is the last time), but after I finished Mamono, I started this story right away. There were times when I was really whining to my editor, but during those times, your letters really saved me. ❀ Knowing that people thought about things after reading what I had written, then wrote me a letter about it--then when I read the letter, and realized something myself, it somehow healed me. (Not just because of the words of sympathy, but that person's resolve. ← Writing it like this is overdramatic, but oh well.) I received a lot of those letters, and they really saved me during some dangerous times. Wow, I'm glad I wrote Mamono. Thank you so much--from the bottom of my heart. ❀

So that being the case, I plan on writing more stories with all the gratitude I feel. So please keep on reading. ❀

And I hope to see you in the next volume!

SHIHO SUGIURA, FALL, 2003

If I draw the snake wrong, people might thing it's something else...

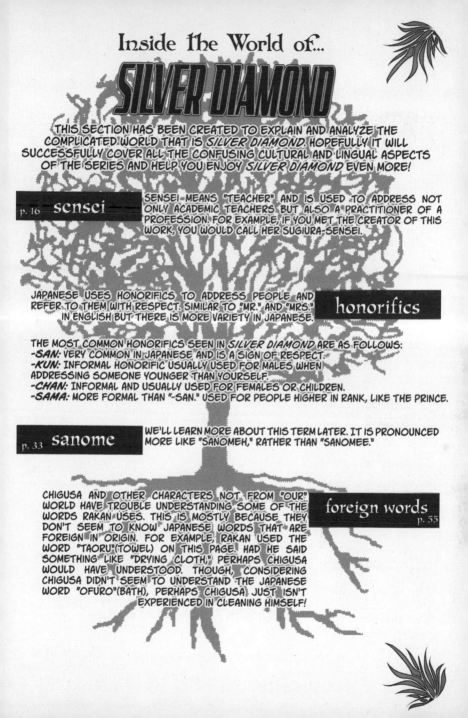

Inside the World of...

SILVER DIAMOND

THIS SECTION HAS BEEN CREATED TO EXPLAIN AND ANALYZE THE COMPLICATED WORLD THAT IS *SILVER DIAMOND*. HOPEFULLY IT WILL SUCCESSFULLY COVER ALL THE CONFUSING CULTURAL AND LINGUAL ASPECTS OF THE SERIES AND HELP YOU ENJOY *SILVER DIAMOND* EVEN MORE!

p. 16 sensei

SENSEI MEANS "TEACHER" AND IS USED TO ADDRESS NOT ONLY ACADEMIC TEACHERS BUT ALSO A PRACTITIONER OF A PROFESSION. FOR EXAMPLE, IF YOU MET THE CREATOR OF THIS WORK, YOU WOULD CALL HER SUGIURA-SENSEI.

honorifics

JAPANESE USES HONORIFICS TO ADDRESS PEOPLE AND REFER TO THEM WITH RESPECT. SIMILAR TO "MR." AND "MRS." IN ENGLISH BUT THERE IS MORE VARIETY IN JAPANESE.

THE MOST COMMON HONORIFICS SEEN IN *SILVER DIAMOND* ARE AS FOLLOWS:
-SAN: VERY COMMON IN JAPANESE AND IS A SIGN OF RESPECT.
-KUN: INFORMAL HONORIFIC USUALLY USED FOR MALES WHEN ADDRESSING SOMEONE YOUNGER THAN YOURSELF.
-CHAN: INFORMAL AND USUALLY USED FOR FEMALES OR CHILDREN.
-SAMA: MORE FORMAL THAN "-SAN." USED FOR PEOPLE HIGHER IN RANK, LIKE THE PRINCE.

p. 33 sanome

WE'LL LEARN MORE ABOUT THIS TERM LATER. IT IS PRONOUNCED MORE LIKE "SANOMEH," RATHER THAN "SANOMEE."

foreign words p. 55

CHIGUSA AND OTHER CHARACTERS NOT FROM "OUR" WORLD HAVE TROUBLE UNDERSTANDING SOME OF THE WORDS RAKAN USES. THIS IS MOSTLY BECAUSE THEY DON'T SEEM TO KNOW JAPANESE WORDS THAT ARE FOREIGN IN ORIGIN. FOR EXAMPLE, RAKAN USED THE WORD "TAORU"(TOWEL) ON THIS PAGE. HAD HE SAID SOMETHING LIKE "DRYING CLOTH," PERHAPS CHIGUSA WOULD HAVE UNDERSTOOD. THOUGH, CONSIDERING CHIGUSA DIDN'T SEEM TO UNDERSTAND THE JAPANESE WORD "OFURO"(BATH), PERHAPS CHIGUSA JUST ISN'T EXPERIENCED IN CLEANING HIMSELF!

Prince vs. Imperial Prince
p. 66

AS YOU CAN SEE ON THE PAGE, THE TWO VERSIONS OF "PRINCE" ARE WRITTEN DIFFERENTLY. RAKAN'S CONFUSION HERE IS THAT HE FIRST IMAGINES A KIND OF HAPPY EUROPEAN PRINCE, WHILE THE PRINCE CHIGUSA IS DESCRIBING HAS A MORE RELIGIOUS CONNOTATION TO IT, LIKE HOW THE EMPEROR OF JAPAN IS THOUGHT TO BE A DESCENDANT OF THE GODS.

Sengin vs. Senroh
p. 76

THIS IS EMBELLISHED ON LATER IN THE VOLUME, BUT TAKE A LOOK AT THE TWO KANJI BELOW. THE DIFFERENCE IS JUST ONE ADDED STROKE TO THE SYMBOL FOR SILVER, GIN, TO TURN IT INTO ROH (THE METALLIC ELEMENT LANTHANUM).

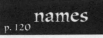

names
p. 120

THE NAMES IN *SILVER DIAMOND* ARE VERY IMPORTANT TO THE PLOT, SO THIS SECTION WILL BE USED EACH VOLUME TO ANALYZE THEM AS WELL AS POSSIBLE. AS RAKAN EXPLAINS ON THIS PAGE, THE NAMES IN THE OTHER WORLD USE RARE KANJI SYMBOLS AND USUALLY HAVE THE SAME SYMBOL REPEAT IN THE FIRST AND LAST NAME. SOMETIMES THE READING OF THE SYMBOL IS THE SAME IN EACH NAME, LIKE WITH KINGEN KINREI. (THIS KANJI FOR "KIN" MEANS "GOLD.") OTHER TIMES, THEY ARE PRONOUNCED DIFFERENTLY LIKE WITH SENROH CHIGUSA. THE SEN AND CHI ARE THE SAME KANJI SYMBOL, WHICH MEANS "THOUSAND." IF ANYONE HAS SEEN THE GHIBLI MOVIE *SPIRITED AWAY*, A SIMILAR PLAY WAS MADE ON THE NAME OF THE MAIN CHARACTER. THE JAPANESE TITLE WAS BASICALLY "SEN AND CHIHIRO'S SPIRITED AWAY ADVENTURE" AND IN THE MOVIE, CHIHIRO'S IDENTITY WAS STOLEN WHEN THE SECOND SYMBOL OF HER NAME WAS TAKEN AND THUS REDUCING HER NAME TO SEN. SHIGEKA NARUSHIGE SHARES THE SYMBOL FOR "WEIGHT/HEAVINESS" IN BOTH NAMES. THERE MAY BE SOME PLOT RELEVANCE TO THE SCENE EARLIER WHEN ONE CHARACTER COMMENTED TO NARUSHIGE ABOUT HIS NAME BEING A HEAVY BURDEN.

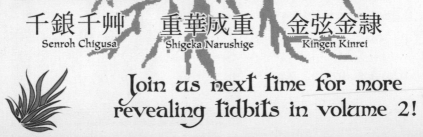

千銀千艸
Senroh Chigusa

重華成重
Shigeka Narushige

金弦金隷
Kingen Kinrei

Join us next time for more revealing tidbits in volume 2!

Silver Diamond
···Fanart···

SAWA RAKAN

Aira···Canada
Aira-chan was the first to send in fanart, and it's gorgeous! Look for more of her work in volume 3!

Shiu-Yee Chu··· Northern Ireland
Rakan is looking adorable with a cascade of flowers around him.

Macky Pierce... Texas

Rakan and Chigusa looking serious in front of a graceful bough of flowers. Great work capturing the complexity of Chigusa's rifle!

Jimena...Bolivia

This one features everyone's favorite snarky snake, Koh! Plus, Chigusa's looking mighty fine. What conditioner does he use?

SHOW YOUR LOVE FOR SILVER DIAMOND! NOW ACCEPTING FANART FOR FUTURE VOLUMES!

ADDRESS: *Silver Diamond* Fanart
c/o TOKYOPOP
5900 Wilshire Blvd, #2000
Los Angeles, CA 90036

See **http://www.tokyopop.com/legal/fan_art_policy.html** and make sure to follow the proper submission guidelines!

In the next...

Silver diamond

Rakan learns more about his secret past, Narushige learns how to make miso soup, Chigusa learns how to hug, and Koh learns the phrase "sexual harassment." The two men from another world (plus the talking snake) are starting to become comfortable with their new surroundings. But coming to disrupt the peace is an assassin sent by the Prince who shares Rakan's face. Will Chigusa save the day again?

See you next time in
Silver Diamond #2:
Master and Servant!

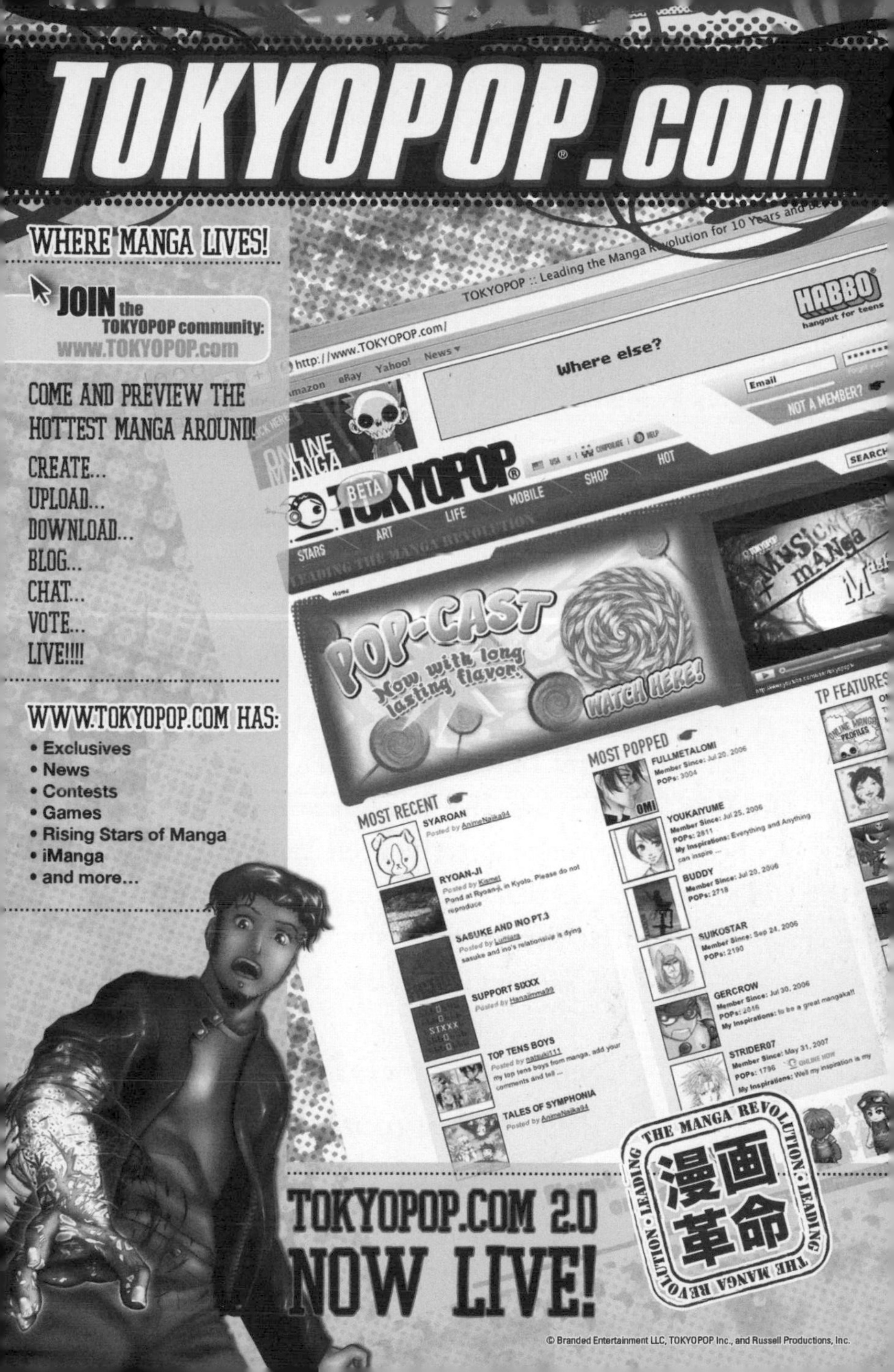
TOKYOPOP®.com
WHERE MANGA LIVES!
JOIN the TOKYOPOP community:
www.TOKYOPOP.com
COME AND PREVIEW THE HOTTEST MANGA AROUND!
CREATE...
UPLOAD...
DOWNLOAD...
BLOG...
CHAT...
VOTE...
LIVE!!!!
WWW.TOKYOPOP.COM HAS:
• Exclusives
• News
• Contests
• Games
• Rising Stars of Manga
• iManga
• and more...
TOKYOPOP :: Leading the Manga Revolution for 10 Years and Beyond
http://www.TOKYOPOP.com/
Where else?
POP-CAST
Now with long lasting flavor!
WATCH HERE!
MOST RECENT
MOST POPPED
TP FEATURES
LEADING THE MANGA REVOLUTION
漫画革命
TOKYOPOP.COM 2.0
NOW LIVE!
© Branded Entertainment LLC, TOKYOPOP Inc., and Russell Productions, Inc.

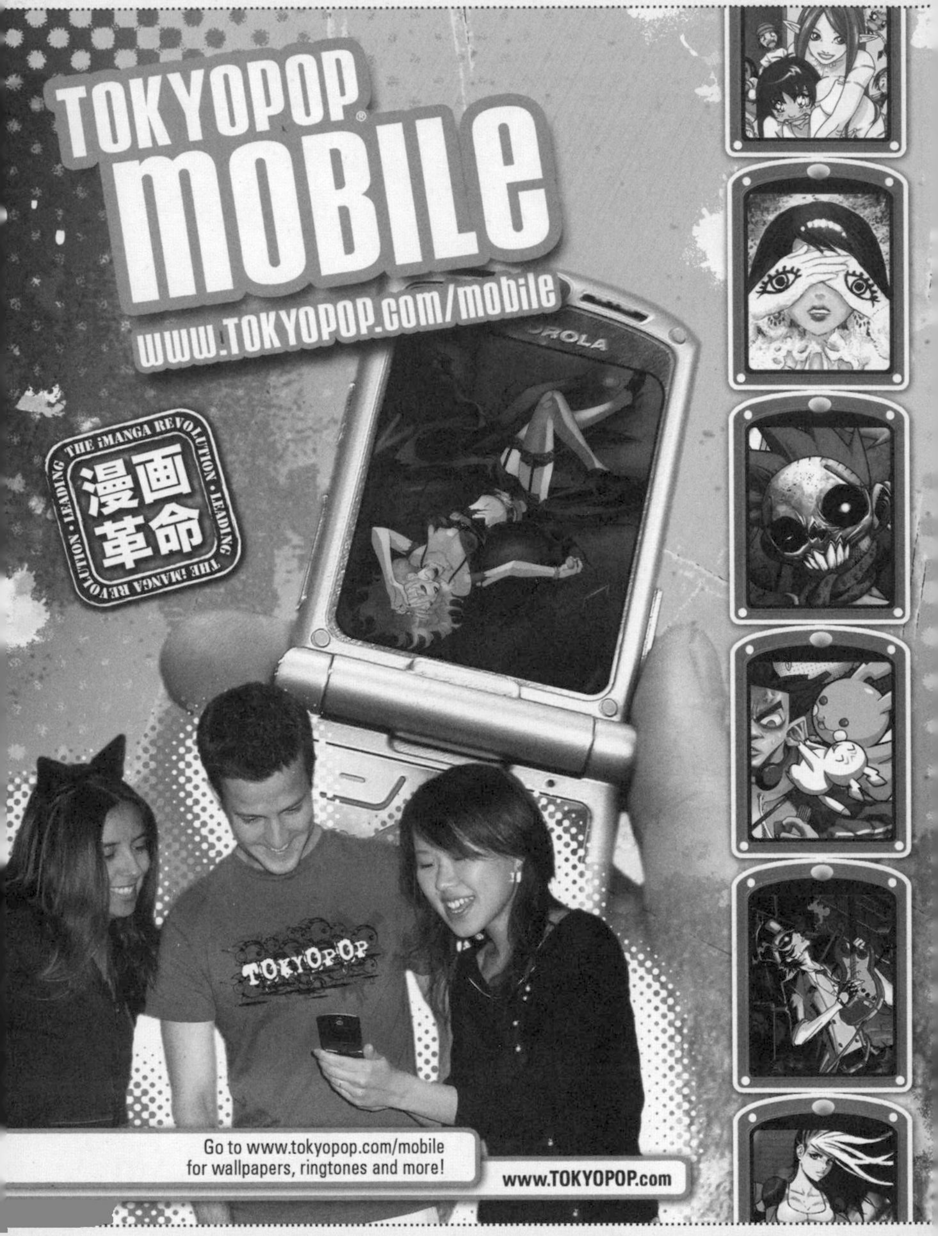
TOKYOPOP® MOBILE
www.TOKYOPOP.com/mobile
LEADING THE iMANGA REVOLUTION · LEADING THE iMANGA REVOLUTION
漫画
革命
TOKYOPOP
Go to www.tokyopop.com/mobile
for wallpapers, ringtones and more!
www.TOKYOPOP.com

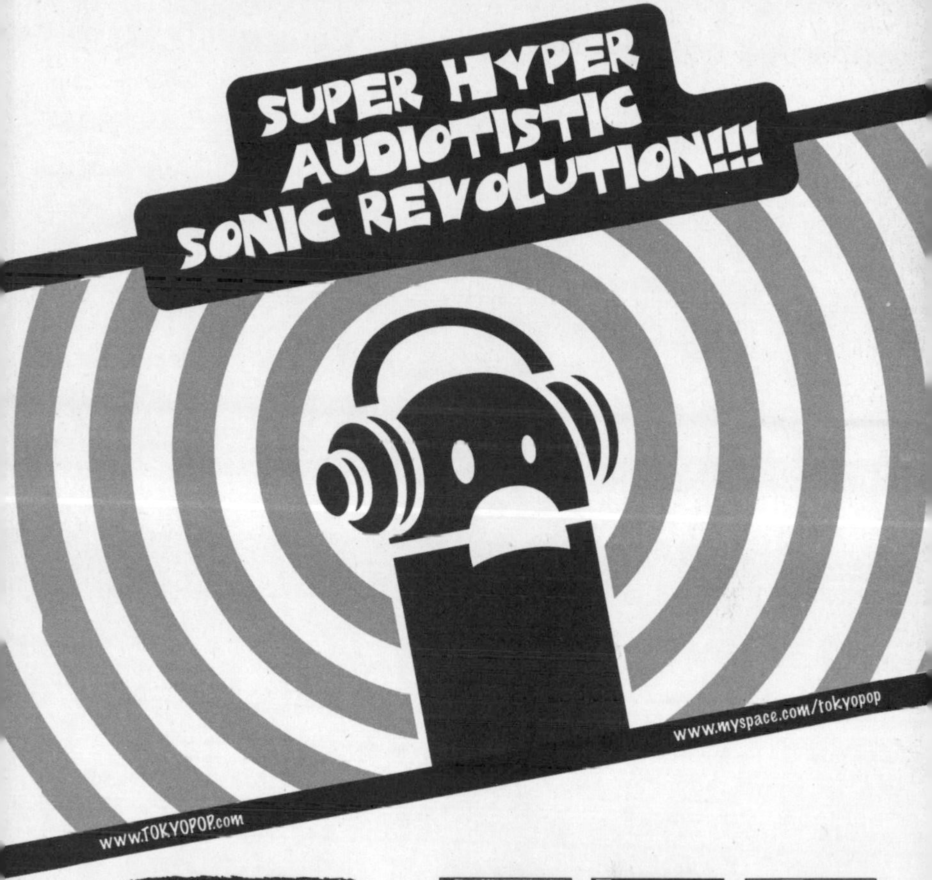

SUPER HYPER
AUDIOTISTIC
SONIC REVOLUTION!!!
www.myspace.com/tokyopop
www.TOKYOPOP.com

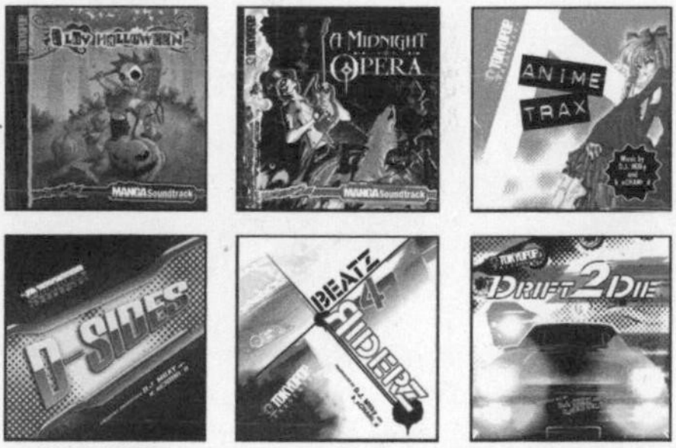

MANGA Soundtrack
A MIDNIGHT OPERA
MANGA Soundtrack
ANIME TRAX
BEATZ 4 RIDERZ
DRIFT 2 DIE

From the creator of *Peace Maker*

ヴァッサロード

+

Nanae Chrono

The Vatican has employed a new assassin who's a vampire, *and* a cyborg. If you think he sounds nasty, wait 'till you see his master! When these two hot guys collide, the good times and carnage will roll like a head off a guillotine!

© NANAE CHRONO/MAG Garden

AS SEEN ON CARTOON NETWORK

TRINITY BLOOD™

TRINITY BLOOD
TOKYOPOP
STORY BY SUNAO YOSHIDA
ART BY KIYO KYUJYO
CHARACTER DESIGNS BY THORES SHIBAMOTO

Trinity Blood Volume 7

While lost in the city, Ion and Esther meet a strange young tea-seller who reveals that Radu may be alive...but not before a fight for their survival against Dietrich's vampire zombie soldiers!

ACTION

OT OLDER TEEN AGE 16+

LET THE BLOODLETTING CONTINUE

THE SOURCE MATERIAL FOR THE ANIME AND MANGA

TOKYOPOP
TRINITY BLOOD

Trinity Blood
Rage Against the Moons
Volumes 1, 2 and 3

TOKYOPOP
TRINITY BLOOD

Trinity Blood
Reborn on the Mars
Volumes 1 and 2

THE ADVENTURES CONTINUE IN THESE EXCITING TRINITY BLOOD NOVELS

POP FICTION

FOR MORE INFORMATION VISIT: WWW.TOKYOPOP.COM

Fruits Basket™

By Natsuki Takaya

Volume 20

Can Tohru deal with the truth?

After running away from his feelings and everyone he knows, Kyo is back with the truth about his role in the death of Tohru's mother. But how will he react when Tohru says that she still loves him?

Winner of the American Anime Award for Best Manga!

The #1 selling shojo manga in America!

FOR MORE INFORMATION VISIT: WWW.TOKYOPOP.COM

STOP!

This is the back of the book.
You wouldn't want to spoil a great ending!

This book is printed "manga-style," in the authentic Japanese right-to-left format. Since none of the artwork has been flipped or altered, readers get to experience the story just as the creator intended. You've been asking for it, so TOKYOPOP® delivered: authentic, hot-off-the-press, and far more fun!

DIRECTIONS

If this is your first time reading manga-style, here's a quick guide to help you understand how it works.

It's easy... just start in the top right panel and follow the numbers. Have fun, and look for more 100% authentic manga from TOKYOPOP®!